Lynching and Mob
Violence in Ohio,
1772–1938

Lynching and Mob Violence in Ohio, 1772–1938

DAVID MEYERS *and*
ELISE MEYERS WALKER

McFarland & Company, Inc., Publishers
Jefferson, North Carolina

Photographs are from the collection
of the author unless credited otherwise.

LIBRARY OF CONGRESS CATALOGUING-IN-PUBLICATION DATA

Names: Meyers, David, 1948– author. | Walker, Elise Meyers, author.
Title: Lynching and mob violence in Ohio, 1772–1938 / David Meyers
and Elise Meyers Walker.
Description: Jefferson, North Carolina : McFarland & Company, Inc.,
Publishers, 2019 | Includes bibliographical references and index.
Identifiers: LCCN 2018048524 | ISBN 9781476673417 (softcover : acid free paper) ♾
Subjects: LCSH: Lynching—Ohio—History. | Mobs—Ohio—History. |
Violence—Ohio—History. | Ohio—Race relations—History.
Classification: LCC HV6462.O3 M49 2019 | DDC 364.1/34—dc23
LC record available at https://lccn.loc.gov/2018048524

BRITISH LIBRARY CATALOGUING DATA ARE AVAILABLE

ISBN (print) 978-1-4766-7341-7
ISBN (ebook) 978-1-4766-3412-8

Front and back cover illustrations: Much of the nation was
in the grip of "Judge Lynch," as portrayed in this illustration
from *Harper's Weekly* in 1884.

Printed in the United States of America

McFarland & Company, Inc., Publishers
Box 611, Jefferson, North Carolina 28640
www.mcfarlandpub.com

For our Ford Friday—
To ensure that there is at least one light
in an otherwise dark book.

Acknowledgments

Students are right; the books are boring.—James Loewen

Dr. James Loewen, author of *Sundown Towns*, served as an inspiration for this book. Not only did he share information from his files, but he also provided us with some advice which, admittedly, we did not always follow, even though he was right.

We are indebted to the Tuskegee University Archive for supplying us with a list of lynchings in Ohio from 1882 to 1932; the Licking County Historical Society, in particular Jenn Lusetti, for providing us with the only reference we have to the lynching of an unidentified cattleman; and Terry Metter of the Cleveland Public Library who helped us to unravel the story of Albert Morrison.

We are also grateful to Jim Bowsher, the Temple of Tolerance, Wapakoneta, Ohio; Natalie Fritz, Archives of the Clark County Historical Society, Springfield, Ohio; and Harvard University, Harvard Art Museums/Fogg Museum, Cambridge, Massachusetts, for permission to republish images from their collections.

To Tom Holton and his sisters, Jan Betz and Julia Todd, we express our deep appreciation for providing us a personal perspective on the subject of intolerance as it touched their family and for the use of a photograph taken by their father.

Special thanks are due to Evelyn Keener Walker for reviewing the manuscript and making suggestions as well as Randy McNutt for his comments and continuing encouragement.

Finally, we want to recognize our spouses, Beverly Meyers and Sam Walker, for their patience and forbearance as we once again took a plunge down the rabbit hole.

Table of Contents

Preface

It may be true that the law cannot make a man love me, but it can stop him from lynching me, and I think that's pretty important.—Martin Luther King, Jr.

On July 13, 1920, Milton Harris died under suspicious circumstances. While working as the chef on a steamer traveling from Duluth, Minnesota, to Toledo, Ohio, Harris drowned, allegedly at the hands of some crew members. His body was subsequently interred in an unmarked grave in Toledo's Forest Cemetery.

The death of Harris, a thirty-five-year-old African American, likely would have been forgotten if not for the Tuskegee Institute (now University). From 1882 to 1968, Tuskegee tracked lynchings by state and race. By its count, the United States had a total of 4,743 lynchings during this period—1,297 white (or 27 percent) and 3,446 black (73 percent). Ohio contributed twenty-six—ten white (38 percent) and sixteen black (62 percent).[1]

During the late nineteenth century, Ohio was reeling from a wave of lynchings and most reasonable people felt something had to be done. On May 21, 1892, Ohio-born Benjamin Harrison was the first U.S. president to call for an anti-lynching legislation. Four years later, his home state responded with the Smith Act—"an Act for the Suppression of Mob Violence." It was a major step forward and the most severe anti-lynching law in the country.

Championed by Harry C. Smith, a black state representative from Cleveland, and Albion W. Tourgée, a white civil rights activist born in Ashtabula County, the Smith Act was intended to discourage all forms of mob violence by allowing victims (or their families) to obtain up to $5,000 in financial compensation from the county where the crime occurred.[2]

The Smith Act established that

> any collection of individuals assembled for an unlawful purpose, intending to do damage or injury to anyone or pretending to exercise correctional power over other persons by violence, and without authority of law, shall for the purpose of this act be regarded as a "mob," and any act of violence exercised by them upon the body of any person, shall constitute a "lynching."[3]

It would become the model for similar legislation in nine other states.

However, there is a difference between hanging a man and, say, shooting him (or drowning him, for that matter). For most people, the term itself—lynching—is unlikely to conjure up the image of someone being shot and, yet, the inclusion of shooting victims alone doubled the number of individuals "lynched" in some states.

To qualify as a lynching, Tuskegee required that these four elements had to be present:

> There must be legal evidence that a person was killed. That person must have met death illegally. A group of three or more persons must have participated in the killing. The group must have acted under the pretext of service to justice, race or tradition.[4]

We have chosen in this work to separate those instances of lynching which involved actual hanging from those that didn't, even though this puts us at odds with most other researchers. Our rationale is that the ritual of hanging a person sets it apart from other forms of extrajudicial punishment. It becomes a sort of street theatre. It conveys an element of quasi-judicial approbation, occasionally including mock trials. It also removes an element of ambiguity when it comes to judging the mob's intent.

In the more traditional sort of lynching, the implication is that the victim has somehow violated community standards and is being punished by representatives of that community. This is not as readily apparent when the victim is shot, stabbed, or beaten to death and the body simply dumped somewhere. A lynching is a lynching is a lynching isn't true.[5]

An overwhelming majority of lynching victims nationally were African American, far exceeding their proportion in the total population. Despite his own racist inclinations, H.L. Mencken launched a crusade against lynching in the *Baltimore Sun* following a case in his beloved Maryland. Linking arms with the NAACP, he promoted the Costigan-Wagner Anti-Lynching Bill which would have made lynching a capital offense. However, President Franklin D. Roosevelt refused to buck the Southern Democrats and allowed the bill to die in Congress.

Between 1882 and 1968, some 200 anti-lynching bills were introduced, but not one passed. The reason seems obvious. To paraphrase historian Barbara J. Fields (who was channeling U.B. Phillips), keeping the United States a white man's country has been the central theme of American history.

In *Lynching and Mob Violence in Ohio, 1772–1938*, we have provided an account of every "lynching" (narrow definition) which took place in the state. We have also attempted to provide a context for them by including every "lynching" (broad definition), attempted lynching, and other significant act of mob violence, such as tar and feathering, we have been able to identify.

Although traditional lynchings in the United States have subsided, incidents of mob violence and extrajudicial punishment continue to periodically raise their ugly heads. It is our hope that this book will be used to inform meaningful discussion of this ongoing problem.

Introduction

American history is longer, larger, more various, more beautiful, and more terrible than anything anyone has ever said about it.—James Baldwin

The metaphor of the United States as the "great melting pot" was first suggested by J. Hector St. John de Crèvecœur, a French immigrant. In *Letters from an American Farmer* (1782), Crèvecœur observed, "Here individuals of all nations are *melted* into a new race of men, whose labors and posterity will one day cause great changes in the world."[1]

But not everyone agreed.

"Ohio was a salad bowl of peoples, not a melting pot," historian George Knepper wrote. "Indeed, Ohio's most important quality has been its representative character, and probably no other state contained so broad a sampling of American types in the nineteenth and early twentieth centuries."[2]

Some of these American types included individuals who had no compunctions about engaging in various acts of mob violence, including lynchings. Babbidon and Green noted in *Race and Crime*: "By the 1880s, lynching, a form of social control, was a crude, cruel, and often ritualized form of murder, especially in the South. Due to prevailing attitudes about both race and crime, lynching was not always viewed as a crime."[3] While Ohio was not the South, that was of little comfort to those who were lynched.[4]

Even before Ohio attained statehood in 1803, migrants began coming to it from three cultural regions of the United States.

New Englanders, mostly American-born, but descended from the British, largely settled in northeastern and north central Ohio's Connecticut Western Reserve and Firelands regions. They also founded such distinctly New England communities as Marietta, Granville, and Worthington (in Washington, Licking, and Franklin counties, respectively).

Migrants from the Middle Atlantic States, mostly Pennsylvania Dutch, but quite a few Scotch-Irish as well, settled in the Connecticut Western Reserve and the United States Military District in the central part of the state. They also could be found along Zane's Trace which cut a swath from Wheeling, (West) Virginia, to Maysville, Kentucky (or Belmont County in the east to Adams County in the southwest).

Southerners, largely Scotch-Irish from Appalachian Virginia and Kentucky in the Upland South, made their homes in the Virginia Military District in the southwestern area of the state, particularly Clinton, Fayette, and Highland counties. They preferred to live in more isolated communities similar to the ones they left.

By 1850, Germans represented nearly half of all immigrants in Ohio and the Irish

Ohio's eighty-eight counties (Elise Meyers Walker).

nearly a quarter. Although many chose to live on farms, significant numbers of Germans were concentrated in such cities as Cincinnati, Columbus, and Cleveland. They collected in areas already staked out by the Pennsylvania Dutch, but also along the Scioto and Miami rivers and in the counties of Auglaize, Stark, and Tuscarawas.

Hundreds of Irish came to Ohio in 1817 to work on the canal system. Thousands more began arriving in 1848, fleeing the potato famine. They gravitated to the cities, but also took jobs on the railroads in more rural areas. The third largest immigrant group in 1850 was the English, who were concentrated along Lake Erie and around Cincinnati.

Adding to this ethnic patchwork quilt were smaller pockets of French (southeastern

Ohio), Swiss (alongside the Pennsylvania Dutch for the most part), Welsh (Gallia and Jackson counties), and Canadian (the Refugee Tract of central Ohio) immigrants. Toward the end of nineteenth century, southern Italians began coming to the United States, driven by the miserable living conditions in their homeland. But not all immigrants to the United States had come of their own volition.

At the beginning of the nineteenth century, there were 337 African Americans—mostly freemen, but, undoubtedly, some fugitive slaves—living within the bounds of the Ohio Country. Although the Ohio Constitution of 1803 outlawed slavery, it did not entirely eliminate it. Some slave owners were known to live in the southern counties and would transport their "property" across the Ohio River to Kentucky or (West) Virginia if the law started closing in on them.

Just a year later in 1804, the Ohio General Assembly passed the first Black Laws (or Code) which imposed restrictions on the rights of the state's few "black and mulatto" residents. Sadly, other states would follow Ohio's lead—Indiana, Illinois, and Michigan as well as Iowa, California, and Oregon. The laws' effect was to discourage black migration into the state. Nevertheless, Ohio's African American population grew at a faster rate than the white population. For many of them, "the Ohio [River] was, in song and lore, the Jordan; across it lay the Promised Land."[5]

Although Ohio's Black Laws were repealed in 1847, this did not result in an immediate change in attitudes toward them. The African American population in Ohio began to soar during the first three decades of the twentieth century in what was called the Great Migration. An estimated 1.5 million African Americans relocated from the rural South to northern cities in Illinois, Indiana, Ohio, Michigan, and Pennsylvania. They came in search of jobs and greater opportunity advancement, economically, socially, and politically.

Three cities in particular saw their African American populations increase dramatically—Cleveland, Cincinnati, and Columbus. No doubt, many of them were also fleeing the specter of lynching which had surged during the 1880s and 1890s in what has been called "the Negro Holocaust."

Of the states which contributed significantly to Ohio's population, four surpassed it when it came to the sheer number of lynchings attributed to them by the Tuskegee Institute: Kentucky (205), Virginia (100), West Virginia (48), and Maryland (29). While there is some room for quibbling about the exact numbers, they do suggest a pattern among some cultural groupings for taking the law into their own hands.

African Americans were disproportionately the victims of lynching. According to social reformer Frederick Douglass, there were three excuses used to justify the lynching of African Americans in the South. As paraphrased by journalist Ida B. Wells-Barnett, "The first excuse given to the civilized world for the murder of unoffending Negroes was the necessity of the white man to repress and stamp out alleged 'race riots.'"[6] Lynching was allegedly a check on the propensity of African Americans to go on the rampage, but, as Wells-Barnett observed, "only Negroes were killed during the rioting, and that all the white men escaped unharmed."[7]

The second excuse given for lynching black men was to discourage them from exercising the right to vote. With the ratification of the Fifteenth Amendment to the United States Constitution on February 3, 1870, no citizen could be denied the right to vote based on "race, color, or previous condition of servitude." However, not only in Ohio, but throughout the country, there was a fear that black voters, working in concert, would come to dominate what was a "white man's government."[8]

The third excuse was to prevent and punish assaults upon (white) women. "I do not deny," Douglass declared, "that they are capable of committing the crime imputed to them, but utterly deny that they are any more addicted to the commission of that crime than is true of any other variety of the human family."[9] This was not the last time the patriarchal need to protect the women would be used as a way to justify violence, victimizing the men who are injured and killed and infantilizing the women who are being "protected." But in the *Red Record*, Wells-Barnett refuted it. Of the 1,115 cases she examined, only 348 (31 percent) were charged with rape, while some were lynched for such trivial offenses as vagrancy or looking suspicious.

"The only excuse for lynch law which has a shadow of support in it is," Douglass wrote, "that the criminal would probably otherwise be allowed to escape the punishment due to his crime. But this excuse is not employed by the lynchers, though it is sometimes so employed by those who apologise [sic] for the lynchers."[10]

Such was the bias against the black man at all levels of society that some defenders of lynching were even willing to accept that the mobs might make mistakes. In a letter to the *New York Times*, one Thomas M. Thorpe spoke for many when he wrote:

> Because innocent persons have been imprisoned under all forms of law, and even executed, we do not abolish the law. Why, then, excoriate lynching for errors of rare occurrence? No human institution can be absolutely perfect; that is for God alone.[11]

Although the number of lynchings would steadily decline during the first half of the twentieth century, it wasn't until 1968 that the Tuskegee Institute quit tracking them.

Definitions

For our purposes, a lynching occurred when the victim was actually hanged with a rope. An attempted lynching was one in which a mob formed and a concerted effort was made to capture the intended victim, but the lynching was not completed for some reason. An expected or anticipated lynching was one in which threats were made or insinuated, but were not acted upon. All incidents classified as lynchings by the Tuskegee Institute [TI] have been so denoted.

We have also identified instances of tar-and-feathering, white capping, and other acts of mob violence we have uncovered. Finally, we have attempted to identify the race of the victims: black or African American [B], white or Caucasian [W], and race unknown or not indicated [unk].

With a few exceptions, we have not included incidents of violence related to labor disputes, such as strikes by coal miners, steel workers, farm laborers, transit employees, etc. We have also omitted such things as temperance riots and Ku Klux Klan cross-burnings, except when they were particularly noteworthy.

Finally, nobody, to the best of our knowledge and per historical record, was lynched in Columbus, Chillicothe, or Waverly—Ohio, that is—despite numerous newspaper articles to the contrary. Now, Columbus, Georgia, Chillicothe, Missouri, and Waverly, Iowa, are an entirely different matter. It's just that sometimes the newspapers got their geography confused. We trust we have not compounded these errors.

1

Antebellum Ohio (1792–1860)

At the time Ohio attained statehood in 1803, there were purportedly 337 African Americans living within its boundaries. A year later, the first Black Laws would be enacted by the Ohio legislature, imposing restrictions on their rights and freedom and discouraging them from settling in the state. Nevertheless, by the time the Civil War broke out in 1861, their numbers had increased 100 fold to nearly 37,000.

Mob Violence, Hamilton County, February 1792—Blanchard, Mr. [W]

Cincinnati was, as Nikki Marie Taylor observed, "northern in its geography, southern in its economy and politics, and western in its commercial aspirations."[1] Founded as Losantiville in 1788, it consisted of eleven families and a couple of dozen single men. The following year, a frontier garrison, Fort Washington, was constructed to protect it, increasing the population to about 500.

On a Sunday, February 12, 1792, Lieutenant Thomas Pasteur lured John Bartle, the owner of a local store, inside the fort. The two men had previously quarreled. Now, surrounded by his fellow soldiers, Pasteur proceeded to give Bartle a severe beating.

When Mr. Blanchard, Bartle's attorney, brought charges against him for assault, Pasteur was so enraged that he dispatched a sergeant and thirty privates to "chastise the lawyer and all who might be disposed to defend him or his cause."[2] A free-for-all ensued on Main Street involving eighteen citizens, including a magistrate named McMillan. The citizens prevailed and the soldiers were driven off.

The sergeant was subsequently reduced in rank, while Pasteur was found guilty of assault and battery and ordered to pay a three-dollar fine.

Lynching, Jackson County, 1803—Unknown man [B]

There may well have been lynchings in Ohio—or what would become Ohio—which went unrecorded. One early lynching occurred at Salt Lick Town. Before there was a city or county of Jackson, there were people living and working at the Scioto Salt Springs. Salt boilers, they were called. It was state's first industry and one of its earliest settlements. The salt springs were considered so vital to the nation's interests that the federal government had retained the rights to them.

Salt Lick Town was a lawless place, as uncivilized as any gold mining camp. As historian Daniel Webster Williams wrote: "It was a common occurrence from 1795 to 1803 to find the corpse of someone murdered overnight floating in a salt water tank, and to discover later that one or two others had departed between two suns without leaving their addresses."[3]

"The last of these murders was committed by a negro," Williams noted, and he was caught and lynched near "the Mitchell rocks."[4] The unidentified man was buried in a local cemetery which quickly fell into disfavor.

Lynching, Licking County, Early 1800s—Unknown drover [W?]

In *Memories of Old Newark*, W. Thomas Huff recalled that the first lynching in Licking County occurred in the early years of the nineteenth century near Kirkersville. Local cattlemen had hired an unidentified man to drive their stock to markets in the east and bring them the proceeds.

When he got back, "the man told the cattlemen that he had been robbed on his return trip and that the money had been taken by the robbers."[5] However, the cattlemen were dubious. After watching him for a week, they discovered where the drover had buried the money.

Writing nearly two centuries later, Huff provided no other details regarding the lynching nor the story's source. Presumably, the man was white because it would have been unlikely for the cattle owners to place their trust in a black man.

Threatened Violence, Warren County, August 1810—Shakers [W]

During the first half of the nineteenth century, the Shakers of Ohio were subjected to mob violence on a periodic basis. Members of the United Society of Believer's in Christ's Second Appearing, the Shakers were followers of Mother Ann Lee, a Charismatic English woman who presented herself as the female Christ. She preached that her followers should remain celibate, give up their worldly goods, and live communally. They were called "Shakers" because of they engaged in an ecstatic form of dancing during their religious services.

Early in June 1810, a declaration authored by Colonel James Smith was published in a local newspaper claiming that the Shakers were guilty of physical, financial, and sexual abuse, and other wrongdoing. Smith's son was a Shaker and he was determined to wrest custody of his grandchildren from him. He was joined by John Davis, John Bedle, and John and Robert Wilson—all former members of the society who had left on bad terms and were seeking revenge.

Although Richard McNemar, a Shaker leader, refuted the accusations in the press, that did not stop the efforts of the apostates to punish the group. During the month of July, Davis and the Wilson brothers actively worked to assemble a mob. By late August, Colonel Smith was purportedly recruiting men in Kentucky for an expedition against the Shakers. They were also threatening to tar and feather McNemar and drive the Shakers out of the region.

Despite warnings by Warren County Sherriff T. McCray and state's attorney J. Collet that the group's intentions were illegal, at eight o'clock in the morning on August 27, 1810, bands of strangers started assembling in Union Village from every direction.

At one o'clock in the afternoon, 500 armed troops entered the village by the Dayton road from the north. They were led by a party of military officers decked out in their uniforms. Walking in front of and behind the militia were an estimated 2,000 spectators who had turned out to watch the anticipated clash between the soldiers and a handful of Shakers, who preached and practiced pacifism.

The troops came to a halt in front of the Shaker meeting house. Some of those in attendance were hoping that violence could be avoided. However, the majority were there to enjoy whatever entertainment value might be had from the anticipated melee.

Not only did the militia want the Shakers to surrender various children and grandchildren who were, apparently, either in the custody of one parent or the other (or both) or, in one case, legal authorities, they also demanded that they renounce their faith, practices, mode of worship, lifestyle, and leave the area by the first Monday in December.

After conferring with one another, the Shakers replied that the demands were unreasonable and unjust. While this was transpiring, some of the armed men and spectators were urging violence and destruction. However, others defended the Shakers' right to exist.

Finally, it was agreed that a committee composed of some members of the mob would proceed through the village, questioning the residents of the village in an effort to ascertain the truth of the charges against the Shakers. After searching every room, Captain Thomas proclaimed that he saw a "decent house with decent people in it."[6]

Much to their chagrin, the committee found that conditions were not as they had been led to believe. And so those who had expected to be entertained by seeing the Shakers destroyed went away disappointed.

Threatened Violence, Warren County, May 1813—Shaker woman [W]

On May 12, 1813, the Shakers had to deal with another angry mob in Union Village. The entry in the Shaker book of records was brief: "Mob at the West Section; trying to take a woman away against her will."[7]

Mob Violence, Warren County, December 1813—Bedle's children [W]

Then on December 16, 1813, James Bedle led a violent mob to the Center House at Union Village, planning to take by force the children he had bound to Peter Pease. "The house doors being closed and barred, [Bedle and his companions] took a battering ram and broke a door in two; they then rushed in and committed considerable violence and abuse; but failed in getting the children. After a shameful day's riot, they dispersed for the night."[8]

Threatened Violence, Warren County, December 1813—Two Bedle children [W]

Two weeks later on December 29, 1813, another mob appeared to be gathering in Union Village, led by James Bedle. They had failed to prove to referees that Bedle's children had been abused by the Shakers. However, the referees did recommend to Peter Pease that he voluntarily surrender the indentured children for the sake of peace. He agreed and the mob dispersed. James Bedle dragged off his two youngest children the next day, while their mother and the two oldest children fled.

Threatened Violence, Warren County, January 1817—Rude, Sarah [W]; Davis, Jonathan [W]

Patty Rude had left the Society of Believers, but her daughter, Sarah, had not. So on January 12, 1817, Patty came with a party of ruffians to Union Village to forcibly take Sarah, by then a young woman, away from the Shakers.

Jonathan Davis, Jr., had also left the Shakers. His father, who remained a member of the sect, authorized several of his Shaker brethren to retrieve Jonathan, which they did. However, John Davis, a cousin with whom Jonathan had been staying, got a party of men from Lebanon to join him in storming the village. They threatened to burn it to the ground if the Shakers did not surrender the youth.

In the end, the constable arrested the Shaker men who had retrieved the boy. Although they were indicted, nothing came of the charges.

Mob Violence, Warren County, August 1819—Johnson, Phoebe [W]; Various Shakers [W]

On August 6, 1819, while the Shakers were at work, some thirty or forty horsemen rode into Union Village from Middletown and continued on until they reached the South House. Forcing their way in, they announced that they had heard one Phoebe Johnson was being held there against her will.

Johnson, who was in the orchard, conversed with the men through a window, insisting that she had no desire to leave, but if she did no one would stop her. However, it was evident that the band intended to compel her to go with them. They finally left when they became convinced that the woman was no longer there.

Three days later, a mob constituting some 200 people on horse and on foot passed through the village and arrived at the South House. This time, they were more agitated and unruly than before. Their purpose was to free the children of David and Anna Johnson, even though both parents were in agreement that they should be brought up among the Shakers.

The rioters were met at the gate by the Deacons of the Society who prohibited them from entering. However, they leaped the fence and rushed the house, attacking those who got in their way with fists, clubs, and whips, whether men or women. This assault continued until Squire Welton showed up and ordered them to leave under threat of law.

Mob Violence, Warren County, September 1824—Drake, Harriet R. [W]

On September 7, 1824, at about eight o'clock in the evening, a party of sixteen men escorted Francis Drake to the East House in Union Village. They were there to take away his daughter, Harriet R. Drake, who chose not to go with them.

After some disturbance, a group of Shakers arrived and somehow took ten of the mob prisoners "without any harsh means, and brought them to the office—fed and lodged them comfortably till morning."[9] The men were then released on their promise that they would behave in the future.

Mob Violence, Hamilton County, August 1829—Black Exodus [B]

Located on the border between the slave and the Free states (and directly across the river from the lynch-happy state of Kentucky), Cincinnati was divided in its allegiance. From an economic standpoint, the city was heavily invested in markets in the Deep South and was a major port on the Ohio River. At the same time, it was an important stop on the Underground Railroad, aided by an active vanguard of abolitionists. Many runaway slaves took their first breath of free air when they reached the north bank of the river.

By 1828, the racial climate in Cincinnati was so heated that many members of the black community were planning to move to rural Ohio where they hoped to establish their own settlement which they would call "Africania." In the span of three years, the number of black residents in the city had jumped from 700 to 2,258 persons or about 10 percent of the population.

Fearful that Cincinnati would soon be overrun by a class of primarily poor and uneducated people of color, the American Colonization Society initiated a campaign of negative propaganda. "[T]he rapid increase of our black population … is of itself a great evil … night walkers, lewd persons, and those who lounge about without any visible means of support, and especially the negro house gamblers."[10] Irish immigrants, in particular, felt threatened by the competition for jobs.

Invoking the 1807 Black Laws or Code, the *Cincinnati Daily Gazette* told all black residents that they had thirty days to post a $500 bond as proof of their respectability.[11] Finally, on August 15, 1829, a largely Irish mob estimated at 300, attacked the black neighborhoods in the city's Fourth Ward. For a full week, black homes, businesses, and properties were under siege and many were destroyed. Neither the police nor the mayor would lift a finger to protect them.

Finally, on August 24, Mayor Jacob Burnet dropped charges against ten African Americans and imposed fines on eight white men. When all was said and done, about 1,200 African Americans had left Cincinnati, eventually resettling in Wilberforce Colony in Ontario, Canada, at the invitation of the Governor of Upper Canada.

Mob Violence, Scioto County, January 1831—Black Friday [B]

According to Andrew Feight, on Friday, January 21, 1831, the following notice appeared in the *Portsmouth Courier*:

> The citizens of Portsmouth are adopting measures to free the town of its colored population. We saw a paper, yesterday, with between one and two hundred names, including most of the house-holders, in which they pledged themselves not to employ any of them who have not complied with the law. The authorities have requested us to give notice that they will hereafter enforce the law indiscriminately.[12]

In recounting this chapter in the city's history some seventy years later, Nelson Evans dubbed it "Black Friday" and wrote that "all the colored people in Portsmouth were forcibly deported from the town. They were not only warned out, but they were driven out. They were forced to leave their homes and belongings."[13] It is estimated that some eighty African Americans were expelled from the city limits, some of them settling in Huston Hollow about eight miles north of town.

However, this was not the first time African Americans had been pressured to leave Portsmouth. Feight discovered that at a meeting on March 2, 1818, the Wayne Township Trustees had authorized special payment of $4.18 to Warren Johnson, the town constable, for "warning out black and mulatto person of the township."[14]

Mob Violence, Pike County, 1830—Love, male [B]; Hill, Dennis [B]

Situated thirty miles north of Portsmouth is Waverly. About a year after its founding in 1829, a half dozen or so African American families arrived in Pike County from Virginia and settled about four miles northwest of town. Although they purportedly worked hard and did not bother anyone, some of their white neighbors resented their presence.

According to Henry Howe, Waverly's "antipathy to the negro" dated back to its earliest days.

> When Waverly was still in its swaddling clothes, there was a "yellow nigger" named Love, living on the outskirts of the town. He was a low-minded, impudent, vicious fellow, with the cheek of a mule. He was very insulting, and made enemies on every hand. His conduct finally became so objectionable, that a lot of the better class of citizens got together one night, made a descent upon his cabin, drove him out, and stoned him a long way in his flight toward Sharonville. He never dared to come back.[15]

During the same period, a black man named Dennis Hill who operated a tanning business at Piketon was "almost harassed to death by the negro-haters" and finally moved to Michigan "where he grew rich."[16]

Joseph Smith, the founder of Mormonism, was tarred and feathered by some of his former followers in 1832, as this illustration from J.H. Beadle's *Polygamy or the Mysteries and Crimes of Mormonism* (1904) shows.

Mob Violence, Lake County, March 1832—Smith, Joseph [W]; Rigdon, Sidney [W]

Tar and feathers was once the recommended punishment for the crime of theft, first appearing in the laws of England and France as early as the Crusades. While it is not considered as deadly as lynching, people were seriously injured at times and some even died.

One of the factors was the temperature of the tar when it was applied. Historically, the tar used was not the thick black tar—bitumen—used today for roads and roofs, but pine tar such as a baseball player might apply to the handle of his bat. Although it was usually brushed on or daubed on with a stick, people sometimes applied it with their bare hands. It could be removed with kerosene and a lot of scrubbing.

The first person known to have been tarred and feathered in Ohio was Joseph Smith. The founder of the Church of the Latter Day Saints or Mormons, Smith had settled his followers in Kirtland, Lake County in 1831, after relocating from upstate New York. He had been emboldened to make the move by the large number of converts in that region. While some of his devotees soon pushed on to Missouri, Smith was happy, for the moment, in what would become Lake County.

While staying at the John Johnson farm, both he and Sidney Rigdon, one of his chief spokesmen, were attacked by a gang of apostates from the faith. Then on March 24, 1832, he experienced his first taste of the persecution that would dog him the rest of his short life. Smith and Rigdon were set upon by a party of drunken thugs who beat them severely, then covered them with tar and feathers.

As biographer Fawn Brodie wrote:

> Fortified by a barrel of whiskey, [the mob] smashed their way into the Johnson home on the night of March 24, 1832, and dragged Joseph from the trundle bed where he had fallen asleep while watching one of the twins. They stripped him, scratched and beat him with savage pleasure, and smeared his bleeding body with tar from head to foot. Ripping a pillow into shreds, they plastered him with feathers. It is said that Eli Johnson demanded that the prophet be castrated, for he suspected Joseph of being too intimate with his sister, Nancy Marinda. But the doctor who had been persuaded to join the mob declined the responsibility at the last moment....[17]

Rigdon got the same treatment. While not everyone accepts Brodie's account, there is no doubt that both men were assaulted by ex-members of the church. For the most part, Smith and the Mormons were tolerated by their non-Mormon neighbors in Kirtland—that is until he established an illegal bank and it failed, bankrupting many investors.

Afterward, all was forgiven and Smith remained in Kirtland for five more years.

Mob Violence, Pike County, 1835—Unknown settlers [B]

Timothy Downing was "the leader of the gang that made almost constant war" on a group of African Americans from Virginia who had settled on Pee-Pee Creek.[18] They burned their wheat and hay, harassed their livestock, and did what they could to interfere in every aspect of their lives. Finally, Downing and his companions, including Williams Burke, made a raid on the black settlement around 1835, intending to kill them all. After surrounding one cabin, they opened fire.

Grabbing a rifle and concealing himself behind the corner of the house, a black settler shot back, nicking the artery in Downing's brother's leg. The raiders threw the wounded man over a horse and immediately took him to Burke's home where he died from blood loss.

A coroner's jury ruled Downing had died as the result of a gunshot wound, but did not identify the person who shot him. Nevertheless, the black settler was arrested and tried for murder. Amazingly, he was acquitted. Consequently, Tim Downing went to the man's house and shot him in the head. Downing was never held accountable for this assault and the victim, who recovered, moved away.

A year passed. One day, Downing's brother confronted an African American near Sharonville where he was making rails. Intending to kill him, he told the man he had only a few minutes "to make his peace with God."[19] Although Downing was sitting on a horse, the black man quickly struck him in the head with an axe before escaping.

Luckier than his brother, Downing wasn't killed, but forever bore the mark of this encounter—a scarred face. Both African American men were put on trial for these assaults, but were acquitted on the grounds of self-defense. "It was under such circumstances as these that the bitter anti-negro feeling at Waverly had its origin," Henry Howe concluded.[20]

Mob Violence, Licking County, April 1835—Robinson, R. [W]; Weld, Theodore D. [W]

When it was announced that the Reverend R. Robinson, a noted abolitionist, would be giving an anti-slavery lecture at the Congregational Church in Newark, a group opposed to his views took him from the pulpit by force and dragged him into the streets where they "treated him in a most brutal manner."[21] Immigrants from Maryland and Virginia were blamed for having brought this "southern prejudice against the negro" with them.[22]

The anti-slavery movement had its first rumblings at nearby Granville in 1834. A Western Reserve College student named Hawley riled things up when he denounced the colonization program supported by some members of the community as a "scheme hatched in Hell."[23] All this supposedly accomplished was to widen the gulf between the moderates and the extremists, and the colonization society profited as a result.

The following year, on April 3, 1835, Theodore D. Weld, a recent ministry student at the Lane Seminary, came to the community to speak on the topic at the Granville Female Academy. His credentials were impressive. He had been one of the sixty-three organizers of the American Anti-Slavery Society two years earlier. He was also a direct descendant of Jonathan Edwards (the great Puritan theologian) and the man who had converted Henry Ward Beecher and Harriet Beecher Stowe to the abolitionist cause.

Because it was a warm evening, the windows of the conference room were open. A throng of people unfriendly to his message gathered and pelted him and his audience—both men and women—with eggs. Nevertheless, Weld wiped the raw egg from his face and continued to speak.

Stymied in their efforts to silence him, the crowd bobbed the tail and mane of his horse. However, the building was owned by the Congregational Church and the demonstration so alarmed the pastor and the trustees that they refused to allow Weld to use it again.

Weld was subsequently invited to speak at a house that stood unfinished, lacking windows and doors. This time, he spoke from an upper window to a large crowd that had assembled outside. Although no eggs were thrown, he was subjected to hoots and hollers from those who objected to his opinions. Consequently, village officials pressured him to leave Granville, which he did.

Mob Violence, Pike County, 1836—Weed, Edward [W]

Dr. William Blackstone of Pike County learned in 1836 that an English abolitionist, George Thompson (actually, the Reverend Edward Weed), was touring Ohio, so he prevailed upon him to give an address on the cause in Waverly.[24]

As soon as the people heard of Blackstone's intentions, they united in protest. He was "warned not to send for Thompson; warned that if Thompson came he would not be allowed to make a public speech, and warned that it would not add any to Dr. Wm. Blackstone's happiness, for him to slap public sentiment in the face."[25]

These threats, issued by a group led by a man named Quill Jordan, only strengthened Blackstone's determination to have Thompson speak. The day before the scheduled lecture, Thompson arrived in Waverly and was warmly received at Blackstone's home. The doctor vowed that he would sacrifice his own life if necessary to ensure that the people of Waverly got to hear Thompson speak against slavery.

The campaign against Thompson began that same night when his horse was taken from the stable, his mane clipped, and his hair shaved. His buggy was painted with some obnoxious substance and hauled to the roof of a house.

Early the next morning, a crowd presented itself in front of Blackstone's house and Jordan informed Blackstone, "Thompson can't speak here to-day. And what's more, he can't speak here any other day. He is a traitor and here for a traitor's purpose; and the sooner he gets out of this community, the better it will be for Dr. William Blackstone and the Honorable George Thompson, of England."[26]

The crowd, which had "grown to threatening proportions," cheered Jordan's declaration. They then began chanting, "Fee, fie, fo, fum! We smell the blood of an Englishman!"[27] The mob became increasingly menacing.

Having heard what was occurring, "Old" Squire Barnes came to the scene and endeavored to read the riot act to the crowd. However, he was quickly seized, loaded into a buggy, and driven away.

Jordan warned Blackstone that if Thompson attempted to make a speech, they would tear down his house, log by log. He gave Thompson fifteen minutes to leave town and five hours to vacate the county. After consulting with Thompson, Blackstone rushed the Englishman out the rear door of the house, placed him on his horse, and pointed him out of town at a full gallop.

Having anticipated this might happen, Jordan had stationed men throughout the town to pelt Thompson with rotten eggs as he fled. The incident so angered Blackstone that he swore he would no longer live in "such a damned intolerant community" and moved to Athens not long afterward.[28]

However, according to a letter later published in the *Chillicothe Gazette*, Samuel Reed, a former Associate Judge of the Court of Common Pleas in Pike County, negotiated Thompson/Weed's peaceful exit. Weed then fled to Piketon, where he spent the night in the home of another supporter before leaving the county the following morning.

While in Piketon, Weed wrote a letter to his new wife, who at the time was living near Cincinnati: "Much violence is abroad in the land. For the last four days"—Weed had apparently lectured in Waverly, contrary to the account provided by Emmitt—"I have been in the midst of an infuriated mob who were seeking my life. But the Lord has delivered me out of their hand.... Now, while I am writing, there are men all around thirsting for my blood, and would kill me, if they had a good opportunity, as soon as they would a snake!"[29]

Mob Violence, Hamilton County, April 1836—Pro-Slavery Riots [B]

One of the darkest stains on Cincinnati's history was the so-called Pro-Slavery Riots of 1836. They were sparked by an incident which occurred on April 11, 1836, in which a white boy and a black boy got into a fight and the white boy lost.

Since there was already a large body of citizens who had no use for African Americans, a mob sprang up almost immediately, ostensibly in support of the white boy, but in reality to drive the blacks out of the community. They moved to an area known as "The Swamp" at Broadway and Sixth streets where "the houses of many negroes were burned to the ground, and their occupants shot down like dogs."[30]

Although the police made an attempt to intervene, they were powerless to stop the vandalism and the killing.

Many of the riot participants and instigators were alleged to have come across the river from Kentucky. Finally, Governor Joseph Vance imposed martial law and sent in troops to restore order.

Historian S.B. Nelson noted, "A remarkable feature connected with these pro slavery demonstrations was the eminent respectability of the men who acted as leaders and urged the rabble to commit deeds of violence and destruction."[31] Harriet Beecher Stowe, a resident of Cincinnati and, later, author of *Uncle Tom's Cabin*, quoted the mayor as saying, "Well, lads, you have done well, so far; go home now before you disgrace yourselves."[32] No arrests were ever made.

Twice in 1836, rioters destroyed the office of James G. Birney, an abolitionist newspaper publisher. A former slave owner from Alabama, Birney incited the wrath of local businessmen who valued their business connections with southern states. At a time when free blacks and escaped slaves were competing for jobs in the local economy, his antislavery stance fanned the flames.

Mob Violence, Licking County, April 1836—Granville Riot [W]

The Ohio State Anti-Slavery Convention met in Granville on April 27, 1836, but was unable to obtain a room within the village because seventy-five men, including the mayor, members of council, and other prominent citizens had signed a petition against it. So the group convened in a large barn outside town they named "The Hall of Freedom."

About 200 people (nearly half the population of the village) collected in Granville on the day of the convention to oppose it. They decided to confront the conventioneers as they marched through town in a procession that afternoon. However, Misses Grant and Bridges happened to suspend classes at their ladies' school at that very time and they and their charges, some forty girls, were caught in between the rival factions. There were also nineteen women delegates and an unknown number of female spectators on the streets.

Some of the male delegates spontaneously fell in beside the academy girls, who were walking in pairs, in order to escort them to their boarding house. With a man walking on either side, they formed a column of fours which seemed to enrage the drunken troublemakers, perhaps because it resembled a military formation.

All at once, a prominent citizen was heard to shout, "Egg the squaws!" and the young women fell under a barrage of eggs and other items.[33] When a college student and his girlfriend were forced into a muddy ditch by the protesters, a free-for-all commenced. Abolitionists and demonstrators tussled in the dirt as eggs continued to fly and women were assaulted. Some eyewitnesses estimated there were 400 or more people on the main street.

Constable Anderson, who had left town earlier to avoid being on hand for the anticipated trouble, rode up and attempted to put a stop to the mayhem. However, he was quickly dragged off his horse. Judge J.G. Birney came riding through, but was driven out of town under a hail of eggs. Squire Elias Gilman tried to read them the riot act, but was shouted down.

For half an hour, the town was totally lawless. At some point, people began swinging clubs. Although no one was killed, many were injured, some seriously. One unconscious victim was found hours later on a Broadway porch.

Finally, a violent thunderstorm came up, driving the throng inside for cover. By early evening, peace had returned and the Granville band played an impromptu concert on the village square.

In the end, the citizens of Granville were ashamed that a riot had occurred in their community. When the abolitionists met that evening in the stone schoolhouse on Welsh Hills, no one bothered them. Soon, their rolls had increased and Granville was established a station on the Underground Railroad.

Mob Violence, Licking County, March 1837—White, Samuel [W]; Spencer, William [W]; Linnell, Knowles [W]; Gunn, Charles [W]

Fifteen miles northwest of Granville at the village of Hartford, Samuel White, a local resident known for his abolitionist sentiments, was assaulted and ridden out of town on a rail in March 1837, in what came to be called the Hartford Riot.

White, the first student to enroll at what became Denison University, had been speaking at a meeting with William Spencer, Knowles Linnell, and Charles Gunn. They also were beaten. White soon left school and enrolled at Oberlin College, where his views were more appreciated.

Mob Violence, Mahoning County, June 1837—Robinson, Marius [W]

Marius Robinson was a student at Cincinnati's Lane Theological Seminary in 1835 when he decided to practice what he preached, namely the abolition of slavery.

Shortly after his marriage to Emily Rakestraw (whose parents promptly disowned her), Robinson set out on a tour of Ohio, speaking and organizing the antislavery movement. In letters home, he described the hardships he and his fellow abolitionists endured, especially the attacks by those opposed to his cause.

In June 1837, ten months after his departure, Robinson, age thirty-one, came to Berlin, Mahoning (formerly Trumbull) County, where he stayed with a Quaker merchant, Jesse Garretson. At about ten o'clock on the evening on June 3, he was sitting in the store with Mr. and Mrs. Garretson when a group of men charged in and grabbed him.

"You have got to leave this town tonight," they said. "You have disturbed the peace of our citizens long enough."[34] Assisted by the Garretsons, Robinson tried to resist them, but they were outnumbered. He was wrestled outside where he was stripped of his clothing and had tar and feathers applied to his body. His left arm near his shoulder was injured in the struggle and bled freely.

After they had dressed him again, Robinson was hauled eleven miles out in the country to a point near the village of Canfield where he was left in the road. He found refuge in a nearby home.

A dozen men were indicted for the assault, but before the case could be tried, each of them agreed to pay Robinson $40. Although he suffered from the effects of his mistreatment the rest of his life, Robinson and his wife continued to promote the abolitionist cause through lectures and the publication of their anti-slavery newspaper, the *Bugle*.

Expected Lynching, Hamilton County, March 1840—Whitewater Shakers [W]

Late in 1839, Mary Black and her two sons left the Whitewater Shaker settlement in Hamilton County for Kentucky. It is likely she sought refuge with the Society of Believers after she was widowed, but had been unable to accept their peculiar religious beliefs—equality of the sexes, pacifism, celibacy, and separation from the world.

In March of the following year, legal authorities in Cincinnati were notified by their counterparts in Bracken County, Kentucky, that the boys had been "emasculated" by the Shakers. Delivered to Cincinnati at once, the two were examined by a couple of doctors who asserted that the accusation was true.

On Wednesday, March 25, the marshal of Cincinnati and a deputy sheriff arrested at least fourteen members of the Whitewater community, including Elder Archibald Meacham, Joseph Agnew, Manley Sherman, William A. Agnew, and John S. Whitney.

By five o'clock that evening, a "multitude" of people had jammed the streets outside the county jail, disturbed by the account of what the Shakers had done to Mrs. Black's sons. For many, the alleged crime was just an excuse. They had never cared for the Shakers and felt threatened by them simply because they were different.

Over the next two days, there was a very real concern that the prisoners might be taken by force from the jail and hanged. At four o'clock on Friday afternoon, the brethren were led into the courthouse where they found their trial was already in progress and testimony was being taken. They remained until sunset when they were returned to their cells.

The trial resumed on Saturday. Defense counsel had succeeded in persuading the mayor and the marshal to have the boys examined by another pair of physicians. This time the medical opinion was that the two suffered from a "medical deformity" and had not been abused by the Shakers in any manner. Consequently, they were acquitted, although the records for Union Village state, "As if to add injury to insult, the greedy cats charged $300 for fees; besides incidental expenses that would of course accrue to the prosecution."[35]

Expected Lynching, Richland County, October 1840—Bushong, Samuel [W]

There was talk of a lynching when Samuel Bushong slaughtered his family. A resident of Chestnut Ridge, not far from Bellville, Bushong was never an agreeable man and was known to mistreat his family, brought on by financial difficulties. But on October 4, 1840, he apparently slipped into insanity. First he split his wife's head open with an axe while she was preparing breakfast. He then went after his two daughters and two sons, killing the former and seriously injuring the latter.

Naturally, the community was abuzz. "Kill him, and throw his body on the pile," some said.[36] Others called for hanging him. However, "a few negative words by Dr. Eels and a few other dispassionate persons calmed their vengeance."[37]

Bushong was handled roughly by his captors who tied him on a horse. Some twenty men or more then escorted him to Bellville. After he entered a plea of insanity, the doctors declared it was a clear case of "monomania," the court found him not guilty, and he was released.

Placed in the custody of his brother-in-law, Bushong was taken to Columbiana County where he died sometime prior to 1850.

Mob Violence, Montgomery County, January–February 1841—Dayton Riot [B]

Though overshadowed by the Cincinnati riot the same year, the Dayton riot had a profound impact on the city's African American population, causing them to withdraw into their own community.

On January 23, 1841, an appearance by antislavery activist Thomas Morris, a former Ohio senator, was disrupted by an anti-abolition mob. Two days later, a similar mob raided a black neighborhood in the vicinity of Fifth, Wayne, and Eagle Streets.

A light complected black woman had moved into a black resort known as the Paul Pry (likely some sort of tavern), but the mob believed she was actually white. During the confusion, a black man killed the mob's white leader, Nat McCleary.

Then on February 3, 1841, during a sub-zero cold spell, another mob returned to the neighborhood, burned a number of cabins, and drove out many of the black residents, some of whom died of exposure. Sixty to seventy African American men, women, and children fled to Detroit.

In its coverage of the incident, the *Signal of Liberty* asked how a black man could respond to the accusation that he could not take care of himself when he had no legal protection when he was attacked and robbed.

Mob Violence, Hamilton County, September 1841—Little Africa [B]

Ohio's white citizens were generally opposed to slavery, but they did not, for the most part, support social equality. Racial prejudice was palpable. When an extended period of drought led to widespread unemployment on the waterfront, a mob of idle whites turned their anger on the African American residents of Cincinnati. It began on August 31, 1841.

The *Daily Gazette* reported a week later: "This city has been in a most alarming condition for several days, and from about eight o'clock on Friday evening until about three o'clock yesterday morning, almost entirely at the mercy of a lawless mob, ranging in number from two to fifteen hundred."[38]

One particular incident involved a fight between a party of Irishmen and several persons of color in which two or three people on each side were wounded. The quarrel continued the following night with an attack upon an African American boarding house on McAlister Street. The Irishmen, armed with clubs, drove the blacks out of the building and threatened their lives. However, the black men in the adjoining houses resisted. Both sides may have employed firearms.

The next several nights were a repetition of the first two. Squabbles in the streets and assaults upon African American residences in the "Little Africa" neighborhood—all without police interference. Finally, a band of men who had formed in Kentucky assembled in the Fifth Street Market and began marching toward Broadway and Sixth Street. Armed with clubs, stones, bricks, etc., they called out the black residents of Cincinnati before laying siege to a black-owned confectionery on Broadway.

When the mayor arrived on the scene and urged them to obey the law, he was shouted down. The mob continued to advance, hurling missiles, until they were met with gunfire. Scattering for cover, they immediately rallied, but were repulsed once more. There were many wounded on both sides and some dead as well.

The African Americans began to push the crowd back and even fired into it. The battle went back and forth all evening until past one o'clock in the morning when someone obtained a six-pound cannon from the riverfront. Loading it with boiler punching (i.e., soot and sediment) and other scrap, it was pointed down Sixth Street. Over the objections of the mayor, it was discharged several times as both groups continued shooting at one another.

In the daylight, the mayor posted sentinels and imposed martial law in the area. Many blacks were rounded up and thrown in jail—some 300 altogether—and held until they paid bond in accordance with the Black Code.

Mob Violence, Clark County, 1844—Fall, Chancey [W]

Although Chancey Fall of Moorehead was said to be a Whig, he was also regarded as an abolitionist. "Mr. Fall harbored runaway slaves, and because his neighbors were intolerant, he was tarred and feathered; they rode him on a rail for it."[39]

Mob Violence, Auglaize/Shelby County, 1846—Randolph slaves [B]

In death, John Randolph was more charitable than in life. When he died in Roanoke, Virginia, in 1846, Randolph left three wills explicitly stating that his slaves should be freed. However, thirteen years would pass while his family contested the bequest which, at $1,000 per slave, would have cost the estate a lot of money.

Finally, William Leigh, the executor of the estate, purchased land for them near Carthagena, Ohio, which was already established as a settlement for free blacks in Mercer County. It had been founded by Augustus Wattles, a white Quaker, in the 1830s.

The freed slaves, numbering 383, left Virginia on June 10, 1846. They ranged in age from less than a year to over 100. They traveled down the Ohio River to Cincinnati, then north on the Miami Canal. Upon reaching New Bremen, ten miles east of Carthagena, on July 12th, 1846, the freemen disembarked and made camp. A Mr. Cardwell, in whose trust they had been placed, went to meet with the local citizenry to discuss the group's plans.

However, the farmers in the area had already considered the prospect of having nearly 400 new black neighbors joining with those already living at Carthagena and they didn't like the idea that the white citizens would be out numbered.

That evening, an armed mob of some fifty to 100 armed white men surrounded the camp and its leader read the following proclamation: "Resolved, that we will not live among Negroes; as we have settled here first, we have fully determined that we will resist the settlement of blacks and mulattoes in the county to the full extent of our means, the bayonet not excepted."

The *Cincinnati Gazette* of July 2, 1846, no doubt captured popular sentiment when it opined,

> The people of Virginia ... hear the call of death ... the first step is to free the slaves, that they may lull the unquiet knawings of conscience next to send them to Ohio so that they may be free. What right have they to be pouring in upon us their helpless, new made free [*sic*]?[40]

The following day, Cardwell, who had been taken into custody, was compelled to pay passage for himself and the freed slaves. They were to return the way they had come, back down the canal, dropping off a portion of the emigrants at each stop. But this did not go smoothly, either. They were first taken to a place in Shelby County called "Carey's Plantation" (possibly Fort Loramie). The July 14, 1893, edition of the *Sidney Journal* recalled:

> In July of 1846 quite a commotion was caused in the village by the arrival of a boat carrying as passengers ... about 100 Randolph slaves, just set free. The boat passed up to the vicinity of Berlin (Now known as Fort Loramie), but were not allowed to land. A mob received them with sticks and stones.[41]

Next, they went to Sidney, where they attracted another mob. After making appeals to their charity, an agreement was reached to allow a number of them to stay. A "good class of white people took some on the farm, and some around to the dwelling houses ... some settled around through Sidney ... and the rest came to Piqua." The remainder of the group reboarded the canal boats. They moved onto Troy, Xenia, West Milton, and elsewhere.

Attempted Lynching, Hamilton County, 1846—Unknown soldiers [W]

Two Mexican-American War veterans came to Cincinnati in 1846. Securing jobs in a downtown factory, the soldiers began boarding with a German family. In exchange for their military service, they had been issued land warrants which their hosts coveted. However, they did not want to give them up. So the proprietor charged the two men with having assaulted his seven-year-old daughter. Unable to pay the $5,000 bail, the suspects were promptly jailed to await trial.

When the public learned of the horrible crime, it didn't take long for a throng of people to collect in front of the jail, threatening to lynch the prisoners. Sheriff Thomas S. Weaver responded by calling out two militia units—the Citizens' Guards and the Cincinnati Greys.

From time to time, Weaver addressed the crowd, urging them to disperse, but as the night wore on they became angrier and restless. He warned them he would shoot them down if they attempted to rush the jail, but they did not listen. When they made a surge toward the jail, the soldiers fired blank cartridges, but these did not frighten them.

At the risk of his own life, Weaver went outside and informed the mob that they would not fire blanks next time, but he was shouted down. Finally, they tore down the fences, ripped up the pavement, and began hurling missiles at the jail.

As they breached the doors, Sheriff Weaver ordered the guard to shoot and eleven people fell dead. That took the fight out of the rest and they immediately scattered to their homes. Unfortunately, several innocent bystanders had died in the volley—a woman working in her house across the street and a workman who was on his way home.

Thousands of people would attend the funerals for the slain, but eventually public sentiment favored the sheriff. This was reinforced when a grand jury heard the case against the men and learned the little girl had been coached by her parents to testify against them, even though the accusation wasn't true. Furthermore, the father had been overheard telling the prisoners that he would go away if they would simply give him the land warrants.

Finally, more than twenty physicians testified that the crime with which they had been charged was an impossible one. If the mother and the father hadn't disappeared with their child, they might have found themselves at the end of a rope.

Mob Violence, Montgomery County, March 1851—"M.N." [W?]

In Montgomery County, a dozen people forced an elderly woman out of her house on the night of March 20, 1851. "M.N." (as she was identified) was then made to walk some 200 yards to the Great Miami River where they cast her into its cold waters. After retrieving the poor creature, they dragged her along the ground another 100 yards to where they covered her with tar and feathers. Finally, she was beaten, kicked, and whipped with switches.

The following day, M.N. died from her injuries and her twelve attackers were indicted for manslaughter.

Expected Lynching, Summit County, April 1853—Parks, James [W]

Thirty-five-year-old James Parks readily acknowledged that he was a person of bad character. He had reportedly been a poacher, burglar, and highwayman in his native England, for which he spent seven years in prison. Then after immigrating to the United States, he participated in a grave robbing while in Rhode Island, for which he served more time. Upon his release, he committed a series of robberies and burglaries in Philadelphia which resulted in four more years in prison.

Finally, he relocated to Cleveland around 1851 and opened one of the most notorious saloons in the city. It was then that he changed his name from Dickinson to Parks, but he couldn't change his broad face, scarred nose, and missing front teeth.

When his companion (possibly brother-in-law), William Beatson, purportedly died from a nasty fall on the wagon road from Cuyahoga Falls to Hudson on April 13, 1853, Parks said he knew no one would believe it was an accident. So after giving the matter some thought, he stripped Beatson's body, cut off his head, and threw both into the river. He then disposed of the clothing as he continued along the road. Even with the aid of a spiritualist, the head was never found.

Parks was right. No one did believe him. He was also charged with cutting Beatson's throat, as well as shooting and striking him in the head with a stone. The motive was robbery. Convicted of murder in the first degree, he was sentenced to be hanged.

On the appointed day, a huge crowd assembled outside the jail, 2,000 of whom were thought to be from outside of Akron.[42] Initially, Parks feared he would be lynched, but was reassured by the sight of so many "ladies" in the throng. He responded by displaying himself in the window of the jail, while pleading his innocence.

However, this served only to fuel the anger of the crowd which sought to punish him themselves. They were further disappointed when Parks was granted a new trial on the basis that the first had not been impartial due to the prejudicial feeling that existed against him.

Transferred to Cuyahoga County, Parks was tried again. But the result was the same: guilty of first degree murder. Sentenced to hang on June 1, 1855, he went to his grave protesting his innocence.

Mob Violence, Hamilton County, December 1853—Bedini Riots (Part I) [W]

Germans who immigrated to Cincinnati following the failed rebellion of 1848 were often called the "Forty-Eighters" or, sometimes, "Society of Freeman." When they heard that Cardinal Gaetano Bedini was being sent to Cincinnati as the Papal Nuncio (Pope's diplomat), they were outraged. They considered the priest to be a traitor for his role in undermining the rebellion—the anti-Papal Roman Republic. So on December 25, 1853, a group of them some 500 strong marched to the cathedral at the corner of Eighth and Plum Streets in protest.

The mayor of Cincinnati promptly dispatched the police to restore order. After one officer was shot, Police Chief Looken ordered his men to use their batons on the protesters. Several men were injured and one died.

The officer's funeral was one of the largest in the city's history. The men charged with his murder were tried the following Friday and acquitted. Although the actions of the chief were deemed "entirely justifiable, [it] aroused bitter feelings against the police, and the mayor was obliged to dismiss Chief Looken, who had done nothing more than his duty."[43]

Mob Violence, Hamilton County, January 1854—Bedini Riot (Part II) [W]

Three weeks later on January 15, 1854, riots broke out in Cincinnati again. Meeting at a vacant lot on Elm Street, a group of Forty-Eighters marched to the archbishop's residence where they burned Cardinal Bedini in effigy. When Marshal Ruffin, Deputy Sheriff Thomas Higdon, and several other law enforcement officers tried to intervene, Higdon was stabbed and Ruffin knocked to the ground and clubbed. Higdon died of his injuries.

Mob Violence, Brown County, June 1854—Temperance Riot [W]

The riot in Ripley on June 24, 1854, was sparked by the customers of a tavern throwing rotten eggs into a coffee house while a temperance meeting was in progress. In response, the temperance men destroyed all the liquor and fixtures in the tavern. They then "visited all the liquor shops in the town, and those that did not agree to give up the business were assaulted."[44] No one was injured.

Mob Violence, Hamilton County, April 1855—Know-Nothing Riot [W]

The American Party, known as the Know-Nothings, despised all foreigners, especially Roman Catholics, and frequently clashed with the German immigrants in the Over-the-Rhine district of Cincinnati. The Know-Nothings were concerned that they would lose the upcoming election in the predominantly German Eleventh Ward if the Germans voted as a bloc for the Democratic ticket.

On April 2, 1855, Election Day, a number of Know-Nothings gathered in the lower part of Cincinnati and began to march north toward the Vine Street Bridge, intending to seize and destroy the ballot boxes. When they reached it, they found that the Germans had a cannon trained on the bridge. Before any serious violence could occur, however, some peaceful citizens intervened.

That evening, a "squad of half grown men and boys with fife, drum and flag" proceeded up Vine Street and across the bridge.[45] The Germans purportedly fired upon them from the windows of their houses, wounding several and driving them back. The Germans then erected a barricade across Vine Street near Freeman's Hall, and also created a wall from drays, wagons, and carts parked along the sidewalks and across the street.

As many as 5,000 Germans stood behind the wall, armed with "stones, sticks, bludgeons, revolvers, muskets, carbines, rifles, slingshots and all the various instruments of offensive and defensive warfare."[46] Among them were members of the Sarsfield Guards, several German military companies, and a fair number of Irish citizens. They remained in place for a day or so until the Know-Nothings had left.

The fight may have been precipitated by the killing of a foreman at Link's brewery by William Brown, a Know-Nothing, on Election Day. Although the story is garbled, a "party of rowdies" was said to have entered a German drinking establishment and ordered beer.[47] After it had been served to them, they tore the place up, knocked the owner senseless, and assaulted his wife and kids. Outside, they encountered four Germans walking along the sidewalk. They knocked down three and stabbed the fourth to death.

But there was also a rumor that the riot was initiated by professional gamblers who had wagered large sums of money on the outcome of the election. They supposedly had infiltrated the Know-Nothing Party and called upon their brethren to destroy the ballot boxes in the strongest German ward. The party members then turned out in force, seized the cannon from the Germans and the Irish, and fired upon them, possibly killing ten or twelve and wounding many others.

On the evening following the election, a resident of Newport named Morgan was shot from a Vine Street window. Whether an innocent bystander or not, over 10,000 Americans wearing a distinctive soft white hat called the Know-Nothing hat attended his funeral.

Mob Violence, Franklin County, May 1855—Turner Riot (Part I) [W]

German immigrants who settled in Columbus, many coming in the wake of the failed revolution of 1848, found they weren't necessarily welcome. The nativist Americans (mostly English-speaking citizens who had been here a generation or more) were often suspicious and mistrustful of them, as they were all foreigners.

The Germans had a different language, different customs, and different institutions. One of these was the Turnverein or Turners, an athletic, social, and political organization that they brought with them from their homeland. The primary purpose of the Turners was to encourage physical education and fitness, but to outsiders such uniformity of appearance and clannishness represented a threat.

On May 29, 1855, some forty members of the Turners marched south out of the city to Stewart's Grove for a picnic. They carried a red silk flag bordered in black with a motto in yellow letters on each side. While the Turners were enjoying their outing—typically open-air gymnastics and the singing of German songs—a rumor began making the rounds that they had been bearing the "Red Republican flag of Germany" and that it bore anti–American slogans.[48]

In truth, the flag was wholly inoffensive. The mottos, written in German, were "Blithe, Merry, and Free" on one side and "Through exercise, strength; through investigation, knowledge. Freedom" on the other.[49] The Turners had planned to carry a United States flag as well, but had yet to obtain one.

That evening as the Turners paraded back into Columbus toward their Turnhall, they were met at the Friend Street canal bridge by a band of thugs and hooligans, likely Know-Nothings, who demanded they lower the flag. When the Turners refused, the mob began throwing stones at them and a struggle ensued. Several people were injured as the flag was wrested away from them. The musicians and boys quickly fled, followed closely by the rest of the Turners. They were chased to Front Street by the rowdies who continued to hurl stones and other missiles. Other "young loafers" joined the pursuit.[50]

Additional fights broke out at South and Front Streets and Mound and High Streets. More rocks were hurled and some of the Germans were severely beaten. The uniform of the Turners was a white coat, which made them an easy target. One man wearing such a coat was chased by a furious crowd, yelling, "Kill the damned Dutchman!"[51] When they caught him, he was savagely beaten. Another man in a white coat was also assaulted and left in the gutter to die.

An hour or two later, six Germans were accosted by about sixty "Americans" who stoned and beat them.[52] The police, all allegedly Know-Nothings, arrested none of the assailants, but several of the victims. One was arrested simply for wearing a white coat and his friend was threatened with arrest for offering to pay his bail. A newspaper blamed the Germans because their attackers did not understand their language.

Mob Violence, Franklin County, July 1855—Turner Riot (Part II) [W]

Barely a month later, on July 4, 1855, the Turners were victimized once again. A fire company of the South Ward, a German Infantry Company, and the Turners had been celebrating Independence Day. At about 6:30 in the evening, they began to parade through the streets, an American flag at the head of the procession, and the Turners, numbering seventy-eight individuals, carrying their customary banner in the rear.

As the procession crossed High Street on State, someone in the crowd made a threat, but no actions were taken. However, as the head of the column turned down High Street from Town, some onlookers began jeering, making threats, and flinging stones at them.

Although subsequent testimony was conflicting, there is no question the Turners did not initiate the dispute. It is believed that it started when a fifteen-year-old boy got in an argument with a Turner and hit him with a stone. Another Turner may have then thrown a stone back at the boy. When he followed the boy to the United States Hotel and was prepared to throw another stone, the landlord, Mr. Simonton, seized the Turner and took the stone away from him.

A second man, John White, who knew the boy, grabbed him and tried to flee. That is when they were allegedly stoned by the Turners. A melee broke out by the hotel between the Turners and the people in the street. Four windows were broken in the hotel and people fled in all directions.

When the Turners reached High Street, they purportedly drew their revolvers (having armed themselves this time) and commenced firing while stones continued to fly.

However, other witnesses asserted that the shots were fired by someone—not a Turner—in the vacant space in front of the basement of the hotel. A bystander, Henry Foster, who was on the east side of High Street, was struck by a bullet and died half an hour later. Both the hotel and Doctor Parson's house were riddled with bullets. The Turners then returned to their position in the ranks of the parade. The whole affair lasted about three minutes.

Nineteen Germans were arrested, some of whom were believed to have been completely innocent. The police rounded them up as they walked along the street or broke into their houses and rousted them from bed. A large crowd had joined in the pursuit, some throwing rocks, yelling, cursing, and calling upon the police to hang the Turners from lampposts and telegraph poles.

A day later, the Turners who had been lodged in jail issued a statement declaring that every one of their members was a naturalized citizen had voted the Republican ticket. Of course, this set them up in opposition to the Know-Nothings.

Nevertheless, some forty-nine Turners were ultimately charged and had to pay about $3,000 in court fees. One of them was killed and many others were injured, including their physical education instructor who sustained a serious wound to the forehead. They subsequently disbanded their organization for about ten years.

Lynching, Adams County, November 1856—Terry, William "Old Bill" [B]

Ohio's first generally recognized lynching took place in Kentucky. Of course, that bit of geographical trivia mattered little to the victim, William "Old Bill" Terry, or to the citizens of Adams County who carried it out on Tuesday, November 25, 1856.

Three days earlier, Terry, a free black, had "committed an outrage on Mrs. Morrison" (some accounts say Morris) of Manchester whose husband was away.[53] The *New York Times* headlined that she was raped ("outrage" and "rape" being nearly synonymous terms during the nineteenth century).

Terry had made his way into her house at about two in the morning by removing the sash from a back window. Surprised in her bed, the woman screamed and jumped to her feet. As he grabbed for her throat, Terry's thumb entered her mouth and fractured her jaw. He then choked her until she was unconscious.

After sexually assaulting the woman, Terry went home to his own bed. When his wife asked him why he was panting so heavily, he replied that "he had run all the way from the river where he had been hard at work pumping out a flatboat."[54]

Mrs. Morrison's screams roused the neighbors. Although she found it difficult to talk, she was able to tell them she had scratched her attacker's face. Suspicion immediately fell on Terry because he was known to have committed or attempted to commit two rapes while living in Ironton. A crowd immediately went to his home where they found him in bed, his face badly bleeding.

Terry was taken by his captors to Manchester Island, located in the Ohio River just above town. With little ceremony, they hanged him from a convenient tree. However, the rope broke and he revived. At this point, he admitted his guilt. While there were those who wanted to continue with the lynching, others counseled them to let the law handle it.[55] So they transported Terry to West Union, some ten miles away, and lodged him in the county jail to await justice.

When Mr. Morrison arrived home and learned what had transpired, he and what must have been most of the male residents of Manchester (population 700 or so) decided that justice delayed was justice denied.

On Tuesday, sixty to 100 men, led by John Dougherty, Mrs. Morrison's brother, set out on horseback for the county seat, accompanied by a wagon. Breaking down the jail door, Dougherty cut Terry's chains with an axe and was stopped short of cleaving his skull. They then seized the frightened prisoner and conveyed him back to Manchester Island, arriving by three o'clock. He was, history notes, given "a little time to arrange his worldly affairs."[56]

Once they reached the Ohio River, Terry was hauled out to the closest of the Manchester Islands (originally three, now two). He was hanged from the limb of a large sycamore tree some twenty-five feet high which stood on the western end near the water's edge. After he had expired, his body was cut down and buried at the base of the tree. However, his remains were soon carted off to be dissected and studied by medical students.

Little is known about William Terry. He was an African American who either looked old or was old. He had few if any friends; certainly none who were willing to defend him. Even if there was nothing more to go on than he-said/she-said, the fact he was black and she was white tipped the scales of justice in her favor.

If convicted of rape in Ohio, Terry could have received a maximum penalty of twenty-one years in prison. However, many of the settlers of Adams County were from Kentucky where the punishment for rape was death when the woman was white and the man was black.

Expected Lynching, Adams County, November 1856—Milligan, Alexander [W]

In sharp contrast to William Terry, Alexander Milligan had been biding his time in the Adams County jail for a few days short of a year when it was stormed by a pack of angry men seeking to hang "Old" Bill. Although Milligan was in the process of being tried for two counts of murder in the first degree, he apparently was not bothered by the mob. This begs the question: why? Was it because he was white?

Late in the autumn of 1855, William H. Senter and his wife, Nancy (both in their mid-forties) had been introduced to Milligan by Clinton Dixon, a relative of theirs who lived in Brown County. They were told that Milligan, a twenty-five-year-old Englishman, had lived in Pennsylvania for several years before coming to Ohio. Upon his arrival, Dixon had given him several months working on his farm. The young man now wanted to buy a small farm and was interested in the Senters' place, located just outside the hamlet of Unity.

On the first day of November, Milligan agreed to pay the couple $1,000 by the first day of December. A contract was drawn up by William B. Brown, a local merchant, and was witnessed by Brown and Dixon. Milligan told the Senters that he would finance the deal by collecting money that was owed him by others in the area. While he set about doing so, they allowed him to move in with them.

In the weeks that followed, Milligan made himself at home and participated in many of the neighborhood social events. He was described "as being of good stature, fair complexioned with blue eyes, sociable, but quiet in his manners, with a broad Yorkshire accent in his speech, and seemingly intelligent in the ordinary affairs of life."[57] Folks back in Brown County had also been favorably impressed during his stay among them.

News of the pending sale quickly spread throughout the vicinity. When George A. Patton, a merchant in Harshaville, got wind of it, he was particularly interested because Senter owed him money.

Only a few days after discussing the matter with William Senter, Patton stopped by the residence on a Sunday and was told by Milligan that the couple had gone away, but he expected them to return on Monday to complete the sale. However, when Patton came back the following day to collect on his debt, he found Nancy Senter's parents were there, too. Milligan informed them all that the Senters had not yet returned from visiting their friends.

By this time, Patton had become concerned about his claim and went to West Union to seek legal advice. While in town, he learned that a few days earlier Milligan had presented himself to Squire William Stevenson, masquerading as William Senter, and requested that a deed be drawn up giving Milligan the farm.

On Tuesday, Patton went back to the Senter homestead where Milligan told him that he had paid the Senters off and they had signed the deed over to him before leaving to see some friends up river. When asked to produce the document, however, he was unable to do so. As it turned out, Squire Stevenson had refused to finalize the transaction until he could meet with Mrs. Senter as well.

Patton, along with Brown and James McClellan, all of whom were owed money by Milligan, accompanied him to West Union where he arranged to pay them by mortgaging the farm. However, when Brown arrived home that night, he found his business overrun with his neighbors who demanded that Milligan be arrested for murder. Squire J.C. Milligan of Oliver Township was rustled out of bed to issue a warrant and the town constable, old Johnny Moore, was dispatched to take him into custody.

Milligan was eating breakfast when Moore and a posse arrived. He would not allow them to take him anywhere until he finished his meal. In the meantime, the premises were thoroughly searched. Initially, blood spots were found on pillows and bed-clothing, then bloody clothing was found hidden in wheat barrels in the smokehouse, and finally two bodies were discovered beneath some logs and brush in the spring branch below the cabin.

It was evident the Senters had been slain with an axe while asleep in bed and then dragged to where they were discovered. The murder weapon had traces of blood and bits of hair on it. Nevertheless, Milligan denied any guilt, even when confronted with the horrific evidence.

Indicted for first degree murder, Milligan was tried over the course of a week, interrupted midway by the lynching of Terry. There were, it is estimated, 1,000 in attendance at his trial. Someone actually proposed to the mob that they wait until Milligan was sentenced to hang Terry. If Milligan did not receive a death sentence, then they could hang the two men together. However, the mob was anxious to complete the job they had undertaken and left Milligan behind while they led Terry to his doom.

For whatever reason, the jury could not agree that the crime had been premeditated and returned a verdict of murder in the second degree. It was determined that Milligan had killed the couple on the night of November 26, 1855, and then slept in the bed until the crime was discovered ten days later. He had even had a visitor during that time who had stayed overnight in the cabin. Sentenced to the penitentiary for life, he died a few years after he was released.

Mob Violence, Madison County, October (?) 1857—Unknown groom [B]

A black man and a "pretty white girl" eloped late in 1857.[58] When the honeymooners arrived in London, some of the local residents suggested that they tar and feather the husband and ride him out of town on a rail. Taking their threats seriously, the newlyweds "absquatulated" (as the *Evansville Daily Journal* put it).[59]

Mob Violence, Ashtabula County, March 1859—Richmond, Dr. B.W [W]

Dr. B.W. Richmond was tarred and feathered on March 31, 1859, at Jefferson. He had allegedly seduced Jane Udell, daughter of Frederick Udell, who had been living in the doctor's house.

On Thursday night, Richmond was lured from his home in the belief that his professional services were required. When he drew near Udell's house, he was jumped by four men who beat him with clubs, covered him in tar, dressed him in women's clothes, placed him in his buggy, and sent back in the direction of his home. As he reached the gate of his own house, his wife heard his groans and found him outside.

By Sunday, Richmond had recovered sufficiently that he was no longer considered to be in any danger. Udell, his two sons, Franklin and George, and three others were indicted for the offense. Both Richmond and Udell were respected men in the community. The disposition of the case is unknown.

Mob Violence, Belmont County, June 1859—Galton, Sarah [W]; Galton (son) [W]; Galton (daughter) [W]

Sarah Galton had been living with a daughter and son in Mount Liberty, but their behavior did not sit well with their neighbors. As the *Wheeling Intelligencer* wrote, "Their house was the resort of men whose names were not altogether unsullied, and the woman lived in open adultery with two persons of the opposite sex, much to the shame and disquietude of the better people of the village."[60]

On June 3, 1859, the Galton home was attacked by a party of men who demolished the front of the building and everything inside. They then severely beat the son and after tarring and feathering him made him promise to leave the house and find work. When they were finished with the son, they turned their attention to the mother and the daughter.

Although the girl was only sixteen, both women were tarred and feathered and then carried through the streets of Mount Liberty on rails, along with the son and a man named Bryan who, apparently, had been caught on the premises. Two other men, Henry Phillips and James Travis, had escaped through a back door during all of the commotion. Incredibly, Mrs. Gatton had been tarred and feathered once or twice before.

Mob Violence, Portage County, June 1860—Tousley, Franklin [W]

Franklin Tousley, wearing a coat of tar and feathers, turned up in the streets of Ravenna on June 24, 1860. He had purportedly been abusing his wife—beating and kicking her, tying her in a chair, forcing her to go without food, and working her nearly to death. She finally fled to her brother's house in Summit County.

Previously, Tousley had killed his cattle and three or four horses to keep creditors from getting them. He had also hitched a starving cow and dragged it around a field until it died. Worst of all, he had held his nine-year-old boy's face against the hot stove to punish him for refusing to do his chores when he lacked suitable clothing to protect him from the elements.

Finally, his neighbors in the village of Nelson had enough of his cruelty and took matters into their own hands.

2

War and Reconstruction (1861–1877)

Civil War was waged in the United States from 1861 to 1865, prompted by the longstanding controversy over slavery. At its conclusion, Congress endeavored to bring the Southern states back into the Union as quickly as possible, rebuilding the former Confederacy economically and socially, while also protecting the rights of African Americans. In most respects, Reconstruction, as it was called, failed.

Meanwhile, the African American population in Ohio had roughly doubled since just before the war.

Attempted Lynching, Hamilton County, January 1861—Lohrer, Constance [W]; Lohrer, Romain [W]

In the second week of January 1861, two Cincinnati police officers—Clairborne Long and Daniel Hallam—were stabbed to death in a brothel. Brothers (or father and son) Constance (or Casimir) and Romain Lohrer were arrested for the crime and placed in the city jail.

According to the *New York Times*, it did not take long for a mob estimated at 2,000 to form, hankering to lynch the prisoners. They tore down a wooden fence and rushed the door of the jail. However, the mayor called up the Guthrie Grays, a local militia group, to defend the building. They quickly dispersed the rioters.

The police determined that the deaths of the two officers was due to "an inscrutable dispensation of divine Providence."[1] The Lohrers were expected to plead not guilty.

Mob Violence, Hocking County, May 1861—Spears, Preacher [B]

On April 12, 1861, the Civil War began when Confederate forces fired on Fort Sumter. However, owing to the Black Laws, the 36,673 African Americans residing in Ohio were not considered citizens of the state. Neither were they welcome in many places.

A preacher named Spears of the Free Wesleyan Church was taken by force from his pulpit at Murray City on May 5, 1861, because he had been telling them to arm themselves. His advice was in response to a series of incidents in which several blacks had been tarred and feathered, and others ordered to leave the Hocking County.

Mob Violence, Hocking County, May 1861—Lett, Joshua [B]; Pumphrey [W]

Six days later, on May 11, 1861, a large group of citizens from Green and Ward townships in Hocking County assembled to warn the Reverend Spears that if he attempted to preach there again he would be summarily dealt with. They then proceeded to the home of Joshua Lett, an African American, who had a white woman named Pumphrey living with him. Both of them were tarred and feathered.

The Lett Settlement, a mixed race community including the Caliman, Guy, and Lett families, was located in nearby Muskingum County.

Mob Violence, Hocking County, May 1861—Mabray, Thomas [B]; Gross, Abraham [B]

Thomas Mabray and Abraham Gross, both black, were tarred and feathered on May 12, 1861, presumably by some of the same people who assaulted Lett and Pumphrey a day earlier. The victims had allegedly "made use of expressions which the citizens did not relish very well."[2]

Mob Violence, Hocking County, May 1861—Norman Settlement [B]

A mob made its way to the Norman settlement in Hocking County on Monday, May 13, 1861, and told several African American families they had to leave within six months. It had been rumored that the black residents of this area, who were more numerous than in the rest of the county, had been arming themselves and making threats, but they denied it.

Mob Violence, Montgomery County, May 1863—Butternut Riot [W]

When Clement Vallandigham was arrested in Dayton on May 5, 1863, for "making disloyal speeches throughout Ohio," some 500 or 600 men took to the streets.[3] In short order, all of the telegraph wires were cut and the *Journal* newspaper building was burned to the ground. The conflagration then spread to adjoining structures.

Dubbed the "Butternut Riot," it pitted the Copperhead (anti-war Democrat) supporters of Vallandigham, their native son, against the pro–Union/anti-slavery supporters of President Abraham Lincoln. Troops had to be sent in from Cincinnati and Columbus to quell the disturbance.

Vallandigham was placed under arrested by General Ambrose E. Burnside acting on President Lincoln's proclamation that disloyal practices were to be tried by military commissions.[4] Whether he had the authority to suspend the writ of habeas corpus is still being debated.

Mob Violence, Holmes County, June 1863—Battle of Fort Fizzle [W]

The Civil War was in its second year when President Abraham Lincoln signed an act on June 5, 1863, requiring all men between the ages of twenty and forty-five to sign up for the military draft. It was not a popular law.

Not long afterward, Elias Robinson arrived in Holmes County to enforce the Enrollment Act, as it was called. He was in the Glenmont (then known as Napoleon) area, recruiting troops for the Union Army, when Peter Stuber threw a rock at him. A scuffle ensued which evolved into a full blown rebellion.

When word of the incident reached the Knights of the Golden Circle, they decided to capitalize on it to intensify anti-draft sentiment in the area. Southern sympathizers, the Knights were against the war, feeling the north had no business meddling in the affairs of the South.

Captain James Drake, provost marshal, quickly hurried to Robinson's rescue. He arrested four of the men who had participated in the affray, but not Stuber (although he would later turn himself in). As he was marching his prisoners toward Napoleon, Drake and his men encountered some members of the Golden Circle and other members of the community who were intent upon freeing the prisoners. Wishing to avoid bloodshed, Drake let them go for the moment.

The prisoners, as well as other men from the Napoleon area, collected at the home of Lorenzo (or Laurant) Blanchard, a farmer. They set about fortifying the stone farmhouse, possibly even installing a few pieces of rusty artillery. They called it Fort Freedom.

In the meantime, Captain William Wallace, commander of the 15th Ohio Volunteer Army, was dispatched to Holmes County to put an end to the rebellion. Traveling from Columbus to Lakeville by train, the troops marched through the countryside to Napoleon. They arrived on June 17, 1863.

Wallace had 420 soldiers, but the anti-draft mob numbered nearly 1,000, drawn from Knox, Coshocton, Muskingum, and Holmes counties. Nevertheless, Wallace fired upon Fort Fizzle, as the stone house came to be called, wounding two men and scattering the rest.

Although forty-three "insurgents" were indicted for assault and interference with the law, Blanchard was the only one convicted.[5] He was sentenced to six months hard labor at the Ohio Penitentiary, but was later pardoned by President Lincoln.

Mob Violence, Columbiana County, June 1863—Morris, Mrs. [W]; Lee, Mrs. [W]; Five other women [W]

On or about the evening of June 16, 1863, thirty women and five men dressed as women went to the homes of seven Democratic women in the town of Liverpool, including two widows, Mrs. Morris and a Mrs. Lee. After persuading them to open the door, they seized them, stripped off nearly all of their clothes, and coated them with tar and feathers.

Mob Violence, Wayne County, July 1863—Limp, Mr. [W]

On Thursday afternoon, July 2, 1863, a train carrying 200 Union soldiers stopped in Wooster. They were headed to Camp Chase in Columbus, where they would be guarding Confederate prisoners of war. Upon arrival, they sought out Ethan A. Brown, an alleged Copperhead, indicating they wanted to kill him. However, he was not in town. So they went to a grocery operated by a man named Limp, who was known to be a Democrat.

Demanding that he serve them drinks and charge it to Clement Vallandigham's account, Limp did. However, he then closed his business for the day. This upset some fifty of them, who broke into the store and forced him to retreat into his home, firing their guns at him several times.

Finally, they apprehended him, after bayoneting him in the hand and terrorizing his family. Stripping off much of his clothing, they dragged him by the hair back to the train. They then took him with them to Columbus where he was released. On the way, he was cursed and physically abused, sustaining severe injuries in the back, arm, and hand. All the soldiers involved were arrested.

Mob Violence, Montgomery County, March 1864—Empire office [W]

The year following the Butternut Riot, twelve to fifteen soldiers on furlough from Company C, Forty-Fourth Ohio Regiment, entered the *Empire* newspaper office in Dayton at noon on March 3, 1864. They proceeded to ransack the place.

Next, they went to the courthouse where their leader made a speech, taking upon himself full responsibility for their actions. When another man in the crowd made an offensive speech about how the government was "protecting the niggers," the soldiers rushed him.[6] Shots were fired. Two soldiers were wounded and a spectator was killed. Captain Bridger, commander of Company C, was arrested.

Mob Violence, Fairfield County, March 1864—Lee's Son [W]

During the Civil War, Lancaster, the county seat of Fairfield County, was a nest of Copperheads. One of the most prominent was a man named Lee.

On a Sunday evening, March 6, 1864, Lee and his son entered a saloon and encountered two soldiers, Nichols and Little, of the Seventeenth Regiment. One of the soldiers addressed the younger Lee, asking him if he was a colonel in the Copperhead militia. "Well," the son replied, "what if I am? What business is it of yours?"[7]

An argument ensued, but was brought to an abrupt end when the elder Lee drew a revolver and shot both soldiers. One died instantly and the other a few hours later. Both Lees jumped on their horses and rode out of town, post haste.

When members of the soldiers' regiment heard of their deaths, they formed a posse and set out in pursuit of the fugitives. They soon overtook the son and clubbed him to death, while the father made good his escape.

The soldiers cleaned out the saloon and would have burned it to the ground if it were not for the intervention of their commander, Colonel Durbin Ward, who urged his 400 charges to remain calm. A short time later, the elder Lee surrendered to county authorities.

A grand jury in Fairfield County indicted a number of the Union soldiers for riot and manslaughter. However, in April 1864, newly-elected Governor John Brough overturned the civil law, declaring the soldiers were still under the command of General Thomas and the general would deal with any crimes they committed while on furlough.

Mob Violence, Greene County, March 1864—Spence, George [W]

With its abolitionist sentiments, portions of Greene County were downright hostile to so-called Peace Democrats or Copperheads. "Our townsman, George Spence, Esq.," wrote the *Springfield Democrat*, "was shamefully treated by the soldiers, Abolitionists and niggers of the sweet-scented town, Xenia, on Saturday last, because he is a Democrat."[8]

On a Saturday morning in March 6, 1864, Spence was followed from the courthouse, where he had conducted business, by a soldier who managed to stir up a mob. A racially mixed crowd dragged him through the streets from the Hivling House, where he had stopped, to the probate judge's office, where he was made to swear an oath of loyalty to the Union.

The newspaper concluded by saying, "Democrats who have business in this God forsaken town, should go prepared to defend themselves from the insults and violence of that niggerloving community."[9]

Mob Violence, Mahoning County, March 1864—Ross, Emma [W]; Stearne, Louisa [W]

An Abolitionist stronghold, Youngstown was prone to frequent outbursts of mob violence. However, what happened to sisters Mrs. Louisa Stearne and Emma C. Ross, residents of nearby Canfield, had nothing to do with their politics. They were accused of keeping a disreputable house and on the evening of March 21, 1864, a group of men and women, all members of the community's "Shoddy aristocracy," took action.[10]

As Ann Niblock later testified, Mrs. Hiram Park came to her sister's house at four o'clock in the afternoon and announced to the women who had gathered that they were going to put down those Ross sisters. Mrs. Park said they would obtain revenge for the sisters' having caused Mrs. Powers' husband to leave her, as well as for Charles Howard's abandoning his wife for Emma when the latter was but sixteen. The women had several revolvers and Mrs. Park pocketed one, saying she knew how to use it. She also said she had cayenne pepper to throw in the women's eyes.

Several hours later. Emma heard someone in the alley ask, "Is this Mr. Ross's house?"[11] Someone else replied yes and then there was a light rap at the door. When she opened it, she was confronted by a man in a wrapper—a nightgown. He grabbed her by the throat and she screamed. Then the mob, including other men dressed as women, rushed in.

Emma told them that her sister was upstairs sick in bed and that their children were also in bed, one upstairs and one down. The angry women pushed her down, tied her hands, hacked off her hair, and put tar on her head. Five or six of them held her while others broke up the furniture. They then took feathers from pillows and forced them into her mouth.

When Louisa came down, she was also seized. Because there was a bright fire in the room, both women could identify many members of the mob. Someone grabbed Louisa by the hair and dragged her into the room. "We will spoil your beauty," they shouted, "we will take the English out of you; your career in Youngstown is ended."[12] They then cut her hair and covered her with tar and feathers, too. Louisa estimated there were about forty or fifty people altogether.

Rescued by three men, Emma fled up the stairs. She was followed by James Ryan who ordered her to open the door or he would shoot her and throw her over the stairs. Although she had no gun, she said she would shoot him. He then said, "Come, boys, let's go down and storm the castle."[13]

Once outside, the men started throwing cinders. The first struck a lamp. The second struck Emma, leaving a mark. Finally, two male friends made their way into the house and took the sisters and their children to Mrs. Simmons' place.

Although the attackers were disguised, the sisters were able to recognize many of them. Emma subsequently sued a total of thirty for $25,000 in damages. Although some of the defendants were able to prove they weren't there, Emma was awarded $5,000 from seventeen men and women.

Expected Lynching, Richland County, March 1867—Various criminals

In the aftermath of the Civil War, Mansfield was a magnet for criminals of every stripe. For the first couple of years, the townsfolk left the law to deal with it. However, it became evident that these crooks were too crafty at evading punishment. Nightly depredations became common with houses and stores being burglarized, and people being assaulted and robbed on the streets. In the vicinity of the railroad depots, it became dangerous to walk alone during the daytime. Patience was wearing thin.

Finally, in March 1867, a "company of regulators was formed" and the following warning was published[14]:

> To thieves, blacklegs, confidence men, etc.: Our city has been infested by, and our citizens suffered as long as they will bear, your depredations on person and property. You are all known to our Regulators. We therefore warn you to leave our city instantly and forever, for we will not tolerate you longer. You are watched and cannot escape. A short shift will be your doom if caught at your wicked business hereafter.[15]

Soon afterward, a committee of vigilantes swept through the Mansfield saloons, took six or eight men into custody, and locked them in jail where they were all photographed for public exhibit.

At a meeting at Miller's Hall on March 12, 1867, there was an open discussion on how best to deal with these undesirables. The room was filled to capacity. "A few were for hanging, but, after much discussion, it was decided to escort them to the depot and place them aboard the first train."[16] And so they were, with the admonition that they would surely be hanged if they returned. Fortunately, the men did not.

Lynching /Attempted Lynching, Mercer County, June 1872—McLeod, Alexander [W]; Kimmel, Absalom [W]; Kimmel, Jacob [W]

The night before she died, Mary Arabella Secaur had a horrible nightmare. In her dream, the thirteen-year-old girl said "her guardian angel had visited her to warn her of approaching danger—danger wherein she saw herself attacked by ruffians and cruelly murdered!"[17]

The following morning, June 23, 1872, Mary went to Sunday school at Liberty Church and then remained for church services. Afterward, she departed for home with several friends until they reached a point about one mile from her rural Mercer County residence. Bidding then goodbye, she continued on to "the terrible fate which awaited her."[18]

Mary lived in Liberty Township outside Rockford on the Indiana border, west of the county seat of Celina. Her mother, Susannah May, had died a few years earlier and her father, Joseph Secaur, more or less abandoned the kids. At the time of his daughter's murder, Joseph was visiting family in Ross County where he was originally from.

According to J.H. Day, Mary "was a gentle, tractable child; being dutiful and of a kind and loving disposition."[19] She had come to live with John Citterly and his wife, who, having no children of their own, planned to adopt her. However, the *Cincinnati Commercial Tribune* added a detail not included in Day's account: "It appears that the girl had a lover—he was arrested for committing the deed, but proved an alibi."[20]

In addition, Day described Mary as a "large and well-developed for a child of her age," suggesting that this was an important factor in her subsequent rape and murder. She had a twin brother, Marion Monroe, as well as a brother, Elias, who was five years older and, in all likelihood, her caretaker in their father's absence. Beyond that, nothing much is known about her circumstances—except that her brothers did not become concerned about her welfare until Monday afternoon when her naked body was found, separated into pieces and being devoured by pigs. She was identified by her clothing.

It appeared that Mary had been overpowered by brute force, dragged into a nearby thicket, and stripped of her clothes. Once she had been molested, she was killed. When she didn't come home that day, the Citterlys assumed she had decided to stay overnight with her grandfather who lived in the vicinity.

Mercer County Sheriff Thornton Spriggs initiated an investigation, but others in the community turned their attention to solving the mystery as well. No one would rest until the guilty party was brought to justice. Suspicion soon settled on some tin ware peddlers from Fort Wayne who had been visiting at the home of their relative, Henry Kimmel. Their names were Alexander McLeod and Andrew J. Kimmel. Henry's sons, Absalom and Jacob, were thought to be guilty by association.

McLeod and the two Kimmel boys had "been seen in close consultation at church an hour or two before the crime was committed" and some remembered that they had left "before the congregation was dismissed."[21] The fact that they all three had departed for the West early on Monday morning was enough to convince many they were guilty.

Sheriff Spriggs sprang into action. Deputizing three others, he set out with his small posse in pursuit of the suspects. On Friday, June 28, they overtook McLeod and Andrew Kimmel in Fort Wayne and brought them back to Celina. On the same day, Absalom, George, and Jacob Kimmel were rounded up by others.

Realizing the seriousness of the charges against him, Andrew Kimmel turned State's evidence, blaming the murder on the other four. A three judge panel heard the case on Sunday, June 30, 1872.

Absalom Kimmel confessed his own guilt and that of McLeod, sharing some details of the crime. Both men had blood on their clothing, as did Jacob Kimmel. And, according to historian James Bowsher, one of them had imprudently identified a box of snuff that was found at the murder scene as his.

Although the public was highly agitated, peace prevailed for more than a week. Then on the morning of July 8, people began to assemble in Celina. As early as four o'clock, they began arriving by ones and twos and small groups. By ten o'clock, the streets were so jammed with humanity that they were nearly impassable. Yet, everyone remained calm, well-behaved, and orderly, though expectant.

At high noon, 200 horseman came riding into town. They rode directly to the jail with a huge crowd trailing behind. Sheriff Spriggs and his officers had locked and barred the door. They refused to admit anyone, but asked that the riders to allow the law to handle it. This did not mollify them.

Breaking through the door, the mob overpowered the lawmen. In irons and manacles, the terrified prisoners were wrestled outside, dumped in a wagon, and driven rapidly out of town surrounded by the horsemen. The excited crowd scrambled to follow along as best it could.

Traveling eleven miles toward the Indiana border at breakneck speed, the mob arrived at the farm of Henry Kimmel, father of Absalom and Jacob. They immediately began erecting a rude gallows. A small tree was cut down and fashioned into a beam then hoisted onto a couple of wooden forks. Then the wagon with the prisoners was drawn up beneath it.

With some 3,000 people surrounding him, McLeod was asked if he wanted to confess, but he continued to proclaim his innocence. Absalom Kimmel, however, repeated his previous confession. Jacob Kimmel continued to deny his guilt, claiming that McLeod had told him that he and Absalom had killed the girl.

At this point, Elias, Mary's brother, pleaded with the vigilantes to release Jacob because of doubts regarding his guilt. Surprisingly, they agreed. Jacob, age sixteen or seventeen, was returned to the county jail where he remained until November before being released.

Two ropes were now thrown over the beam and nooses dropped around the necks of McLeod, age twenty-one, and Kimmel, nineteen. Their hands and feet were tied. At ten minutes before four o'clock on July 8, 1872, the wagon was driven out from under the men, and "their souls were launched into eternity."[22]

As intended, the whole horrible spectacle could be seen by Absalom's mother from her parlor window. After their bodies were cut down, they were given to physicians in Shanesville and Fort Recovery for dissection.

Little is known about Alexander McLeod, save that he was born in Canada. The

Kimmel family, however, were not strangers to the community. Henry and Susanna Kimmel presided over a large family of seven sons and four daughters. While her husband had been born in Pennsylvania, Mrs. Kimmel, had been born in Mercer County, the daughter of Amos Hines. Just prior to the murder of little Mary, Mrs. Kimmel had been found guilty of assault.

Less than two years later, a story emerged from Denver, Colorado, that a man named Thomas Bradwell Douglass had confessed on his deathbed that he had raped and murdered Mary. He blamed the crime on drunkenness which had left him a madman, unable to control his actions. Furthermore, he admitted that he had been a leader of the lynch mob, urging the others to do it to save his own neck.

"The hanging of the two men, McLeod and Kimball [*sic*], was as vile a murder as was ever perpetrated," Douglass said. "I was one of the mob that executed them."[23] Afterward, he had moved out to Denver due to his health.

Lynching, Tuscarawas County, July 1873—Davis, Jeff [W]

When they finally got around to hanging Jeff Davis, John Foanbieger, John Smith, John Miller, and Richard Roe died as well. They were all aliases Davis had used at one time or another.

A "notoriously feckless character," Davis was no stranger to the court system.[24] Swiss by birth, his real name was John Miller and he had settled in Stark County with his parents. Large, muscular, weighing, perhaps, 200 pounds, he was an intimidating figure. And trouble. His criminal pursuits began before he reached the age of sixteen and led to a stay in the Ohio Penitentiary.

Davis's life outside of prison fell into a predictable pattern. He first took revenge on the jurors who had convicted him by burning down their barns, one by one. He then shifted his criminal operations to Holmes, Wayne, and Tuscarawas counties. Roaming the countryside, he worked for bed and board when necessary, stole whatever he could, and molested women.

On August 7, 1867, Davis grabbed a Miss Taylor in the public market house and tried to force her to kiss him. Refusing to pay a $13.80 fine for his indecent behavior, he was given fifteen days on the chain gang. Another assault on a married woman in the same community led to another stint in prison. During his arrest, Day had stabbed H.H. Scheu, a member of the posse.

Altogether, Davis served three terms in prison for grand larceny and a fourth for assault with intent to commit rape. Upon his release in September 1872, he returned to his old stomping grounds, determined to get even with those who had testified against him. He purportedly threatened to cut out the heart, lungs, and liver of every man who had a hand in arresting him. He also resumed insulting the women of the community, regardless of age.

The following summer, Davis returned to Wayne County, got himself arrested once more for some crime or another, and was tossed in the jail at Wooster. Stupidly, the sheriff left the keys in the cell door when he delivered Davis's evening meal. Seizing the opportunity, Davis slipped out, locking the officer in the cell, and made his escape. It took a trio of locksmiths to free the sheriff from his own jail.

Meanwhile, Davis paid a visit on Mr. Scheu, threatening not only to kill him, but also the constable of Ragersville the next time they crossed paths.

On Sunday, July 20, 1873, Davis assaulted Miss Hunjerikhouse while she and another girl were on the highway near Ragersville. The same day, he molested an eight-year-old girl named Flora Lehn near Stonecreek. Upon learning of the incident, Flora's father filed charges in Ragersville and an arrest warrant was issued to Constable D. Neff. However, Davis could not be located.

According to the *Ohio Democrat*, Neff immediately organized a search for Davis. On July 26, he was arrested at Bakersville in Coshocton County, six miles south of Newcomerstown. Conveyed to Ragersville by Constable Neff, he arrived about sundown. A preliminary hearing was held that evening before Judge Levi Travis.

Some twenty to thirty townspeople crowded into the town hall to witness it. As they awaited the arrival of witnesses, the spectators became increasingly upset by the prisoner's brashness and vulgarity. When Davis insulted one man's wife, the man punched him and another struck him on the head with a fire poker.

No one knows who extinguished the lamps in the town hall, but in the ensuing darkness five to seven shots were fired at Davis, three of which penetrated his head. But he did not die. Despite the efforts of the law officers to protect him, they were overpowered by a mob of twenty to thirty men.

A rope was then tied around his feet and he was dragged out of the building by his heels and through town to the intersection of Ragersville and Crooked Run Roads. Here, the mob stopped to hang their seriously injured captive from a tree, even as he pleaded for mercy. This time he did die and for many years thereafter Ragersville was known as Hangtown.

Five months later, the *Cambridge Jeffersonian* revealed that there were now doubts that Davis had committed the rape. Furthermore, a grand jury had returned indictments against four men for their participations in the lynching. However, after one was found not guilty, charges were dropped against the other three.

Meanwhile, even in death, Davis did not find any rest.

After his body was cut down, it was hidden in a pile of sawdust one mile south of Shanesville in Holmes County—a site still known as Jeff Davis Hill. It may or may not have been buried there, but wound up in the hands of a local doctor who tucked it away in his attic, that is until the local authorities found out and demanded he bury it.

Presumably, he complied, but later Dr. Herman Peters somehow obtained it. He preserved the skeleton for use in his medical practice, except for a few parts he distributed as souvenirs. When he died, his son traded the bones for a box of cigars, whether to a saloonkeeper or a doctor in Lorain is in dispute.

Finally, Davis's remains came into the possession of an undertaker who passed them onto his daughter. She finally donated them to the Ragersville Historical Society where they are still on view.

Expected Lynching, Trumbull County, July 1874—Watson, William [W]

Described as a "villain from New Jersey," William Watson purportedly came close to being lynched in Warren on July 27, 1874, for the rape of a six-year-old child.[25]

Watson had stopped at the home of John Lowhorn, asked for something to eat, and was fed. After he departed, he encountered the girl on the road. Her screams alerted her brother and others in the area who wrangled him off to jail despite cries of "Lynch him!" from those who followed behind.[26]

Lynching, Champaign County, January 1875—Ullery, George W. [B]

Not much is known about George W. (Washington?) Ullery. An African American,

Ullery was thirty years of age, purportedly from Buchanan, Michigan, and engaged in the grocery business with his brother. However, a bad drinking problem had led to his becoming a "common tramp."[27] He likely was just passing through Urbana on January 12, 1876, when a white girl of nine or ten was "ravished" (another euphemism for rape) after being lured just outside the city limits.

Although the girl, Nellie, daughter of J.B. Morgan, would die within the year from the effects of "exposure and nervous prostration" brought on by molestation, she must have identified Ullery or someone who resembled him—a black man, anyway—as her attacker.[28] Two days later, he was apprehended not far from Marysville by Dr. S.M. Mosgrove and Captain John O. Dye. He was wearing blood-stained underclothing. They brought the suspect back to Urbana and secured him in the jail on Thursday.

He purportedly confessed to the crime.

At a preliminary hearing on Friday morning, January 15, 1875, before Mayor Joseph Brand, Ullery was scheduled for trial. That night, a group of men tried to take him from the jail, but were fought off by Sheriff Benjamin Ganson.

A mob of forty or fifty returned on Saturday night—described as the third attempt to seize him, suggesting there had been one on Thursday as well. This time they broke through the doors, captured the sheriff and his deputies, and forced their way into his cell. Seizing the prisoner, they marched him out onto the courthouse lawn. The crowd was considerably larger, but kept at bay by a guard posted by the lynchers.

By one account, the mob was additionally outraged by a report that two tramps had raped and killed a twelve-year-old girl in London, twenty-five miles away.

Made to stand on a wooden box beneath a catalpa tree, Ullery was given two minutes to prepare to die. When the time was up, he was hanged early on Sunday, January 17, 1875. Although they made no effort to conceal their identities, no one was ever prosecuted for Ullery's murder. His corpse remained hanging for an hour before it was taken down by the coroner.

Ullery's unclaimed body was interred in Oak Dale Cemetery. Several nights later, a handful of young medical students were caught in the act of stealing it. They were driven off and the corpse was reburied where, presumably, it was left undisturbed.

Lynching, Logan County, September 1875—Schell, James W [W]

James W. Schell was accused by his own wife of murdering Alice "Allie" Laughlin, the daughter of a respected and well-to-do farmer, at the Lewistown Reservoir. Arrested and locked up in the county jail, he was subsequently lynched on the lawn of the Logan County courthouse on September 24, 1875. But evidence would later suggest that his wife may have committed the crime.

Thirty-one-year-old "Jim" Schell, his wife, and son lived near Belle Center as tenants on the farm of Josiah Laughlin. On September 22, 1875, James and Josiah's sixteen-year-old daughter, Alice or Allie, went to the Lewiston Reservoir "to fish and pick berries."[29]

Late that afternoon, the girl's mother reported that she was missing. Her father immediately commenced a search, but found no sign of her until the next day when her dead body was recovered from a swamp. Allie's face was gashed and her skull crushed. James Schell was immediately suspected and locked up in the county jail.

At the coroner's inquest, Mrs. Schell was the key, in fact the only, witness against him. She testified that on the day Allie disappeared, she had accompanied her husband and the teenage girl on a trip to the reservoir to hunt plums. At seven o'clock that morning,

James had gone to Belle Center and hired a spring wagon from E.E. Nafus. Returning home, he picked up his wife and two children, then proceeded to the Laughlin home where Allie joined them.

They then drove seven or eight miles to the reservoir, arriving between eleven o'clock and noon. They had a picnic lunch about 500 feet southeast of the Scott House. Making an excuse that she had a headache, Mrs. Schell remained at the wagon while James and Allie went into the thicket to pick plums. Two hours later, he returned alone and from a different direction.

When Mrs. Schell asked him where Allie was, James purportedly said, "I have killed her. If you peep, I will kill you. I will knock your brains out with a club."[30] He said the girl offered to submit to him, but knowing she would tell her father, he had to kill her. James allegedly told his wife that he planned to make a "pretense" of looking for the girl and walked to the Scott house. When he reached it, he told Mrs. Bailey that Allie has disappeared.

James then led a party of men to a mill, telling them the girl was either lost or murdered. They laughed because they thought he was joking. George Brandon had asked him, "Who in thunder would murder her?"[31] He replied that he didn't know, but that's what he felt.

Meanwhile, Mrs. Schell returned home with her children in the wagon. She was met by Mrs. Loughlin who asked her where Jim and Allie were. She told her that Allie was lost. At that moment, Josiah Laughlin arrived, jumped into the wagon, and returned with Mrs. Schell to the last place his teenage girl had been seen.

The search party continued to look for the girl throughout the night, riding back and forth, calling her name and firing their guns. At ten o'clock, Laughlin and Schell left to rouse the residents of Belle Centre, then returned to the reservoir about four hours later. During the interim, Schell changed his clothes. This seemed suspicious to the workers at Nafus's shop who realized right away that he had done so. They began watching him even closer.

Thursday morning, the searchers formed a line that swept through the woods from Huntsville Pike to the creek, some fifty rods and back. Another pass was made, each ten feet apart, when roughly 200 men had joined them.

Finally, Brandon found the body lying partly in the swamp grass and partly in the wood. The grass, twigs, and ground gave evidence of a violent struggle. She was lying on her sun bonnet, her bucket and tin cup some eight feet away with a few plums in it. Her right arm was bare to the elbow, her dress and skirts pulled up to her knees and cut down her left side.

Although her underclothes were torn, Allie had not been raped according to the physicians who examined her. She had been stabbed twenty-one times—in the back, head, neck, side, and face. In addition, her skull had been crushed beneath the heel of a boot, nearly severing her ear.

While Shell was not upset by the sight of her dead body, one of the other searchers said he had been crying in the woods shortly before she was found. The men prevented the Laughlins from viewing their daughter's corpse. They also ensured that Schell did not leave, most of them now having decided he was guilty of the crime. A rope was produced and they began making preparations to lynch him, but a few of them were not convinced.

On Friday, an inquest was held at Huntsville. It was then that Mrs. Schell claimed that her husband had murdered the girl. She said she would have told it sooner if she had known he was safe in jail, but feared for her life. She claimed that for years she had lived in fear of being murdered. Furthermore, she accused him of once raping a black woman (and threatening to cut her throat if she told) and of burning down Laughlin's old house as well as his new one for revenge. She said her mother had warned her he was a bad man and would have preferred she went to her grave rather than marry him.

Mrs. Schell's statement electrified the crowd. With a cry of "Bellefontaine!" the race was on. One hundred or so men boarded a passing freight train, while others piled into wagons, rushing full tilt to the county seat. By dusk, the city of 3,500 citizens was packed with "strangers"—as often seems to be the case. A makeshift guard had encircled the jail, while people poured in from all directions.

As the evening wore on, men stood in groups, discussing the situation: "There was no brag, no bluster, no whiskey."[32] The *New York Times* would report, "it became evident from the demonstrations of the populace that he would be dangling between heaven and earth before sunrise the next day."[33]

About half past eleven, some came through the crowd carrying a railroad rail about twenty-six feet long. At 11:53 they stood outside the door. Their leader knocked on it and said three times, "Sheriff, open the door, we are bound to execute justice."[34] When the door was not opened, he said, "Number one, do your duty and do it well" and the first squad of men rammed the rail through the door in a double column, nearly toppling Deputy Sheriff McCracken, whom they immediately detained.[35] Sheriff Chandler was also captured.

Both men were searched for keys, but none were not found. Consequently, they attacked the hinges of the first door with sledgehammers and chisels. Breaking through, they continued to the next, smashing padlocks and slides to gain access to the prisoner. Sixty to 75 people had actually stormed the jail, while another 1,000–1,500 waited outside.

It took about half an hour to wrestle Schell from the cell to the wooden box placed under a silver maple tree at the south end corner of the courthouse yard. Although he was given time to pray, he declined the offer of a minister and asked only that he be buried with his little boy and that his parents in western Canada be notified he died an innocent man. He accused his wife of having done the deed and lying to save herself. She was jealous, he said, because he had given Allie a box of candy.

Some lynchers had tied handkerchiefs around their faces and turned their coats inside out, but many made no attempt to disguise themselves. At 12:33 in the morning, the box was kicked out from under him. The doomed man's last words were, "I would like to see Mr. Laughlin, but I see he is not here."[36]

Thirty minutes passed before Dr. Cretcher pronounced Schell dead. He had strangled to death because the noose had not been tied properly. He was buried in Potter's field. Some of those in attendance cut the hanging tree to pieces to obtain souvenirs of the hanging. The rope and the box were divided up as well.

As it turned out, the hair found clutched in the hands of the murdered girl did not match James Schell's, being ten to fourteen inches long. However, it did match Mrs. Schell's in both length and color. She was thrown in jail as an accomplice.

Even as some of the mob began to experience remorse for their actions, there was talk of lynching Mrs. Schell as well. And it was women who were doing the talking.[37] However, she was soon released instead.

Expected Lynching, Mahoning County, January 1876—Sterling, Charles [W]

The body of a young German girl was found stashed in a thicket about three miles from Youngstown on the morning of January 21, 1876. Her name was Elizabeth "Lizzie" Grombacher (or Gronebacher), age fourteen. Described as "short, heavy set, with finely cut features ... altogether she was very good looking."[38]

Elizabeth was the daughter of a poor widow who lived in nearby Powerstown. She had been living with her mother and three sisters for a while, but previously was employed by Mrs. H. Heasley, who lived about three quarters of a mile from where the slain girl's body was found.

On Friday, Elizabeth left home to go to Mrs. Heasley's to collect her clothing. No more than an hour or two later, a man ventured some fifty yards off the trail to obtain a stick and happened upon her body. The veil which she had been wearing was twisted about her neck and embedded in the flesh. "Her little black winter hat was lying close to her head, her face was somewhat discolored, foam was oozing from her mouth and nostrils."[39] Her waterproof cloak had a torn pocket, apparently from when she was pulled over the fence.

Just before she was slain, a Mr. Coover had encountered her on the trail, not less than 250 yards away. He said he had noticed a suspicious-looking character walking just ahead of her in the same direction. A Mr. Stevens said he also ran into a man of the same description on the path that day.

An immediate search was begun for the suspect and he was taken into custody later that day a few miles distant. Identified by both men, the suspect—Charles Sterling—was locked up in Youngstown, while authorities continued to look for another tramp who had been seen not far from the site of the murder. Sterling's throat was scratched and bleeding; he had blood stains on his shirt.

At the coroner's inquest, Sterling, who hailed from Dover in Ashtabula County, vigorously denied the charges. He said he had last lived at New Castle and was a carpenter by trade. Although he admitted being on the road, he said he had not seen any girl walking behind him on the road. However, the jury concluded that Elizabeth had been strangled to death by Sterling.

A boisterous crowd of miners and other laborers from the girl's neighborhood, as well as throngs of people from surrounding counties, crowded around the jail. Many of them had been drinking and they were threatening to lynch the tramp if they got the opportunity. The guard on the prisoner was increased as a precaution.

The *Stark County Democrat* reported that Sterling had dined at Field & Dewalt's Grand Pacific soup house a few days before the murder. "He did not look like a character who could perpetrate such a deed."[40] Nevertheless, he was convicted of first degree murder on largely circumstantial evidence and hanged at Youngstown on April 21, 1877.

Expected Lynching, Holmes County, February 1876—Mosenbaugh, Henry [W]

In November 1874, Henry Mosenbaugh (or Mosenbach), his wife, Mary, and their five-year-old child came from Baltimore, Maryland, and settled in Walnut Creek. A German by birth, he spoke no English, but made a comfortable living as a day laborer. However, after the birth of a second child, he began quarreling with his wife, accusing her of infidelity.

According to the *Holmes County Farmer*, Peter Ettlinger, a neighbor, called at the Mosenbaughs on February 13, 1876. Sensing that there was tension between the two, he continued on to the home of Emanuel Beechey and shared his concerns. At about eleven o'clock, Beechey decided to check on them. Upon entering the one-room cabin, he found Mary dead and her four-month-old baby on the floor crying. Beechey rushed to Berlin to report his discovery.

When several men returned to search the property, they encountered the older Mosenbaugh child who told them his father had gone into the woods. Splitting up into several search parties, they soon located Henry standing behind a large beech tree north of the road. He confessed at once he had beaten Mary with the rung of a ladder, but claimed he did not intend to kill her. He was immediately taken to Millersburg and locked in the jail. Not only had he struck his wife on the forehead the ladder rung, but also on the back, arms, and legs with an axe handle before strangling her to death.

A murder case in Holmes County was a novel thing. And there were rumors of some feeling in the county for lynching Henry Mosenbach. However, the *Holmes County Farmer* pronounced them untrue. "The people all expressed a willingness to let the law take its own course."[41] Many of them would have been Amish.

In the end, Henry Mosenbaugh pleaded guilty to murder in the second degree and spent the next sixteen years of his life at the Ohio Penitentiary.

Lynching, Clermont County, July 1876—Mangrum, George [W]

On Thursday, July 6, 1876, George Williams (aka Mangrum) stopped at the home of Charles Hooper, a carpenter, in New Richmond, a town of 2,500 people. Claiming to be from Lexington, Kentucky, he said he had set up housekeeping a few miles north of New Richmond and was looking for help. He hired Hooper's daughter, Mrs. Mary Hooper Bennett, to work for him and that same evening set out with her by foot for his purported residence. After they were outside of town, he raped and murdered her.

The very next day, Williams returned to New Richmond and hired Amanda Abbott under the same pretext—to perform housework. He told her he and his wife needed help because she had just given birth.

Mrs. Abbott, Amanda's mother, remembered having seen the gentleman around town previously and was reassured by his appearance. Also, they were a poor family, living hand-to-mouth, so the opportunity for Amanda to secure a job was seen as a godsend. Once again, while ostensibly walking to his house, he turned on the young woman, raping and choking her. He then left her for dead and returned to New Richmond.

Regaining consciousness, Amanda manage to drag herself home, stumbling through the door as her family was eating dinner. She looked close to death and quickly collapsed. When she was revived, Amanda reported that George Williams had "ravished" her.[42] Naturally, her story created a sensation.

A search was immediately undertaken for Hooper's daughter, but without success. However, on Saturday evening, Williams was captured and promptly jailed. Behind bars, Williams said he had a wife and two children (one had died) living in Bethel, Ohio.

Saturday night, July 8, "about a thousand citizens surrounded the jail and gained entry, overpowering the jailor."[43] They may have used chisels and hammers to break through the doors. After "gaining" the prisoner's confession, they took him outside and hanged him from a tree.

The story pieced together by Gary Knepp provides additional and, at times, varying details than reported above. He wrote that Williams was described as "a large man of superb build and gigantic proportions" who had told people he was seeking to hire "three or four young women to work on his Kentucky dairy farm."[44] Williams and Mary Hooper, the first victim, had left New Richmond in his "fine carriage," headed in the direction of Cincinnati.[45]

In Knepp's account, the rape and murder took place at "a wooded spot near the farm of Jonathan Corbly," and Williams dispatched the twenty-year-old woman with "a sharpened hickory sapling."[46] After driving back to New Richmond, he "spent the night drinking, plotting his next outrage."[47]

The very next morning, Williams drove Amanda Abbott eastward—or the opposite direction from the first—until he reached another isolated spot about a half hour away. Here he "forced the young woman at gunpoint to go into the woods with him."[48]

According to Amanda, Williams at first talked to her about his business and his family as they traveled in his buggy. But when they passed from farmlands to forests, he embraced her and began to make "dishonorable" entreaties.[49] When she resisted, he told her it was his only purpose in taking her from her mother's home and that he had done to same to Mary Hooper. Amanda tried to cry out and make her escape, but he covered her mouth and choked her. Stopping the wagon in a small woods, he threw her to the ground, raped her, and beat her until she lost consciousness. Leaving her for dead, he drove back to town.

At Mont's Saloon on Front Street, Williams resumed his drinking. Meanwhile, Amanda had "manage to crawl back to town and told her story."[50] The accused was promptly arrested and hauled off to jail where "he begged like a whipped cur to be taken to Batavia."[51]

The town marshal quickly capitulated to the mob's demands and surrendered Williams to them for swift and sure justice "untrammeled by red tape, unhindered by the delays, and subterfuges of the law."[52] Taken to Ashburn Hill on the outskirts of town, the prisoner allegedly confessed to his crimes and begged for mercy.

By some accounts, Williams offered to show them the body of Mary Hooper Bennett in exchange for his life. He also revealed that his true name was George Mangrum, age thirty-one, and that he lived in Campbell County, Kentucky. Then as 200 people looked on, he was hanged from the limb of an elm tree. However, because his toes still touched the ground, someone had to climb the tree to lift the rope up higher.

The body of young Mary Hooper Bennett was subsequently found in the woods, horribly mutilated, the skull crushed like an egg. Although the perpetrator was dead, this did not satisfy everyone. Rumor had it that Williams's brother lived somewhere nearby, so parties of men began to search for him and might have hanged him, too, had he been found. But the lingering question is whether Williams killed anyone else.

As far as the disposition of Williams's body was concerned, Knepp discovered two different stories. In one, he was buried in an unmarked grave in Collard Cemetery. In the other, his remains were interred near the Ohio River and later moved to higher ground until it was dug up by two medical students a year later. The head was missing, having previously been removed by Dr. William Kinkaid of New Richmond who kept it as a keepsake in a jar of alcohol. However, the torso was stuffed in a coffee sack and given to Dr. Cyrus Gaskins of Amelia who allowed his anatomy students to dissect it. The bones were then passed around as souvenirs, or so it was said.

Late the following year, $24,000 mysteriously disappeared from the Clermont County treasury. In a letter to the editor of the Clermont County *Courier*, one citizen wrote, "In general, we don't advocate hanging, but we could serenely view an accident of this kind if it should happen to the man that robbed the county safe, and this with a conscience void of remorse, together with the opinion that if there isn't any hell there ought, at least, to be a small one established for his especial benefit."[53]

Attempted Lynching, Hamilton County, November 1876—Unknown man [B]

The Democrats were parading through the streets of Cincinnati on November 4, 1876, three days ahead of the hotly contested presidential election. Ohio governor Rutherford B. Hayes headed the Republican ticket and William Wheeler was his running mate.

At eleven o'clock, the procession split up and many of the Democrats continued on to the Republican headquarters on Fifth Street. As the *New York Times* reported, "A number of colored men were standing in front of the head-quarters and when the Democrats approached they shouted for Hayes and Wheeler."[54]

Angered by their remarks, the Democrats, many of whom were intoxicated, gave chase to the black men who retreated into the Republican headquarters. The Democrats pursued them, tossing chairs and stones, and causing serious damage to the building.

Just minutes later, an African American man was driving an express wagon along Sixth Street when he was attacked by one of the Democrats who beat him over the head with a torch. Although he begged the man and his companion to quit, they would not, so he drew his revolver and shot one of them in the hip.

Promptly arrested and carted off to the station house, the black man was followed by a mob of Democrats who threatened his life. Shots were fired at him and one man managed to stab him even thought he had a police escort. After he was locked up, the mob continued to grow. Threats of lynching became so loud that the police sounded the riot alarm, summoning other officers to the station. A standoff ensued.

At midnight, Mayor George Johnston, himself a Democrat, urged the crowd to go home. While many people were still riled up "at this unprovoked attack by Democrats on peaceful Republicans," they did as they were asked and a lynching was averted.[55]

Attempted Lynching, Butler County, September 1877—Garnett, Jim [B]

Jim (or, perhaps, Simon, Simeon, or Clem—the newspapers couldn't agree) Garnett was a twenty-five-year-old African American man residing in Oxford. On the afternoon of Saturday, September 1, 1877, he went to the house of Perry Kingrey, a mile and a half southeast of town, somehow knowing that Kingrey would not be there. A man "of bad character," Garnett allegedly raped Kingrey's wife.[56]

As soon as she was able, Mrs. Kingrey grabbed her baby and ran a mile to where her husband, Perry, was working. She told him what had happened and described her attacker. He was quickly apprehended. Early the next morning, Mrs. Kingrey went to the jail and positively identified Garnett as her assailant. She also tried to shoot him. Although she was prevented from doing so, a party of her relatives and friends stood guard outside, vowing to hang him.

The Kingreys were regarded as "one of the first families" of Butler County."[57] The sympathies of the community, many of whom blockaded the streets of Oxford, were entirely with Mrs. Kingrey. No one was on the side of the "black brute," as one newspaper described Garnett, who had purportedly attempted to rape five other women in the community on previous occasions.[58]

Around noon (or ten or one o'clock), "a party of furious men—mainly relatives of the victim—broke into the jail, battered down the cell door, dragged Garnett out, and called for a rope." When Marshal Henry L. Kyler came running, someone shot Garnett before they all bolted. They expected him to die, but the ball had passed just to the right of his spinal column and lodged in his right hip. Another attempt was made to kill the prisoner at four o'clock, but it also failed.

Unable to protect his prisoner, Marshal Kyler telegraphed the sheriff of Butler County to come and take charge of him. Upon arriving in Oxford, Sheriff Marcellus Thomas and a deputy found the jail surrounded by a mob that threatened to shoot Garnett if they tried to remove him from the building.[59] When someone shouted, "Boys, do your duty!" men came running from all parts of town and packed into the yard around the jail until no movement was possible.[60]

According to the *Cincinnati Gazette*, the mob was "led by first-class farmers, nearly all of whom are friends of the injured woman."[61] However, when Jim Hann, "a notorious rough," tried to lead the mob, they refused to follow him.[62]

At eight-thirty Monday morning, Mrs. Kingrey, escorted by her husband and a large party of men, arrived at the town hall. Garnett was going to be placed on trial, but the crowd was so large that it was "impossible to get any ways near the justice room."[63] Furthermore, some of Garnett's witnesses were missing, so the trial was postponed until one o'clock. Although the accused claimed he was at the depot at the time of the rape, his alibi did not hold up.

The general impression was that the law was going to be allowed to take its course. However, at around eleven o'clock, Perry Kingrey went to the jail. Facing the door behind which the prisoner was being kept, he shouted, "Boys, for the sake of my poor wife, I want vengeance!"[64] He then kicked it. Others began heaving stones against the door, but to no effect. A sledge hammer was produced and the door was quickly demolished.

Because the cells had been broken open the day before, Garnett tried to escape into an adjoining room, but was seized by the mob. A blow to the head with the sledge hammer knocked him senseless and three bullets killed him. Still intending to hang him, the mob dragged him outside onto the sidewalk. However, they did not do so.

Someone fired another bullet into Garnett and his body was left for the coroner. An hour later, Marshal Kyler retrieved it and summoned Coroner Spencer from Hamilton.

"A jury was impaneled, an inquest held, and a verdict returned that the deceased came to his death from the effects of a pistol shot from the hands of a mob, to the jurors unknown."[65] The remains were then given over to some unrecorded African Americans who sent it to Garnett's home near College Corner.

Mob Violence, Darke County, October 1877—Geyer, Wesley [W]; Quakenbush [W]

A series of crimes occurred in two bordering counties—Darke in Ohio and Randolph in Indiana. While there were two or three prosperous families in these communities, most were branded as "a shiftless, worthless set, who subsist in the main by thieving."[66]

The farmers in the vicinity, having endured enough of their plundering, organized for the purpose of eliminating the "pests." The first person to die was Wesley Geyer. Although he was slain in, 1877, the story begins many years before that.

A resident of Palestine, eight miles from Greenville, Geyer, an undertaker, never enjoyed a good reputation. He had accused David Putnam, a local lawyer, of criminal intimacy with his wife and they had become bitter enemies. Yet, when the Civil War broke out, Geyer enlisted in the company commanded by Putnam. It wasn't long until his stealing got him into trouble and Colonel Putnam had him arrested and confined at Camp Chase. After the unit disbanded, the two men continued their feud.

Not only was Geyer a notorious thief, but his two sons as well. Their home became a hangout for other bad characters. When Geyer was accused of passing counterfeit money, he fingered Putnam. After a horse was stolen, the farmers' Self-Protective Association, headed by Putnam, blamed it on a young man named Reed who was apprehended in Illinois. Reed implicated both Geyer and Putnam. It was thought that Putnam subsequently aided Reed in his successful escape.

Numerous other crimes were attributed to Geyer, including shooting at Putnam, but none of the charges could be made to stick. Then one day he received a notice from a group of Regulators (i.e., vigilantes) to leave the township. He ignored it.

Finally, on October 24, 1877, at about 7:30 in the evening, a group of about forty masked men marched up to Geyer's door and knocked. Mrs. Geyer, accompanied by her daughter, age seven, answered it in her nightclothes and asked what they wanted. The leader replied that he wanted Geyer "damned quick."[67]

Mrs. Geyer immediately summoned her husband who stepped outside the door to talk to the men. While he was standing with his hand on the gatepost, one of the men took aim and shot him. Although he staggered, he did not fall until he was hit in the neck with two more gun blasts. He fell to the ground and the rest of the mob riddled him with bullets. Before marching off, the leader warned Mrs. Geyer to leave or she would meet the same fate.

About two blocks away, the mob paid a visit on a man named Quakenbush, whom they suspected of theft, and told him he had ten days to disappear. Even though many people saw and recognized some of the mob, including children playing in the street, they would not tell authorities who they were. Mrs. Geyer claimed that her husband was killed by his own confederates and she was able to identify five of them, but law enforcement did not give her statement any credence.

Putnam was not in Ohio at the time, but it was suspected he had organized and paid the group $1,000 to do the deed. Furthermore, it was believed Geyer was not killed because of his crimes, but for fear he would reveal who had committed other crimes. Consequently, the culprits were never brought to justice and the motive for Geyer's murder remained a mystery, "save a charge of petty thieving."[68]

Attempted Lynching, Geauga County, November 1877—Scott, Luther [W]

Some lynchings appear to have been half-hearted affairs whose true purpose was open to dispute. Such was the case when Luther Scott (aka Levi) was lynched. He had been arrested for robbing Church & Company, a Middlefield clothing store, on November 15, 1877.

Middlefield was a little way station on the Painesville & Youngstown Railroad in Geauga County. "A case of peculiar horror" occurred there when the clothing store of Church & Company was burglarized at a loss of $600 in goods.[69] It was only the latest in series of burglaries and, clearly, the community was getting fed up. They "all turned detectives."[70]

According to the *New York Herald*, an attempt was made to lynch Scott on the night of November 20, 1877. A "gang of desperadoes, of which he was a member," hoped, it was thought, to keep him from telling authorities about their criminal activities.[71] However, he was rescued by a constable from Middlefield who cut him down and successfully resuscitated him.

The *New York Times* gave a slightly different account. Scott and some other prisoners were being driven through a woods at night by three officers when they encountered a group of masked men with guns. "All were dragged out of the wagon in which they were riding."[72] The officers were tied up and a guard placed over them.

An effort was then made to elicit a confession from Scott by hanging him from a tree. After drawing him up into the air three times, the leader of the band said, "Gents of Vigilance, I wish to consult you."[73] (The dialogue seems to have been lifted from a Ned Buntline novel.)

Four of the men then broke off to confer with one another while the others kept guard. When the men returned, the leader said, "Vigilants disperse."[74] With that, the vigilantes vanished into the darkness. Throughout the ordeal, the officers were gagged and bound, but could see what was happening. Loosening their bonds and rushing to check on their prisoner's health, they found Scott was trembling in fear, but not seriously injured (or, perhaps, he seemed dead—sources differ). He was revived at the village, but could not (or would not) identify any of the men.

Some believed the mob was actually Scott's accomplices who were worried he would "peach" (snitch) on them.[75] If so, he seemed to have passed that test. In any event, the reporter did not believe the townspeople had been responsible. Scott was handed over to the sheriff and then released for insufficient evidence

The *Rome Daily Sentinel*, published an account of the aborted lynching that was clearly tongue-in-cheek. The officers, it seems, were conveying the prisoners from Middlefield to the Chardon jail when they were intercepted. The vigilantes hanged Scott three times in an effort to make him confess to a series of burglaries in which he had been implicated. After they failed, Scott was subsequently released for lack of evidence.

3

Disenfranchisement (1878–1885)

Nearly as quickly as the slaves were given their freedom, concerted efforts were being made to curtail their civil rights, especially the right to vote. In 1883, the United States Supreme Court declared that the federal government cannot prohibit businesses or individuals from engaging in racial discrimination.

Expected Lynching, Richland County, May 1878—Webb, Edward [B]

Newspapers reported that "a burglar Thursday night, Dec. 6 [1877], entered the house of William Finney, a farmer living two miles south of Mansfield, and murdered [him] and so severely injured his wife that it is expected she will die in a few hours."[1]

Edward Webb, a Mansfield resident and former slave, was arrested a few days later and tried for Finney's slaying. The key prosecution witness was eleven-year-old Minnehaha "Minnie" Finney, the victim's eleven-year-old daughter. Webb was convicted largely on her testimony, but took little interest in his own defense. He was sentenced to hang.

Although the crime occurred in Richland County, adjacent Crawford County took it personally. As Marilyn Howard noted, "Located in the central portion of the state, Galion [the county seat] was home to a very small population of blacks who had little contact with the white population, although some blacks did work on farms owned by whites or as day laborers in white homes."[2] Her point was that Ohio's black and white citizens, in many respects, occupied very separate worlds.

Whether Webb was given a fair trial or not is debatable. The overt racism of some newspapers at the time certainly created a hostile atmosphere. The *Crestline Advocate*, a newspaper published a dozen miles west of Mansfield, repeatedly kicked the hornet's nest by referring to Webb as a "black devil," "his niggership," and a "copper-colored potato trap," while dubbing his impending execution as a "gallows polka."[3]

While there were threats that Webb would be lynched, in the end he wasn't. However, his public execution on May 31, 1878, proved to be a particularly unruly affair attended by more than 10,000 people who had come to "see the nigger hung."[4]

Expected Lynching, Hocking County, June 1878—Terrell, William [W]

On the afternoon of June 22, 1878, three members of the Welden family were brutally murdered at their farm just outside the village of Gore. John Welden, his sister, Susanna McClurg, both in their early fifties, and her daughter, Nancy Hite (or Hetty), age eighteen, were slain by a neighbor, William V. Terrell.

The body of Welden was found the next day in a cornfield. He had been shot two or three times and stabbed with a corn-cutter. The two women were lying close to the house and had been killed with an axe.

Terrill supposedly had asked Welden to loan him money, as he had done before, and flew into a rage when he refused. Upon his arrest, Terrell immediately claimed that another boy his age, Joseph King, was actually the culprit and that he had no hand in it. However, authorities suspected King was innocent of any wrongdoing.

When word got out that the two suspects were confined in the Logan jail, the town's citizens began to flood the streets. There was considerable excitement as some 500 people collected.

Fearing either a riot or a lynching, Mayor G.W. Bohm, as well as the captain of the local guards, S.W. Bright, sent a telegram to Governor Thomas L. Young on June 24 requesting support from the militia. The governor responded immediately that he did not have the authority to do so.

Ultimately, Terrell, age eighteen or nineteen, was found guilty of the murder and sentenced to the Ohio Penitentiary where he spent much of his time in the prison's insane asylum.

Lynching, Erie County, September 1878—Taylor, William [B]

Alice O'Donnell, a servant girl of Sandusky, had disappeared under mysterious circumstances on September 2, 1878. William Taylor, an African American, was arrested the next day on the suspicion that he knew what happened to her. Likely under duress, he confessed to having helped hide her body in McCartney's Woods near Venice. However, he insisted that another black man had killed her.

Taken to the scene, Taylor pointed out where he had left her and it did not take long to recover her body. Alice was delivered to Ruff & Son's Undertakers, while the suspect was carted off to jail. Taylor's confession was soon known throughout Sandusky and an estimated 7,000 people (about half the population) began forming at the jail. They angrily demanded that the prisoner be released to them.

Sheriff Merrill L. Starr attempted to smuggle Taylor out of the jail by a back way, but his effort was so badly bungled that the mob soon discovered it. They set off in pursuit of the sheriff and the girl's accused murderer.

Cornered in the infirmary, Starr was "bulldozed" into surrendering Taylor to them.[5] The mob immediately marched him over to a pagoda in East Washington Park. Procuring a rope, they looped it around his neck and yanked him headlong out of the pagoda. They then dragged the hapless prisoner, arms bound, across the park and down Columbus Avenue as far as Market Street, more than a mile in all, before hanging him from a lamp post. What became of his body is unknown.

While the local bar association met and recommended the arrest and punishment of the ringleaders, a group of prominent citizens had their meeting disrupted by rioters who voted down their similar recommendation. The coroner's inquest was cancelled for lack of evidence.

According to the *New York Times*, "The town is governed by Democratic officials, mostly Irish Catholics, and they seem to be in sympathy, many of them, with the rioters."[6] In fact, members of the lynch mob subsequently held a meeting "for the purpose of mutual protection against the civil authorities if any attempts at arrest she be made."[7] And the citizens of color were threatened with violence if they dared to speak out.

Expected Lynching, Huron County, September 1878—Emory, George [W]

Threats to lynch George Emory (or Emery) were taken seriously at Norwalk. He had assaulted and beaten Kate "Katie" Dern on August 30, 1878, in what was called "one of the worst outrages ever perpetrated in this part of the State."[8] He then fled to White Pigeon, Michigan.

The incident happened when Emory, age thirty, invited eighteen-year-old Katie out one evening. When they were two and one-half miles outside town (possibly Milan), he threw her out of the buggy and attempted to rape her. She resisted him so forcefully that he gave her a vicious beating, cutting her neck, bruising her face, and nearly dislodging an eye from its socket.

During the attack, the horse became frightened and ran off. As Emory ran to catch it, Katie scrambled over a fence and concealed herself in the darkness. He searched for her with a lantern, but soon abandoned the effort and returned to town with the buggy. Then at 9:35 the same evening, he boarded the westbound train on the Lake Shore Railroad. His victim remained in hiding all night.

In the morning, Katie sought out the nearest house and the residents drove her back to where she was boarding. Not only were the citizens of Norwalk incensed by this affair, but also those in Katie's hometown of Tiffin. She was regarded as a very respectable young lady. Following Emory's capture five days later, he was returned to Norwalk in a roundabout way to "to avoid trouble with the indignant crowd who threatened to lynch him."[9]

Expected Lynching, Licking County, October 1878—Two tramps [unk]

Two tramps brutally assaulted Caroline McMillen, a forty-four-year-old widow, at her farm on Ramp Creek near Newark on October 1, 1878. While she was home alone, they entered her house, threw her down, placed a pillow over her head, and raped her. "She was found insensible some time afterward" by her son, Cary, and a hired hand.[10]

The neighbors were, naturally, in a state of intense excitement and a vigilance committee composed of 150 men went in search of the culprits. "[I]f they are caught, a lynching will surely follow," wrote an anonymous reporter.[11] But they apparently were not caught.

Mob Violence, Darke County, October 1878—Wade, Stephen "Steve" [B]

Stephen "Steve" Wade (or White), age sixty, was, according to the *Cincinnati Enquirer*, "a quiet, peaceable old colored man, who lived on the outskirts of the Ohio colored settlement, against who no one, even at the present time, will speak a hard word."[12] However, the same could not be said of his sons.

One of them, William, was kidnapped in June 1878 by an armed band of thirty men who came over from Indiana. He had been accused of stealing a pig. He was removed to the village of Winchester, Indiana, tried, and convicted of grand larceny, receiving a one year sentence to the penitentiary. He was later given a new trial.

That same night William was taken, the remaining Wades were left a warning in red ink: "To Stephen Wade, Robert, Benjamin, and Philip Wade—you are each and every one of you hereby advised to leave and stay away from Darke County within thirty days from date, or suffer the penalty."[13] A second warning was received on October 1, which included a picture of a coffin. And a third followed. Stephen ignored them all.

Then at midnight on October 24, 1878, Wade's house was surrounded by a mob. One of them shouted, "Come out; the night of your resurrection has come, and you must go to hell before us."[14] When Stephen did not do so, one of them fired a shot through the front window, striking a clock above his bed. He returned fire, but did not hit anyone. The mob then began shooting into the dwelling at random.

Endeavoring to escape, Stephen threw open the back door and was hit full in the left eye with sixteen pellets of number one shot. The blast penetrated his brain and he died at once.

Shortly before Stephen was slain, a white man named Ike Shiveley had warned him that he better leave because there was a band of men planning to "Geyer" him. Shiveley purportedly told several other black men the same thing, adding that the band had drafted a constitution and rules and were holding meeting in his school house.

Then on the night Stephen died, his daughter, who was also in the house, recognized Shively in the mob and spoke to him. He told her that she had no need to be afraid because they would not harm her. After they left, a hat was found on the ground that was identified as belonging to Shively's son, Webb.

Shively later claimed that three or four years earlier, an African American man named Sanford Holty had asked him to prepare documents like the ones he had described and he thought he might have done so. Holty later told him that the group had met several times at the school house, but failed to get organized.

Local law officers made no effort to track the mob. However, a grand jury decided the same people who kidnapped William had killed his father. It returned indictments against John Archie, Jacob Burdie, William Shumate, Albert Dickey, Solomon Ferguson, Oliver Morgan, and Robert Hart for kidnapping Wade. All were arrested by Marshal Shafer, including Shumate who had an estimated worth of $50,000.

In response, the Regulators issued warnings to ten well-known citizens to leave the county under penalty of death. Nevertheless, three of those arrested were eventually sentenced to the penitentiary, nine more were taken into custody, and ten others fled to avoid arrest. The arrests were made on the strength of a confession by one of the gang.

Expected Lynching, Crawford County, April 1879—Storer, Jacob [W]

Sometimes described as a "prominent citizen," Jacob Storer was charged with the attempted rape of eleven-year-old Estella Bauer near Bucyrus.[15] The offense allegedly occurred at various times before and after Christmas 1878.

Fearing she might be punished for not resisting Storer's advances, Estella did not tell her parents. However, she did confide in a classmate who went public with the story in April. Estella's father, Abraham Bauer, subsequently swore out an affidavit, charging Jacob Storer with the crime. Storer, a resident of Auburn Township and a neighbor of the victim, was swiftly apprehended and jailed.

Described as a "hoary-headed old sinner of over sixty," Storer was accused of having attempted to "debauch" numerous young girls in the community.[16] He was the defendant in a "bastardy suit" six years earlier and had a history of "lustful crimes."[17] He had seduced another young woman whom he married after impregnating her. She subsequently obtained a divorce due to his "lascivious nature."[18]

Storer then married "a woman in whose veins there is a slight tinge of African blood."[19] They were still together at the time of his alleged molestation of Estella.

"Such conduct as is revealed in his testimony is unparalleled in this county," the *Cincinnati Enquirer* noted. "The excitement is great, and threats of lynching are, freely made."[20] However, Storer, a white man of Swiss descent, was not lynched, despite a reporter's bringing up the miscegenation angle. History suggests a black man almost certainly would not have fared as well.

Attempted Lynching, Clermont County, May 1879—Storey, William [W]

Leaving her home near Afton Station in Clermont County, Jennie Atchley, the young wife of Charles Atchley, packed her bags and boarded a train at Batavia Junction on Monday, May 26, 1879. She intended to rendezvous with William Storey, her lover, in Cincinnati. However, she mistakenly caught an east-bound train.

When Jennie discovered her error, she leaped from the train and rolled down an embankment. Uninjured, she grabbed the next train going the opposite way and met up with Storey, who was described as "a restless young masher from St. Louis."[21] However, her husband had wired ahead and the couple were apprehended by two detectives.

Storey, who had claimed that he could have the pick of any woman in Afton, had stayed at the Atchley home for a couple of nights while visiting them to collect final payment on some property he sold Mr. Atchley. Having grown up in an adjoining county, he had known Jennie since childhood. However, her husband became suspicious of their conduct and angrily confronted her about it on Sunday morning.

A "violent scene ensued," concluding when Jennie announced she was going to church.[22] Charles told her if she did, she could never come back. Later, she found all of her possessions dumped on the lawn and the house locked. With the help of neighbors and Storey, she gathered all of her property, placed it in storage, and spent the night in Williamsburg. The next day, she set out to join her lover.

The two of them were arrested at the Great Western Hotel. Storey had purchased a pair of tickets for them to St. Louis and had checked her luggage. In Storey's satchel were the following: a set of false whiskers, $50 in silver, two watches, a revolver, and a pair of brass knuckles. He had on his person a navy revolver and $115 in cash. While he was placed in jail, Jennie was released into the custody of her husband.

Charged with "stealing Atchley's goods," Storey was transported back to Batavia for trial.[23] He probably did not anticipate how much ill feeling he had engendered among the menfolk in Atchley's Clermont County neighbors.

Afton Station was not known as "Hell's Half Acre" for nothing[24] As the *Cincinnati Commercial* reported, "Thirty men, coal-blacked and with masks, armed with revolvers, shot guns and corn-knives" went to Batavia at two o'clock in the morning.[25] (Or it could have been seventy-five men at three o'clock.) Halting in front of the Munson House where Storey was being held, eight or ten entered the building and seized the constable and town marshal. The rest broke into the bedroom and put a rope around the occupant's neck.

It was only after they had adjusted the rope that they realized that he was not Storey, but M.R. Rybolt, a plasterer who bore a resemblance to him. Turning him loose, they continued searching the building and located Storey in another room.

Surprised in his bed, Storey offered to fight any five of them. But there were no takers. Hauling him out of bed, they fixed a rope around his neck, and bound his hands behind him with a handkerchief. They then paraded him down the street to an iron bridge over the East Fork of the Little Miami River.

Upon reaching the center of the bridge, the mob tied the free end of the rope to an iron strut. Several of them then picked up Storey and dumped him over the railing head first. He fell about eight feet until the rope either broke or slipped over his head. Storey continued plummeting headlong twenty more feet into the water.

Unbeknownst to the mob, Storey had managed to free his hands, which may have enabled him to break his fall. After firing a few shots in his direction, they left the scene.

The mob's activities had not gone unnoticed by the citizens of Batavia, many of whom were now taking to the streets. The "raiders" (as the reporter called them) left town in a hurry, instructing those who had been left guarding the constable and sheriff to leave as well. But in parting, they told the law enforcement officers where to find their man. Several men searched the banks of the river for a body.

Instead, they found evidence that Storey had crawled out of the water by the left bank and wandered along the creek until he reached the home of an African American named Hampton. He had begged the black man to give him shelter and clothing, but Hampton refused to admit him.

Eventually, Storey stumbled back to Batavia and surrendered to the officers. His neck and wrists bore bruises and abrasions which attested to his ordeal. When the story of his miraculous escape got out, some believed it was divine intervention.

The *New York Times* reported that the citizens of Batavia, a town of 3,000, were indignant over the attempted lynching and the bad light in which it placed their community. They also tended to sympathize with pretty young Jennie Atchley, "the best horsewoman in the county," and handsome William Storey who claimed he was only trying to help her escape from her cruel husband.[26]

The *Weekly Chillicothe* (Missouri) *Crisis* reported on May 27, 1880, that Storey, who had apparently returned to St. Louis, was suing thirty residents of Clermont County for trying to lynch him a year earlier for being "unduly intimate with a married woman."[27]

Lynching, Pickaway County, August 1880—McDonald, Thomas [W]

The 1880 census lists Thomas McDonald's occupation as "an outlaw." Whether based on reputation or he actually claimed to be one is unknown, but to the citizens of Commercial Point, population 169, there was no question about it.

For the best part of a decade, McDonald had terrorized them, men and women alike. Recently, he had upped the stakes by boasting he would kill them all and reduce the town to ashes. But before he had a chance to carry out his threat, he was lynched by a deputation of his neighbors who had had enough.

What's known about McDonald (aka McDaniel) isn't flattering. As one reporter summed it up, "His chief passion had been to cut, carve and shoot. His greatest weakness had been for brass handled pistols and two-edged knifes."[28] Following his death, one headline branded him "A HUMAN WOLF."[29]

At the age of fourteen, McDonald had come to the area from Falmouth, Kentucky, to evade arrest "for engaging in a cutting scrape."[30] He picked up odd jobs here and there and then about 1870 was hired as a farmhand by a wealthy land owner named Decker.

It didn't take McDonald, now twenty-four or so and by some accounts a handsome young man, very long to cast a spell over Decker's sixteen-year-old daughter, Alice. Scandalizing the community, the couple ran off and got married.

Alice's brothers, Boone and Peter, vowed they would kill McDonald if they ever saw him again. But a week later, he returned "with his brass pistols and his bride, panting for gore and eager for a fray that would enable them to decimate the Decker heirs, and thus increase his wife's share of her father's vast property."[31] The brothers chose not to bother him.

Hoping to make the best of the situation, Decker set aside 150 of his 900 acres for the newlyweds, built them a cottage on the edge of a woods, and waited to see what McDonald would make of it. What he made of it was nothing, refusing to do a lick of farm work and allowing the place to gradually run down.

One day while passing through Commercial Point on his way to a wolf hunt, McDonald "became offended at Thomas Beckett, a dry good merchant."[32] Springing from his horse, he began beating Beckett unmercifully while 100 people looked on, fearing to get involved. Finally, a bystander did pull him off the storekeeper, preventing him from bashing in the poor man's head with "a piece of buggy shaft."[33] There is no indication the law got involved.

In the late 1870s, McDonald decided to crash a house-warming party at Barron's Cavern in southern Franklin County. No one dared to challenge him. However, during a dance, he "provoked a quarrel by stepping on the toe of a country gentlemen who was fastidious enough to object."[34] Whipping out one of his beloved pistols, McDonald fired into the crowd, striking one of the guests, Hock Breckenridge, in the thigh. Once again, he escaped arrest.

Likely based on his reputation as a tough guy, McDonald was hired as town constable of Mount Sterling in 1878–1879. It didn't take him long to show his true colors. On one occasion, he tracked down a man named Crawford who had allegedly thrown stones at a train on the Muskingum Valley line, outside Washington Court House. Surprising the suspect while he was dining, McDonald shot Crawford in the face without warning and then arrested him. Again, there were no repercussions for his misbehavior.

Not long after, McDonald "became enamored of a fair maiden of doubtful repute at the American House" in Darbyville.[35] Late one night, he climbed atop a peddler's wagon and through the woman's window. He found she was entertaining a "sport" named O.S. Renick. A fight ensued which spilled out of her room and down the stairs "until the house was as bloody as a butcher's pen."[36]

Although he was not called to task for this assault, McDonald did get thrown into the Circleville jail for stealing a buggy. Upon his release, he went directly to a neighbor's house and stole another one. Clearly, he had not reformed.

In the spring of 1880, while out squirrel hunting, McDonald was blinded when he fired a shotgun and "a piece of the cap flew into his right eye, which ran out of the socket."[37] Amazingly, he ignored this injury, seemingly impervious to pain. Then in July, he ambled into Martin V. Beaver's grocery store in Commercial Point.

Beaver, a relative of McDonald's wife, was, according to the reporter, "a magnificent specimen of physical manhood."[38] He also was one of the few men who wasn't intimidated by him. When McDonald informed the merchant that he intended to shoot him, Beaver responded by tackling him. The two men wrestled about the store until Beaver was able to gain possession of his pistols.

On Monday, August 30, 1880, McDonald returned to Beaver's grocery brandishing a knife and told Beaver he intended to kill him. This was after he had already gone about the town, threatening to kill John Bolin, a candidate for sheriff, and several others. Kicking the knife out of McDonald's hand, Beaver grabbed his would-be killer and "they had it rough and tumble, pound and pummeling."[39]

This time, Beaver decided to gouge out McDonald's left eye, his only good one. As a bystander recalled, Beaver made two or three attempts to dislodge the eyeball from its socket, but each time it would snap back with a popping sound "like a cork flying out of a champagne bottle."[40] All the while, McDonald didn't even wince.

Having administered a thorough beating, Beaver rolled McDonald's body out into the gutter and warned everybody not to touch him. For the next three hours, McDonald lay there in the dirt before he was finally carted home to his wife. She tended to his injuries as best she could and McDonald even seemed to be recovering the use of his eye.

The following night, August 31, Mrs. McDonald came face-to-face with eight armed men at about 11:30. She had gone to close the door of their dwelling which she had left open due to the summer heat. The men ordered her out as they surrounded McDonald in his bed. Some accounts say they had made no attempt to disguise themselves, but others mention masks or visors. Sitting up, McDonald asked, "Boys, are you going to kill me?"[41]

There was no reply as the men bound his hands, slipped a noose made out of a halter-rope over his head, and drew it tight. "They dragged him over a rail fence, over logs, through bushes for about four hundred yards to a little red oak near the road side, where he was strung up."[42] He was likely dead by the time they reached the tree.

The following morning, his body—naked save for a band of shirt around his neck and a strip down his back—was still swinging from a tree limb, visible to all who passed by the spot. Those who approached close enough could read a card pinned to it: "Take Notice!—Any or all person interfering will meet the same fate. We will protect all law abiding citizens. VIGILANCE COMMITTEE."[43]

Justice of the Peace Thomas Beaver conducted an inquest. After questioning Mrs. McDonald and five other witnesses, the coroner ruled, "Death by a person or persons unknown."[44] However, this was not exactly true. Mrs. McDonald had recognized town constable Satterfield when his mask fell off. And an intrepid reporter was able to determine that ten to twenty people had been involved, some from Jacktown and the rest from Commercial Point. Twice before they had called at the house, planning to lynch him, but he had not been at home.

Afterward, the reporter dined with McDonald's widow and learned that she had not slept in four weeks for fear that the house would be set ablaze during the night. "His death is a relief," she said.[45]

No one seemed to be grieving his passing, although his funeral attracted people from miles around. In the weeks that passed, however, there was a change of heart. Although McDonald was guilty of disturbing the peace, he had never killed anyone and, many began to think, did not deserve to die.

Mob Violence, Perry County, September 1880—McMahon, Thomas [W]

If there was any place you'd expect to find trouble it was Rendville. Founded in 1879 by the Ohio Central Coal Company, Rendville took its name from the company's owner, William P. Rend, generally regarded as one of the more benevolent mine owners in Ohio. Over the objection of white miners, Rend hired black miners and also Europeans. To overcome the fear they would drive down wages, Rend paid them all the same.

On September 19, 1880, white miners from Corning and other nearby communities marched on Rendville, intent upon driving the African Americans out of town. To conceal their plan, the white miners smuggled firearms into Rendville in wagons hidden under hay. They charged Mine No. 3 and were met with gunfire. Although it would be dubbed "The Corning War," very little happened.[46]

There were a few minor skirmishes. Thomas McMahon was killed and eight others wounded, one perhaps mortally. Still, Governor Charles Foster sent in the Ewing Guard as a precaution and they dispersed the mob before the week was out. The miners claimed that if the mine operator, Colonel Leinert, had allowed them to speak with the black strikebreakers, they could have persuaded them to quit working. Racial tensions did not go away, but an uneasy truce prevailed.

Expected Lynching, Stark County, December 1880—Kline, Joseph [W]

Simon Kline, a stone mason, died unexpectedly on Saturday night, December 11, 1880, in Canton. On Monday, his son, Joseph, was arrested on suspicion of murder. The coroner's inquest revealed that Joseph had tried to administer arsenic to both his father and the housekeeper, Mrs. Boyle, by putting it in their coffee. However, an overdose resulted in it functioning as an emetic instead.

Undeterred, Joseph bought morphine and gave it to his father. This had the desired effect. Just before he died, Simon purportedly said, "Joe has given me a bad dose this time."[47]

Joseph's motive was to prevent his father from marrying Mrs. Boyle and, thereby, depriving him of his father's estate. According to some reports, however, Mrs. Boyle promised to marry the son after she became a widow. Evidently, he didn't want to wait that long. Due to fear of a lynching, the jail was securely guarded.

There was a large crowd outside the courthouse waiting for the verdict and when he was convicted of second, rather than first degree murder, the people were highly disappointed. As if to assuage them, Judge Seraphim Meyers gave him the most severe sentence possible: life in the Ohio Penitentiary with solitary confinement every other six months. However, the penitentiary physician refused to place him in solitary. Kline served eighteen years before he was pardoned late in 1899.

Lynching, Athens County, November 1881—Davis, Christopher C. [B]

Christopher C. Davis was a farmhand who worked on occasion for Mrs. Lucinda Luckey, a fifty-two-year-old widow who lived near Albany. On the evening of October 29, 1881, Davis went to Luckey's home between eight and nine o'clock and "made indecent proposals to her, which were indignantly repelled."[48] Somehow the woman persuaded him to leave, only for him to return around midnight. Axe in hand, he broke into her house, striking her in the face, knocking her to the floor, and choking her.

After raping the helpless woman, Davis began hacking at her face and about the head, fracturing bone and partially scalping her. Thinking her dead, he ran off. However, by morning she had recovered enough to make her way to a neighbor's house. It didn't take long for Davis to be arrested and arraigned before a justice at Albany.

Bound over to the court, the suspect was transported to Athens and locked in the county jail. However, as word of the crime became known throughout the community, Sheriff Tim Warden was alerted that people were making threats against the prisoner. He took Davis to Chillicothe to protect him until the excitement died down, then brought him back to Athens.

This was a mistake, for on November 21, 1881, between one and two o'clock in the morning, some thirty armed men arrived in Athens for the purpose of lynching Davis. They had come primarily from Albany, but also other parts of the county that shared their outrage against the "mulatto," as he was called.

The vigilantes posted guards at Marshal Scott's house and the Brown House (where Deputy Sheriff Sands was thought to room), as well as at the churches and city hall to ensure no bells could ring an alarm. With everyone in their assigned positions, they directed their attention to the residence of the sheriff warden. After overpowering him, they obtained the keys to the jail and released Davis from his cell. A noose was placed around his neck and he was led to South Bridge with a crowd surging around him.

Despite initially protesting his innocence, Davis finally admitted he had assaulted the woman after being told he would be returned to the jail if he did. "I'm the man," he said, only to be answered with cries of, "Throw him off!"[49]

Tying the end of the rope to the bridge, the ringleaders gave him three minutes to say a prayer (he didn't) and then pushed him over the side. His neck was broken in the fall. Once they were certain he was dead, they quietly dispersed.

In a subsequent grand jury hearing, testimony failed to identify the leaders of the mob and no one was ever indicted for his role in the lynching. But, then, there was little effort to investigate the crime.

Ira Graham, an ex-prosecutor for Meigs County who grew up in Athens County told the *Pomeroy Telegraph* that the lynching of Davis was because "the administration of justice in that county has in the past been a failure."[50] He referenced a half dozen murder cases in which the authorities either made no attempt to bring the guilty parties to justice or allowed them to escape punishment. The *Shawnee Banner* termed it a "monkey show."[51]

Expected Lynching, Hocking County, December 1881—Richards, Morgan [W]

Mary Terrell, the mother of murderer William Terrell, was shot to death by her nephew, Morgan Richards, on December 28, 1881, near Gore. He had purchased a revolver the previous Friday, planning to kill her. Richards, age twenty-six and described as a half-wit, knocked on Mary's door and shot her in the abdomen. He then ran.

As he was being transported to jail, Richards claimed Mary had defrauded him out of his share of his parents' estate. However, it was also said that he believed she was trying to poison him. Regardless, there was "strong talk" in Logan of lynching him.[52]

Lynching [TI]/Attempted Lynching, Lawrence County, January 1882—Wagoner, John [W]; Zeek, Bill [W]

Fresh out of college and working as a stenographer and court reporter, John K. "Jack" Richards happened upon a lynching while passing the Ironton courthouse on the night of January 10, 1882.[53]

John Wagoner had been confined in the county jail for a number of months on the charge of slaying a Dr. Joseph Biggs (or Beggs or Byers), a chemist for the Aetna Iron Works and/or treasurer of the Alice Furnace Company. Beggs had been shot at night on a lonely path near the Aetna Iron Works while on his way home from a saloon.

Richards later wrote that "Beggs was a trespasser on the premises of Wagoner and it could probably have been proved that he was hanging round against the wishes of Wagoner, trying to entice some of the women from the house."[54] Personally, he doubted Wagoner could have been convicted of anything more than manslaughter.

Because of the passage of time, interest in the crime seemed to have subsided. However, a double murder of two young girls at Ashland, Kentucky, five miles away, had "exasperated the people of the country on both sides of the river for miles around" because the prosecution had failed to obtain a conviction.[55]

On the night Wagoner was lynched, Richards was headed home. It was about eleven o'clock when he reached the jail and noticed the door was standing open. He then saw a large crowd of masked men congregating in the alley. Almost immediately, two of the men confronted him, shoving revolvers in his face, and ordered him to come with them. They escorted him some distance away from the jail, but still in clear view of it.

"We are going to succeed in what we are attempting tonight," one of them said.[56] He asked what they were attempting, but neither answered, possibly fearing that he was trying to identify them by their voices. As they guarded him, Richards was a witness to everything that took place.

"It was the finest organized body of men I ever saw, to be only a mob," Richards would recall. "They were perfectly drilled. The leader was distinguished by a white baton that he carried. With this he gave signs and conveyed commands to the members of the band."[57]

The men had obtained keys to the jail and Richards could hear them moving through the jail corridor. At this point, his guards left him in order to get a better view of what was taking place, so he took the opportunity to walk away. He quickly found himself standing in the midst of the lynch mob watching Wagoner's body swing from a tree. As the only one in the crowd of forty or fifty who was not masked, he was singled out. Several men then took charge of him and separated him from the rest of the group. He was ordered to go up town.

As soon as the lynchers were out of sight, Richards returned to the jail yard to see whether Wagoner was still alive. He wasn't. Entering the jail, he learned from the sheriff that he had refused to surrender the keys to the mob, but when they pulled out their guns, his wife was frightened and told them where the keys could be found.

Although Richards didn't mention it, the mob first took Wagoner's co-defendant, Bill Zeek (or Seek). They placed a noose around his neck and "swung him up, whereupon he made a confession implicating others not yet arrested, and the crowd allowed him to live for the present."[58]

Although he insisted he was in the house at the time, Zeek claimed it was an organized band of robbers and they had killed Beggs for his money, which amounted to one silver dollar. He believed the person who pulled the trigger was either John Wagoner, Sarah Zeek (his own wife), or Frank Marshall.

Furthermore, Zeek said that Wagoner's mother suggested they tie a bar of pig iron around the doctor's neck and drop him in the river, but they decided against it. Instead, they carried the body to where it was found and then sought out police officers, telling them that they had slain him in self-defense.

Wagoner refused to say anything.

With regard to Wagoner's lynching, readers of the *Jackson Standard* were informed that the newspaper editors "believe, the way the criminal law is now not being administered, that this was right."[59] They went on to argue that the terror of lynch law needed to be extended "in some cases" to judges and jurors.[60]

Once again, the coroner's jury and the grand jury could not identify any of the perpetrators and it was generally felt that the community—some 8,900 strong—supported the mob's actions.

Expected Lynching, Crawford County, April 1882—Hogan, James [W]

Marshal David Snodgrass was shot to death at half past seven on the evening of April 21, 1882, in Crestline, a railroad town. He left behind a widow and six children. The marshal was attempting to arrest a tramp, James Hogan (aka John Smith), whom he had been keeping an eye on for several days.

Snodgrass was in Casell & Zint's hardware store when Hogan entered and inquired about some cartridges. Snodgrass asked him if he had a revolver and he replied that he had one at home. At that point, the lawman seized Hogan, but he broke loose and ran out of the store. Snodgrass and another man gave chase.

Hogan had gone about sixty feet when he turned and fired at Snodgrass, striking him near the heart. Carried into a drug store, the marshal died seven minutes later.

Despite being captured by a mob determined to lynch him, Hogan wasn't. After punching and beating him over the head, they took him to Bucyrus, thirteen miles away, and locked him in the county jail. The *New York Times* reported that the marshal's killer would likely be lynched before morning, but that didn't happen, either. As the *Cincinnati Enquirer* noted, "All that was needed was a determined leader to have taken and lynched him."[61]

Hogan, age twenty-one, was subsequently tried at Bucyrus, convicted of murder in the second degree, and sentenced to life imprisonment.

Lynching [TI], Crawford County, April 1882—Fisher, Frank [B]

"The most exciting day in the history of Galion," as some called it, was April 30, 1882.[62] The reason for all the excitement was the lynching of Frank Fisher, an African American, who was accused of ravishing a thirteen-year-old German girl, Barbara Retting (or Ketting).

The crime occurred on the previous Friday while Fisher was chopping wood in a grove. He promptly fled to Knox County where he was apprehended by police officers T.J. Wurts and W.H. Nichols at five o'clock in the morning as he was preparing to leave Fredericktown on foot. His clothes appeared to be bloodstained.

As soon as Fisher was lodged in the Galion jail, the mayor and the police started planning to move him again, either to Bucyrus or some other neighboring town, fearing that he might be lynched if he remained in their custody. Word of his apprehension had quickly spread throughout the countryside.

By three in the afternoon, a large crowd of men—perhaps 200—assembled outside city hall. Making no attempt to disguise their identities, they brandished hammers, crowbars, and other tools that could be employed in breaking into the jail. The throng demanded that Fisher be turned over to them, but the police refused.

The *Wheeling Daily Intelligencer* reported that many African Americans joined in the mob and one emerged as a leader. As locomotives whistled and fire-bells clanged, over 2,000 people rushed the jail. The door was quickly breached and a black man "broke open the cell" where Fisher was being held.[63] Seizing the prisoner, the vigilantes pulled him out into the street.

Fisher was marched to the home of the German girl, "preceded by men carrying a rope, and surrounded by a howling rabble."[64] She had said she had often seen her attacker chopping wood near her home. When Fisher was presented to her, Barbara declared, "That is the man," before fainting away.[65] Immediately, a noose was placed around his neck and he was dragged to a tree behind the girl's house.

Someone suggested that Fisher should be hanged at the scene of the crime. All agreed and they took him to the spot. By then, some 2,000 to 4,000 spectators (in a community of 5,700) had assembled. About 200 of them were active participants.

Given time to pray, Fisher insisted he was innocent. His last words were, "O Lord take care of me; I know I am going to die, but I have many friends."[66] His hands were then tied behind his back, his feet pinioned, and a handkerchief draped over his face. A number of men pulled the rope, lifting him off the ground at ten minutes past four o'clock on Sunday afternoon.

At some point, his body was shot full of bullets while men, women, and children, having come from Bucyrus, Mount Gilead, Crestline, and other neighboring towns, looked on. His corpse was left hanging from the tree limb for at least five hours.

Fisher had dared to cross the color line. Had he been white and his victim black, he probably would have escaped with his life. One "leading journal" in South Carolina had asserted "it is not the same thing for a white man to assault a colored woman as for a colored man to assault a white woman, because the colored woman had no finer feelings nor virtue to be outraged!"[67]

The participation of (and leadership by) African Americans in the lynch mob probably arose out of their own indignation over Fisher's criminal behavior, a need to distance themselves from him, and a desire to express their unity with the white citizens of Galion. However, in doing so they ran the risk of inviting more violence against other blacks.

Expected Lynching, Montgomery County, August 1882—Guenther, Henry [W]

Henry Guenther's wife was poisoned under suspicious circumstances early in August 1882. Married but two weeks earlier, she died on August 11 from the effects of poison in her coffee. Several other members of the family also were sickened, but recovered. It was suggested that something had gotten into the coffee during the manufacturing process. There was nothing to indicate criminality. Still, four days later, there was an expectation that Henry might be lynched.

A prosperous Dayton gardener, Guenther was not prosecuted for his wife's death. However, nine years later on August 4, 1891, he was charged with poisoning his third wife. When the coroner had her body disinterred, he discovered strong traces of arsenic in the dead woman's stomach. The deceased wife, Sophia "Sofi" Winkler, had borne him two children. The year before, she sued him for seduction and breach of contract, and was awarded $5,000 in damages.

Rather than pay her, Guenther married the woman on April 16, 1891. However, she soon suspected he planned to kill her and a man swore out an affidavit in which he claimed Guenther offered him $1,000 to do so.

The fact is, Guenther might have gotten away with it. Winkler had been his housekeeper and had been adopted by him some time before his second wife died. (The cause of her death is unknown.) Before he persuaded her to marry him, he deeded his farm and all his property to a friend, retaining a lifetime dower (or interest) for himself.

After a few weeks, Guenther brought his wife to town, left her on the street, and said he did not want to see her again. She brought suit against him, but was persuaded by her friends to return to him and did so.

Guenther said she would not live a month and he was right. She had violent spells of vomiting and her stomach was in fearful condition. He would claim she had been unfaithful and died of diphtheria.

Sentenced to a twelve-year term for manslaughter, Guenther was pardoned by Governor William McKinley in December 1892, in the expectation he would die at any moment.

Attempted Lynching, Meigs County, August 1882—Holmes, William "Bill" [B]

There is little doubt the mob of 100 to 600 men who nearly broke through the jail walls in Pomeroy at midnight on August 6, 1882, planned to hang William "Bill" Holmes.

While out hunting on Saturday evening, August 5, 1882, Holmes, a black man, happened upon several white girls picking blackberries. Scaring the youngest away, he seized the oldest, Hysell, and brutally raped her. He was soon caught and placed in the Rutland jail by the police, while the girl's neighbors searched the woods for him with shotguns, vowing to lynch him.

The *Newark Advocate* asserted, "Holmes has a reputation for general cussedness and lynching would be too good for him."[68] However, after nearly breaching the jail wall, the mob found he was not there. He had been hidden in a coal bank and soon was on his way to Columbus for his protection.

The would-be lynchers were well known men from the community who made no effort to disguise themselves. It was suggested they would be arrested. In fact, two men from Middleport were: one a saloonkeeper and the other a newspaperman for the Middleport *Republican*. When they realized that none of their compatriots from the mob would gain their release, they bailed themselves out.

False Report of Lynching [TI], Wood County, July 1883—Butterfield, Orville Orlando [W]

The Tuskegee Institute reported that a white man named Butterfield was lynched in North Baltimore, on July 24, 1883, for murder. According to the *Democratic Northwest*, "On Friday afternoon last two farmers in Wood county, named Jerry Bowman and O.O. Butterfield, got into an altercation over a line fence, when Bowman was shot through the body by Butterfield, dying soon after."[69] The incident occurred at Hoytsville. However, reports that Butterfield was lynched were false.

O.O. Butterfield shows up in the 1880 census for Wood County. Born in Chautauqua, New York, June 6, 1838, his full name was Orville Orlando Butterfield. He was a married farmer with four daughters and a son living in Jackson Township. Also a surveyor, Butterfield specialized in ditching and tiling projects and played a part in draining the Great Black Swamp of northwestern Ohio.

Butterfield can be documented as a resident of Wood County until 1883, when his daughter, Jennie, died. Everyone except him then moved to Meeker County, Minnesota, according to the 1885 state census. The reason becomes clear in an article published in the *Perrysburg Journal* in February 1884: "Butterfield Gets Four Years."[70] Tried for the shooting of Bowman, Butterfield was convicted of manslaughter. Charges against his daughter, Ella, for shooting with intent to kill, were dropped.

By January 1887, when his last child was born, Orville was living with his family in Minnesota. A letter to his daughter, Ella, dated May 3, 1887, has survived and he also appears in the 1895 state census. On October 9, 1813, Orville died in Port Williams, Washington, after suffering two strokes.[71]

Mob Violence, Licking County, June 1883—Erenier [W]

In the village of Granville, a blacksmith named Erenier was dragged from his home on the night of June 18, 1883, and horse-whipped by some of the local citizens for mistreating his wife.

Expected Lynching, Henry County, October 1883—Johnson, Wesley [W]

On October 23, 1883, Wesley Johnson, a convicted thief, slew George Williams and his wife, Isabella, with an axe outside of Napoleon. The motive was robbery.

Two days later, their corpses were found by a neighbor, Addison Crew, who had stumbled across George's lifeless body in the barn at about one o'clock—head split open and his throat cut.

Raising an alarm, Crew then joined several others in entering the house where George's wife was lying dead on the floor of their bedroom, her head similarly gashed. A starving two-month-old infant, Charles Foster Williams, was on the bed, crying and sucking on his bloody fingers.

It was apparent that the Williamses had been slain several days earlier—Tuesday evening, most likely. Suspicion immediately fell on Wesley Johnson. A suit of bloody clothes, identified as the ones he was wearing, were found beside the road where he flung them while fleeing to Kendalville.

A newspaper reported, "it is not improbable that had it not been for the extraordinary precautions of the officials of [Henry] and Fulton county, Judge Lynch would have revenged, so far as possible, this awful murder and the gallows cheated out of its own."[72]

Johnson was placed on trial instead, convicted of murder, and hanged on May 29, 1884.

Expected Lynching, Montgomery County, December 1883—Two tramps [unk]

Fourteen-year-old Clara May Eby was raped by two tramps on December 13, 1883, near her Vandalia residence. Soon thereafter, two tramps were rounded up.

"The country people are gathering in large crowds, and if identified beyond a doubt the tramps will surely be lynched," it was reported.[73]

However, Clara did not identify either of them, nor a third man who was picked up. A week later, Charles Kelley was arrested in Piqua. Although he insisted he maintained he was innocent, Clara positively identified him, but the fever for lynching had apparently subsided.

Lynching [TI]/Attempted Lynching, Perry County, February 1884—Hickey, Richard [W]; Reddy, Joseph [W]

At about midnight Saturday, February 2, 1884, Peter Clifford, a brakeman on the Ohio Central Railroad, heard a knock at his door in Rendville. Thinking it might have something to do with his mother who lived a mile away and had been taken ill, Clifford asked, "Who's there?" "A friend," said the voice. "Come quick."[74]

As soon as Clifford opened the door, he was shot through both lungs and his arms. Before he died, he gasped, "The Hickeys have killed me."[75]

Clifford's brother, Bill, had married Richard Hickey's sister, Mary, and there were some bad feelings over this union. On Saturday night, Peter Clifford and Mike Glenn, a son of Mary's former marriage, got into a fight in a billiard saloon, with Glenn coming out on the losing end. (Alternately, Peter went to Hickey's "dive" and gave Hickey "a sound drubbing."[76]) He presumably went home and told what had befallen him.

As a result, Glenn, Richard Hickey (his uncle), Joseph Reddy (another uncle), and Mary set off to even the score. Before they reached Peter's house between Corning and Rendville, Glenn and Mary split off and returned home. However, Hickey and Reddy continued on with the result that Peter was murderered.

While fleeing the scene, the killers encountered a black man and warned him not to say anything. However, he did tell and within an hour Hickey and Reddy were arrested. The following day, people came to Rendville from all over, drawn by the excitement of the murder. Word was sent to New Lexington, asking the county sheriff to send a company of militia because trouble was expected.

That evening, a large number of miners and railroad men met a short distance outside Rendville and planned their attack. About twelve to twenty masked men subsequently interrupted a preliminary hearing conducted before the mayor, seizing the prisoners. The guards on duty immediately dropped their weapons and ran.

The lynch party took Hickey, his nephew, and brother-in-law outside to a small grove of sycamore trees in the center of town. First Reddy was strung up by the neck and kept there until he was close to death. When he was lowered to the ground, he was asked if he shot Peter Clifford and he said he did not.

Glenn then swore that he had not done it. When asked who did, he pointed to his uncle, Hickey. Hickey was jerked up by his neck again, but the rope broke and he fell unconscious to the ground. That rope was replaced and he was lifted up once more and left there. When asked the same question, he did not directly answer, but responded that if they intended to hang him, he would die like a man. With that, the mob pulled him up into the air a third time and left him hanging there until he was dead. Meanwhile, Reddy was released and promptly fled for parts unknown.

About forty years old, Richard Hickey was a native of Ireland who had lived in Shawnee before coming to Rendville. He operated a saloon and resort for the worst sorts of people. Joseph Reddy was also an Irishman who had come to the United States only ten months earlier. Both had bad reputations. Peter Clifford, on the other hand, was seen a sober, hardworking, and generally well liked.

The number of men in the lynch party was estimated to range from a dozen to fifty. Hundreds of others looked on as they went about their work.

According to a reporter, the general feeling in the community was that the law had been too lenient in dealing with previous homicides. In that respect, there was hope that the lynching might be of some benefit. When Mary and Glenn were arrested on Monday, it was rumored they might be lynched as well.

Having completed their task, the avengers quietly dispersed after warning the rest of Hickey's gang to leave Sunday Creek Valley within twenty-four hours. The family was regarded as a curse upon the community and everyone was grateful when they were gone.

Mob Violence, Hamilton County, March 1884—Courthouse Riot

The Courthouse Riot of 1884 was the low water mark in the history of Cincinnati. The city was four years shy of a century old, yet far from being civilized, if the events of March 24–26 were any indication. In the final reckoning, fifty-six people died, some 300 were wounded, and the Hamilton County courthouse was a smoldering ruin.

Three months earlier, William Berner, a German, and Joseph Palmer, a "mulatto," had murdered their employer, William Kirk, the owner of a west end livery stable. Their motive was to rob him of $285 he had received for the sale of a horse. His body was found where they dumped it, near the Mill Creek on the Northside. They were immediately suspected and placed under arrest.

A jury was seated from a pool of more than 500. Over the course of several weeks, seven different witnesses testified that Berner, who was being tried first, had confessed to the murder. However, on March 26, 1884, the jury found Berner guilty of manslaughter. In handing down a sentence of twenty years, the judge pronounced the verdict "a damned outrage."[77] The newspapers agreed that such leniency was a travesty of justice and called for a public meeting to protest the verdict.

A vast throng numbering in the thousands attempted to break into the Hamilton County jail in 1884.

Under orders from the deputy sheriff, the police and the militia battled the rioters in the tunnel leading to the jail.

Several members of the jury soon felt the public's displeasure in various ways: threatened with hanging, severely beaten, pelted with rotten eggs, and even fired from a job. One man's house was vandalized with dead cats and rotten eggs thrown through the windows until the mob discovered they had the wrong person. All or nearly all jurors would be compelled to leave town.

Two nights later at the music hall, a large gathering of at least 6,000 people listened to the fiery oratory of several community leaders—a doctor, a judge, and a general—denouncing the verdict and the methods of the attorneys for the defense, implying that bribery had been involved. Afterwards, they flooded Elm Street and swarmed the county jail on Sycamore above Court Street.

The ranks of the howling mob swelled. While some hurled bricks and stones at the building, others battered down the basement doors, and still others the main doors of the jail. Once they gave way, the mob rushed into the office where they encountered iron grated doors.

Although county sheriff Morton L. Hawkins and a handful of deputies tried to face them down, he had ordered his officers not to fire their weapons. So the mob surged through the jail, scouring it for the murderer Berner. But he was nowhere to be found.

What they did not know is that an effort had been made to take Berner to Columbus immediately after the verdict was handed down. However, through the negligence of a deputy, he had escaped while on board a train at Loveland. Other accounts are that he was attacked by a mob trying to take his prisoner.

A squad of fifteen police officers came to the aid of the sheriff and his deputies, but they were ineffectual in clearing the mob. Then at 9:55 p.m., the riot alarm was sounded. Even more citizens came to the scene, most of whom fell in with the mob.

Police from other stations also began arriving and were divided into two groups, one above and one below the jail. With patrol wagons in the lead, they began advancing in two columns upon the crowd, which was now estimated at close to 10,000.

The rioters began to stampede, fleeing in all directions. Some of the ringleaders were apprehended and carted off to the station house. However, as soon as they had departed, the rioters closed ranks and once more assailed the jail, this time having armed themselves with axes, stones, and bricks.

The mob made two or three assaults upon the jail house, breaking down doors and gates with sledgehammers. At about midnight, they were inside, engaging the police in hand-to-hand combat. Six men, two militia and four officers, were shot, while none of the mob were injured. Afterward, they retreated outside where they began setting fires in the jail yard and around the courthouse.

Once more, the mob rushed the jail. This time they were fired upon by the militia. The rioters were unaware that the troopers were using blank cartridges. Bolstered by reinforcements, the militia was able to force them to retreat.

The rioters then began looting several gun stores, stealing firearms and ammunition. At the same time, others had set additional fires around the courthouse and jail, fueling them with coal oil and powder stolen from neighboring stores.

The fires were so bright that hundreds of people were drawn to the scene from the suburbs, attracted by the flames. By morning, the fires had been extinguished and many

Opposite: **After seizing the Hamilton County courthouse, the rioters set several fires and the entire structure erupted into flames.**

of the rioters had returned home, exhausted by their labors. However, others replaced them.

A tense stand-off took place all day Saturday. That evening, the streets were once again choked with people and another attack—the most serious of all—was made upon the jail. Breaking into the courthouse, the mob set multiple fires, and it seemed as if the entire structure burst into flame at once. The building soon burned to the ground, destroying all of the county records housed there.

Despite his reluctance to get involved, Governor George Hoadly finally sent in the state militia. The troops began arriving by train, one after another. Their appearance on the streets of Cincinnati incensed the mob. It was all out war and blood began to flow. These troops did not fire blanks, but mowed down the rioters "like grass under the keen sweep of a scythe."[78] Many well-known citizens were wounded by stray shots.

After three days, the Thirteenth Regiment from Hillsboro and the Fourteenth Regiment, Governor's guards, and Duffy Rifles (an African American unit), all from Columbus, were allowed to return home. They had been in the thick of things, defending the barricades at the most dangerous points. They were replaced by the First, Second, Fifth, Fifteenth, Sixteenth, and Seventeenth Regiments.

While all of this was taking place, detectives recaptured Berner late Saturday afternoon, playing cards at a cabin in the woods near Loveland. He was taken directly to Columbus and locked up in the Ohio Penitentiary to begin his twenty-year sentence. As far as his accomplice is concerned, Joseph Palmer was found guilty of first degree murder in a separate trial and hanged. The evidence was the same and the guilt was equal, but the penalty was greater for Palmer, either because he was black or as a consequence of the rioting.

Although the Berner trial verdict was the ostensible reason for the riot, it was just another example of the underlying corruption that had rankled the citizens of Cincinnati for ten years. According to an article reprinted in several newspapers around the country, criminal lawyer Thomas C. Campbell, a Republican, and newspaper editor John McLean, a Democrat, were the ringleaders. They were backed by local gamblers, saloonkeepers, brothel owners, and "common roughs of both parties," not to mention "southern lottery schemes."[79]

The two men combined to control members of the police force, the judiciary, and office holders. McLean used his newspaper, the *Enquirer*, to attack their enemies and Campbell would defend him in lawsuits. He also represented murderers with money and, at the time, there were some forty who had yet to be convicted or acquitted due to his efforts. Three of those walking the streets were then made ward captains so they could deliver votes.

In the aftermath of the rioting, there was a strong belief among the citizenry that those tried for murder going forward would not as easily escape the noose.

Victor Hugo and other observers from across the ocean drew parallels between the events in Cincinnati and the storming of the Bastille at the onset of the French Revolution. The *Dayton Daily Democrat* did likewise, but didn't mean it as a compliment when it called Cincinnati "the Paris of America," recalling the Reign of Terror.[80]

In the aftermath, both McLean and Campbell were toppled from power, with Campbell departing for New York City. Although it has been claimed that thirty to seventy-five murderers awaiting trial were in the Hamilton County jail at the time of the riot, twenty years later a historian asserted, "The fact is, as shown by the records in the county jail ... that the number of prisoners in the county jail at that time charged with homicide was only ten."[81]

Expected Lynching, Seneca County, July 1884—Beach, James [W]

Rich people rarely are lynched, so threats to lynch James Beach weren't likely to be carried out, despite what the *New York Times* termed his "unnatural crime."[82]

On July 25, 1884, workmen engaged in tearing down the wooden steps leading up to the front door of his "mansion" in Attica, Seneca County, discovered the skeleton of an infant buried in the soft ground. Although Beach instructed them to rebury it, the workmen took it to the authorities.

An investigation followed in which Beach's college educated daughter admitted the child was hers—and her father's. Immediately after it was born, they had strangled and buried it where it was found. "The mother knew of her daughter's indiscretion, but never suspected her husband of the crime."[83] The daughter was engaged to marry a man she met in college.

Both the father and daughter were jailed while awaiting the grand jury, but certain members of the community talked of lynching James Beach. They did not carry out those threats, however.

Attempted Lynching, Athens County, August 1884—Two unknown men [unk]

Some 300 to 400 masked and heavily armed men descended upon Snake Hollow near Nelsonville at midnight on August 29, 1884. Their purpose was to seek "revenge for the many insults thrust upon them since the strike began."[84] They were met by gunfire from the guards who had been posted at the mine. The vigilantes returned fire.

When the smoke cleared, William Hare, the acting captain of the guard, was found dead with several bullet holes in his body. Two other guards were wounded. The miners were said to be carrying ropes with which to hang the blacklegs (non-union miners) and they had actually placed nooses around the necks of two men.

On September 1, David Woody, a Nelsonville miner, was arrested and charged with complicity in the Saturday night attack. He was transported to Logan on a special train and confined in the jail. The Lancaster guard was assigned to protect the jail.

Expected Lynching, Preble County, October 1884—Ellis, William [W]

Marshal Michael Ryan of Eaton was murdered on the evening of October 28, 1884, and there was some fear that his suspected killer might be lynched. After all, the former drayman was a popular figure in town, especially among his fellow Irishmen.

Little is known about the events surrounding the officer's death, but it is believed he encountered William Ellis at around seven o'clock and they became involved in an altercation. Ellis may have been the same person Ryan had arrested previously on suspicion of murder and soundly beat with a club before tossing him in jail.

Newspaper accounts diverge on the issue of which man drew his revolver and shot first. However, Ryan was hit three times (or possibly five), once fatally, and Ellis not at all.

In the end, calmer heads prevailed and Ellis escaped the noose. The *Eaton Democrat* declared, "Marshal Ryan will be the most missed person that ever went out of Eaton."[85] A few months later, Ellis was found not guilty.

Attempted Lynching, Sandusky County, February 1885—Muntz, Charles [W]

Twenty miles from Sandusky was the village of Graytown. On February 25, 1885, thirteen-year-old Pauline Scheuster was returning home from school when she was criminally assaulted by Charles Muntz (alias Brunner), who also lived in the community.

Despite his neighbors' efforts to capture and lynch him, Muntz managed to jump aboard a train to Sandusky where he hid out in the home of a relative. Discovered by the police the very next day, he was sent under guard to a jail at Port Clinton.

Mob Violence, Belmont County, April 1885—Bellville, Thomas [W]

The citizens of Mead Township had banded together to protect themselves from petty theft and other crimes. They suspected several local families of harboring thieves and possibly being involved in the crimes. So about April 13–15, 1885, a group of them called on William Bellville, who had a boat moored the mouth of Pipe Creek. But they found he had floated away. Next, they visited Andy Doty. Because he had a sick child, he was given time to travel. David Little also had a sick child and was given some time to depart.

However, Thomas Bellville, who resided on one of the Day farms in a cabin, had a wife and no sickness. Visiting him at midnight, they hauled his household goods out into the yard before demolishing his house. He was given twenty-four hours to leave under threat of death. He used part of his time to obtain warrants for the arrest of three of the fifteen to twenty people in the gang.

"There has been considerable stealing in that part of the country, and farmers have become very tired of it," the *Wheeling Daily Intelligencer* opined. "A little such rough work will have a good effect, no doubt."[86]

Mob Violence, Huron County, May 1885—Hathaway, Ray S [W]

Ray S. Hathaway, city editor of the *Toledo Sunday Democrat*, visited Norwalk a few days after "he published an obscene article, coupling the names of several prominent young Norwalk business men with that of a respectable married lady."[87] Dated May 17, 1885, it accused them of stealing the woman's affections and breaking up her marriage.

It had been Hathaway's practice to visit Norwalk and report on any gossip he heard. He would also bring with him copies of the latest newspaper to hawk. Bad decision. He was quickly waylaid by several prominent citizens of Norwalk, who took objection to what he had written about them. Lured into the barn behind the St. Charles Hotel to look at a horse, he was seized by W.H. Peters while Henry E. Smith and C.L. Merry bound his hands and feet.

Coated with tar and feathers in the presence of a physician, he had a placard hung around his neck which read, "Compliments of the Peek-a-boo Club."[88] A revolver and a billy club taken from his pockets were turned over to the town marshal. Hathaway was told to tell his editor that if he ever appeared in Norwalk again, he would be lynched.

It took about an hour for a group of people to clean Hathaway up sufficiently that he could grab the next train out of town. When he reached Toledo, Hathaway was nearly dead and expected to lose the sight in both eyes. "No sympathy is wasted on him," one paper wrote, "as the *Democrat* has long preyed upon the best people in this part of the state."[89]

Afterward, the men who had assaulted him were eager to make a financial settlement owing to the adverse publicity, but Hathaway was intent upon seeing them prosecuted for assault and battery, highway robbery, and creating a mob. He also sued them for $25,000.

Lynching [TI], Perry County, May 1885—Guest, Albert [W]

The lynching of Albert Guest (aka Guess) was probably inevitable, given the trajectory of his miserable life. Guest was born on a farm three miles outside of Carbon Hill to "respectable and well-to-do parents."[90] They later sold their farm to the Akron Iron Company and moved to one near Delaware. As a boy, Guest was quiet and reserved, but he grew up to be a bully with a serious drinking problem.

About 1866, Guest and another young man went to Gore where they met up with a young miner from Kentucky. The trio spent the evening carousing. The next morning, the body of the miner was found entangled in the cowcatcher of a locomotive which had traveled from Gore to Straitsville. Guest and his companion were arrested and found to have the miner's watch in their possession.

Charged with robbery, Guest was sent to the Ohio Penitentiary. Although his codefendant was cleared, he confessed before he died a few years later that the two of them held the Kentuckian's head under water until he drowned then placed his body on the railroad track.

After serving three years of a seven year sentence, Guest was pardoned by Governor Charles Foster on the condition that he not partake of alcoholic beverages. Although many prominent citizens of Logan had signed the petition for the pardon, Guest was seldom sober upon his release. Then in 1873, he became embroiled in an affair when he attended the local agricultural fair with two young women "of questionable character."[91]

The threesome subsequently took a room at the Buntz Hotel in Logan. That evening, four men entered their room, planning to carry off the women. They began beating Guest, but he retaliated with a pocket knife, slashing at them until they fled for his lives. Although he was arrested for assault, he was acquitted when the case went to trial. But he acquired the reputation of being a bully and started drinking heavily.

For two years, Guest held a job in a Straitsville coal mine to provide for his wife and children. However, any thoughts that he had turned over a new leaf were dashed when he and William Tandy, a night watchman, paid a call on William Wallace in New Straitsville on the night of May 20, 1885. Both men were conducting themselves in a manner that made Wallace wary of admitting them to his house. But, he relented when they threatened to break down the door. Once inside, they proceeded to rape a Miss Anderson. As they left the around four o'clock the next morning, they fired several shots at the house, nearly wounding the inhabitants.

Later the same morning, a warrant was sworn out, charging Guest and Tandy with rape. Marshall Henry Auer soon located Tandy, who readily surrendered and was locked up in the jail. Guest, however, having boasted that he would never allow himself to be arrested again, met the marshal in front of the United States Hotel. Drawing a 45-calibre revolver, he shot Auer three times, striking him in the thigh, abdomen, and neck. He then fired two more shots into the crowd. One of these struck a boy named Hugh McTague, age eleven, in the stomach, damaging his spine. Marshall Auer only managed to get off one shot, which missed.

Guest took off in the direction of the Plummer Hill mine. Hundreds of men, women, and children came running into the streets to see what had happened. As Auer and McTague were tended by physicians, who declared the wounds to be fatal, the whole town was buzzing with excitement. A group of men, including two Pinkerton detectives, set out to capture the killer and found him in the woods, prepared to shoot if necessary.

One burly German, training a Winchester rifle on Guest, shouted, "Throw up your hands." When the killer raised only one hand, the German ordered, "Throw up both hands this minute. Give yourself up, Goddamn you. Throw up both hands, for I'm going to shoot you through the heart if you don't."[92]

Despite his vow to never surrender, Guest gave up. There were some who clamored to lynch him on the spot, but they were overruled and he was taken to jail. Nevertheless, they did not abandon the idea. Throughout the day, people talked of little else wherever they gathered.

The towns of Logan and New Lexington offered to provide Mayor Spurrier with assistance in maintaining order, but he turned them down. Then, at about two o'clock in the morning on May 21, 1885, a mob of 200 masked men approached the jail. Breaking into the building, they placed revolvers to the heads of the officers in charge and forced them to hand over the keys. Unlocking Guest's cell, they dragged him out.

By the time the mob had walked from the jail to the place of execution near Plummer Hill mine, it had doubled in size. As he was being hanged, Guest shouted out the names of those he thought he recognized. A number of the men then drew their revolvers and shot him ten times, ensuring his death. He was cut down by Coroner Stebbs at 7:30 Friday morning. Twenty-three-hours later, Marshall Auer succumbed to his wounds. The boy, Hugh McTague, revived somewhat, giving false hope for his recovery, before expiring at one o'clock the same afternoon.

Mob Violence, Gallia County, May 1885—Herder, Ella [W]

Late in May 1885, Annie Rhodes, age fifteen, came from Middleport to Gallipolis in search of a woman for whom her mother used to sew. She wound up at the house of Ella Herder, who hired her to do kitchen work. Apparently, Herder operated a brothel. At the end of the week, she proposed that she become a "boarder" (prostitute), which the girl refused.

About ten o'clock that evening, a strange man tried to molest Annie, but she was able to drive him off. The following day, she moved out, but Herder would not allow her to take her clothes with her until she got the mayor to intercede. Then on the night of May 31, a mob of 100 converged on the Herder house, took her beyond the city limits, and coated her with tar and feathers. They then ordered her to leave Gallipolis forever.

Mob Violence [TI], Darke County, June 1885—Graham, Turner [B]; Graham, Fanny [B]

As the *Topeka Daily Capital* reported, "Turner Graham and wife (colored), were killed by a mob, armed with shotguns, after midnight Thursday."[93] That would have been June 11, 1885.

The incident occurred in the village of Osgood, where Turner made his living as a barber. The couple were known to drink heavily and quarrel frequently with one another. While they were regarded as "obnoxious," they did not seem to bother others.[94] Still, there was a group of citizens who resented the presence of African Americans in their community, peaceful or not.

During the early hours of the evening, the Grahams—Turner and Fanny—had been away from their home "on a spree."[95] When they returned, a mob was lying in wait for them and "riddled them with shot."[96] One newspaper headlined, "Negroes Hunted Like Beasts."[97] It charged that for an hour or more, the couple had been stalked through town until they were finally cut down in a hail of shotgun fire.

Four men were subsequently arrested and indicted for the murders—or at least the murder of Fanny (Turner evidently did not die)—and jailed in Greenville: Dr. Aaron R. Greer, town council member; Jacob "Job" Gosley (or Goslee), corporation treasurer; Nicholas Wynant "Wes" Mills, clerk; and Isaac N. "Ike" Medford, mayor of Osgood. All were regarded as prominent citizens in the community.

The wife of Mills subsequently died in September due to "a broken heart" (actually tuberculosis, possibly complicated by childbirth and depression) resulting from her husband's involvement in the murder.[98]

Genealogist Audrey Hancock has written about this incident and, specifically, its impact on the Mills family. By his own testimony, Turner and his wife moved to Osgood in August 1884, where Mills operated a tavern. "According to a Mills family story/legend," Hancock wrote,

> One night about six or seven white men were drinking heavily, and they decided to scare the two into leaving town. They asked Wynant to loan them his revolver. He did.... The men went to the house. When the couple came out, the men supposedly shot over the man's head. The man fell down, pretending to be dead. The wife began screaming and the men shot her, believing they had also killed the husband. All the men were sent to prison, as was Nicholas [Wynant Mills] for providing the gun, for the unplanned murder of Fanny Graham.[99]

However, as Hancock pointed out, Mills was convicted of shooting with intent to wound, which suggests he took a more active role in the affair than family history would admit. Given a sentence of one to twenty years in prison, he died at the Ohio Penitentiary on June 7, 1888.

Dr. Greer, meanwhile, escaped from jail and went south where he changed his name. He died in 1917 and his body was buried in Versailles.

Lynching [TI], Coshocton County, June 1885—Howard, Henry [B]

Two young women, Eliza Bache, age seventeen or eighteen, and Ellen Phillips, twenty, were picking strawberries along the Pan-Handle Railroad line four miles outside Newcomerstown when they were attacked by an African American man. The stranger clubbed Phillips on the back of the head, knocking her to the ground, and then raped Bache at knifepoint.

Newspapers reported, that Phillips "called for help and the negro was pursued and captured near West Lafayette in an old barn."[100] He identified himself as Henry Howard. He claimed to be from Apalachicola, Florida, and had come north five years before as a laborer with John Robinson's circus.

At the time of the assault, Howard said he could prove he was working at a coal mine just outside town. However, given that Bache had been rendered unconscious and was expected to die, there was immediate talk of lynching him.

During the preliminary hearing on June 19, 1885, Phillips, her head wrapped in bandages, identified Howard as the man who had raped her companion. A physician who examined the prisoner stated that he was wearing freshly washed clothes and was suffering from a "loathsome disease."[101] The father of the young woman had to be restrained from killing him there and then.

A mob soon formed about one mile east of Coshocton. Hordes of people converged on the town from all directions and by evening the streets were packed with strangers. Entering the town, the mob marched down Chestnut Street to the jail. It has been kept under surveillance to ensure no attempt was made to move Howard to another county.

At about eleven o'clock, Howard was taken from the Coshocton jail by a band of masked men, numbering nearly 200.[102] Most were armed and one carried a sledge hammer. The mob's demands to be admitted were met with no resistance. As Howard was brought out, "deafening cheers" went up from the enormous crowd that had assembled.[103]

A noose was quickly placed around his neck and he was propelled across the street to the courthouse yard. An attempt was made to hang him from a tree, but it proved too small, so they took him to a larger one, an elm. Several men climbed it, each eager to be the one to arrange the gallows.

In front of at least 1,000 spectators, Howard, his hands and feet tied, purportedly confessed to the crime three times and said he was sorry. They then "put a strong hemp rope around his neck, threw it over a limb, and strung him up, everybody being eager to lend a hand."[104]

The correspondent for the *Springfield Globe-Republic* "asked the deputy sheriff how they gained an entrance into the cells so soon, and was informed that the mob overpowered the sheriff and took the keys away from him."[105] It took no more than three minutes. The sheriff had earlier been dissuaded from contacting Governor George Hoadly for assistance.

Another reporter wrote that he "talked with some of the masked men, whom he knew well, and they are men of property and well respected citizens of the community."[106]

Expected Lynching, Perry County, August 1885—Unknown bomber [unk]

While Hugh Kinney was asleep in his apartment on the night of August 17, 1885, in the mining town of Shawnee, someone threw a bomb through the window. Kenny, a miner, was "badly mangled and his wife wounded."[107]

The whole community was riled up by this cowardly attack and threatened to lynch the guilty party should they be caught. They were already angered by the recent cut in wages and the failure of a strike the previous week. Kenny was believed to be an informer, providing information to the mine operators.

Then on December 10, 1885, John E. Mason of New Straitsville, a strike organizer, was arrested and charged with the crime. By then, thoughts of lynching had gone by the wayside.

Expected Lynching, Stark County, December 1885—Green, George [B]

Sixty-year-old D.J. Begges of Canton was robbed, his throat and face gashed, and left for dead on Christmas Day, 1885. When he regained consciousness the next day, he exclaimed, "Hang that damned nigger. He tried to kill me."[108]

The suspect, George Green, who had been hired to clean the elderly man's room, had been captured earlier. Begges's identification was considered conclusive and there were written threats to lynch Green. (Ray Bour, who managed a chinaware ship owned by Begges, was even asked to provide a "leader" for the mob.) However, nothing came of them.

4

Segregation (1886–1889)

The Ohio Accommodations Law of 1884 prohibited discrimination on the basis of race in all public buildings, including schools. Nevertheless, African Americans were routinely denied admittance to hotels, bars, swimming pools, theaters, skating rinks, restaurants, etc., until the 1960s. De facto segregation was everywhere.

Attempted Lynching, Erie County, January 1886—Horn, John [W]

John Horn's neighbors complained to Justice Childs of Vermillion that the forty-five-year-old widower had indecently assaulted his daughter, Alice, age fourteen, on New Year's Day, 1886. The mechanic, who lived in Birmingham with his four children, admitted his guilt.

While the hearing was taking place, hundreds of incensed citizens collected in the streets and began planning "to lynch the brute."[1] However, the authorities placed him on a fast train to Sandusky where he was locked up. He immediately asked for a Bible.

Expected Lynching, Darke County, March 1886—McVey, John [W]

On March 17, 1886, fourteen-year-old Cora Green escaped from John McVey, a gypsy, and his two female companions near Greenville. She told authorities that he had kidnapped her from her home near Lebanon, Indiana, over a year earlier. Since then, she had been forced to travel around the country with his gypsy band.

"McVey, she says, shot her in the head, kicked her, cut her on the body with a hatchet, beat her with a club, flogged her with a buggy whip, and outraged her. He also drove a nail through her foot, fastening her to a board, and swung her up to the wagon bows."[2]

As soon as he realized the girl was gone, McVey and his companions decamped. "A large number of citizens are hunting for the party, and, if they are captured, a lynching will probably follow" the *New York Times* reported.[3]

Attempted Lynching [TI], Paulding County, April 1886—Haley, Bill [W]

A former brakeman for the Chicago & Alton railroad, William "Bill" Haley murdered Matthew Crosby in the village of Latty, some twenty-eight miles east of Fort Wayne, Indiana, on April 3, 1886. Haley was arguing with another man in the middle of the street when Crosby tried to intervene. Angered, Haley ran into a butcher shop, picked up a knife, and threw it at Crosby, striking him in the back.

Crosby hung on for two days before dying. "On hearing the news Mrs. Crosby died in hysterics."[4] Haley then fled into the woods. Several days later, he was arrested near

Convoy, Indiana, "in a starving condition and nearly frozen."[5] Apparently, Haley had been hiding out in the woods ever since the murder and a heavy snow had driven him out into the open. He was taken to the Fort Wayne jail.

Following Haley's capture, there was talk of lynching him, but he was moved to the Putnam County jail at Ottawa for protection. Paulding County "wood-choppers," as they were called, twice made attempts to lynch him due to his bad reputation. Haley had lived in Monroeville and was known to the court for multiple larcenies and fights.

In time, Haley was returned to Paulding County for trial. At two o'clock in the morning on July 22, 1886, Sheriff Parr was awakened by a mob of 150 masked and armed men who surrounded his jail. They demanded he give them the keys so they could hang the prisoner.

Most newspapers, including the *New York Times*, reported that the sheriff tried to reason with the men, stalling for time while a deputy tried to sneak the prisoner out a side door. But, the gang was not fooled. Grabbing Haley, they took him a mile outside of town and hanged him from a tree. "The crowd immediately and quietly dispersed, and no one appears to know who they were."[6]

However, most newspapers were wrong. According to the *Hicksville News*, "The sheriff, good humoredly, told them he would conduct them through all the cells, and did so. Word of the intended mobbing had been received, and, the evening before, Deputy Sheriff Swain had taken the murderer out of the county."[7] The *Toledo Blade* described it as "an attempted lynching bee."[8]

The mistake became apparent when the following items appeared in the November 18, 1886, issue of the *Democratic Northwest*: "Haley, the Paulding county murderer, has been found guilty of murder in the second degree."[9] He was sentenced to life in the Ohio Penitentiary.

Ten years later, Haley's sentence was "commuted to fifteen years (August 6), owing to mitigating circumstances and numerous petitioners."[10]

Expected Lynching, Auglaize County, June 1886—Hendershot, Daniel [W]

In the first week of June 1886, Daniel Hendershot entered the saloon of Henry Schwers in New Bremen. He got into an argument with Schwers because the saloonkeeper purportedly refused to serve him a drink.

Hendershot drew a gun and shot Schwers in the jaw just below the mouth. The slug struck his teeth and he promptly spit the bullet out on the floor. Fortunately for both of them, it was "of a caliber known as 22-short and was fired from a small pistol."[11]

Although he tried to make a run for it, Hendershot was apprehended a short way out of town. "He was in danger of being lynched, but cool heads prevailed upon the posse to permit the law to take its course, and the accused was placed on trial and sentenced to 3 years in the penitentiary."[12]

While Hendershot was in the Wapakoneta jail, there apparently still was some talk of lynching him. In September 1886, he was convicted of shooting with attempt to kill and sentenced to the Ohio Penitentiary.

Expected Lynching, Montgomery County, July 1886—Russell, Rolla [B]

When thirteen-year-old Mary (or Mamie) Halweger was found gruesomely murdered outside Franklin on July 22, 1886, Rolla Russell was arrested. Considered weak-minded, Russell, age twenty-two, admitted a knife found near the scene belonged to him, but not everyone was convinced he did it. Despite the father's insistence that he was guilty, Russell had a sound alibi.

A one-armed peddler (or tramp), John Taylor, was also arrested a mile away, but there was reason to doubt his guilt as well. "The town is in great excitement, and should evidence point clearly to any one immediate lynching will result"—or so wrote the *New York Times*.[13]

The following month, however, it was reported that the girl had been killed by her father, Chris Halweger, who was enraged when she did not return from buying groceries in a timely manner. After striking her with a club, he mutilated her body and spread the story that she had been raped.

Apparently, Detective Cooney Kuntz had suspected the father from the beginning because he did not seem interested in solving the mystery and tried to prevent them from exhuming the body.

Mob Violence, Allen County, August 1886—Gray, Al and wife [unk]

There was an outbreak of vigilantism in August 1886 when Al Gray (or Gay) and his wife, who lived near Lima, were tarred and feathered for blackmailing a neighbor and refusing "to leave the country."[14]

Attempted Lynching, Richland County, August 1886—Dolph, Simon [W]

Simon Dolph, a farmer near Mansfield, had a reputation for spreading scandalous rumors about local women. On the evening of August 25, 1886, Dolph was out rounding up his cows when "a sentinel on the road" spotted him and fired a shot.[15] This was the signal for four other men who had been hiding in the cornfield to rush him. Unable to restrain him, they called for four other men to assist.

Once Dolph was securely bound and his wife driven off at the muzzle of a gun, the men tied a rope around his neck. They then dragged him through a woods to where the free end of the rope was thrown over a limb and then pulled up him into the air.

Apparently, Dolph passed out. When he regained his senses, he was lying on a log and a man was blowing air into his mouth. Taken to a graveyard, he was stripped of his clothing, covered in tar, and made to roll in several bushels of feathers. The men also patted feathers on him and stuck some in his hair to make him look like an Indian.

Dolph was then led by the rope over rocks and through bushes to the village of Rome. A bonfire was built and Dolph was forced to march around it to music.

Although most of the village turned out to see this spectacle, no one attempted to help Dolph, including the constable and the justice of the peace. They stood by as he was kicked and beaten with sticks. When they were finished marching him around, the men gave Dolph a kick and sent him on his way, but not before telling him that if he did not leave town in ten days they would kill him and his family and burn his house to the ground.

Several hours later and on the verge of collapse, Dolph manage to reach home. Three days before, he had been warned by two masked men to leave the country and, once again, the night before he was assaulted, this time by two women in disguise. He did not heed them and somehow a man was shot during the confrontation.

Dolph knew who his enemies were; many of them were, purportedly, wealthy men. A local newspaper suggested "the best thing Dolph can do is emigrate."[16] He sold the lease on his farm and the expectation was that he would move away. Instead, he relocated to Mansfield and filed a suit for $20,000 damages. Twelve or thirteen people were indicted for the crime. It took four years to reach a settlement.

Mob Violence, Ross County, August 1886—Follis, John W [W]; Potts, Henry [W]

In late August 1886, John W. Follis and Henry Potts were tarred and feathered by their neighbors for allegedly living in adultery.

Expected Lynching, Perry County, November 1886—Inman, Joseph [W]

Five years after Rendville's founding, the town was a rowdy, violent place with one saloon for every twenty-five citizens. Fights, including shootings, were commonplace. Murders, too.

In November 1882, Marshal Joseph Inman confronted the Murray brothers outside a wedding reception. He felled one with a "mace" and shot the other.

Four years later, Inman killed a black man, Moses Hatchet, during a barroom dispute. Feelings against him ran so strong that he was jailed in Lexington for "fear he would be lynched by enrage citizens, both white and colored," according to the May 22, 1886, *Cleveland Gazette*.[17]

Lynching [TI], Preble County, December 1886—Mussel, William [W]

William Mussel (or Mansell) had gone to the home of Daniel Christman, a seventy-five-year-old farmer, on the night of December 7, 1886, to rob him. He had worked for Christman on a number of occasions during the past eight years and knew him to be a wealthy man.

Arriving after Christman and his wife had retired for the night, Mussel knocked at the door of their impressive two-story home. The unsuspecting farmer rose from his bed to let Mussel in and agreed to let him stay the night. However, Christman later heard his guest leave. His curiosity piqued, Christman got up to investigate. He encountered Mussel at the front gate and they started to walk back to the house together. It was then that Mussel struck him in the head with an axe.

Mrs. Christman had also risen from bed and was standing at the window. She saw her husband's murder. When he returned to the house, Mussel demanded that she give him the money which he assumed they had hidden somewhere. She gave him ten cents from her dress pocket and denied there was more.

After conducting a search on his own and failing to find what he was looking for, Mussel clubbed the elderly woman on the head with a piece of stove wood and pushed her onto the bed. Thinking the woman was unconscious, Mussel threw a lamp on the bed, setting it aflame. As he fled from the house, Mrs. Christman put out the fire. Although her condition was precarious owning to her injures and shock, she positively identified Mussel as the perpetrator of the crime which netted him no more than $20. Before he died, Daniel Christman was able to confirm her account: "William Mussel has killed me."[18]

Five days later on a Sunday morning, George Glidewell headed out to his barn after breakfast only to encounter what he took to be a tramp. A farmer living some two miles southwest of Greencastle, Indiana, Glidewell said the man gave his name as William Olds and begged for food and work. So he hired the stranger for twenty-five cents a day and board to help him around his place.

Olds proved to be a very good worker. Several days later, they struck a deal for him to clear out the brush near the railroad for $10 and his board. Olds also asked that Glidewell build a shanty for him there so he could be close to his work site all the time.

Glidewell began to be troubled by the fact that Olds brought his axe into his room every night, storing it under his bed so that the frost wouldn't warp the handle—or so he said. He even had a dream in which Olds was standing over him with the axe upraised, threatening to kill him.

The next day, Glidewell went into town to pick up his mail, including a copy of the Cincinnati *Enquirer*. But he didn't get around to reading it until a day later. It was then he learned about the horrible murder that had been committed near Eaton, Ohio, by a man named William Mussel. The portrait of the wanted man and the accompanying description fit that of William Olds to a T.

Certain he was housing a murderer, Glidewell didn't know what he should do about it. Hiding the newspaper, he decided to sleep on the matter, but sleep eluded him. Fearful that he might give his suspicions away, he tried to behave as normally as possible.

Glidewell needed an excuse to return to town, but didn't come up with a good one until the following afternoon. He then confided his suspicions to Detective Stone. Along with his right hand man, Lewis Parker, they armed themselves with shotguns and went out rabbit hunting. When they were within thirty yards of Mussel, they aimed their weapons at him. Stone ordered him to throw down his axe. Mussel obeyed. As he was being handcuffed, he asked, "What is the matter, boys? What is this all about?"[19]

The two men asked the man if he was William Mussel and he didn't deny it. However, he claimed he didn't kill Daniel Christman. Held in the local jail until midnight, Mussel was then placed on the 2:37 a.m. Vandalia train by Detective Stone, accompanied by a reporter. After changing trains in Indianapolis, they arrived in Richmond at 6:50, on December 21, 1886.

Although they were only sixteen miles from Eaton, they had to wait three and one half hours to make their connection. During this time, a mass of people assembled. Mussel told them that the day after the murder, he had walked through the town without being recognized even though people were actively hunting him.

In Richmond, the sheriff of Preble County, marshal of Eaton, and ex-sheriff Gorman of Wayne County took custody of Mussel. They reached Eaton just before eleven o'clock.

A large crowd was already waiting at the depot. The train continued to the main cross street where Mussel was bundled into a closed carriage. From there it was a race with the mob to the city jail. Men, women, and children converged on them, yelling, "Kill him! Shoot him!"[20]

Another crowd had assembled at the courthouse yard, hoping to intercept him. There were at least 500 people. However, the law officers drew their pistols and hurried their prisoner through a side gate, running over anyone who got in their way.

For his efforts in apprehending Mussel, Detective Stone was paid $200 by Mrs. Christman and another $200 by the county commissioners (he gave $75 to Glidewell and $50 to Parker). He asked the sheriff if he wasn't concerned that the prisoner might be lynched, but was told the danger had passed. The sheriff evidently wasn't aware that during a town meeting attended by many of Eaton's most prominent citizens, a group of men were assigned to the task. They proceeded to the jail, seized the sheriff, and locked him in a woodshed.

Using sledgehammers and chisels, the mob battered down the three doors that separated them from Mussel. While he admitted assaulting the farmer's wife, he continued to insist he had not killed Christman. It didn't matter.

After Mussel said, "If you're going to hang me, be quick about it," a rope was thrown over the crossbeam of the wooden electrical tower.[21] The leader of the mob ordered, "Pull the rope," and several men obliged.[22] As Mussel's body dangled in the air, the crowd cheered and clapped.

Detective Stone, who had started for home at 7:20 p.m., learned just thirty-five minutes later that Mussel was dead. For one hour, Mussel was left hanging from the makeshift gallows while women and children came to gawk at it. Finally, he was cut down and his body given to the undertaker. His last request had been that his coat and letters be given to his wife.

Lynching [TI], Greene County, June 1887—Betters, Peter [B]

Early on a Sunday morning, June 12, 1887, Marshal Ballard of Jamestown arrested Peter Betters, an African American, for the brutal beating of Mrs. Martha Thomas the night before. Also black, the victim's age was given as between fifty and seventy-five.

Since his release from the Ohio Penitentiary, Betters had been living with "a much respected" elderly woman and her husband in her home one to three miles outside of town on Waynesville Pike.[23] However, he moved out after her husband passed away a few months before.

Betters, age thirty-five to thirty-eight, had served two terms in prison—one for stealing a horse and the other for the rape of a seventy-year-old woman. Still, he had managed to get a job as a hand at the Stinson Brothers livery stable.

On a Saturday night, Betters went to the home of Thomas while drunk, crawled under the house and emerged through the old brick hearth by removing the bricks. Once inside, he savagely attacked her while she was asleep in the house with her two grandchildren. The children fled in terror to the closest neighbors.

When Thomas was found, she was unconscious, her arm and two or three ribs broken and skull crushed, but alive. It is believed he jumped on her with both feet and struck her in the face with a coal oil lamp. The stuffing from a feather bed covered her like snow. However, the woman had gotten a good look at her assailant by the light of the lamp and identified him. A posse formed to hunt him down and he was captured at the fairgrounds.

Throughout the day, Jamestown was buzzing with news of the outrage. Despite rumors that Betters would be lynched, the sheriff did not post any special guard. Then, just before midnight, a mob—mostly consisting of black people, but also a few whites—invaded the village and marched on the jail, a small brick building on the main street. Breaking a window (or, perhaps, a door) and prying open the cell where Betters was confined with a crowbar, they handed him to those who were awaiting outside.

According to newspaper accounts, "the trembling wretch manifested the most pitiable cowardice, yelling and struggling so that he could be heard a mile away."[24] Betters supposedly cried out, "Murder! Save me!" while the crowd answered with "Hang him! Shoot him!" and fired their guns.[25] He was then dragged up the street to the fairgrounds, "yelling like a spaniel," practically at a run, about half a mile away.[26]

Once there, Betters was lynched from an oak tree which was one of many that had been broken in half during a recent storm, the top resting on the ground "forming an admirable gallows."[27] A large man who appeared to be the mob's leader then said, "Now disperse and go home. We have done good work; we have nothing to be sorry for. Now keep quiet and all will be well. Colored people are as true to virtue and justice as steel."[28] (An artist by the names of James Watson photographed the scene.)

Around five o'clock Monday morning, Horace D. Buckles passed the fairgrounds on his way to the depot to catch a train for Dayton. He discovered the "lifeless carcass of

Betters was hanging from the tree. His toes were only a couple of feet from the ground."[29] The coroner was sent for to verify that he was dead.

While there was some suggestion Betters had committed suicide, everyone knew better. Few people mourned his passing and most thought it was for the best. After all, Mrs. Thomas, who had survived the attack, was a respected member of the community and he was the antithesis. The *Xenia Democrat News* was one newspaper that described the lynch mob as "composed seemingly of all colored men."[30] The same reporter noted "few men could have managed a hanging bee so well or so quietly."[31]

Mob Violence, Adams County, June 1887—Martin, Mrs. [W]; Martin, Lillie [W]

On the night of June 28, 1887, more than twenty riders armed with shotguns and hickory switches descended on the home of a woman named Martin and her daughter, Lillie, in Jefferson Township. Known as "women of easy virtue," they had been notified several days earlier to leave Adams County.[32] They didn't. When the men demanded entrance to their home, they refused, only to have the door battered down. Two men—apparently customers—who were inside tried to resist, but were overpowered after several shots were fired.

Dragged from their beds, the women were stripped, tied to the door frame, and then beaten with switches until they lost consciousness, their bodies "a shocking mass of bruised and bleeding flesh."[33] The mother came to first and was told if they didn't leave within twenty-four hours, they would be killed. The men, two married farmers, were warned that if they were ever again found in a house-of-ill-repute, they would be killed as well. The Knights of the Switch, as they called themselves, then rode off.

Expected Lynching, Mahoning County, August 1887—Robinson, Alexander [B]

In August 1887, a thirty-three-year-old black man, Alexander Robinson, was charged with raping a ten- (or eleven-)year-old white girl, Essie Hoover. Although he was not lynched, he might as well have been.

The only support for his widowed mother, Robinson was considered an exemplary young man. The shame and disgrace of the charges, coupled with threats of lynching from an enraged populace in Youngstown, resulted in Robinson's death from fright while in jail. As the *St. Paul Minnesota Western Appeal* observed, "Colored men are not always guilty, and these dispensers of justice become murderers in many cases."[34]

Later, the little girl confessed that the guilty party was actually Charles Bishop, a sewing machine salesman who had left town after he heard the girl had named him. She said he had threatened to kill her if she told on him. Bishop was later located in Pulaski, Pennsylvania. He professed his innocence and vowed to return to Youngstown once he had hired a lawyer. However, he disappeared instead.

Mob Violence, Adams County, March 1888—Two Mormon men [W]

Two Mormon elders were attempting to hold meetings at the Brier Ridge school house near Winchester on March 15, 1888, when they were seized by an angry mob of farmers, stripped, and tarred and feathered. Afterward, the missionaries were chased to the Ohio River, which they gladly crossed.

Mob Violence, Allen County, April 1888—Election Day Riot [B]

In his history of Allen County, William Rusler wrote,

> It is said the negroes do not live north of the Pennsylvania railway tracks in Lima.... Once in a while the color line is drawn, and the negroes remain south of the railway tracks for safety. They are represented on the Lima police force, and they do not unnecessarily antagonize the Irish.[35]

But in 1888, a few did antagonize the Irish and vice versa.

Election Day was Monday, April 2, 1888. On Friday, the *Allen County Democrat* reported, "The streets from eight o'clock in the evening until late the next morning were given up to an infuriated mob, who were thirsting for revenge for the killing of an inoffensive and highly respected Irish boy by one of a crowd of drunken negroes."[36] It acknowledged there had been "ill feeling" between some of the Irish and the African Americans for several years and it "needed only the fire of whisky to kindle it into a consuming passion."[37]

Whiskey and elections went together in those days and the former was used to influence the latter. When Tim Casey (Irish) bested Williams Goins (black) at the De La Flora Saloon & Restaurant, Goins gathered reinforcements, including his companions Sam Thomas, Frank Crowder, and Frederick Harrison. Crossing paths with some Irish men at Harper's Corner, a fight broke out between the two groups which sent bystanders scattering for cover.

Patrick Hughes, age sixteen, and David Gallagher were getting a drink from the pump when someone threw a brick from their direction that struck one of Goins's party. The African Americans immediately set out after the two Irish men, slashing them with a knife. Hughes struggled to reach Manning Brothers' pool hall where he died. Gallagher was treated for his wounds at the Lima Curative Institute, then released. Several other Irishmen were injured.

News of Hughes's death quickly spread throughout Lima and the blame was placed squarely on Goins and Crowder, although neither of them was armed. A mob rose up at once and headed for the city jail where it was believed the two suspects were being held. Quickly growing to 500 strong, they marched through the streets, throwing stones, swinging clubs, and waving pistols.

Arriving at the jail, they tore down the doors and searched the cells, only to find the prisoners were not there. At the urging of Hughes's cousin, they turned their attention to the county jail. Although they overwhelmed the sheriff, they still did not find the men they were looking for. During the commotion, several inmates escaped. Goins and Crowder, who had been hidden away, were taken to Kenton the following morning.

Coverage of the riot broke down along party lines. The *Allen County Republican Gazette* blamed the Democrats for pouring whiskey and money into the election "in a way never seen here before."[38] The *Lima Daily Democratic Times* insisted it was the fault of "a party of colored men inflamed with whiskey."[39] An investigation into the death of Hughes concluded that he had been stabbed by Frederick Harrison, aided and abetted by Goins, Crowder, Thomas, and William Standup.

The first to be tried, Harrison was found guilty of manslaughter and sentenced to twenty years in prison. Thomas received twenty years for his attack on Gallagher. Since public interest in the case had died down considerably, it was expected that Goins would receive a similar sentence. However, he was found guilty of murder in the second degree and sentenced to life at hard labor, even though he had only used his fists. It turned out that the jury had been deadlocked between murder and manslaughter and decided the matter by drawing slips of paper out of a hat.

The *Ohio Law Reporter* noted in 1913, that

> these four colored men were set upon by twenty times their number armed with stones and clubs, and while they were all badly beaten one of the assailants was killed, presumably by Harrison, who was tried on a murder charge but convicted of manslaughter. Goins was a good citizen, member of a

poor but respected family of large connections, and on the night in question he was in the peace of the state, but he received internal injuries at the hands of this mob from the results of which he died a couple of years later. With anything like a fair trial he would never have been convicted, as was proved by his subsequent acquittal by a jury after the Supreme Court reversed the case for numerous errors occurring at the trial.[40]

Following his release from prison, Harrison killed a soldier and was promptly returned to the Ohio Penitentiary.

Mob Violence, Pickaway County, May 1888—Milligan, William [W]

Early in May 1888, William Milligan was tarred and feathered after he was caught with Mrs. Bertha (or Kara) Doddroe in a Circleville house of assignation. He had purportedly induced the woman to leave her family and elope with him. He was seized by a group of men from Darbyville who treated him quite roughly.

Attempted Lynching, Franklin County, May 1888—Umphreys [B]

Perhaps, the best known attempted lynching in the history of Columbus was that of "Umphreys, the negro." Arrested for assaulting a little white girl, nine-year-old Stella Couch, on May 16, 1888, he was confined in the city jail. As soon as the other inmates learned his identity, they crowded around him and announced they would kill him at two o'clock. He was then handed a Bible and told to get down on his knees and pray. Declaring he could not pray, he read a chapter instead.

When Umphreys had finished, the inmates told him he needed to be washed. "After throwing him into a bath tub and nearly drowning him, the prisoners secured a rope, placed it around his neck and dragged him about the corridors, ending the performance by drawing him up from the floor."[41] All the while, Umphreys pleaded with them, "For god's sake, don't murder me!"[42] He likely would have strangled to death except for the intervention of another prisoner or two who cut him down before the jailers responded.

False Report of Rape, Lorain County, Autumn 1888—Offet, William [B]

The Reverend J.S. Underwood, his wife Julia, and three children lived in Elyria. He was away from home during the autumn of 1888, campaigning on behalf of prohibition candidates in West Virginia.

Upon her husband's return, Julia told him a horrifying story, one she had not mentioned in any of her letters. She said that one day a black man had knocked on her kitchen door. When she opened it, he stepped inside and propositioned her. She, naturally, ordered him to leave, but he grabbed her and placed a cloth soaked in chloroform under her nose, even as she was trying to defend herself with a fireplace poker. After coming to her senses, she found her clothes were ripped and her body was in a "horrible condition."[43]

Incensed by what he heard, the Reverend Underwood said he would kill the man if he ever encountered him. Julia said she would recognize her assailant if she saw him, so Underwood began taking her on walks along the streets of Elyria to see if they could find him. And, one day, they did.

When Mrs. Underwood pointed him out, the Reverend Underwood pulled out his revolver and threatened to shoot the man on the spot. Instead, with the assistance of some bystanders, they took him into custody.

The suspect's name was William Offet. Charged with rape, he adamantly denied being guilty, but admitted to having had sexual relations with the minister's wife at her invitation. Of course, he wasn't believed. Indicted and tried for the offense, he was found guilty and sentenced to fifteen years in the Ohio Penitentiary. He entered the prison on December 14, 1888.

As soon as Offet was locked away, Mrs. Underwood's emotional well-being began to decline. It was evident something was preying upon her mind. At the same time, her husband became desperately ill and it was thought he might die.

When she could bear it no longer, Mrs. Underwood confessed to her husband (on what she thought was his deathbed) that Offet was innocent. She had initially met him at the post office and he had volunteered to carry some packages home for her. After that, he came to visit her on occasion and eventually they became sexually intimate. "I did not care after the first time," she told him. "In fact I could not have resisted and had no desire to resist."[44]

Mrs. Underwood said she had lied about the affair for several reasons:

> One was the neighbors saw the fellow here, another was, I was afraid I had contracted a loathsome disease, and still another was that I feared I might give birth to a Negro baby. I hoped to save my reputation by telling you a deliberate lie.[45]

Now, the problem was how best to undo the tangled web she had woven.

Upon the advice of an attorney, the Underwoods moved out of state where the Reverend quietly obtained a divorce to avoid scandal. Mrs. Underwood went on to sign an affidavit in which she admitted she had lied about the whole affair.

With the aid of two members of the Ohio legislature, Offet received a pardon and had his citizenship restored. He walked out of prison a free man during the week of January 4, 1892, having served four years for a crime he didn't commit, but, presumably, thankful to have escaped with his life.

The Offet case was cited by Ida B. Wells-Barnett as an example of how African American men were frequently accused of rape by white women when the relationship was consensual. "[T]he relationship sustained between the man and woman was voluntary and clandestine, and that in no court of law could even the charge of assault have been successfully maintained."[46]

Mob Violence, Hardin County, September 1888—Strunk, Mrs. [W]

The vigilante movement known as the White Caps was born in Indiana and spread to Ohio, where it first surfaced in the southeastern counties of Brown and Adams. Composed largely of local farmers, they were sometimes called "regulators" because they regulated behavior or morals. However, even the best intentioned bands tended to degenerate into bullies and terrorists.

At midnight on September 4, 1888, a band of thirty White Caps rode to a house-of-ill-fame at Ada operated by a woman named Strunk. When she answered the door dressed only in a chemise, they seized her and tied her garment over her head. They then led her a short distance away to where they had a kettle of tar and a bag of feathers ready. "Strong hands scooped up the sticky fluid and plastered it over the terrified victim and then a thick coating of feathers was added."[47]

When they were finished, the White Caps told Mrs. Strunk she had twenty-four hours to get out of town. They then left the following notice at the office of the *Ada Recorder*:

> We are a band of White Caps, thirty in number, request you to publish that we raided the Strunk mansion, tarred and feathered her and a certain young man, smashed the windows and doors, and

gave them notice to leave in ten days or they would get a worse dose. There are other ranches in town that will be treated likewise if not stopped also.

A hell hole run as a restaurant, or a first class saloon, should take warning and stop, or you will be visited in ten days. Leave town, both of you, as we don't need you, and mean it. COMMITTEE.[48]

In response, the newspaper received a letter a week later signed by Garibaldi, secretary of the Black Caps. This new secret order directed people to pay no attention to the White Caps because the Black Caps, "a body of orderly citizens, and a band organized not after the style of the White Caps, Molly Maguires, or Bald Knobbers, but for the purpose of self-protection and extermination, if necessary, of the so-called White Caps, will stand by him."[49]

Mob Violence, Brown County, November 1888—Vance, Aaron [W]

Over time, the White Caps broadened their original focus in order to perpetuate their own existence. For example, the attack on Aaron Vance of Sardinia on November 9, 1888, was due to his efforts to expose the Brown County White Caps. He had picked up his nephew, Eddison Vance, at the train station in a horse and buggy and they were returning to his farm shortly after nine o'clock when they encountered a man on horseback, a white cloth wrapping his head, riding swiftly in the opposite direction. Aaron remarked, "There goes one of those cursed White Caps; somebody will get whipped tonight."[50]

A half mile further on, they stopped at a water trough so the horse could have a drink. As they were waiting, Aaron told Eddison, "I know two of them, and have engaged spies to discover the rest. As soon as we can get evidence enough I will spend every dollar I possess, if necessary, to land the villains in the penitentiary."[51]

Aaron was a wealthy bachelor who had a reputation for finishing what he started. They continued on to his house, arriving at about 11 o'clock. Eddison woke early, before his uncle and the servants. Upon opening the front door, he found a drawing of a heart, a skull and crossbones, and a coffin on a piece of paper stuck to the door with a knife. There was an inscription: "Aaron Vance, you'd better be careful as to what you says and does. This is a warnin.' If you try to do us harm you will get the worst of it. WHITE CAPS."[52]

When Aaron heard what had transpired, his first response was, "The devils must have been in the woods last night when we watered the horse."[53]

After breakfast, Aaron went to town and purchased two shotguns, three revolvers, and a supply of ammunition. Calling their bluff, he posted a sign on his fence informing the White Caps that he didn't fear them. So they warned him again and once again he paid no attention.

On their third visit, a masked gang numbering about thirty announced, "We want you and we are going to have you."[54] Aaron told them to come on and fired into the middle of the group. There was a yell and a man fell off his horse. Picking him up, they left, but returned two hours later. As they rode into the yard, the two men began blasting them with bird shot. Again, they fled.

Three nights later, they heard a noise in the barn around 10 o'clock. Eddison and Harwick, a guard they had hired, went to investigate and were immediately jumped by masked men. They were tied up and taken to the barn. A man was left to guard them while the others went to the house to get Aaron. However, the uncle drove them away with gunfire.

Despite a threat to obtain revenge if it took all winter, Vance wasn't intimidated.

Mob Violence, Brown County, November 1888—Berkes, Adam [W]

Before midnight on Saturday, November 17, 1888, a group of riders started from Mount Orab to Burford, passing out of Brown into Highland County. They then cut back into Brown and arrived at Sardinia, having followed a triangular course. They wore masks over their heads with cutouts for the eyes and coarse coats. Their horses were draped in white and black sheets. It was impossible to recognize any individual in the group.

They first visited the home of Bill Eiler, just outside Mount Orab on the Ohio and Northwestern Railroad. The leader demanded Eiler come out. He refused until they threatened to smash down his door. Eiler then obliged, quaking in his boots. He was warned if he stole any more chickens or coal he would be flogged within an inch of his life. Eiler protested his innocence and was allowed to slink back inside the house to his wife and two children.

Two miles further along, they dragged Jim Donnelly out of his house. Sometime before, they had whipped Aaron Conover for stealing chickens and wood. At that time, his brother, Tom Conover, and Donnelly remarked that if anyone beat them, they would be riddled with bullets. They gave Donnelly a chance to carry out his threats, but he begged for mercy. They threatened him with blacksnake whips and hangman's nooses if he ever threaten them again. A few minutes later, Conover was given the same treatment.

Just before midnight, the band reached Buford, where Henry Whitley and Bill Berry were warned to keep their hands off their neighbors' property. They had previously received notices. Both protested their innocence and were allowed to return to their homes.

Six miles further, they reached the home of Adam Berkes, an old shoemaker, in Sardinia, at about one o'clock, Sunday morning. Two of them pounded on his door and shouted for him to come out, alarming the neighbors who were told to shut their windows and mind their own business (emphasized at the point of a gun).

Mrs. Berkes was awake with a sick child in her arms. She told the men her husband was asleep. They replied that no one intended to hurt him. Then Berkes appeared at the door, dressed in trousers and a thin undershirt. He was hurried into the backyard as his wife followed, wailing in fear. She was told she would be whipped if she didn't go back inside so she did.

A little man, less than 100 pounds, Berkes was accused of having stolen coal from the railroad and wood from proprietor Nathan Dunn of the village hotel. Although somewhat shiftless and desperately poor, he was considered to be doing what he could to provide for his family.

For ten minutes, Mrs. Berkes heard the frightful sound of her husband being beaten by six men with whips, demanding that he confess to the thefts. He said he had only picked up coal that had fallen off the train and had not taken any wood. He asked to be taken to Mr. Dunn.

After twenty lashes, he was asked why he didn't pay his debts. He said he didn't owe as much as $10 and would pay up as soon as he could. Then the beating resumed. After fifteen more lashes, he was dragged to his front door, thrust inside, and told they would be back if he didn't do better. The White Caps then returned to Mount Orab, peeling off their disguises as they rode.

Berkes was born in Cincinnati and was a veteran of the war. He had been married twice and had a pretty fifteen-year-old daughter who worked in Sardinia. His neighbors said if they had no objections to him living among them, outsiders shouldn't, either.

Following the visit, Berkes suffered terribly and, less than a week later, he had become "a raving maniac."[55] However, he apparently recovered because he was subsequently placed on "exhibit" at Kohl & Middleton's dime museum in Cincinnati.[56] Chief of Police Colonel Deitsch was warned that he personally would be White Capped if he didn't put a stop to it.

Mob Violence, Brown County, November 1888—Tumbelson, Frank [W]; Smiley, Jim [W]

A week following the Berkes beating, Frank Tumbleson received a letter from Mount Orab dated November 25, 1888, with a black snake whip drawn across the top. It read: "Your brags amount to a mule without any feet. Take warning as you will get the above." It was signed "Office of the White Caps."[57]

Others in Brown and Highland counties had received similar, but distinctive, missives, including prominent businessmen and even Company D of the Thirteenth Regiment. Constable Jim Smiley of Georgetown was warned: "Look out for us. You insulted one of our members upon your streets November 21. Keep your mouth shut and keep off the streets or you will get the whip."[58]

Mob Violence, Brown/Highland County, November 1888—Jester, Anna and two daughters [W]

When the White Caps broke into the Sardinia home of Mrs. Anna Jester and her two grown daughters on the night of November 29, 1888, and whipped them on their bare backs with switches, it set off a firestorm of criticism.

The women were purportedly warned they would be tarred and feathered if they did not mend their ways and their houses would be destroyed. They lived two miles outside town and the daughters did not have good reputations.

However, papers in various parts of the nation such as the *Bossier Banner* in Louisiana pointed out that the White Caps had stooped to levels that even the original Ku Klux Klan did not go. Some people even questioned whether it was true.

Threatened Violence, Adams County, November 1888—Notice in Manchester

The black community in Adams County was so alarmed by the threats that everyone armed himself when he went out at night. Various people reported encountering White Caps in the countryside. Notices were also posted in Manchester on November 29, 1888: "Evil doers, men and women, take warning. First, the visitor; second, the persuaders; third, the helper; fourth the regulator. We are coming. Prepare for better or worse. WHIPS, Advance Agent."[59]

Mob Violence, Brown County, December 1888—Courthouse fire

On December 3, 1888, a fire broke out in the Brown County courthouse in Georgetown, damaging the basement and a portion of the first floor. It was widely believed that it had been set by the White Caps in order to destroy evidence that was being prepared for the grand jury. While repairs were being made, court was held in the Methodist church.

Just before Christmas, a White Cap warning was delivered to B.P. Long, business manager of the *Georgetown News Democrat*. It read:

> To the Citizens of Georgetown:
>
> We want to say now that they have seen what we can do, that if they do not quit making threats as to what they will do if we come to your town we will burn every house in the place. The exhibition of

the night of the 3d (courthouse fire) is not to be thought of in comparison to what we will do, for we must succeed at any cost. So take warning and you will have less use for your fire engines.

WHITE CAPS[60]

The letter was addressed Mount Orab, the purported headquarters for the group. It was believed it had been written in response to a conference in Cincinnati conducted by the prosecuting attorney and the expressed intent of the citizens of Georgetown to assist in "quieting this trouble."[61]

The courthouse reopened in March 1889.

Mob Violence, Allen County, December 1888—Casey, Thomas [W]

Notices had been served to several houses of ill-repute in Lima telling them to close up and leave town. Then, on Wednesday night, December 5, 1888, one was posted at Thomas Casey's saloon in Lima, warning him that he had twenty-four hours to leave or the building would be burned to the ground. Then on Saturday night, December 8, it was.

The White Caps also dropped off notices at several other saloons warning them they were in line for the same. But, a week later, a report out of Chicago asserted that stories of White Cap activities in Northern Ohio were "destitute of any foundation."[62] There may have been bands of self-appointed regulators in two or three counties bordering the river in Southern Ohio, the newspapers stated, but there was no evidence they existed elsewhere.

Yet, in the same issue there was a report of notices being posted by White Caps in Batavia (Clermont County), Lebanon (Warren County), and West Union (Adams), as well as Shane's Crossing (Mercer County)—the latter most definitely not in Southern Ohio.

Mob Violence, Fayette County, December 1888—Lawhead, Charles [W]; Gleason, John [W]

It has been estimated that Ohio had about 300 White Caps in 1888, a number comparable to the rolls of the Ku Klux Klan in the South some years before. What was known about them indicates that they were "composed of those who are law-abiding citizens who have become tired of seeking Justice in the channels from where it was originally designed that it should come"—or so the newspapers claimed and many people believed.[63]

Washington Court House was given as an example of the White Caps at work. There was a rash of break-ins recently—coal houses, chicken coops, cellars. The police force was powerless to suppress it, so the White Caps took it upon themselves to do so.

Charles Lawhead's and John Gleason's saloons were hit on the night of December 6, 1888. The following night, White Caps began posting notices in blood, warning the offenders that their crimes must stop. "Beware, the White Caps have come, and are determined to enforce and preserve order. This is the blood of our last victim. Beware."[64]

Whether that did the trick or not is unknown, but it suggests that some citizens of Fayette County still felt they needed to take the law into their own hands.

Mob Violence, Brown County, December 1888—Whitley, Bill [W]; Berry, Bell [W]

During the month of December 1888, White Cap activity in Ohio would reach a peak that it would never approach again. The night riders would administer more whippings and post more threatening notices than during any other period. Their victims tended to be the obvious targets: those considered lazy, shiftless, abusive, intemperate, and/or immoral. They focused their attacks on prostitutes, gamblers, wife-beaters, drunks, and those of otherwise poor repute.

An editorial in the *New York Times* asserted that the lack of excitement and diversions for the youth of that region were factors. The young men who joined the White Caps found it exciting to be meting out punishment to transgressors and welcomed the break from the monotony of everyday life. Fortunately, the Ohio White Caps were nowhere near as violent as their counterparts in Indiana and other states.

On December 6, 1888, the *Stark County Democrat* reported that there were 300 White Caps in Brown County and 200 each in Adams and Highland counties. The paper stated, "The persons whipped or encouraged by the White Caps are all bad eggs, both male and female."[65]

A correspondent from Brown County wrote that there was a rivalry between the villages of Sardinia and Mount Orab, with each telling scandalous stories about the other. There were believed to be at least three men in the vicinity of Sardinia who were members of the White Caps, led by a prominent farmer who lived near Greenbush.

Until the regulators began to operate, Mount Orab was a place where you couldn't leave your whip and lap-robe in your buggy without fear of it being stolen. "There have been many crimes in Mount Orab which would seem to justify such measures" because of its deplorable moral condition. "Of course the White Caps are to be denounced," the *Democrat* observed, "but what shall we say of the condition of society that prompts the organization of the White Caps."[66]

For example, one resident of Mount Orab lived openly with a prostitute who had driven his wife away. The White Caps informed him that his presence was an insult to the "pure wives and mothers of the community."[67] He had been given two weeks to leave or be thrashed. Bill Whitley and Bell Berry, two men accused of wife-beating and petty theft, reportedly were "doing much better" after a visit from the White Caps.[68] They were working steadily and their neighbors were no longer missing firewood and chickens.

The newspaper concluded by stating that it is only the evil doers who are terrorized by them.

Mob Violence, Putnam County, December 1888—Slick, James [W?]; Miller [W?]

James Slick of Leipsic was brutally beaten by "a party of veritable White Caps" on the night of December 8, 1888, for the offense of whipping his wife and abusing his family.[69] At about the same time, another Leipsic man named Miller, received a similar notice. Thinking it was a practical joke, he ignored it. Miller was subsequently taken from his home and lashed.

The White Capers had also struck at Defiance, Perrysburg, Napoleon, Maumee, putting the lie to the contention that they were strictly limited to the Southern counties. At Napoleon, they posted a notice which read, "God hates liars, perjurers, adulterers. The White Cappers are the Lord's chosen people to wreak out his vengeance on the wicked and unjust."[70]

Mob Violence, Harrison County, December 1888—Parkhill, Dr. John [W]

In Hopedale, a village seven miles east of Cadiz, the White Caps appeared on Sunday night, December 9, 1888. They posted notices warning a local physician to leave the county. But he vowed to remain and threatened to give the night riders "a warm reception" if they came after him.[71]

Presumably, the physician in question was Dr. John Parkhall, for he was whipped by the White Caps on Christmas night. His office boy had gotten drunk and the doctor was accused of having drugged him. They stripped off his clothes and beat him within an inch of his life. More threatening notices were also posted all over town.

Attempted Lynching, Wood County, December 1888—Martin [W?]

A man named Martin who lived a few miles outside of Bowling Green was warned that if he did not go to work and support his family he would be punished. The note was signed, "Wood County Vigilantes."[72] He did not heed it. On the evening of December 11, 1888, when he started home intoxicated, he was intercepted by a band of masked men and taken into the woods.

A rope was tied around his neck and the other end was thrown over a tree limb. He began to pray. Twice he was lifted off his feet and dangled in the air. Then they stripped off his clothing and beat his back with beech switches until it was bloody. He was placed back in his clothes and taken home where he continued to suffer from his injuries.

Mob Violence, Adams and Brown Counties, December 1888—White Caps disbanded

Governor Joseph Benson Foraker of Ohio conferred with David R. Watson, his attorney general, on the White Cap issue early in December 1888. They decided the best course of action would be to meet with the prosecuting attorneys of Adams and Brown counties to plan their strategy for suppressing their activities.

When S.V. Pearson, the Brown County prosecutor, was asked what sort of men they were dealing with, he replied:

> I cannot say they belong to what people call the best class, but they are men who have been engaged as sewing machines agents, feather cleaners, and others whose business takes them all over the country. They are the same class who ten years ago were known as "Regulators."[73]

On December 15, 1888, Governor Foraker announced:

> The so-called White Cap organization has been permanently disbanded and there will be no more meetings, raids, threatenings, whippings, or terrorizings of any kind by those who composed the membership, but should there be any repetition of any such practices the state is in command of testimony and the facilities generally to enable it to promptly bring the leaders to justice.[74]

Somehow, Foraker had struck a deal with the leaders of the White Caps, even though there was not thought to be any extensive system of organization. In retrospect, he had been mistaken in believing that their activities were restricted to Brown County. The following month, H.C. Newcomb, former editor of the *Ohio Sentinel* at Mount Orab, began publishing a weekly newspaper devoted to the White Caps at Winchester, Adams County.

Two days later, the governor announced that a detective had been among the White Caps since their earlier depredations and had secured the names of all the members as well as the order's secrets. He had met with some of them and they had agreed to permanently disband. There were nine lodges in Ohio with about 1,000 members, including many of the best citizens in their communities.

Newspapers around the State did not feel that Foraker's truce was sufficient. Quoting the *Dayton Monitor*, the *Democratic Northwest* encouraged Governor Foraker to take action against the White Caps in the same way he had used the militia "against a few starving miners" to stop them from whipping defenseless men and women.[75] And Albion Tourgée criticized the governor and others for his defense of the White Caps as "men of the highest respectability."[76]

Adam Berkes was, according to Governor Foraker, the only man in Ohio actually whipped by the White Caps. So when he created a treaty with the Brown County night riders, he was holding some unspecified evidence that he would use against them if they broke the deal.

However, Berkes moved into another county and initiated a suit against sixteen of the White Caps asking for $10,000 in damages for the beating they gave him. This raised the question over whether he would subpoena Foraker's testimony based on this information he had in his possession. The *Cleveland Plain Dealer* posed the question of whether Foraker might have been bluffing.

Attempted Lynching, Summit County, December 1888—Carn, Joseph [W]

In Akron, a sixty-year-old widower, Joseph Carn, was attacked on December 18, 1888, by a small band of White Caps in "a lonely part of the city."[77] It was after midnight and he was on his way home. They told him he was being punished for "immoral conduct." A rope was looped around his neck and thrown over a tree limb. He was then raised into the air until he was close to being choked to death.

At that point, they lowered him and began conferring among themselves. Seizing his opportunity, Carn made a run for it. A notice was later posted to his door notifying him that he would be hanged if he didn't feed his livestock better. As it turned out, the perpetrators were well known in the community and insisted it was all a joke.

Mob Violence, Carroll County, December 1888—Wycoff, James [W]

On December 18, 1888, James Wycoff of Watsville was seized by eight or ten masked men in the home of a woman "with whom he had been intimate."[78] Taken outside, he was stripped to the waist and severely beaten with willow branches. He was then warned to leave or else he would be whipped again.

Not long before this, he had been tarred for his alleged immorality. The newspapers reported that "the parties who did the flogging are said to be respectable citizens and not allied with the Ohio White Caps."[79]

Mob Violence, Hancock County, December 1888—Messamon, John [W]

Early on the morning of December 19, 1888, White Caps entered the saloon of John Messamon at Rawson. After pouring all of the liquor into the street, the totally demolished the place. Before leaving, they left Messamon a warning not to resume business.

Mob Violence, December 1888—Ashton, Jim [W]; Harris, Bob [W]

Chief Thompson of Ripley received a post card dated December 1, 1888, directing him to notify some of the "Ripleyites" that the Advance Guard of the White Caps was onto them. It was written in red ink and stated, "We have heard of Bob Harris, Jim Ashton and others that are living with niggers; so they had better beware, for we will use the whip."[80] Ashton quickly departed.

Mob Violence, Madison County, January 1889—Silvers, Clark [W]

Three or four White Caps visited the homes of J.S. Stone and Clark Silvers, about five miles from West Jefferson in Glade Run, on the night of January 3, 1889. They threw rocks at Silvers's house, waking him. He grabbed a double-barreled shotgun and fired both barrels into the crowd at short range. One or more of the men howled and rode away.

In the morning, blood was found on the ground. Not long afterward, Stone went to town to buy ammunition so he would be prepared if they came back.

Mob Violence, Ashland County, January 1889—McColman, William [W]; Eddy, Nathan [W]; Chesrown, John [W]; Chesrown, Adam [W]

On February 25, 1888, the Chesrown brothers, wealthy farmers, were involved in a struggle over custody of their father. In resisting the execution of a writ of habeas corpus, they shot to death Constable William H. Kelly and Special Deputy Jacob Holdert (or Helbert). The four brothers—Elias, Wesley, Adam, and John—as well as Wesley's son, Mervin, were individually indicted for the murders.

Although Elias confessed to firing the shots that killed both men, he was acquitted when tried for the death of Kelly. The other brothers got off with a slap on the wrist. This did not sit well with the residents of Jeromesville, ninety percent of whom were friends of the murdered men.

Around midnight on Friday, January 25, 1889, a party of forty mounted men and another thirty on foot occupied the village. They began firing guns and revolvers and ordering everyone off the street. They were all disguised in various fashions, some wearing white coverings over their faces.

The houses of William McColman and Nathan Eddy, two supporters of the Chesrowns, were demolished. They also threatened to hang McColman and his wife, but they managed to escape, while another Chesrown sympathizer was chased out of town.

The riders then set off for the house of John and Adam Chesrown, several miles away. However, the Chesrowns had been warned that the mob was coming for them and fled. The vigilantes had to satisfy themselves with wrecking their houses. A written notice was found Saturday morning in Jeromesville which said: "If any of the Chesrowns or Chesrown sympathizers are caught they will be lynched."[81]

Mob Violence, Brown County, February 1889—Jackson [B]

Thirty-five masked men rode through Mount Orab on February 5, 1889, in search of a black man named Jackson. Adam Berkes had brought suit against fifty of them in Highland County and had named Jackson as a witness against them. They did not find him. If they had, he would have been lynched.

Foraker's deal with the White Cappers remained intact until a strict anti-conspiracy bill was enacted through the governor's efforts on March 28, 1889. The statute specifically stated

> that when three or more persons unite or combine together and commit any misdemeanor, while wearing white caps, masks or other disguise, they shall be guilty of a riotous conspiracy, and, upon conviction thereof shall each be imprisoned in the penitentiary not more than ten years nor less than two years, fined in any sum not exceeding two thousand dollars.[82]

Obviously, the White Caps had quickly proven to be a significant nuisance and the law had the desired result. The incident of White Cap activity declined precipitously, but did not stop.

Mob Violence, Tuscarawas County, February 1889—Meloy, Billy [W]

On Saturday, February 9, 1889, White Cappers struck at the home of Billy Meloy in Glasgow. Several days earlier, Meloy had received a notice warning him to quit drinking, return to work, and stop mistreating his family. He ignored it. But on Saturday, five masked men called at his residence, forced him to go outside, stripped him to the waist, and tied him up.

Each of the men administered five lashes and then rubbed salt in the bleeding wounds. After making him promise not to abuse his family again, they "left a notice with Meloy giving him nineteen days to recover and go to work."[83]

Mob Violence, Allen County, April 1889—Kessler, David [W?]

David Kessler of Sugar Creek Township, near Lima, was warned to leave the city. When he failed to do so after a couple of weeks, his house was burned to the ground on April 8, 1889, while no one was home.

Attempted Lynching, Greene County, April 1889—Jackson, Sherman [B]

At about two o'clock in the morning on April 2, 1889, Sherman Jackson killed Frank Lawrence with a knife. Both men were African Americans and the motive was jealousy.

Lawrence was holding a dance at the Schmidt Building in Xenia. Jackson, a notorious criminal, was conducting himself in an obnoxious fashion and Lawrence tried to calm him down. Instead, Jackson stabbed him in the sternum, breaking the knife, and then stuck him twice more in the groin, twisting the weapon to create a gaping wound.

When the police found Jackson later that afternoon hiding in the house of a black woman, a mob collected to lynch him. It was led by Thomas and William Lawrence, the murdered man's uncles. However, the police refused to surrender their prisoner to the crowd and were twice attacked "in the heart of the city," a short distance from the jail.[84]

Despite wielding clubs to defend themselves, the police were outnumbered and the horde of 1,000 wrestled Jackson out of their custody. Aided by Sheriff C.W. Linkhart and a posse, the police then drew their revolvers and retook the suspect. He was locked in the local jail where a heavy guard was posted. In June, Jackson was convicted of murder and sentence to life in the penitentiary.

Mob Violence, Hamilton County, April 1889—Gehrline, Frank [W]

Although Governor Joseph Foraker believed he had reached an agreement with the White Caps which would curb vigilantism statewide, he quickly realized that the problem was greater than he had thought. So he initiated legislation that would tackle them head-on.

A month after the White Caps were specifically outlawed, Frank Gehrline, a resident of Riverside just west of Cincinnati, was set upon by a band of masked men on the night of April 27, 1889. His alleged offense was "general worthlessness" (his wife supported to family by taking in boarders) and spousal abuse.[85] He had been observed knocking his wife down in the yard.

Gehrline was in a saloon getting a drink when a boy entered and told him there was a man outside who wanted to see him. When he stepped to the door, he was seized, stripped to the waist, tied to a tree, and beaten with willow switches for half an hour as a crowd cheered his attackers.

After he was released, Gehrline pulled a knife, causing everyone to scatter. Though he threatened to kill them, he wisely went home to bed instead.

Mob Violence, Hancock County, April–May 1889—Messamore, Jack [W]

Early in April 1889, Jack Messamore at Rawson near Findlay was visited by White Caps who cleaned out his saloon and destroyed it, pouring the liquor into the street. They left a note that said they would do it again if he reopened. He did, after hiring a watchman.

On the night of May 1, 1889, he withdrew the watchman, figuring they were bluffing. Later in the evening, they demolished his saloon again so Messamore prepared to move to another town.

Mob Violence, Champaign County, August 1889—Middleton, Arthur N [W]

Arthur N. Middleton was the ex-city solicitor of Urbana, brother of county prosecutor Perry N. Middleton, and, it was alleged, an abusive father and husband. On the night of August 1, 1889, several days after he most recently beat his wife, a party of twelve to fifteen masked men came to his house about midnight to teach him a lesson.

Entering through the rear door, they took Arthur by surprise. After barring the doors, they bound him with rope, stripped him of his clothing, and whipped him until he passed out. An African American servant jumped out of the upstairs window and ran for help.

Although the incident generated considerable excitement in Urbana, there was little sympathy expressed for Arthur. His drinking and cruelty had already caused his wife to leave and seek shelter with friends. She would file for divorce the same month. The police had twice locked him up recently because of his behavior. And, finally, his "bright and beautiful little daughter" had just died and he was felt to be partially to blame for her death.[86]

Arthur Middleton passed away in on December 23, 1889, three days after his divorce was finalized.

Mob Violence, Harrison County, October 1889—West, Mrs. James and children [B]

Between eleven o'clock and midnight on October 5, 1889, about twenty White Caps visited the residence of James West in Cadiz. A respected African American gentleman, West was not at home. So the night riders forced his wife and children out into the street, half-clothed, then demolished the house and its contents.

Charles Greene and George Steinrod, well known young men in the community, were arrested, but it is not known if they were prosecuted. The *Belmont Chronicle* declared, "No Mississippi methods should be countenanced in these parts."[87] Yet a month later, the same newspaper opined, "If reports are true there is a man in town who is a fit subject for White Cap visitation."[88]

The effort to quash the White Caps had turned into a recruiting tool. Ironically, the *Ohio State Journal* called upon other vigilantes to help stamp out the White Caps. But, then, the *New York Times* had done the same when it came to the White Caps in Indiana. It was a mixed message for certain: some vigilantes were bad, but others were good.

5

Reign of Terror (1890–1895)

The number of lynchings in the United States increased dramatically following the emancipation of the slaves, peaking at 230 in 1892. This was especially true in the South, which was suffering from great economic distress, and would eventually lead to an extensive northward migration by African Americans.

Threatened Violence, Greene County, January 1890—Hammons, Riley [W]

By 1890, Ohio had 87,000 African Americans residents and one of the more racially diverse spots in the state was the village of Yellow Springs. In 1862, a Cincinnati minister named Moncure Conway, settled a group of about thirty former slaves nearby.

Known as the Conway Colony, they gradually became an accepted part of the community, although they did not enjoy equal status with their white neighbors. Even after Ohio schools were officially desegregated in 1887, there was resistance.

A notice was posted on the door of Riley Hammons, a Yellow Springs school teacher, on January 10, 1890. Dated three days earlier, it read:

> Mr. Hammons
>
> We have consulted over the case and if you do not quit your posish as teacher at that school the White Capps will pay you a visit within three days to W.A.
>
> From the Captain of the White Caps.[1]

It was accompanied by a bundle of switches, a symbol of the White Caps. The author purportedly made no attempt to disguise his handwriting.

The local school board had integrated the village schools, opening up what had formerly been an African American school in the south end of town to both races. In an odd twist, one newspaper reported that the notice was "supposed to be the work of some colored men, who are under the impression that we are to have separate schools again.[2]"

Expected Lynching, Union County, January 1890—Miller, Ellis [W]

Ellis Miller of Union County was hanged at the Ohio Penitentiary on December 2, 1890, for the murder of Emma Johnson. He had lived four miles outside of Marysville with his wife and family. His wife's sister, Mrs. Benjamin Johnson, and her husband, lived nearby.

Miller was known to be a brute who regularly beat his wife. For his deplorable treatment of his family, he had been visited by White Caps who gave him the customary flogging for his sins. Instead of being chastened by the beating, he swore vengeance against his wife, his sister-in-law, and various others.

On the day of the murder, January 16, 1890, Miller was at home, drunk, brooding over his situation, when he spotted Mrs. Johnson passing by his house. Rushing out to the road to intercept her, he demanded she tell him where his wife had gone after he had driven her away at the point of a shotgun. When she didn't, Miller drew a revolver and shot her as she was walking away. Afterward, he covered her face with a shawl and left with the intention of killing her husband as well.

Miller was soon seized by a mob (which included the victim's husband), disarmed, and tied to a tree. Although there was some sentiment for lynching him, they refrained from doing so, perhaps because Emma Johnson was still alive. She would pass away four days later.

Expected Lynching, Van Wert County, April 1890—Six tramps [W?]

Six tramps scrambled into a boxcar a half mile west of Lima, Allen County, on April 6, 1890. They were discovered by Conductor Tucker who ordered them out. When they refused, he climbed in after them. One of the men fired a shot that went wide of the mark. Tucker then proceeded to wrestle with the gang who tossed him off the car before jumping out on the opposite side.

After climbing over the train, Tucker confronted a member of the gang who waved a gun at him. Although he wrenched it out of the man's hands, Tucker was unable to defend himself when the man's companions grabbed his arms. One of the men then stuck the gun in his left side and fired, fatally wounding him. Two of the men escaped, but the others were arrested. The newspaper noted hopefully that the "Crime Would Justify a Lynching."[3] But there was none.

Attempted Lynching, Ross County, May 1890—Gardner, Richard [B]

Richard Gardner (or Gardiner) murdered Ethel Long, who was in her early teens, near Austin on May 22, 1890. It was a particularly horrific crime in that he ripped her open with a knife, raped her, and then slashed her throat.

The son of slaves, Gardner was born in Tallahassee, Florida, and was living in Cincinnati. On the day of the crime, he was returning home from a trip to Washington C.H. when he saw Ethel leave her home with a bucket to fetch water from a spring. Following her, Gardner asked the girl where her parents were. She told him her mother was in the house and her father at work in the field. He then propositioned her twice, but she rebuffed him.

When Gardner grabbed her hand, she screamed and he struck her on the head with an iron rod eighteen inches in length, stunning her. Then, placing his handkerchief over Ethel's mouth, he molested her. Afterward, he watched for five minutes before killing her to "put her out of her misery."[4]

Gardner didn't realize that Ethel's brother had witnessed his attack. It was only a few hours before he was captured and taken to jail in Athens, owing to the highly charged atmosphere in Chillicothe.

Over 500 men traveled to Athens from Ross County where they battered down the doors of the jail and demanded that the prisoner be turned over to them. When told he wasn't there, they conducted a search of the entire building. As they did so, a carriage carrying a "phony negro" was driven rapidly away from the rear of the jail.[5] Thinking it contained Gardner, they took off in pursuit. However, Sheriff C.H. Porter had hidden Gardner in the courthouse when he heard the mob was on the way.

Marshal Peter Finsterwald and Sheriff Porter smuggled Gardner on a Toledo & Ohio

Central train to Columbus. Even as they disembarked in the capital city, there were shouts of "Someone get a rope" and "Lynch the brute," although no one made any attempt to follow through.[6]

Indicted by a special grand jury, he was returned to Chillicothe where he received a speedy trial and was sentenced to death for first degree murder.[7] Prior to his execution at the Ohio Penitentiary on November 9, 1900, he found religion, made a full confession to the girl's parents, and begged their forgiveness. He was hypnotized prior to being put to death in the electric chair.

Mob Violence, Seneca County, June 1890—Miller, Sarah [W]

Fifteen White Caps visited the Bloomville home of Sarah Miller, a partially demented woman with an unsavory reputation, on June 30, 1890. Breaking in, they dragged Miller from her bed, stripped her, smeared her body with tar and threatened to cover her with feathers if she did not leave the village at once.

Miller went to Attica where she hired an attorney to prosecute the men, a few of whom she recognized. They were described as fifteen "prominent citizens."[8] The woman purportedly had "both money and friends" and promised "to make things exceedingly lively."[9]

Attempted Lynching, Wood County, July 1890—Burkett, William [W]

About twenty miles south of Toledo was Bairdstown. Although it was an oil town on the Baltimore and Ohio Railroad, an ordinance was passed banning the drilling of any gas or oil well within the village limits. Those who had purchased lots in anticipation of selling them to oil men found themselves blindsided.

So in July 1890, someone decided to eliminate the town by setting fire to every building housing a business. The first occurred on July 8, followed by the 17, 26, and 28. Of the dozen business houses, only one remained standing.

A detective from Cincinnati named William Burkett was hired to investigate the crimes and reported that several prominent citizens were engaged in a conspiracy to destroy the town. In response to his allegations, some of these citizens hatched a plan to hang him. Sprung from the local jail, the detective was taken out into the woods and a noose placed around his neck.

Although they claimed they only intended to scare him, he was already being lifted off his feet when Mayor Nusbaum came across the scene. "Half dead with fright he begged piteously for mercy, and promised to leave town."[10] He was beaten and sent on his way to Bowling Green.

As a result, armed men were assigned to patrol the streets as a check on further arsons. Everyone lived in fear of having their homes torched. Three families barely escaped in time, while one merchant had to relocate three times in a week. The town council subsequently voted to go into the gas business.

Expected Lynching, Van Wert County, July 1890—Roodhouse, Samuel [W]

As a train neared Van Wert on the night of July 21, 1890, Engineer Vandevanter and Fireman Samuel Roodhouse were engaged in a deadly fight in the locomotive's cab. They had been quarreling throughout the trip, with the engineer accusing the fireman of having reported him for drunkenness.

According to Roodhouse, Vandevanter charged him, cursing and saying he would fix him. He then struck him in the face, knocking him to the floor and cutting his head.

Grabbing a copper hammer, Roodhouse retaliated by hitting the engineer several times on the head, "knocking him insensible."[11] The fireman then took control of the locomotive as they were entering the switch.

When Vandevanter climbed to his feet once again, Roodhouse struck him one more time, killing him. Out of control, the train ran past Van Wert and into the yard where it collided with the switch engine. He was terribly burned on the face and hands as a result of the collision.

Originally, Roodhouse claimed that they both had been attacked in an attempted robbery by an unknown man who boarded the train. Suspicion fell on Blair Mock, a man who had killed Vandevanter's son at Huntington, Indiana, six years before. Vandevanter had been the principle witness against Mock who purportedly swore to get even with him.

However, Roodhouse had been overheard by several men at Franklin arguing with Vandevanter, so he finally confessed. It was all he could do to keep from breaking down when the warrant for his arrest was read. There were fears that the engineer's friends were planning to lynch Roodhouse, but a report that he was taken to Lima for safekeeping proved to be false.

Mob Violence, Defiance County, February 1891—Moll, John H [W]

In February 1891, Superintendent C.W. Butler of the Defiance Public Schools noticed John H. Moll (or Mull), a janitor, watching him through a trapdoor in the ceiling of his office. An argument ensued, climaxing in an appearance by Moll before the school board during which he charged Butler and three of the female teachers with engaging in inappropriate behavior (from kissing and hugging to "criminal intimacy").[12] His story was collaborated by William Wyant, the assistant janitor, as well as by a Mr. Betke, "a highly respected citizen."[13]

Moll was originally from Napoleon where he was regarded as an exemplary citizen, which may account for why the town's *Democratic Northwest* newspaper trumpeted the crime with the headline "Wicked Defiance!"[14] Initially, the trio's stories were believed, despite the sterling reputations of Butler and the women. However, a subsequent investigation revealed that the school superintendent was miles away at the time the incidents allegedly occurred.

Both janitors were promptly fired from their jobs.

The townsfolk, who had been quite indignant about the whole affair, redirected their anger from Butler and the women to the janitors and warned them to leave town. When they didn't, an armed mob of twenty-five or so paid a visit to Moll's house late one evening after attending a masked carnival at the roller rink. He was not home.

Having been frightened by the rumors that he was to be lynched, Moll had sought refuge with a friend near the Wabash Railroad. But at two o'clock in the morning, he became uneasy and decided to go back to his own place. He never made it.

Four hours later, Moll's mangled body was discovered between the railroad tracks by a tramp named Parker. The janitor was still alive, but soon expired. Before the train nearly severed his legs, he had had his throat cut and been stabbed twice in the chest. A pocket knife was found nearby. Moll had manure and straw grasped in his hands, even though there was none in the immediate vicinity. Wyant was also missing and a rumor was circulating that his body had been dumped in the canal.

Moll's friends, of which there were many, threatened to kill Butler. As the "wildest excitement" gripped the streets, women and children wisely stayed away.[15] The sheriff deputized extra men to increase the size of the police force. But then something changed. Suddenly, it was being argued that fifty-two-year-old Moll had killed himself in order to keep from being held responsible for his slanderous statements or, perhaps, out of despair over losing his job. And as far as Wyant was concerned, no one seems to have lost any sleep worrying about what had become of him.

Not everyone, however, wanted to sweep the matter under the rug. "That school teachers unhappily possess an inordinate proclivity for hugging and kissing, is a well-known fact," wrote "Javert, Jr." in the *Democratic Northwest*. "There should be no doubt that Moll was murdered."[16] The Defiance coroner agreed: Moll had been murdered. A dozen or two men were ultimately indicted for riot, but none for murder.

Lynching [TI], Hardin County, April 1891—Boles, William

On Tuesday night, March 31, William Boles (or Bales) and two other men, Lake and Noel, killed Edward Harper, a Kenton police officer, as he was trying to place Boles under arrest. Plans to lynch the men began to form from the moment they were jailed. And every citizen in Kenton, a town of 5,600 people, purportedly knew it was going to happen.

During the evening of April 10, 1891, small groups of men began congregating at the agreed upon meeting place. Then at about midnight (or, perhaps, two a.m.), fifty to 100 masked men marched upon the jail. Breaking down the exterior doors, they entered the building. A reporter marveled at how well "organized and drilled" they were, communicating in whispers and signals.[17]

The leader wore a white mask while the others wore black hoods, long overcoats, and rubber boots. They had assembled an hour before outside the county jail in Kenton and posted armed guards to ensure no one could pass by their lines. They then battered in the side door of the jail.

As seventy-five of their number poured inside, they seized Sheriff William Neville who was coming down the stairs and, shoving four guns in his face, demanded the keys. Although he did not have them on him, they located them in an adjoining room. Rushing down the corridors of the jail, they hurriedly unlocked the cell in which a terror-stricken Boles cowered in a corner.

The mob ordered the prisoner to put on pants and slippers, and hastily escorted him outside. He was taken to a maple tree that stood just across the road to the intersection of Wayne and North Streets fifty yards distant where at least 500 people had gathered. Originally, the mob planned to hang his two accomplices as well, but there was some uncertainty about their guilt so they were spared. However, Boles was "not considered very strong mentally," which may have been the reason he was singled out.[18]

As Boles begged for his life, a noose was slipped over his head, quickly adjusted, and the rope thrown over a tree limb. Many hands reached for the rope and pulled down, swinging the writhing form several feet off the ground. They held him there until his struggles ceased and they were certain he was dead. The rope was then tied to the trunk and he was left there, "dangling between earth and sky."[19]

It was all over in twenty minutes. Sentinels had guarded all approaches to the jail so that the only witnesses to the execution were members of the mob. Members of the lynch mob soon disappeared, blending into the crowd. Suddenly, the fire bell rang and people dashed about in all directions, few choosing to remain at home. At three o'clock, his lifeless body was cut down by order of Justice F.H. Rummel and removed to city hall.

Some law enforcement officers were undoubtedly witnesses to the lynching, but the sympathies of the townsfolk were with the mob. "Who the mob were and where they came from is a mystery," the reporter for the *Salem Daily News* wrote.[20] The reporter for the *Marion Star* observed, "This should be a lesson to a gang of toughs who infest the city, prowling about a night, robbing whoever they chanced to meet."[21]

Expected Lynching, Vinton County, August 1891—Woolweaver, Michael [W]; Woolweaver, Henry [W]; Woolweaver, Cobb [W]

Frank Leamon was a car inspector for the Columbus, Hocking Valley & Toledo railroad at McArthur Junction. Each morning, he traveled by railroad tricycle from his home in McArthur to the junction and then back again at night. A quiet man of excellent habits and devoted to family, he was never known to quarrel with anyone.

On August 1, 1891, Leamon was in front of the ladies' waiting area of the depot, repairing a car, when Michael Woolweaver approached him. Woolweaver and his sons, Henry and Cobb (or Colby), operated a nearby saloon. In the past, Michael had had problems with the railroad and had no use for anyone connected with it. Several times that day, he had come to the depot, possibly drunk, hoping to provoke a fight.

Although there were several witnesses, accounts of what happened differ. In one version, Woolweaver was being loud and obnoxious when he spotted Leamon at work. "You son of a bitch," he said, "you are another one of 'em."[22] He then took a swing at Leamon with a beer bottle.

Springing up, Leamon blocked the bottle with a hammer or monkey wrench. It shattered and both men were cut by the flying glass, Leamon severely as it sliced his face. Responding to the noise, Depot Agent Ewing came running just as Henry Woolweaver rounded a corner.

Standing just fifteen feet away, Henry began firing his pistol. One bullet hit Leamon in the back and pierced his heart. A second struck Ewing in the leg and a third hit Cobb, who had also fired at least one shot, in the arm. Leamon ran a few paces before collapsing. A fourth shot missed everyone.

Sheriff Frank E. Jennings responded to a telegram regarding the fracas and placed all three Woolweavers under arrest. They were jailed in McArthur, while Leamon's body was taken to Logan for burial. A large company of Knights of Labor from Zaleski, as well as some from Hamden, attended the funeral services. By the evening of August 3, 1891, there were concerns that there might be an attack on the jail to lynch the Woolweavers.

When the sheriff started for Jackson with the three culprits on Monday, August 3, 1891, he was forced to turn back because of the large crowd blocking his way. Concerned they might be lynched, he returned them to the county jail to await a preliminary trial in McArthur.

The *Hocking Sentinel* insisted that a trial should be dispensed with since there is no question of guilt. "Will the State of Ohio put up thousands of dollars to protect and support this hellish fiend and let the poor wife that he made a helpless widow toil with weary hands to support herself and orphaned children?" it asked.[23] "Hemp is the avenger and hemp is what ought to be used."[24]

Nevertheless, the trial proceeded and Michael Woolweaver was convicted of manslaughter.

Expected Lynching, Putnam County, August 1891—Roberts, James [W?]

The citizens of Columbus Grove turned out as a body on August 22, 1891, to meet the north bound train on the Cincinnati, Hamilton & Dayton railroad. They expected that James Roberts, who had been arrested for robbery and murder, would be on it and planned to lynch him. However, he wasn't.

When Roberts was later jailed in Cleveland, he was regarded as a second Jesse James and there was more talk of lynching him.

Mob Violence, Warren County, September 1891—Henson, Solomon [W]

On September 1, 1891, a young Warren County man, Solomon Henson, was tarred and feathered by a group of White Caps. He was working on the farm of a man named Pence.

About nightfall, the two men climbed into a cart to go to Genntown. Along the way, they were met by four to six masked men on horses. As one of them seized their horse, two others dragged Henson out of the cart at gunpoint. Pence was then ordered to drive away.

The men proceeded to bind Henson. They removed his coat and stripped off his trousers, vest, and shirt, and coated his arms and lower body with tar and feathers. During the scuffle, the masks where "thrown up" and Henson recognized three of them.[25] When the vigilantes were done, they told Henson to go and warned him to leave the neighborhood within four days.

Henson made a complaint to the authorities and they quickly arrested John Kenter, Benjamin Kenter, and Herman Kenter under the White Cap statute. He claimed they had attacked him because he owed them money for a boar he had purchased. However, others believed that Henson had been too intimate with a woman at Genntown and that the tar and featherings was intended to drive him out of the community.

Mob Violence, Mercer County, November 1891—Disreputable House [W]

About forty or fifty masked women made a raid on a disreputable house in Coldwater, a predominantly Roman Catholic town, on Sunday evening, November 22, 1891. Four women had taken up residence in a frame house just outside the corporation limit. The raiders surrounded the place at about nine o'clock and battered in the doors.

Several men ran from the house, but the four women were captured and beaten on their bare backs with switches until the blood ran. One was taken to a nearby stream and dunked into the cold water until she nearly drowned. The women were told they had twenty minutes to get out of sight. The White Cappers then tore down the house and broke up the furniture. The White Cappers were described as the "best ladies" of the town.[26]

Lynching [TI], Butler County, January 1892—Corbin, Henry [B]

Two days after slaying Mrs. Georgianna Horner by bashing in her head with a piece of stove-wood, Henry Corbin shot himself as his pursuers were closing in. When they reached him, he was lying on his back in the snow, bleeding from a wound above his eye. The young man had hoped to cheat the gallows, but he wound up being strung up on a tree even as the mayor of Oxford begged the mob to let the man die.

For two years, Corbin had been employed in the Horner household as a servant. A twenty-five-year-old African American, Corbin had the confidence of Mrs. Horner, age fifty-two, and her daughter, Lizzie. A graduate of Oxford Female Institute, Lizzie was engaged to an attorney in Hamilton and their impending wedding was sure to be a major social event in the community.

The Horners were one of the most prominent and wealthiest families in Oxford. The former Georgianna Markel, Mrs. Horner was the niece of Thomas McCullough, the town banker, and Lizzie was, by all accounts, the belle of the village.

Then on January 12, 1892, things fell apart. For some reason, Corbin purportedly tried to "outrage" Mrs. Horner.[27] When she resisted, he threw her to the floor and cracked her skull with a piece of fire wood. Hearing the struggle, Lizzie rushed into the room just in time to see Corbin standing over her mother, the gore-covered club in his hand.

Although Corbin seized her, "she fought heroically for her honor and finally escaped from his clutches and ran out into the street where she where she fell exhausted and lay for almost an hour"—apparently unnoticed.[28] It was only after she had revived that she continued on to a neighbor's house and raised the alarm.

When the neighbors found Mrs. Horner, she was still breathing, but soon expired. A search for Corbin was quickly organized. For two days, all business in the community was suspended while everybody aided in the search for the fugitive. Rewards were offered to incentivize his capture—$200 from Lizzie, $800 from the village, and $500 from the county commissioners—although they were hardly needed.

It was thought that Corbin had fled the area, but it turned out that he had never left Oxford. The police picked up on a rumor that he had been hiding in some out-buildings on property belonging to friends. Having grown hungry, he unwisely dispatched a black youth to get him something to eat. The youth's behavior aroused curiosity and the police soon found Corbin in a shed within a few hundred feet of the scene of the crime.

At first, Corbin attempted to keep the posse away by waving a .22 caliber pistol at them. However, once he realized that escape was impossible, he shot himself above the right eye and was quickly taken into custody. It was a serious wound and there was little question it would prove fatal, so he was locked up in the village jail. But the authorities knew they could not hold him there long. They hoped to keep his capture secret until he could be transported to Hamilton, but word got out before they could put their plan into effect.

Soon crowds were collecting in the streets. "The public blood was boiling over the outrage with which the fair name of classic Oxford had been so recently sullied and the opinion prevailed that there was but one proper way to wipe out the disgrace."[29] After a short interval, "an orderly mob of disguised men whom no one seemed to know" converged on the jail from all directions.[30]

Breaking down the door, the mob had little difficulty disarming the law officers. They removed Corbin from his cell and carried him outside to a neighboring tree. Within moments, they had slipped a noose around his neck, tossed the rope over a limb, and had him dangling in mid-air. But it did not end there. The men drew their pistols and began firing volley after volley into Corbin's body as he gasped "in the agonies of death."[31] His body was pierced by as many as 400 pistol balls.

By this time, the crowd was enormous. Many remained at the spot all night long, while hundreds did not return to their beds as the corpse remained hanging in the public square. As one reporter observed, "while it was not in accordance with law and order, the majority of the people of Oxford are satisfied."[32]

Corbin was buried in the Oxford cemetery. Lizzie later said that she believed that Corbin's motive was robbery since some money and items of value were missing.

Mob Violence, Auglaize County, January 1892—Shelbrook, Mary [W]; Peterson, Charles [W]

For several months, Mary Shelbrook had been living in adultery with twenty-five-year-old Charles Peterson in an abandoned hut in the woods near St. Johns. Although Peterson was a hardworking man, they were destitute and scarcely had enough clothing to stay warm.

On Thursday night, January 14, 1892, Peterson was given notice to leave the area within twenty four hours or he would be tarred and feathered. When he did not, a dozen masked men visited the pathetic couple the following night.

Taken from their hovel to Green Creek, they were repeatedly dunked through a hole cut in the ice. They were then allowed to take whatever they could carry and compelled to leave, while the mob burned their hut to the ground.

Mary Shelbrook had already been sick for several weeks and it was believed she would not recover. A farmer named Henley took her in and cared for her. Authorities had their sights set upon a dozen local farmers, some of them well-to-do, and planned to arrest them once they knew Shelbrook's fate.

A man named Culbertson who was traveling through St. Johns said it was the worst case of White Capping he knew of. It is unknown whether Shelbrook actually died.

Expected Lynching, Hardin County, January 1892—Stephenson, John; Smith, Burt; Spurlock, William; Spurlock, Charles [W]

In Kenton, four young murderers—John Stephenson, Burt Smith, and William and Charles Spurlock—purportedly came close to winding up at the end of a rope on January 22, 1892. Ranging in age from twelve to seventeen, they had attacked their teacher, Miss McLaughlin, for admonishing them about their behavior.

When they began to beat her, Frank, the teacher's twelve-year-old brother, tried to protect her and was pummeled into insensibility, dying within a few hours. Miss McLaughlin also died, having sustained a serious head wound. Not surprisingly, there were threats of lynching and the juveniles were closely guarded.

Lynching [TI], Hancock County, March 1892—Lytle, Joseph [W]

Joseph Lytle was deranged. Not quite fifty years old, he was "guilty of many inhuman acts" and had once served a term in the Ohio Penitentiary for "shooting his little son."[33] Many referred to him as "an old soldier" due to his service in the Civil War.[34] While his wife and daughters were "respectable and hard-working women," Lytle was known for his drinking and bad character.[35] Then one day he crossed the line and the citizens of Findlay decided that they had had enough.

Lytle had married Sarah Jane Heck in 1863. They had at least seven children, all but two of whom were girls.

For some reason, likely his mental instability, Lytle had lived for a time at the Soldiers' Home in Dayton. However, toward the last week of March in 1892, he returned to Findlay and resumed abusing his family.

After breakfast on a Wednesday morning, Lytle picked up a hatchet and began chopping away at two of his daughters, both grown women. He crushed Della's skull, but succeeded only in delivering a nasty blow to the back of Emma's head as she fled. He purportedly blamed the girls for the problems in his marriage.

Cornering his wife, who was a sickly woman, Lytle hit her six times on the head, but did not fracture the bone until he struck her with the "pole" (the hammer side) of the tool. She also lost a finger while trying to ward off the blows.

Still in a rage, Lytle hacked up all of the photographs in the house and destroyed the keyboard of the piano and much of the furnishings before pausing to wash the blood off his body. When the neighbors arrived, they found both Mrs. Lytle and Della near death in pools of blood, but expected Emma to recover. Lytle was soon apprehended by the police.

Fearing there might be trouble, the authorities worked out a plan to smuggle him out of the local jail about one o'clock in the morning on March 31, 1892. He would be taken to a suburb of the city where a train was to carry him to Lima. However, before they had a chance, 1,000 men or more had surrounded the Findlay jail where Lytle was being held, intent on seeing that he paid for his crimes. They broke out the building's windows, but when they found they could not get to his cell, they applied oil well drills to the doors for nearly an hour until they were demolished. The prisoner was now in their hands.

Dragging the old man out into the street, they took him to the Main Street Bridge. After tying a rope around his neck, they tossed the other end over a girder. The mob then hoisted him into the air. However, the lynching was interrupted by a shot from a revolver which cut the rope. Still alive, Lytle dropped to the ground.

The mob seized the loose end of the rope and pulled him 200 feet through the street to the nearest telegraph pole where they hanged him once again. He purportedly died without a struggle, no doubt having been struck by some of the dozen shots that were fired at his body.

"The mob is said to have been composed of the best citizens, but was poorly organized."[36] Lytle had evidently suspected he might be lynched and left a note asking that his body be turned over to his brother for burial beside his mother.

As it turned out, Lytle's wife and two daughters survived the attacks. However, the population of Findlay, which peaked at 18,553 in 1890, dropped by 4,000 over the next twenty years.

False Report of Lynching [TI], Holmes County, April 1892—"Unknown negro"

As the citizens of Millersburg began stirring early on a Friday morning, April 1, 1892, they were "horrified" to see the "lifeless" form of the "Only Colored Man in Holmes County" hanging from the limb of a sugar maple tree in front of the courthouse.[37] This "unknown negro"—his body "stiff and cold"—was shoeless, bareheaded, and dead as a doornail—presenting an altogether "hideous appearance."[38]

In a story that was widely circulated, several people reported hearing noises during the night, but did not suspect a lynch mob was at work. The deceased had, it was said, been "sneaking" around town for several weeks, "lounging" on people's doorsteps, "frightening" women, and "staring" at citizens.[39] He had been ordered to leave because many found his behavior annoying. Nothing was known of his history, although someone suggested he had come from Mount Vernon or Wooster. Most certainly a tramp (although one wag suggested a "hosteller"), he was described as "the hardest looking man ever seen here."[40]

Due to the condition of the body, no autopsy was performed and no effort made to identify those responsible. As an article in the *Aurora Daily Express* noted, Millersburg was "populated chiefly by the Omish [*sic*] sect and a class of ignorant whites."[41]

Given that Amish are confirmed pacifists, it seems unlikely that they would have had any involvement in a lynching, so suspicion fell on the "ignorant whites."[42] The *Ohio State Journal*, though, entertained another possibility: suicide.

But things weren't necessarily what they seemed. To begin with, the lynching took place on April 1st—known since the nineteenth century as April Fool's Day. And the victim was a cast iron figure of a black man used as a sign and hitching post at T. A. Lowther's, a local bakery. No wonder he was so "hard" looking and the coroner found it "difficult to ascertain the cause of death."[43] In all likelihood, several men had gotten drunk and strung up the figure as a prank.

Ironically, newspaper coverage of this incident has resulted in its being counted among Ohio's lynchings, although the *Cleveland Gazette* insisted from the beginning the story was false.

Attempted Lynching, Licking County, April 1892—Stottsberry, George [W]

Jailed in Newark for the attempted rape of a school girl, George Stottsberry, age thirty, came close to being lynched shortly before midnight on April 12, 1892. He purportedly assaulted Edna Alward, age seven or eight, at 2:30 that afternoon, just as she stepped outside her classroom to use the outhouse. Stottsberry "forced his entrance to the place where the child was and horribly mutilated her."[44]

Alerted by the little girl's screams, teachers came running to her aid. While they could not catch the suspect, they recognized him as a former player for the Newark baseball team. The police were immediately notified and the city marshal had Stottsberry under arrest within minutes.

As soon as the prisoner was lodged in the city jail, huge crowds began to surround the building and fill the nearby hotels. They talked of nothing but the awful crime which had been perpetrated in their community. Then at seven o'clock that evening, the marshal elected to move Stottsberry to the county jail for his own protection.

About 100 people swarmed the jail and at nine-thirty battered down the door, while thousands (3,000, according to *the Chicago Tribune*) of others remained outside, yelling "hang the ______ scoundrel [*sic*]."[45] The mob reached the prisoner's cell, despite the best efforts of the sheriff to deter them. However, he was rescued at the last minute by Mayor Bell, leading "a fresh squad of men."[46] They succeeded in driving the mob out into the street and saving the prisoner's life.

At eleven, the angry horde had a council to discuss further action. While some favored hauling Stottsberry before the girl so she could identify him, "The mob seem [*sic*] to lack leadership and spirit" and the police successfully dispersed them by two in the morning.[47] (Alternatively, the mob broke into the jail at one o'clock, but failed to find Stottsberry who had somehow hidden himself in the corridor.)

Throughout the affair, the prisoner proclaimed his innocence and begged to be allowed to live until the next day. Later, he was sentenced to five years in prison.

Expected Lynching, Franklin County, November 1892—Holland, Jud [B]

A "cow ripper" was terrorizing Columbus in the early 1890s. It is estimated that he slaughtered some eight to a dozen animals before he was finally captured.[48]

When he killed a cow owned by Clarence L. Powell, vice president of a brick company, on November 29, 1892, newspapers suggested that the culprit would be lynched if not judged insane. The police took Jud Holland into custody three days later and he was sentenced to prison.

Mob Violence, Logan County, December 1892—Jackson, John [B]

Grant Jackson, a waiter at the Grand Hotel in Springfield, enticed Bessie Winkle (or Hinkle), "a pretty white waitress" from White Sulfur Springs, to elope with him in December 1892.[49] A notorious character, Jackson was tracked down by his wife, Nell, who horsewhipped the girl and then left for Urbana in his company.

Winkle told authorities she had been held against her will and he was soon apprehended and jailed in West Liberty (or Huntsville or Springfield). As a result, on the evening of December 26, 1892, Jackson was taken from the jail by a gang of masked men and tarred and feathered.

A year later, Jackson was killed on Christmas Day when he got into a fight with A.S. Piatt. Both men were drunk. Piatt fractured Jackson's skull with a slung shot (or blackjack). He was subsequently arrested and charged with manslaughter. Unlike Jackson, Piatt came from a prominent family. He was the son of the former postmaster and the nephew of Colonel Donn Piatt, a writer and diplomat of note.

Expected Lynching, Montgomery County, June 1893—Grady, George [W]

George Grady, a twenty-year-old farmhand, attempted to rape thirteen-year-old Laura Woodward on June 7, 1893, near a schoolhouse south of Blavertown. Thought to be of low intelligence, Grady was not previously considered dangerous.

As news of the incident spread, farmers armed with shotguns rushed in to save the little girl. Grady did not seem to fear their threats, but grinned like the "simple-minded fellow" they took him to be.[50] Fortunately, the constable was able to rescue him before the ad hoc posse had a chance to lynch him.[51]

Attempted Lynching, Wood County, July 1893—Cook, William [W]

On Wednesday night, July 12, 1893, William Cook, a railroad section foreman, went home to Pemberville drunk. Cook had recently moved with his brood from Rising Sun, after his wife had run off with a "handsomer man" from Cygnet.[52] Abusing his children was nothing new, but on that particular night he went berserk.

Grabbing five-year-old Gilbert, Cook slammed the boy's head against the wall, tossed him against the ceiling, and let him fall to the floor. The child sustained several cuts and broken bones, eventually dying. Thirteen-year-old Mary had the fingers of her right hand broken and suffered a gash in her cheek. Her eleven-year-old sister was kicked, pounded, and hurled against the wall until she was unconscious. The fourth child, a boy, was also beaten up, but manage to escape with his life.

At least two of the children were expected to die from their injuries. The entire village was in an uproar and many were advocating that the brute be lynched.

Confined in the village jail, Cook cowered in fear and wept as he heard a mob of some 400 people demanding that he be turned over to them. It required three or four attempts for the police officers to wrestle him through the crowd and into a waiting buggy which took him to the county jail in Bowling Green for safekeeping. The mob pursued them for several miles before giving up.

The *San Francisco Call* suggested the citizens of Pemberville needed to be "better organized" if they were to succeed in lynching Cook.[53]

Mob Violence, Clark County, August 1893—Rutherford, James S.; Rutherford, Mrs. [W]

Around August 25, 1893, at Thorpe's Station (alternately, Dolly Varden) near Springfield, a group of six masked men entered the Rutherford residence and dragged James S.

Rutherford and his wife from their beds and into a nearby woods. Both were stripped and James was tied to a post and beaten into unconsciousness. Mrs. Rutherford was tarred and feathered. Afterward, she walked half a mile to a neighbor's home to summon help.

The Rutherfords had moved into the village the year before and had "made many enemies since their arrival."[54] Marshal Buffenbarger of South Charleston found the club used on James and the rail used to break into the couple's house. Although Mrs. Rutherford identified Squire Stout as one of her attackers, he had eleven witnesses who claimed he was at home as the time.

The only reason given for the attack was that Mrs. Rutherford had previously filed charges against a neighbor named Willis (or Willie) Whitridge for assault, possibly in an extortion attempt. A couple of weeks later, the Rutherfords had disappeared, leaving all of their possessions behind.

Attempted Lynching, Stark County, November 1893—Davidson, Curtis [W]

Thomas Strawn, age forty-seven, was staying at the C.C. Baugh farm a mile west of Alliance while his sister and her husband were away visiting friends in Pennsylvania.

Rising early on the morning of November 14, 1893, Strawn went down to the sitting room to poke up the fire. He paused to awaken his seventeen year-old nephew, Norman, and then tried to wake his niece, Birdie, but she was not in her room.

When they attempted to enter the kitchen, they found the inside door was locked, so Strawn sent Norman around to try the outside door. As the young man walked into the kitchen, he let out a horrified cry. Racing out the backdoor, he returned to the sitting room and told his uncle something terrible had occurred. Strawn kicked in the kitchen door. The room was "swimming in blood."[55]

Norman immediately summoned help from a neighbor, Jud Wood. As Wood approached the Baugh house, he could see a trail of blood that led from the kitchen to a barn some 100–400 yards away. Inside the barn, a gruesome sight met their eyes. Beautiful Birdie was dead. They immediately suspected their farmhand, Curtis Davidson (or Davison), had done it.

S.S. Scranton owned a farm a mile away. At 6:30 that morning, he went out to feed his stock. As he was about to unlock the barn, he noticed a body on a pile of barnyard refuse. He recognized it as that of Davidson. He was saturated with blood and gasping for breath, his throat cut and a keen-edged razor by his side. Scranton contacted Marshal McFarland of Alliance and he sent a patrol wagon out to pick up the wounded man.

Davidson was transported to Shaw's boarding house not far from the Union Depot. Three physicians were brought in to attend him. He was unable to speak and gasped for breath. His jugular vein had not been cut, but his windpipe had been completely severed. The physicians made an attempt to sew it back together and believed he had a good chance of pulling through. However, the stitches soon ripped out.

Back at the Baugh farm, McFarland began to reconstruct the crime. Davidson, age forty-five, had worked for the Baughs, a well-to-do family, for several years. He also boarded with them, even though they did not trust him. While he conducted himself well enough in their presence, he was considered eccentric and frequently was absent at night. He was not at home on Monday evening and left again on Tuesday after supper.

Birdie, age twenty or twenty-one, was a vivacious young woman, the belle of local society, and a college student. She did not care for Davidson, seldom spoke to him if she could help it, and had asked her father to discharge him on more than one occasion. Their neighbors had also urged Baugh to fire the man, but he would not hear of it.

On Tuesday evening, Birdie's uncle Thomas and her two teenage brothers, Norman and Garfield, had retired for the night. After covering the fire, she had sat down in the kitchen and removed her shoes. Davidson soon came in.

It is not known what provoked it, but Davidson struck her on the head with a poker, stunning her. He then dragged the woman to the barn where he raped her and then cut her throat from ear to ear. Her lifeless and mutilated body, nearly naked, was found by her brother the following morning on the floor of the barn.

Word of the tragedy raced through the community. Many expressed their misgivings regarding Davidson. For example, Mrs. Eli Grant said that Davidson had worked at their farm, but she was always afraid of him. He was in the habit of rising at three o'clock every morning and roaming about the house.

While the physicians gave Davidson a chance of surviving his injury, it was feared that he would be lynched. Therefore, the mayor wired Sheriff Charles Krider to come at once from Canton. He arrived shortly after ten o'clock. Despite reinforcing the guard on the prisoner, the situation became so volatile that Company K of the Eighth Regiment, Ohio National Guard, was called up. After conferring amongst themselves, city officials decided to transfer the prisoner to New Lisbon.

Davidson was driven to the railroad depot in an ambulance under escort by police and militia. A mob followed the vehicle the entire way and made an attempt to kidnap the prisoner, but were repulsed by the guard.

For twenty days, Davidson clung to life. During that time, he was fed by having food pushed through the wound and into his stomach. He finally died at two-thirty in the morning on December 4, 1893, purportedly of blood poisoning, thereby cheating those people who had hoped he would eventually become healthy enough to hang.

Lynching [TI], Adams County, January 1894—Parker, Roscoe [B]

A little more than a mile outside of the village of Winchester by Elk Run was the home of an elderly couple, Luther Pittston "Pitt" Rhine (or Ryan) and his wife, Mary J. Farquhar Rhine. "Old and feeble, the husband past eighty and the wife upwards of seventy, and were living alone."[56] However, they sometimes received assistance from "a family of colored people named Parker."[57]

Consisting of a mother and several children, the Parkers performed odd jobs for the elderly couple. In December, Roscoe Parker, age ten to sixteen, assisted Luther Rhine in driving a calf to Winchester where he sold it to butcher for $13.

On December 19, 1893, a week or so later, the Rhines were found dead, their throats cut from ear to ear. It was suspected they had surprised someone in the act of burglarizing their home. Although Mary Rhine was an invalid who seldom left her room and her husband was a cripple as well, a violent struggle ensued and a double murder was the result. It did not take long for word of the "diabolical and heartless" crime to spread throughout the community.[58]

The Parkers were suspected. A search of their house turned up some stockings that were recognized as being the property of the Rhines and a $5 bill hidden in a bed. But the most damning evidence was the presence of what appeared to be blood stains on young Roscoe's clothing.

Immediately placed under arrest, the teenager was secretly conveyed in closed carriage to the jail in West Union, such was the fear for his safety. Parker implicated his half-brother, Sam Johnson, in the crime. Johnson, however, was able to easily prove his innocence.

Talk of lynching Parker and the formation of a mob in Winchester had led Sheriff Greene X. McMannis to announce he was moving the prisoner to Georgetown (or, perhaps, Hillsboro), but instead he took him overland to the jail in Portsmouth. Such talk had pretty much died down when newly elected Sheriff Marion Dunlap took office and he brought Parker back to West Union, a town of no more than 900 citizens, for the grand jury hearing.

As soon as it was learned that Parker was back in town, messengers were dispatched, and a band of 400 men assembled at Pan Handle crossing on January 12, 1894, and rode to West Union. It was four weeks after his arrest. While some stood guard over their vehicles, the rest moved toward the jail. They battered down the doors of the jail and constrained Dunlap and his deputy, James McKee.

Cornered in his cell, Parker tried to fight back, disfiguring several of the faces of his attackers, but was quickly overpowered. "I'll tell all tomorrow," Parker pleaded. "Sam Johnson did it. I would also like to see my mother before I die."[59] However, no one was interested in hearing what he had to say.

Parker was removed, taken a half mile beyond North Liberty toward Winchester. Driven ten miles in his underwear on a stingingly cold night, Parker was said to have been sweating as though it was the heat of summer. Just after midnight, they threw the rope over the limb of an ash tree. When their leader shouted, "Now, boys!" they proceeded to hang him.[60]

Twice he was swung up and let down in the hope that he could be induced to make a full confession, but refused. Finally, he said only that he knew nothing whatsoever about the murders. He declined to say a prayer for himself.

The next morning, his bullet riddled corpse was found still hanging from the tree, near a little wooden bridge. A grain sack that had been placed over his head by the mob had fallen to the ground and was carried off by a former slave who was ignorant of its purpose. The tree was soon stripped of its branches by those seeking souvenirs of the grisly incident.

After an inquest by the coroner, there was some debate about the disposition of Parker's body. He was buried two days later at Cherry Fork Cemetery, but was promptly disinterred by medical students and his skull was thought to be in the possession of a local physician.

The case against those who had lynched Parker was put before the Grand Jury on January 16, 1894. Judge Davis excoriated the local newspapers, asserting that they had become an "accessory to murder and crime" and declared that the reporters should be indicted.[61]

Governor William McKinley assured three African American members of the Ohio Legislature that he fully expected the grand jury in Adams County to indict and prosecute all who were involved in the lynching and, if it failed to do so, he would take action to ensure justice was served. But the lynchers were not indicted and McKinley was powerless to do anything about it.

Then on January 13, Jesse Prewell, a well-to-do bachelor farmer, had blown his own head off with a shotgun after leaving a note expressing his remorse for having helped to lynch Roscoe Parker.

Mob Violence, Belmont County, February 1894—Chapel, Robert [W]

Masked riders visited Robert Chapel of near Caldwell on February 13, 1894. When they knocked on the door, his wife answered and told them he wasn't there, but could be found at the "home of a disreputable woman."[62]

Rushing to the woman's dwelling, they seized Chapel, dragged him outside, tied him to a fence, and whipped him with switches. They then threw him in Duck Creek and warned him to leave, which he did before daylight. He had been accused of beating his wife.

Lynching [TI], Logan County, April 1894—Newlin, Seymour [B]

When Seymour Newlin (aka Neville or Newland) criminally assaulted Mrs. Eliza Anne Knowles on April 14, 1894, it was the last straw. A resident of Rushsylvania, the eighty- or eighty-one-year-old widow was alone in her house on Saturday night when a black man entered her bedroom, slapped a hand across her mouth, and violated her. After he left, she dragged herself to a neighbor's house and told her story in a few broken sentences before collapsing. News of the crime rapidly spread throughout the village of 500 or so.

Having previously served three stints in the Ohio Penitentiary, Newlin, age thirty-one, had a bad reputation. A mob overtook him the following morning a few miles outside of town and he was taken back to Rushsylvania. He was placed in "lockup, a plain little shell," and a guard was placed outside the flimsy structure, while someone was sent to get a rope.[63]

When Logan County Sheriff John Sullivan arrived to transport Newlin back to Bellefontaine, a mob of as many as 1,500 men and women stood their ground and refused to surrender the prisoner. Even after he summoned a posse, they wouldn't yield. So he telegraphed for a company of militia which left from Bellefontaine late Sunday afternoon.

Learning that the troops were on the way, the villagers were prepared. They armed themselves and encircled the jail. It was sometime after five o'clock when Company F, Second Infantry, arrived. The unit was warned by a chorus of 100 voices that dynamite charges had been placed beneath the building and "the prisoner would be blown to atoms" if they made an attempt to take him.[64] The militia stopped one man from actually lighting the dynamite and a total of six bombs were later found under the jail.

Sheriff Sullivan was able to negotiate an agreement with the ringleaders. He would order the militia back to Bellefontaine, while a deputation of citizens would continue to guard the jail and a hearing would be held the next morning. Although Sullivan undoubtedly thought he had averted a crisis, the angry citizens still weren't appeased.

With the departure of the National Guard, the promised protection disappeared and the mob rushed the jail. Using rails gathered from nearby fences, they overturned the structure, knocking it off its foundation. Unable to resist the onslaught by himself, Sullivan could not stop the mob from taking charge of Newlin.

Looping a noose around Newlin's neck, they dragged him about 100–150 yards to a cottonwood tree. Little was said; he was given neither an opportunity to pray nor confess. An attempt was made to hold a mock trial, but the mob was impatient to get to the execution part. He had been found guilty of a previous outrage, which sealed his fate. The free end of the rope was tossed over a limb. "A dozen willing hands grasped the rope and the negro was swung into the air. As his body rose above the mob the air was rent with the shouts of the men and women who had assembled to witness the lynching."[65]

Many residents of Marion, thirty-five miles away, purportedly helped to swell the crowd at Rushsylvania—estimated at over 2,000. Its work completed, the mob quietly dispersed and order returned to the usually quite community.

In the days that followed, the ailing Mrs. Knowles expressed some uncertainty about whether she had identified the right man. It was thought she probably would not recover from the experience, but, in fact, she lived another fourteen years.

Mob Violence, Wayne County, May 1894—Mishler, John [W]

A band of White Caps paid a visit to John Mishler of Smithville on the night of May 6, 1894. He had been repeatedly warned to stop physically abusing his family. However, earlier that day, he had nearly killed his wife and caused his eldest son to flee. The vigilantes called Mishler out of the house and beat him with horse whips and switches until he begged for mercy.

Mob Violence, Adams County, June 1894—Gilley, Henry [W]

On the night of June 26, 1894, White Caps took Henry Gilley from his home in West Union and gave him fifty lashes, even though he was regarded as "a good citizen."[66]

Originally from Kentucky, Gilley was said to have married a respectable woman. However, he had received several warnings from "The Knights of the Switch."[67] After they had nearly beaten him to death, he was warned they would be back if he didn't treat his wife better.

Expected Lynching, Perry County, July 1894—Underwood, John [W]

At about 10 o'clock on the evening of July 6, 1894, Officer A.R. Koon was shot to death by John Underwood in New Straitsville. Both Underwood and his son, Frank, were drunk and creating a disturbance when the policeman ordered them to go home. Underwood replied by telling Koon he would shoot him if he came any closer.

Unwisely, Koon took a step toward him and Underwood began blazing away with his revolver. One shot struck Koon in the chest. Before he fell and died, Koon fired back, wounding Underwood who fled. Several posses were sent in pursuit of him and the city council offered up a reward of $300 for his capture. "Threats of lynch are heard," the *Marion Star* reported.[68]

Attempted Lynching, Morgan County, August 1894—Cheadle, Madison [W]

During the first week of August 1894, Madison "Madge" Cheadle, a Morgan County farmer, was visited by eight men one evening when he was home alone. His door was locked, so they bashed it in and forced him to accompany them outside where they beat him with whips, clubs, and stones until he had nearly lost consciousness. They then suspended him from a tree limb and left him. Cheadle likely would have died if a tramp who was in a nearby barn hadn't come along and cut him down.

According to the *Morgan County Democrat*, Cheadle was "a very disturbing element in that neighborhood" due to his propensity to gossip and steal from others. Earlier, he had been accused of setting fire to Todd's church schoolhouse, but the charges were dismissed. The general belief was that his neighbors had tired of his behavior.

Five men were soon arrested for the assault: John Leasure, George Greathouse, William Daugherty, John Carr, and Elmer Cheadle. It turned out to be a family affair; Elmer was Madge's brother, George and John were brothers-in-law, and William was his niece's husband.

False Report of Mob Violence, Summit County, September 1894—Three unknown men [B]

One of the most memorable racial incidents in Akron was a hoax.

On September 13, 1894, three African Americans, two men and a woman, stopped at George Woehlhueter's saloon while his wife was alone. They demanded that she fix them breakfast, so she did, although she said she was frightened.

Later, the trio returned to the establishment, broke through the door, entered Mrs. Woehlhueter's living quarters, and severely thrashed and assaulted her. When they were finished, they bound and gagged her before tossing her into the cellar. The men then doused the carpets and bedding with oil and set the place on fire.

If someone hadn't spotted the flames, Mrs. Woehlhueter would have surely died. As it was, she was in critical condition.

Police and citizens throughout Akron searched for Mrs. Woehlhueter's assailants. As far away as Washington, D.C., newspapers were outraged by the crime. The *Alexandria Gazette* suggested that the British committee commissioned by the "Duke of Argile" (likely Argyll) to look into the lynchings in the South should first visit Akron, presumably to have a firsthand look at why African Americans were being lynched.

Fortunately, no one was lynched over the Woehlhueter affair. In fact, no one was even punished, once the police decided the woman was insane and had done it to herself.

Attempted Lynching, Fayette County, October 1894—Dolby, William "Jasper" [B]

William McKinley has gotten a raw deal from history. Gunned down after a little more than four years in office, he is seldom given credit for his actual accomplishments, let alone his bright promise. As governor of Ohio, he was generally on the right side of all major issues, particularly in matters of workers' rights and race relations. He was also tested repeatedly during his administration, no more so than when he ordered National Guard troops into Washington Court House on October 17, 1894.

Two years later, McKinley would tell the Ohio General Assembly that "lynchings must not be tolerated in Ohio," while heaping praise on three men who had died preventing one.[69]

William "Jasper" Dolby, a black (or biracial) man, was accused of raping a white woman, Mrs. Mary C. Boyd, near Parrett's Station, on October 9 (or 10), 1894. Fifty-two-year-old Mrs. Boyd was alone in her farmhouse, nine miles outside of town, when Dolby turned up at her door, demanding to be fed. He had just been released from the county jail where he had served time for a misdemeanor. As she started to prepare food for him, he attacked her, leaving her for dead on the floor. A week later, it was still uncertain whether she would recover.

Arrested sixty miles away at Delaware a week later, Dolby was transported by the sheriff back to Fayette County on October 16, 1894. Taken to the Boyd farm (or the sheriff's residence; again, sources differ), he was positively identified by Mrs. Boyd as well as a neighbor who had seen him leave the house on the day of the attack.

By 1890, 742 Washington C.H. residents—13 percent of the population—were African Americans, mostly families. Both whites and blacks in the community were incensed by the assault and both groups freely discussed lynching him. That night, a crowd gathered outside the courthouse, but local law enforcement aided by locally based Company E of the Fourteenth Regiment were able to keep them at bay. Fearing the worst, Sheriff James F. Cook wired Governor McKinley for help.

At six o'clock the next morning, Colonel Alonzo B. Coit of the Fourteenth Regiment of the Ohio National Guard arrived in Washington C.H. to take charge of the situation. He was accompanied by Companies A and B. He immediately placed a line of guards around the perimeter of the courthouse grounds. That afternoon, a special grand jury was impaneled and Dolby was indicted for the crime. However, he was still entitled to his day in court.

Companies of soldiers formed at the west side of the courthouse while Sheriff Cook and Deputy James Busick went to fetch the prisoner from the jail. The distance between the courthouse and the jail was approximately forty feet and there was a flight of high steps leading to the jail. A thousand people had gathered around the courthouse, vowing that Dolby would not pass by them.

The sheriff and deputies had barely emerged from the jail door when Henry Kirk, Mrs. Boyd's nephew, rushed toward Dolby, broke through his guard, and seized him. Instantly, a soldier struck Kirk in the face with his musket. The crowd rushed madly ahead, cursing and threatening the prisoner, who nearly collapsed in fright. Colonel Coit rallied his troops who pushed forward, virtually carrying Dolby into the courthouse.

Men brandishing wooden staves and whatever other makeshift weapons they could find charged the soldiers who faced them with fixed bayonets. Deputy Busick and Detective Caldwell stood their ground on either side of the prisoner whose hands were manacled. Having obtained medical attention, Kirk returned with a huge bandage on his face. His friends—from farmers to businessmen—swore they would get the prisoner yet before he could be taken to the depot.

Coit, standing on the steps of the courthouse, warned the people to disperse. When they didn't, he ordered, "Load," and the soldiers cocked their weapons.[70] This caused the surprised crowd to retreat a few steps. But within moments, they rushed in again and were held back by the wall of soldiers. Sergeant Andrews of Company A and Private Lenhart of Company B were struck with stones, but did not retreat.

Taken to the courtroom on the third floor of the courthouse, Dolby confessed to the crime. He was sentenced to twenty years' imprisonment, ten days a year to be spent in solitary. Outside, the mob was clamoring to get in. Coit's challenge was to ensure the prisoner was on the train to Columbus so he could begin serving his sentence at the Ohio Penitentiary.

Placing a call to Columbus, Coit asked for 200 more troops. "If you want me to bring the man to Columbus, I will do it," he said, "but it will cost blood."[71] He then addressed the throng, warning them there would be trouble if they attacked and urging all law-abiding citizens to go home.

The soldiers failed to get him to the depot in time to catch the 4:30 p.m. train, so the prisoner was kept in the sheriff's office on the third floor. At 6:10 in the evening, the crowd was augmented by the arrival of additional men with huge battering rams. They surrounded the building and began pounding the doors in rapid succession. The soldiers were called upon to barricade all the entrances with furniture. And then stood ready to repel the mob with their bayonets.

As darkness fell, the people continued their assault, yelling and hurling large stones against the doors. Some 1,500 to 3,000 people crowded around the jail, shouting, "Lynch him! Lynch him!"[72] Someone then threw a stone which hit a soldier in the chest. Angrily, Colonel Coit shouted, "If you want to injure any one, hit me, and not these young men!"

NATIONAL BANK

His hat uplifted, he boldly walked into the midst of the crowd. "Here I am!" he said.[73] "If any man of you hits one of my men, I will direct them to aim directly at the man's heart."[74]

At 7:55 in the evening, the south doors gave way and the soldiers began firing their muskets. Pandemonium broke out both inside and out. In all, five would die—the youngest age fourteen—and twenty would be wounded. The mob turned and ran. They then cautiously returned to carry away the dead and wounded. Word was received by Coit that men were gathering dynamite from all over town. He cleared the courtyard. Hundreds of men now congregated at the southwest corner of the square.

Mayor Eugene Creamer ordered all of the saloons closed and implored the rioters to clear the streets, but they ignored his pleas. Businesses and the engine house were quickly converted into hospitals. All the surgeons in the city were mobilized. Mothers, sisters, wives, and sweethearts crowded around the dead and injured.

The mood had changed. Before the crowd wanted to avenge the rape of Mrs. Boyd. Now, they sought to punish the soldiers and especially Colonel Coit. There was talk of dynamiting the courthouse. Instead of shrinking, the mob continued to grow. People raced through the streets in search of arms and ammunition, shouting, "Down with the militia!" and "Blow up the dogs!"[75] Some of the soldiers would later admit they expected Coit to be lynched.

Fortunately, the excitement began to wear off as the night wore on. When a rumor began circulating that Governor McKinley was in route by special train with several carloads of militia, Elmer Boyd, son of the victim, asked permission to address the crowd from the courthouse steps. He requested that they disperse and allow the courts to dispense justice. However, his speech was met by hoots and jeers as he disappeared back into the crowd.

At 1:30 in the morning, the streets were still clogged with men, congregating in knots. But the violence had ceased. Coit had stationed his men in the darkened windows of the courthouse. A telegram informed him that the First Regiment was on its way and that two remaining companies from Columbus were at Mount Sterling waiting to accompany the first. They were expected to arrive at two o'clock. Meanwhile, many restaurants remained open to serve the people who hung around waiting to see what would happen next.

Unbeknownst to the rioters, the train pulled in before dawn and Dolby had secretly boarded it. Under escort of six companies of the Fourteenth Regiment, he was transported to the Ohio Penitentiary in Columbus where he would spend the next twenty years at hard labor.

Shortly after six o'clock in the morning, McKinley's train pulled into the depot at Washington Court House. Although there were still large crowds abroad, they were contained by the arrival of imposing forces of militia ordered in place by Adjutant General Howe. There were still threats to burn down the jail and commit violence against the sheriff and his deputies. Protected by his men, Colonel Coit marched to the depot to join the governor, whose life was as endangered as Dolby's.

After Governor McKinley arrived back in Columbus, he met with Sheriff Cook and

***Opposite:* In 1894, an enormous mob surrounded the Fayette County courthouse, bent on lynching William "Jasper" Dolby. In order to get a better view, spectators climbed onto roofs and into the telephone wires across from the courthouse. The mob was repelled by the Ohio National Guard.**

reviewed a number of telegrams from prominent citizens in Fayette County assuring him that there would be no further lawlessness. He then ordered all remaining troops to return to their homes.

What had transpired in Washington Court House informed the editorials of newspapers throughout Ohio and the nation. The *Chicago Tribune* praised the authorities of Ohio for enforcing the law, while deploring the loss of life. "The troops did their duty. The governor acted promptly and decisively."[76] McKinley may not have been able to avenge Roscoe Parker's murder, but he had saved William Dolby.

Twenty-four people in all had been struck by bullets and there was pressure on McKinley to dismiss Colonel Coit from the National Guard. Only his departure from Washington Court House that morning had prevented another riot.

Coit was subsequently charged with manslaughter by the Fayette County prosecutor. The trial began the following October and lasted four months. After fifty hours of deliberation, the jury acquitted Coit, although the public did not. When the Ohio legislature later passed a bill authorizing payment of nearly $18,000 in legal expenses, the controversy continued. To this day, there are bullet holes in the south doors of the courthouse.

Attempted Lynching, Defiance County, October 1894—O'Neill, Charles [B]

Charles O'Neill was accused of sexually assaulting three-year-old Harriet C. "Hattie" Heckerman (or Hickerman) near the village of Hicksville. The child was found unconscious in a barn on Sunday afternoon, October 21, 1894. When she came to, she said that O'Neill, a black man, had carried her there.

O'Neill had been hired to work on the farm owned by Mrs. Harriet Crowl, a widow. Living with her were little Hattie, as well as her own daughter, Mrs. Daniel Heckerman, Hattie's mother. Described as "a powerful man and as black as night," O'Neill doted on Hattie and spent a lot of time in her company.[77]

On Saturday, Hattie had gone to the stable with O'Neill. When she didn't return, her mother went in search of her. She found her on the stable floor, unconscious, her clothes torn and soaked with blood. Although she was in critical condition, Hattie was able to describe the assault to Marshal Frey.

Accompanied by six deputies, the marshal soon captured O'Neill. They dragged him through Hicksville, a furious throng hounding their every step. Once they arrive at the village jail, they barricaded the doors and held off the throng with clubs and pistols throughout the night. The people finally dispersed at dawn, but swore to kill the prisoner if he fell into their hands.

Although small groups lingered around town through the day, they did not reach a critical mass again. O'Neill would confess to his crime and, presumably, serve time at the Ohio Penitentiary.

The only newspaper that came to O'Neill's defense was the *Cleveland Leader*. It charged that O'Neill had worked all winter without compensation and that the story was fabricated to frighten him out of the country. Little Hattie, meanwhile, recovered and was married in 1907.

Expected Lynching, Licking County, October 1894—Ward, Benjamin [B]

On the afternoon of October 19, 1894, a man knocked at the door of Mrs. Adelbert Neibling (aka Catherine Swigart) of Newark, a fifty-three-year-old widow, asking for food and water. He then immediately knocked her down, hitting her in the face three times before she had a chance to respond.

Pulling a rope out of his pocket, he tied her hands, looped the rope around her neck, stuffed a rag in her mouth, and raped her. Afterwards, he pushed her down the basement steps.

When she regained consciousness, Mrs. Neibling began screaming and her neighbors came to her assistance. She was in sad shape. Her clothes hung in rags, her face was badly disfigured, and she could barely talk because of a knotted piece of clothing around her throat. Later, however, the widow provided a detailed description of her assailant, a "large and dark Negro [who] wore a dark slouch hat and dark sack coat."[78]

It wasn't long before someone matching that description was seen in the north end of town. A manhunt, led by Marshal Griffith, was soon underway. They found Benjamin Ward busy digging a pit outside a boarding house he frequented. Promptly arrested and carted off to jail, he said he was thirty nine years old, a native of Columbus, and had come to Newark a week before in search of work.

A reporter tried to pressure Ward into admitting to the rape, asserting that the only reason Jasper Dolby hadn't been lynched in Washington Court House was due to his confession. Nevertheless, Ward continued to proclaim his innocence.

The victim, Mrs. Neibling, a white woman, was brought to the jail to identify her attacker. Shown Ward and two other African Americans, she singled out Ward: "Yes, I know that's the one."[79] When word of her positive identification spread across the community, several hundred people collected at the courthouse.

The next day, a gold watch that had been stolen from the Neibling house was turned into the police, having been found in the yard where Ward was digging. A Zanesville man told police that Ward had just been released from the Muskingum County Jail for some misdemeanor. He also insisted Ward was from Dresden, not Columbus.

Other rumors came out of the woodwork: Ward had frightened several other woman before he arrived at Mrs. Neibling's; he had been convicted of second degree murder (and later pardoned when his brother made a deathbed confession); he had served time in either Illinois or Indiana. The deck was stacked against him. Convicted of the rape, he was sentenced to the Ohio Penitentiary.

Attempted Lynching, Paulding County, November 1894—Hart, Charles [W]; Cain, Leo [B]

Nine-year-old George and six-year-old Nellie Good were playing in the road near their home three miles north of Paulding, on November 5, 1894, when they wandered into the woods. After the children failed to return home for supper, a search party was organized. No trace of them was found until eight o'clock the next morning. Their bodies had been tied-together and dumped in a brush heap some distance from the road. An attempt had been made to burn them, but the wood was too damp.

Nellie had been beheaded and disemboweled; George's head was nearly severed from his body. Both children were horribly mangled. Two hours later, Sheriff Edward Staley arrived at the scene and arrested Charles Hart because he behaved oddly when the bodies were discovered. Nineteen and illiterate, Hart was a neighbor of the murdered children. Some people believed he was insane.

Also arrested and jailed was Leo Cain, twenty-one, an African American man described as someone who has been a companion of Hart's. When the streets of Paulding began to fill with 300–500 men "who were talking wildly of lynching," Judge John Snook and other leading citizens of the community addressed them in an effort to smooth things over.[80]

However, the mob continued to increase in size and the talk became angrier. Sheriff Staley quietly took the prisoners to Van Wert for safekeeping. Rumors reached him that a mob was on the move. Later, Clarence Brindle was also arrested on suspicion.

Ultimately (some might say astonishingly), Cain was released, but the other two were bound over. Hart had known that the children were dismembered without having seen the remains, while Brindle confessed to an African American preacher while they both were in jail. Hart was convicted of murdered and hanged at the Ohio Penitentiary. Brindle, a brother-in-law, was released.

Had the lynch mob acted on their emotions, they would have murdered two men, one guilty and one not.

Mob Violence, Ross County, December 1894—Criestlay, Miss [W]

On Sunday, December 9, 1894, vigilantes struck at Bainbridge, tar-and-feathering a seventeen-year-old white girl named Criestlay who had been "keeping company with a negro named Buck."[81] It was alleged that they were "bold in their billing and cooing."[82]

While Buck made good his escape, some fifty men detained the girl. Taking her into an alley, they stripped off her clothing and "decorated her from head to feet."[83] The girl had to walk home some seven miles to Cynthia in that woeful condition, while her boyfriend was not seen in the vicinity thereafter.

Mob Violence, Adams County, December 1894—Shreever, Henry [W]; Longley, Mrs. [W]

Forty White Caps visited a farmer named Henry Shreever who lived near Peebles on Christmas Eve, 1894. He was taken from his house and, after admitting to petty thefts, flogged. His cries aroused Samuel Longley, who lived nearby. Longley fled in fear, but his wife stood her ground. So the White Caps whipped her, too.

False Report of Lynching [TI], Hocking County, May 1895—Fetherolf, Nelson C [W]

From the newspaper accounts, Nelson C. Fetherolf was lynched on May 30, 1895. The *Evening News* of Indianapolis reported that a mob had taken Fetherolf from the lock-up in Laurelville and hanged him. Fifty years old and the father of six daughters, he was accused of brutally assaulting a little girl, Dora Lee Whistler, age eight, "whom he overtook in the roads."[84]

The crime occurred on May 23, 1895, three miles west of Adelphi when Fetherolf talked the girl into joining him in his buggy. He then drove her to a woods where he tried to assault her. After threatening to kill her if she told anyone, he turned her loose. Although Dora was seriously injured, she kept quiet about the assault for five days.

Many similar stories appeared in other papers throughout the country, but there were no additional details. In fact, there was no mention at all of Fetherolf's demise in any of the newspapers serving the area. It was as though it hadn't happened. The *Hocking Sentinel* of June 6, 1895, dismissed it as a rumor.

Fetherolf (aka Federoff/Fitterolf/Fetherroff) was born in Perry Township, Hocking County, in 1845. He was the son of William and Mary Cupp Fetherolf, both natives of Pennsylvania. In 1868, at the age of twenty-three, he married Amelia Bailer (or Bailor). She was nineteen.

Over the years, Fetherolf was involved in a series of lawsuits over various land deals. He also acquired a reputation for larceny that led to several stints in jail. However, the alleged assault on the little girl that resulted in his purported lynching seemed out of character.

It is possible that some men did take Fetherolf from the Laurelville jail to lynch him, but were either thwarted in their plan or intended only to scare him. According to the 1900 census, he was not dead, but confined at the Ohio Penitentiary in Columbus. Thirty years later, Fetherolf was now an inmate of the Fairfield County Home. He evidently died in 1932—thirty-seven years after he was allegedly lynched!

Mob Violence, Henry County, May 1895—Handst, Joel [W]

Joel Handst, an Amish farmer, moved to Henry County from Pennsylvania about a year earlier. He would not associate with his neighbors, nor would he fight with any man including through the courts. Consequently, numerous depredations were made on his farm and no one was punished for it.

Handst's neighbors grew suspicious of him because of his pacifism. Many of them began to think he might have somehow been involved in "several mysterious disappearances" of farmers during the past year."[85] Finally, he was visited by White Caps on May 31, 1895.

A handful of masked men went to his cottage and conducted a search. Handst was praying when they forced their way into his home and continued to do so while they ransacked the place. However, they found no evidence that would confirm their suspicions.

Amazingly, Handst did not resist as the gang deliberately cut off one ear and sliced the other. "He said he would leave their punishment to their Maker. His wounds were dressed by his wife who was as accepting of the outrage as he was."[86] Although the authorities investigated, Handst declined to press charges.

Mob Violence, Henry County, May 1895—Anker, Henry [unk]

The details are minimal and it can only be presumed it happened in Henry County because it was buried in an article about Joel Handst. However, White Caps took Henry Anker into the woods later in May 1895, tied him to a tree, and nearly flayed him to death.

Expected Lynching, Paulding County, June 1895—Smith, Andrew [B?]

Mary McCune, nine-year-old daughter of W.T. McCune, was allegedly assaulted by Andrew Smith near Briceton about June 28, 1895. Captured by a "colored detective in Troy," he was taken to Delphos.[87] The local farmers threatened to lynch him if he was brought to their county for trial. Nevertheless, Marshal Palmer of Latty took his prisoner directly to the county jail in Paulding.

Mob Violence, Fayette/Pickaway Counties, July 1895—Cummings, Bertha [W]

Bertha Cummings (aka Minnie Lewis or Faynor), described as a "female ghost" (because she wore "ghostly attire") was well-known in the village of New Holland. When she was caught entertaining four "tough characters" beneath an apple tree on July 11, 1895, by a mob numbered sixty or so, she was tarred and feathered, egged, and told she had five minutes to leave town. The men escaped unscathed.[88]

Cummings subsequently sued ten prominent and wealthy men in the community for $10,000.

Mob Violence, Columbiana County, October 1895—Humphreys, Thomas [W]

It wasn't unusual for Thomas Humphreys and his wife to drink and when they did they were apt to fight. Apparently, a band of East Liverpool White Caps decided it was time to teach him a lesson. So, on the night of October 4, 1895, they dragged the old fellow out of his bed and forced him to walk to a remote spot on the outskirts of town.

Barefoot and clad only a night shirt, Humphreys was savagely beaten and left hanging by his wrists from a tree. After freeing himself, he sought help at a nearby pottery. The identities of his assailants were unknown.

Lynching [TI], Clermont County, August 1895—Anderson, Noah [B]

One of the surest ways to get lynched was for a person of low station in life to murder a person of high station. This was the case when Noah Anderson, an itinerant paper-hanger who happened to be black, killed Franklin Fridman, an elderly bank president who happened to be white. And, on the surface, the crime doesn't make any sense.

What happened was this. On August 21, 1895, Fridman, New Richmond's wealthiest citizen and the beloved president of the First National Bank, was on his way into town from his home in Clermontville when he stopped his buggy at one of several farms he owned. He had tied his horse up at the dooryard and entered an adjoining field when Anderson jumped him for some unknown reason. (Another account stated that Anderson was living in the house and had frequently threatened to kill anyone who came near it.) The muscular assailant had no weapons, but threw the old man to the ground and choked the life out of him "with the power of a demon."[89]

Satisfied that Fridman was dead, Anderson ran off. The whole spectacle was witnessed by several men who were at work in an adjacent field, but were too far away to intervene. Rushing to the banker's body, they carried it inside the farmhouse.

News of the crime traveled quickly and Anderson was soon apprehended. Taken to the jail early, he readily confessed to killing Fridman, insisting he had deserved it because the banker had deprived him of a great sum of money—$200,000,000! It was obvious to all that Anderson "was not right in his mind" and experiencing delusions because he had never had any interaction with Fridman.[90] He had arrived in New Richmond only a few months earlier on a shanty boat.

Meanwhile, a great crowd gathered outside the jail, preventing the sheriff from entering the "frail" structure until Mayor Dawson accompanied him. The crowd became wildly excited when word of Anderson's confession reached them. Cries of "Lynch him!" and "Hang the coward!" filled the air.[91]

Hearing them, Anderson dropped to his knees, begging for mercy. Someone then produced a rope which had the same effect as a fuse on a powder keg. Despite the admonition of several prominent citizens imploring moderation, the mob worked itself into a frenzy.

In an effort to take advantage of a momentary lull, the sheriff moved Anderson out of the jail at about four o'clock in the afternoon. His plan was to transport his prisoner to Batavia. He immediately regretted his decision, however. As soon as the two of them were spotted, the mob rushed at them, ripping Anderson free of his custody and encircling his neck with a rope. "This is no bluff; we must have him," they warned the lawman.[92] They then moved as one, surging in the direction of Washington and Western Avenues, dragging Anderson behind them in the dust.

Reaching the corner, they tossed the rope over the limb of a poplar tree. At that moment, some of the crowd seemed to lose their will. But then a man who appeared to be their leader cried out, "You're a nice lot of nervy fellows."[93] And with that, he gave the rope a downward tug and tied it off to the trunk.

Anderson did not struggle, so it is believed he had already strangled to death while being dragged through the dust. It had only been three and one half hours since Fridman died.

The members of the lynch mob had not taken any pains to conceal their identities. Each man present was known to the others, not excluding the sheriff. As the *Columbus Evening Dispatch* reported, "It was simply an act of frenzy under most aggravating circumstances. The murdered man … was endeared to every citizen and his taking off was so sudden that his friends and neighbors seemed to have lost their reason."[94]

At the time of the lynching, the population of New Richmond was around 2,300. It would drop precipitously, never topping that mark again for sixty years.

Attempted Lynching, Seneca County, October 1895—Martin, Leander J. [W]

Leander J. Martin (alias Williams), a farmer from Watson Station, six miles south of Tiffin, had quarreled with the fifteen-year-old son of a neighboring farmer on Wednesday afternoon. The boy had refused to carry out some request that Martin made. Flying into a rage, Martin struck the boy with his fist and then grabbed him by the neck and began to strangle him. After he managed to break free, the boy ran into town and told the police what had happened.

Marshal August Shultz and Officer Pat Sweeney set out at once for the Martin farm. When he saw them coming, Martin barricaded himself inside his house. Imprudently, Shultz and Sweeney walked up to the door. He immediately fired a half dozen shots at them from his window, striking them both at close range. Shultz died as soon as he fell to the ground. Sweeney, struck twice, succeeded in getting away. He was soon joined by reinforcements from the town. Seeing he was outnumbered, Martin laid down his gun and gave himself up.

Following Shultz's funeral, few farmers returned to their fields. Instead, they went into town, began drinking heavily, and talked about lynching Martin. Sheriff Joseph Van Nest was prepared, though, having placed four or five guards, armed with rifles, in the jail "just to be on the safe side."[95] The saloons closed at midnight and the streets quickly emptied. What the sheriff and his men didn't realize is that there was a meeting out at the fairgrounds, one mile east of the jail. The crowd was increasing in size by the minute.

At half past one on the morning of October 27, 1895, a mob of 150 infuriated men out to avenge the murder of Marshal Schultz four days earlier stormed the jail where his killer was confined. They spilled into Market Street, just east of Heidelberg College, and reached the rear of the jail at 1:30. Two or three minutes later, they let out a yell and charged through the yard between the Seneca County courthouse and the jail, demanding that they been admitted to the sheriff's residence and the jail. Some were carrying sledge hammers which they swung at the door, destroying it with a few sharp blows. They then surged inside the jail.

Sheriff Van Nest, revolver in hand, threatened them with the law and physical harm if they advanced any further, but was quickly overpowered by the press of humanity. They next encountered six heavily armed deputies, arranged in advantageous positions within the jail. Breaking down the solid steel door which separated them from the jail, the determined mob fell upon the next door with their sledgehammers. The guards warned them to stop and then fired their guns into the ceiling. As a last resort, the sheriff ordered them to shoot into the midst of the crowd. A volley from a half dozen Winchester rifles cut down Henry Mutchler, Jr., and Christian Matz. Mutchler was one of the loudest voices inciting the mob and one of them carried the rope.

The bodies of the dead were carried out while the mob renewed their attack. They paused only when several of their number went to procure dynamite, unaware that during the break Officers Sweeney and Faulkner slipped into Martin's cell, unlocked the door, handcuffed him, and left the building by a rear door. There they jumped into a waiting cab and were driven twenty-four miles to Fremont at top speed. As soon as the guards heard Martin was on the road, they disappeared from their posts and the jail.

Unable to find any dynamite and alerted to the fact that Martin was no longer in jail, the would-be lynchers searched for the deputies who had killed Mutchler and Matz, but they could not learn their names. As daylight broke, a crowd began to assemble in the vicinity of the jail. Sheriff Van Nest, concerned that there would be more trouble, called for Company C of the Sixteenth Regiment of the Ohio National guard to assist him in maintaining order. However, feeling that their numbers were insufficient to cope with a large uprising, the sheriff also telegraphed Governor William McKinley for reinforcements. In response, McKinley sent in three additional companies from Fremont, Sandusky, and Kenton—300 men in all.

The crowd did not accept the fact that the prisoner was no longer there, even when several of their own confirmed it after scouring the building.

Mob Violence, Seneca County, November 1895—Martin, Leander J. [W]

A month earlier, a mob had been foiled in their attempt to lynch Leander J. Martin for the killing of Marshal August Shultz. So on November 24, 1895, 100 men paid him a visit at his hotel, gave him a coating of tar and feathers, and rode him out of town on a three-cornered rail.

Mob Violence, Washington County, November 1895—Rogers, C.H. [W]

C.H. (or H.M.) Rogers, a crayon artist from London, Ohio, was tarred, feathered, and ridden on a three-cornered rail at the fairgrounds in McArthur on the night of November 24, 1895. His offense was speaking disrespectfully to a local school mistress. As a result, 100 men abducted him from his hotel. When the county sheriff arrived, he prevented further mistreatment, but advised the victim to take to the woods. He evidently complied.

Mob Violence, Wood County, December 1895—Schaad, Jacob [W}; Schaad, Catherine [W]; Schaad, Henry [W]; Schaad, Rosa [W]

The Schaad family of near Marietta was visited by the White Caps on the night of December 10, 1895. Three masked men clothed as women dragged the wife, Catherine Schaad, by the hair and clubbed her unconscious with a heavy stick. When the daughter, Rosa, age twenty, tried to help her, she was knocked to the ground and seriously injured. Jacob F. Schaad, age fifty, and his son Henry, age fourteen, were both beaten with clubs.

Other people also joined in beating them after they were taken from their home. "The matter is supposed to have been the result of a road case of long standing" (possibly a dispute over use of a road).[96]

Less than a week later, five well-to-do farmers were arrested and charged with the assault on the Schaad family. Jacob and Catherine Schaad and their daughter filed suit for damages against Peter Andrews, Frank Schwindermann, and James (or Joseph) and John Kerns (or Koerns). They sought a total of $50,000.

About three months later, something resembling justice was served when the men were found guilty of housebreaking. They were fined $300 and sentenced to thirty days in jail apiece, although the total cost to the defendants was $3,000 (the equivalent of $81,000 today).

Mob Violence, Butler County, December 1895—Wescoe, Mrs. [W]

If, as has been suggested, White Capping was just a means for young men to blow off steam, especially in rural communities where entertainment was scarce, that might explain why Daniel William Daub got involved. A pitcher for the Brooklyn Bridegrooms baseball club, Daub joined a band of night riders while spending his winters at Mintonville, near Middletown.

On the night December 20, 1895, Daub was one of twenty young men who stoned the house of Mrs. Wescoe. The daughter of a well-known local farmer, she grabbed a shotgun and sent them fleeing into the darkness. However, they later returned and shot out every window in her home. She subsequently swore out arrest warrants for Daub and many of the others. Clint Crow, well known in local politics, was also arrested.

The White Caps accused Mrs. Wescoe of receiving visits from her neighbor, Snider, on a frequent basis. Her husband purportedly believed she was innocent of the charges.

6

Separate but Equal (1896–1900)

In 1896, the U.S. Supreme Court upheld the constitutionality of racial segregation in the case of Plessy vs. Ferguson, in which Homer Plessy, an African American passenger on a train, refused to sit in the Jim Crow car designated for blacks.[1] By a 7–1 vote, the Court ruled that African Americans could be denied the use of certain public facilities as long as they were provided with "separate but equal" ones.

At the beginning of the new century, the African American population of Ohio numbered nearly 97,000, but its proportion of the overall population of the state had remained about the same for thirty years.

Expected Lynching, Summit County, March 1896—Cotell, Romulus [B]

At one o'clock in the morning on March 29, 1896, Alvin Stone and his wife were savagely murdered in their beds—cut to pieces and beaten—while they slept. Their daughters Hattie, age twenty-nine, and Emma, twenty-seven, as well as their servant, A.F. (or Ira) Stillson, were also clubbed in their Talmadge home. Members of one of the wealthiest and most prominent families in the region, the Stones, surprisingly, were not the victims of a burglary-gone-bad. Numerous articles of value, including two gold watches, were in plain sight.

Only one member of the family escaped unharmed: sixteen-year-old Flora, the youngest. Jumping out of bed, she observed a masked man hitting "Hattie over the head with what looked like a crow-bar."[2] As Hattie fell to the floor, Flora returned to her own room and hid under the bedclothes. A few minutes later, Hattie made her way to Flora's room where Flora asked her to "throw something over her head," but her younger sister was too frightened to move.[3]

Hattie then went to Emma's room, saw a ladder leaning against the house beneath an open window. She climbed down and hurried to a nearby farm to get help. Very quickly, the entire neighborhood was awake and hundreds gathered at the Stone house. The Akron police were summoned, arriving at nine o'clock that morning. Unfortunately, a steady downpour had washed away any trace of the culprit's trail.

Suspicion immediately fell upon John (or Frank) Smith. Two weeks earlier, he had been fired by Stone in a bitter dispute. However, most doubted he was guilty and police soon dismissed him as a suspect. Next, they turned their attention to Romulus Cotell (aka Lyman Strong or Antone B). Three years before, Stone had been largely responsible for convicting Cotell of horse theft. As a result, he was sentenced to three years at the Ohio Penitentiary.

Upon the arrest of Cotell for murder, there were fears that he might be lynched: "lynching is uppermost in everybody's mind."[4] He was confined in the Akron city jail, while Mayor Erastus R. Harper called for assistance from the Ohio National Guard on March 30, 1896. Company B, 8th Infantry, and Battery F, 1st Light Artillery—six officers and 101 men altogether—were immediately ordered to assemble at their armories. Both units were based in Akron and remained on duty for two full days.

While Cotell was in jail, Lillian Allen (alias Marion Archer), a Cleveland detective, coaxed a confession out of him, for which she was paid $100 by the county commissioners. Allen related that she had gone to Cotell's jail cell in Akron in the company of a group of women who conducted religious services. She assisted them and Cotell took a liking to her. By reading the Bible to him and praying with him, she won his confidence.[5] When asked whether she had made love to "Romie M.," Allen answered that she told him they could discuss it in further detail following his release from jail: "We detectives, you know, can't always choose our methods."[6]

Following arraignment before the mayor, Cotell was transferred to the Summit County jail. By then, the excitement in the streets had dissipated. A week later, Cotell claimed that he had nothing to do with the supposed confession. His attorneys were prepared to assert that he made the confession under duress and that he was not himself when he made it.

Nevertheless, Judge Kohler was satisfied the confession had been uncoerced. Flora would later claim that Cotell had entered her room the night of the crime and attempted to outrage her, possibly the original purpose for his breaking into the house.

Sentenced to be executed on November 6, 1896, Cotell was transferred to the Ohio Penitentiary in July 1896. However, doubts lingered about his guilt and his sentence was reduced to second degree murder. Finally, after seventeen years in prison, Romulus Cotell, age thirty-five, was released. The presiding judge, J.A. Kohler, had been seeking to have him freed for some time, suspecting Cleveland detectives had trumped up a case against him to collect the $1,500 reward money.

Mob Violence, Mahoning County, April 1896—Irey, William [W]

The Anti-Mob Violence Act (aka Anti-Lynching Law) introduced by Representative Harry C. Smith was passed by the Ohio General Assembly on April 10, 1896. Five days later, at the Quaker village of Damascus, a group of masked men called William Irey out of his house in the evening and covered him in tar and feathers. He had testified against two men for the dynamiting of the stone crusher at the county work house.

The previous winter, Irey had run away with the wife of George Enlett and had been living with her ever since. After he was released, he was threatened with hanging if he didn't leave the village. He said he would leave as soon as he had picked off all the feathers which was expected to take a couple of days.

Mob Violence, Logan County, May 1896—Benton. Mrs. [W]

Late in May 1896, a Mrs. Benton was removed from her home in West Liberty by a party of men and women who tarred and feathered her and then dunked her in a creek. She was warned to leave or they would be back to do it again. She was described as "a young woman whose manner of life was considered obnoxious."[7]

After they were gone, she crawled out of the creek and made her way home. The victim said she could not identify any of her attackers and no effort was made to round them up. Unfazed by her mistreatment, "Mrs. Benton was out early and paraded the streets, profusely decorated with flowers and wearing a large bunch of carnations on her breast."[8]

Attempted Lynching, Greene County, June 1896—Murray, Rome [unk]

On June 6, 1896, Rome Murray of Cedarville attempted to kill his wife and baby with a hatchet while drunk. They were left in precarious condition. "A crowd of enraged citizens seized and tried to lynch Murray, but he was taken to jail at Xenia before they could act."[9]

Mob Violence, Lucas County, September 1896—Huntsman family [W]

Huntsman, a wealthy farmer in Holland, ten miles from Toledo, was buried alive by White Caps on September 9, 1896. The incident began when two of his children were walking home from the post office. A couple of men in a buggy came driving up and accused them of stealing a pocketbook containing $80. Although the kids denied it, the men forced them to get into the buggy and drove them to the Huntsman farm before releasing them.

The next night, a party of men rode up to the Huntsman house and called the father out of bed. They seized him and dragged him outside where they administered a terrible beating. When they were finished, they carried him to a hole they had dug. Placing him in the ground, they covered him with dirt.

After a while, the men dug Huntsman up and beat him again before burying him once more. After more time had passed, they dug him up, repeated the beating, and warned him he had to leave the county within twelve hours. The two children had also been lashed.

For several days, the entire family hid out in the woods, afraid to return home. They were reluctant to notify the authorities so their neighbors did.

Attempted Lynching, Cuyahoga County, September 1896—Wald, Edward [B]

Edward Wald, a Cleveland ship carpenter, returned home intoxicated on the evening of September 27, 1896, and got into an argument with his wife. After he struck her, his fourteen-year-old son grabbed his arm and tried to calm him down. Instead, Wald hurled the boy down a twenty-foot stairway to the street, rousing the neighbors.

Some forty men forced their way into Wald's residence, broke down the bedroom door, and dragged him outside. A rope was called for, but the police arrived before it was produced. A tug of war ensued over Wald, who somehow broke loose and scurried down the alley toward the river. The mob gave chase.

Realizing he would likely die if apprehended, the fugitive plunged into the cold and muddy water of the Cuyahoga and drowned. His son was expected to die from his injuries and possibly his wife as well.

Mob Violence, Henry County, November 1896—W., Jim [W]

White Caps struck in Monroe Township on November 29, 1896. In reporting the tale, the *Democratic Northwest* omitted names, although everyone was well known. Apparently, a local farmer had died two years before, leaving a widow and seven children, two of them minors. Not long afterward, a tramp from Pickaway County stopped by and soon moved in. There was never any evidence of difficulties in the household, although the children were bothered by the outward appearance of this relationship.

Then on Sunday night, the widow and the tramp went to church as was their routine. When they returned home, they found the home fires were out and children were gone.

They rekindled the fires and were settling down when they heard a knock at both the front and rear doors simultaneously. Peering outside, they saw white robed figures moving about. The tramp—"a small, harmless creature"—was terrified.[10] The woman convinced him they should make a dash for the neighbor's house.

As soon as they slipped out the back door, they were chased down by five of the White Caps and captured at the barnyard gate. The tramp was knocked to the ground and lashed with rawhide until his entire body was seared and scarred. They only stopped beating him due to the pleading of the woman. The couple was allowed to return to the house only when the tramp promised to go back to where he came from the very next day.

The woman recognized the voices of some of their assailants and revealed their names.

The first thing Monday morning, the couple drove to Napoleon to get married. It was there they revealed what had happened:

> Now, Squire, you don't blame me for not going back on Jim after he had sparked me and gone with me for two hull years, do you? And I cared enough for him, too, to go through all this an' with three other fellows after me too, an' all three saloon keepers. I jest said to Jim, I'll die for you, Jim, an' Jim jest said to me, "Lavinia, I'll die for you," and we made up our minds to get married and stay right by 'em.[11]

The newspaper added that the accused White Caps "all live near Malinta and were well known and well-to-do citizens."[12]

However, an anonymous letter to the editor date December 7, sought to correct some of these facts. The author claimed that "Mr. W." was not a tramp, but came to the area three years before to work for a farmer. While he did make his home with the widow and her family, the husband had been dead seven years, not two. Furthermore, he was described as industrious, with no bad habits, and a member of the Knights of Pythias Lodge. Finally, he was on good terms with the widow's children and they had no objections to his marrying her. However, that changed when the home was offered for sale and they feared they might not get their share.

Threatened Violence, Clark County, March 1897—Jackson, George [B]

It was nearly four years later before another White Cap incident was reported. George Jackson, a black cabman who claimed to have driven Pearl Bryan, of Greencastle, Indiana, to her death and whose testimony was used as evidence against the defendants, Jackson and Walling, received a letter signed "Buckeye Regulators" on or about March 11, 1897.[13] It informed him that his coffin was ready unless he told the truth about the two dental students who were slated to be hanged at Ft. Thomas, Kentucky, for the murder of Bryan.

Expected Lynching, Richland County, June 1897—Pate, E. Hollis [B]

When Officer John E. Sellers, stationed at the junction of the Baltimore & Ohio and the Big Four railroads, about a mile and a half north of Shelby, attempted to arrest a tramp on June 3, 1897, he was shot through the stomach. He died the following morning at five o'clock, leaving behind a wife and children. His slayer, an African American man, was "captured after a hard struggle and taken to the town lockup."[14]

A mob collected within minutes, but chose not to lynch him for some reason. The grand jury subsequently charged E. Hollis Pate with first degree murder and he was convicted of manslaughter.

Lynching [TI], Champaign County, June 1897—Mitchell, Charles [B]

The lynching of Charles W. "Click" Mitchell on June 4, 1897, more than a year after the passage of the Smith Act, horrified the nation. The *New York Times* wrote, "There has not been and could not be a more inexcusable lynching."[15] It wasn't so much the way it happened, but where—not in the Deep South, but in Ohio.

Mitchell, a twenty-three-year-old hotel porter, was initially accused by Elizabeth "Eliza" Gaumer, forty-five, of coming to her Urbana home and beating her when she refused to sign a check for $500. However, when the charge was elevated to rape, Mitchell became a dead man walking. The widow of well-known newspaper publisher Dr. T. M. Gaumer was white, while her accused assailant black.

Using a wooden pencil as a clue, Officer Wooten tracked down the suspect. Upon his arrest, Mitchell was taken to the woman's bedside so she could identify him. She is reported to have said, "Hang the brute. How dare he face me?"[16]

Just two days later, Mitchell waived the reading of the indictment and pled guilty to the charge. Rumors soon spread that he had scratched, choked, and bitten the woman, and also suffered from a "loathsome disease."[17] He was sentenced to twenty years in the Ohio Penitentiary, the maximum penalty for the crime under state law. The news was quickly conveyed to the dozens of people standing outside the courthouse.

The *New York Journal* reported that "an excited mob surged around the Court House and jail," standing guard over every street leading from them.[18] An attempt to place Mitchell on a train to Columbus failed, despite the presence of the militia, because the station was overrun by an ever-increasing horde. So Sheriff Louis McLain prepared to defend the prisoner in the Urbana jailhouse and summoned a local militia unit, Company D of the Ohio National Guard, to assist him and his officers.

During an assault on the rear door of the building with sledgehammers, the troops opened fire. Two men fell dead in their tracks, two more died later, another was paralyzed for life, and at least seven others were wounded. Taking their dead and wounded with them, the mob retreated to the front lawn.

Despite the hostilities and the continued presence of an angry mob, Company D prepared to leave at seven o'clock the following morning. They fully expected that Company B, Third Infantry, from Springfield would be replacing them upon orders of Governor Asa Bushnell.

Telling them he hoped there would be no more shooting, Mayor C.H. Ganson asked the guard to put down their arms. He then addressed the crowd. He instructed them to remain orderly and control their feelings, although he seemed to approve their demand for vengeance. At that point, the Honorable Jesse M. Lewis, who had been present during the negotiations with the National Guard, shouted out, "There won't be any more shooting."[19]

Company B, under Captain Bradbury, arrived on a special train from Springfield at 7:10 in the morning. They disembarked just outside of town near the water works. Thirty-six strong, they marched through town, followed by a mob that hissed at them and pelted them with mud. Arriving at the jail, they found that 2,000 more people had assembled.

"We don't want you now," Jesse M. Lewis, a deputy sheriff, informed the captain.[20] Then Mayor Ganson stepped forward to address the militia. He assured them their services were not necessary because the people of Urbana were law abiding. He was confident they would assist him in preserving order. Finally, he told Company B they could leave the courthouse yard and he would send for them if they were needed. With that, the soldiers turned around and marched back to the depot.

Company D, meanwhile, having refused to stand guard any longer, made their way to the second floor of the sheriff's house where they tried to get some sleep. Already inflamed by a speech from Charles Gaumer, the victim's son, the mob, now estimated at 1,500 to 5,000, saw their opportunity and attacked the jail once more. This time, they met with no resistance.

Somebody had located the keys which had been hidden upstairs, but the crowd was too excited to wait, breaking the cell lock with a sledgehammer. While the local military and Sheriff McLain remained out of sight, Mitchell was forcibly removed from his cell, stumbling and falling on the steps, as the crowd shouted in triumph. He was beaten and kicked, and a noose was tightened around his neck. Those who had been successful in injuring him would later boast about it.

Mayor Ganson claimed he decided to surrender Mitchell to the mob in order to save lives. Seeing the horde of men, women, and children surrounding the court house, he was worried that someone might set off dynamite or that there would be a shootout between the troops and the citizens. "The sheriff was prostrated, worn out, and could do nothing," he said, "so I acted with his consent."[21]

Moving out to the public square, the mob stopped under a maple tree—not far from where Ullery had met a similar fate—while one of them flipped the rope over a limb. Mitchell was jerked up and down like a marionette, his head slamming against the tree limb a half dozen times, until his executioners were satisfied he was dead and tied the rope to an iron fence. Even then, some of them continued to strike and hack at Mitchell's corpse.

Many were so proud of their work that they did not shy away from being photographed beneath the dead man while he still was suspended by the rope. It was 7:20 a.m. before Mitchell's nearly unrecognizable corpse was at last dropped in a "rude box" beneath the tree so people from far and wide—men, women, and children—could parade by to view "that dead face, repulsive with bruises and blood" until three o'clock when it was removed by Humphrey, the undertaker.[22]

"Lawyers, doctors, merchants, bankers, owners of broad acres, the cultivated and intelligent of the little city came and looked and praised the deed. Their wives came, matrons and dames who lead the society of the place."[23] Souvenir hunters quickly stripped the corpse. They also peeled away the bark of the lynching tree and snipped off and passed around pieces of the rope. Mayor Ganson had attempted to have it removed from public display, but the crowd would not permit it.

As the *New York Times* reported,

> The body of Charles Mitchell, who was the cause of all the trouble, is an elephant on the hands of the city. Unclaimed by relatives, it was driven, amid the jeers of the crowd, to an undertaking establishment and then hidden. Threats of getting and burning it were freely made. Before being removed from the Court House yard relic hunters had nearly cut the coat off the dead man. Every button was gone, and even his shoes and stockings were taken off and carried away.[24]

The body was refused by a Columbus medical college, so it was carted off to the potter's field.

The animosity toward Sheriff McLain, Mayor Ganson, Captain Leonard, reached such a fever pitch that they fled town on a train to Springfield to save their own necks. At the same time, the local militia donned civilian clothes and quietly blended in with the crowd. Left unguarded, four other inmates in the jail escaped. Despite photographs

of the lynch mob and the fact that it took place in broad daylight, the grand jury failed to indict anyone for Mitchell's murder, claiming they lacked evidence.

When the family of Charles Mitchell sued Champaign County (specifically Sheriff McLain and Mayor Ganson) under the Smith Act, Judge Duston of the Common Pleas Court at Urbana declared that it was unconstitutional and that they were not entitled to collect damages. His opinion, however, was reversed by the Ohio Supreme Court a few months later. It wasn't until five years passed that a settlement was reached: $5,000 plus another $500 interest.

Journalist and anti-lynching crusader Ida B. Wells would later visit Urbana to investigate the truth of this matter and write a report debunking both the details of the crime, including the disease allegation, and Mitchell's alleged confession.

Attempted Lynching, Clermont County, June 1897—Unknown tramp [W?]

The tramp who assaulted Mrs. Emma (or Anna) Curds (or Curlis) on June 9, 1897, was very lucky he didn't get lynched. A highly regarded resident of Williamsburg, Mrs. Curds was left in critical condition.

In no time at all, a posse was on the trail of the culprit. "He was captured at Budd's brickyard, and Constable Bucker had all he could do to prevent a lynching, but the prisoner was removed secretly to Batavia to save his life."[25]

Presumably, the suspect was tried and convicted, but people had likely lost interest in the story by then.

Expected Lynching, Clark County, August 1897—Shafsall, Rollo [W]; Snyder, Dayton [W]

Rollo Shafsall and Dayton Snyder, two wealthy Dayton boys, allegedly assaulted two girls at St. Paris while out driving with them. Soon, residents of St. Paris and vicinity were organizing a band to lynch them.

When word reached Sheriff Thomas Shocknessy on the evening of August 27, 1897, he said he wasn't alarmed. Sheriff Louis McLain of Urbana had agreed "to let him know of any serious turn, and he had not heard from him," he said.[26] McLain had failed to protect Charles "Click" Mitchell at Urbana two months before.

Expected Lynching, Greene County, October 1897—Carter, William [B]

On the night of October 22, 1897, William Carter attacked Katie (or Kate) Swabb in a cruel and inhuman manner. She was on her way home from the fuse factory when he jumped her, beating and choking her before dragging her "to a lonely place."[27] Her cries were heard by Mrs. George Thornhill who rushed to her aid, striking Carter with a club until he ran off.

Throughout the night, crowds of angry citizens milled about in the streets of Xenia, "their mutterings were like the forecast of a storm which might break out at any time."[28] Meanwhile, a posse scoured the countryside in search of the accused.

In the midst of the excitement over the assault of a white woman by a black man, "Joseph McDonald, a prominent contractor, was sandbagged in the heart of the city by

Opposite: **When Charles Mitchell was lynched in Urbana on June 4, 1897, the deed was roundly praised by the most "cultivated and intelligent" citizens (gelatin silver print; image: 15.9 × 10.2 cm [6¼ × 4 in.], Harvard Art Museums/Fogg Museum, transfer from the Carpenter Center for the Visual Arts, 2.2002.3604. Imaging Department © President and Fellows of Harvard College).**

two colored men," presumably because of his stance on the Carter case.[29] James Townley, another white man, was attacked by another African American, but chased him off by shooting at him.

The *Maysville Evening Bulletin* claimed that the city was on the verge of a race war. Feelings were so intense that a lynching was expected and Governor Asa Bushnell asked to be kept informed of any developments. As one newspaper put it, "If the negro is apprehended there may be serious trouble."[30] The suspect had previously served a term at the Ohio Penitentiary for a similar offense.

When Carter was finally caught, Sheriff Grieve took him to Springfield where he pleaded guilty to criminal assault. A mob of several hundred had already congregated in anticipation of his arrival by train, but he was not on it, having been sneaked into town by the sheriff.

Just six months earlier, Carter had been fined and jailed for fifteen days for going "on a wild-west frolic"—i.e., brandishing a firearm while drunk, so he already had something of a reputation in the community.[31] The consensus was to get the trial over quickly. Described as the "Negro ravisher" in more than one newspaper, he was sent back to prison for fifteen more years.[32]

Expected Lynching, Brown County, November 1897—Davis, John [B]

On November 3, 1897, John Davis was talking to Judge John M. Markley in Georgetown about a burglary charge on which he had been found not guilty. Markley started to walk away and Davis called to him. When the judge turned to face him, Davis shot him in the center of the forehead.

Because there was strong sentiment for lynching Davis, he was taken to jail in Cincinnati. Although Markley was expected to die, he served two terms, ending in 1908.

Mob Violence, Henry County, November 1897—Roberts, May [W]; Roberts, Edith [W]

Two Ohio teenage girls were abducted by a group of White Caps who whipped, tarred, and feathered them. They were then left in a wood, "more dead than alive."[33] Their names were May and Edith Roberts, ages seventeen and nineteen respectively, and they lived in the village of Oakwood, twenty-five miles south of Holgate.

On the night of November 10 or 11, 1897, the young women were awakened by a band of eight to ten men entering their rooms. Ten days earlier, they had received a notice from the white caps warning them to leave the county, but they had not complied. Dragged from their beds dressed only in their night robes, the two women were taken out to the road. After being beaten with a cat o' nine tails, they were coated with tar and feathers and returned to their house.

The following morning, they were found unconscious by a passersby. May was in critical condition, her flesh having been cut to the bone by the tines of the whip. A card listing ten names had been attached to the front door, but none of them were recognized.

The St. George, Utah, *Union* editorialized: "Such accursed brutes should be promptly dealt with and rooted out of decent society. But what can you expect? Wickedness, murder, and riot are stalking abroad through the land and continues to grow worse and worse each year."[34]

Expected Lynching, Greene County, November 1897—Unknown man [B]

Mary Shepherd, age seventeen, of Cincinnati was visiting James Walters in Xenia.

On the night of November 16, 1897, she stepped out of the house to get a drink when she was jumped by a black man who choked and attempted to rape her. Newspapers reported, "If the negro is caught, a lynching will follow."[35]

Attempted Lynching, Hocking County, February 1898—Samson, Dr. S.H. [W]

Dr. S.H. Samson (or Sampson), was a physician in Laurelville. On February 5, 1898, he was charged with the murder of Bessie B. Neff, the daughter of a farmer residing at Adelphi.

After the coroner ruled that the girl had died in Samson's house as a result of "some drug" administered by him "for the purpose of performing a criminal operation" (undoubtedly an abortion), a mob of 300 quickly surrounded his home.[36] Its intent was to hang the doctor from the nearest tree. However, the local constable, accompanied by a group of some twenty armed men, was able to rescue Dr. Samson from the mob's clutches and spirit him off to the Laurelville jail.

There were two theories as to why the girl died. The first (and most probable) was that Dr. Sampson had accidentally given her an overdose of chloroform in preparation for the procedure. The other was that he had intentionally murdered her to prevent her from disclosing the father of her child. In either case, they felt the "quack" should die.[37]

The next day, there was an influx of people into the small community. An estimated 700 had come to attend the girl's funeral, but most remained to loiter about the jail. There was fear that another attempt to lynch Dr. Samson would occur before the next sunrise. But, evidently, he was not harmed. Instead, Marshal George Martin drove him to Logan and placed him in the jail there.

Apparently, Samson was released shortly thereafter for on May 11, 1898, the *Logan* (Ohio) *Democrat* reported that he was treating a fifteen-year-old boy for typhoid.

Expected Lynching, Hamilton County, November 1898—Unknown man [B]

Madisonville was considered "one of the most aristocratic suburbs" of Cincinnati, so there was great "indignation and excitement" when one of their own was assaulted by "an unknown negro" on November 17, 1898.[38] Sixteen-year-old Susan Williams was riding on horseback into town when the crime occurred. Afterward, she lay unconscious for three hours before crawling to a nearby house for help.

Officers at once set out with bloodhounds, scouring the countryside for her assailant. "If he is caught and identified a lynching is probable," wrote the *New York Times* correspondent.[39] A newspaper in Oklahoma editorialized, "The negro is a fiendish brute whether he lives in the North or South."[40] A Los Angeles newspaper simply headlined "A Case in Point"—the point being that a black man had not only crossed the color line, but also the class line.[41]

The following day, Thomas Fletcher was apprehended on an east bound train for matching the young woman's description of her assailant. He said he was from Georgia, but had boarded the train at Madisonville. There were other suspects rounded up as well, focusing on the "Bucktown" area of Cincinnati—Henry Collins, George Compton, and Edward Graham.

When presented to the victim, Susan immediately registered fright and recoiled when she saw Collins, saying that he looked very much like the man who had attacked her. However, they seemed to have narrowed their search to Squire Smith, "a degenerate of the worst type" who had "confessed that he has an uncontrollable fascination for white women."[42]

Attempted Lynching, Muskingum County, January 1899—Wright, E.S [W]

Fifty-year-old E.S. Wright had been jailed in Zanesville for criminally assaulting Sylva Taylor, the eighteen-year-old daughter of Edwin Taylor of Bridgeville. While he was being arraigned in court on January 21, 1899, some 500 people, many farmers, gathered outside, threatening to lynch him.

When an attempt was made to sneak him out of the building by a rear door, he was spotted and the crowd converged on him. Four officers surrounded him, their revolvers drawn, and were able to walk him safely back to the jail. It was feared that there might be additional trouble, but apparently nothing came of it.

Attempted Lynching, Wood County, March 1899—Zeltner, Paul [W]; Zeltner, John [W]

After killing an attorney named G.H. Westernhaver in Hoytville on March 25, 1899, two brothers named Zeltner went home to their farm three miles away. Once there, they took the wife of one of them into the cellar where they barricaded themselves against all comers. Even though a mob surrounded the house, it feared to venture too near because each time they approached they were fired upon.

One man was killed, one wounded, and a third pinned down behind a log. All that was keeping the posse from setting fire to the house was the presence of the woman, but it turned out that she was the one shooting at them.

After a company of militia arrived, the Zeltners were talked into surrendering. Marched to the railway station, they were placed on a train to the county seat of Bowling Green. Some 1,500 people had gathered there to see them. Companies H and K of the Second Regiment were brought in to provide protection.

The brothers, Paul and John, had previously killed the attorney after chasing him out of the courtroom at gunpoint, because he filed a suit against them to recover fees they owed him for another case. "From these facts," a reporter wrote, "it would appear that the Zeltners were of an ignorant, suspicious, revengeful nature, and the wonder is that they did not sooner commit murder."[43] Perhaps, they did.

John was sentenced to twenty years in prison and Paul to life. However, he was pardoned in 1913 following the release of his brother.

Expected Lynching, Clark County, April 1899—Lecknan, Carl [W]

Twenty-two-year-old Carl Lecknan (or Leckleben), a German tramp, entered the farmhouse of Mrs. James Hutseler near South Charleston, Clark County, on April 11, 1899, and shot her four times while her children looked on. He then picked her up and tried to stuff her into a burning stove.

Captured at Jeffersonville, Lecknan was jailed in London "to escape lynching at the hands of neighbors of the murdered woman."[44] He was later hustled off to Washington Court House when word reached London that a mob of 175 were in route from South Charleston. His motive was thought to be robbery.

Mob Violence, Ross County, April 1899—Kiniman, William [W]

By April 13, 1899, William Kiniman was noticeably absent from Deerfield Township after he had been tarried and feathered by his neighbors who objected to his relationship with a local woman.

Expected Lynching, Logan County, May 1899—Austin, Ernest [W]

After killing his mother and his brother in Middleburg on May 21, 1899, Ernest

Austin tried to kill himself—but failed. A coroner's inquest was held at the home of a neighbor where Austin was recuperating. Early on Sunday morning, Charles Haines was awakened by Ernest coming down the lane crying, "My God have mercy on me."[45]

After waking his father, the two men went out to the front porch where Ernest was lying in a growing pool of blood, a bullet wound in his chest. He said he had been shot by a stranger or strangers—robbers, probably—and pointed back toward his house which was in flames.

Ernest did not mention Mrs. Rachel Austin or her son Willie, who were lying dead inside the burning house, and the men were too preoccupied with ministering to him to ask about them. It was not until after a doctor was summoned and treated his wounds and they all walked back to his house that Ernest said anything about the other members of his family. It was speculated that Ernest had killed them, set fire to the house, and tried to kill himself. However, the flames stirred his sense of survival.

The Austins were notorious quarrelers and Ernest was known to be hot-headed. A servant who had left the house earlier reported that they were embroiled in a fight over some property. His mother said she would seek to have the court settle the matter on Monday, but Ernest said he wouldn't allow it. Placed under arrest, Ernest was kept under guard. Meanwhile, there was talk of lynching him if he recovered.

Dr. H.C. Rutter, superintendent of the state asylum in Gallipolis, was firmly convinced that for some days after the tragedy in which his mother and brother lost their lives, [Austin's] mental condition was such as to render him irresponsible for his acts or statements.[46] However, he emphasized it was a cautious statement. "It goes just far enough back to cover the prisoner's slips, and is not extended so far down the lines as to endanger the deeds he made."[47]

Ernest left a Bible in his cell in which he wrote that he was innocent of the charge. However, many in Logan County supposedly disagreed. They believed he was "possessed of the devil."[48] Three days after Christmas, the jury in Bellefontaine found Ernest guilty of "killing his mother and brother with an axe."[49] The defense planned to appeal.

Satisfied that he had been imprisoned for his crimes, the citizens of Logan County gave up any plans to administer their own brand of justice.

Expected Lynching, Lake County, May 1899—Kelly, Jefferson [B]

Jefferson Kelly, an African American, already had a bad reputation. He had recently been released from the workhouse when, on May 20, 1899, he saw Mrs. Wilhelmina Tucker, a fifty-year-old widow from Cleveland, walking down a country road. She was on her way to visit her sister in Painesville.

Approaching her from behind, Kelly threw her to the ground, but was scared off. He soon returned, choked and bruised her and tore off most of her clothes, but was frightened away once again by her screams. At this point, he attracted the attention of I.J. Taylor, a farmer, who shot him in the shoulder as he tried to flee. Taylor then placed him under arrest.

It was learned that Kelly had also encountered Mrs. Chilson and her daughter, Mrs. Manchester, on their way to church. He had tried to climb into their buggy, but they beat him off with a whip. There were conflicting reports that local farmers had collected, wearing masks, carrying revolvers, and talking of lynching the prisoner.

Sheriff St. John was aware of the threats, but not overly concerned. It was thought that Kelly was insane.

Mob Violence, Logan County, November 1899—Jackson, Nell [W]; Jackson, Edward [B]; Rickman, Dave [B]

On the evening of November 17, 1899, a masked mob numbering 100 broke into the "frail jail" at West Liberty, battering down the door.[50] Earlier, they had visited the home of the town marshal and demanded the keys, but he drove them away.

Their motive was to get their hands on thirty-five-year-old Nell Jackson, the widow of Grant Jackson (who had been tarred and feathered in 1892); Edward Jackson, age seventy, the widow's father-in-law; and Dave Rickman from Bellefontaine. Nell was white; the men were black.

All of them were given a severe whipping, stripped of their clothes, and tarred and feathered. They were then thrown into a stream, only to be pulled out again and driven out of town with clubs, stones, and occasional pistol shots.

The trio had been arrested for arson after a barn owned by City Marshal Krabell burned to the ground. Nell was suspected because of threats she had made previously. When the officers came to arrest the woman, Edward Jackson tried to stop them. Rickman was rounded up as well simply because he was staying with them. Not surprisingly, the arrests caused excitement in the town and the vicinity.

After the trio was tarred and feathered, Edward Jackson's barn was torn down and his horses turned loose. At first, Nell laid down on the ground and refused to move, but the mob beat her until she joined her companions. They made their way to Bellefontaine where Nell was in critical condition as a result of internal injuries sustained in the beating. Edward Jackson was nearly blind from vitriol thrown in his eyes and purportedly died.

However, in May 1901, Rickman was award $3,000 in damages, Jackson $1,000, and Nell $7,000.

Attempted Lynching, Portage County, January 1900—McGowan, Joseph [W]; Snyder, Dan [W]; Summers, Frank [W]

Burglars murdered Nathan K. Goss of Edinburg on January 13, 1900.

A leading merchant, Goss, age fifty-two, had been robbed so often that he installed an electric burglar alarm that was connected to his nearby residence. At one o'clock Saturday morning, it sounded. After hastily dressing, he asked a neighbor to join him and went to his store. As he entered by the front door, which had been forced open, the neighbor guarded the rear.

Goss was struck down by a volley of shots as three men rushed past him. The neighbor caught a glimpse of the trio as they continued in the direction of Palmyra. The suspects, described as tramps, were overtaken by a posse not far from town in an old barn. They were marched off to jail in Ravenna where over 1,000 people collected, threatening to lynch them.

On Sunday night, County Recorder F.W. Jones had a dream in which he found the murder weapon. "It was such a vivid dream that Mr. Jones, in company with Officer Goodenough, Detective Fowler, and Prosecutor Beckley visited the old barn yesterday."[51] However, by the time they arrived, an Edinburg resident had found the gun—a .32 caliber revolver—under a large plank nearby the granary, not more than twenty feet from where the suspects had been apprehended.

The three men gave fictitious names. Joseph McGowan identified himself as John McGowan, Dan Snyder as Frank Hull, and Frank Summers as Frank Hall. All three were indicted for first degree murder. During their confinement, a man called to see Snyder.

When Jailer John Washer told him there was no one there by that name, he pointed out the one who called himself as Hull. Furthermore, Washer recognized McGowan and Snyder as two of a number of tramps that had been locked up at Akron the previous week.

Summers was soon identified as the person who had bought a half-dozen .32 caliber cartridges from a Ravenna hardware store on Friday. And Pittsburgh Detective Perkins asserted that McGowan was "a dangerous crook."[52] It was suspected the same trio had committed a recent burglary in Greentown.

In March, all three men were sentenced to life at the Ohio Penitentiary for Goss's murder.

Expected lynching, Montgomery County, April 1900—Carter, John [B]

While strolling along a Dayton street on the evening of April 23, 1900, Harry and Daisy Frank, the children of Judge Frank, were assaulted by a black man who attempted to rape the young woman. As he came to his sister's defense, Harry, a high school student, was shot in the neck below the left ear. He was expected to die. But he had saved the honor of his sister, a teacher.

Although their attacker fled, it was felt that he "can hardly escape lynching" if caught.[53] Bloodhounds followed the trail to one John Carter. While he admitted having been close enough that he heard Daisy's screams, Carter denied being involved.

About 200 men bent upon lynching the suspect called upon the Frank home, but Daisy was in no condition to identify the man and the judge said the description did not match the suspect.

In the middle of May, Isaac Bass was arrested by Dayton police and identified by Harry as their assailant. The following month, Daisy failed to identify another suspect, which suggests Bass had been exonerated.

Attempted Lynching, Summit County, August 1900—Peck, Louis [B]

On August 21, 1900, six-year-old Christina Maas was abducted from in front of her home, taken to Perkins Woods and raped. She was white. The alleged assailant was Louis Peck, an African American, age forty or so. He had come to Akron not long before from Patterson, New Jersey, and taken a job as a bartender. About 5'4" and 157 pounds, Peck sported tattoos on his hand and arms. He also bore several scars on his face.

Having rented a horse and buggy under his boss's name, Peck was driving along Perkins Hill when he encountered the Maas children playing outside their home. He invited them to ride along with him, but quickly dropped the older children off (alternately, he offered Christina candy and left the others behind). At about dusk, Christina was found, bloody and beaten, wandering on Merriman Road, and the alarm went out.

A little after midnight, a freight train rolled into the Union Depot. Officer Duffy, who was patrolling the downtown railroad yard, was startled when Peck leaped from the moving train "almost into his arms."[54] Peck was immediately taken to the jail in the basement of the City Building at the corner of Quarry (now Bowery) and Main Streets. Left alone with John E. Washer, the keeper of the jail, he purportedly made a full confession which was taken down verbatim by a stenographer in the presence of R.W. Wanamaker, the prosecuting attorney. They learned that Peck was wanted back in New Jersey for a whole host of crimes.

After the newspapers got hold of the story, public sentiment against Peck was quickly whipped into a frenzy. They even went so far as to print his supposed confession in red ink. At five o'clock that evening, one "professional man" was heard to boast, "I'll be one of a hundred to go over and take him out of the jail and hang him."[55] He was not the first to make such a threat.

To his credit, Police Chief Hughlin Harrison, the city's first police chief, knew he had to act fast and did. He directed Sheriff Frank G. Kelly to take Peck and another black prisoner, William "Bug" Howard, to Cleveland at noon on April 22, where they were lodged out of harm's way in the Cuyahoga County jail.

Mob Violence, Summit County, August 1900—Akron Riot

The Akron Riot was one of the worst episodes of racial intolerance in Ohio history. Historian William B. Doyle would later describe it as the "perfect picture of hell" and the "Darkest Night" in the city's history.[56]

Throughout the afternoon of April 22, 1900, men began milling about the intersection of Howard and Main Streets. By evening, a mob had formed and marched on the City Building, demanding the surrender of the prisoner—Louis Peck—to them. However, he had already been moved to Cleveland.

The atmosphere was tense; rocks and bricks were tossed through the windows. A battering-ram was procured and an effort was made to break the north doors which led into the Mayor's Court. When it appeared they would give way, a policeman opened a window and fired his revolver above the heads of the mob (alternately, one of the rioters fired first).

There is some question about how much ammunition the police had on hand. By Doyle's account, they had only what was already in their revolvers and part of a box which was in Washer's possession. However, it was enough to slay four-year-old Rhoda Davidson, who was in a carriage with her parents. She was struck in the head by one of the officer's bullets. Similarly, ten-year-old Glen Wade also died when hit by one of the shots. In the hail of over 100 bullets, these two children were the only fatalities. Inside, Mayor Young, four city commissioners, Chief Harrison, and eight of his officers watched as tensions escalated.

From the window of the City Building, the mayor, whose offices were on the ground floor, attempted to explain that Peck had been moved to Cleveland, but the crowd didn't believe him. They demanded to see for themselves, so the mayor agreed to allow a half-dozen of the demonstrators (including one member of city council) to search the building. However, once the doors were open, the crowd poured in. When they did not find the prisoner, they turned their attention to the county jail.

Proceeding up the hill to the county buildings, the mob was stopped by Deputy Sheriff Simon Stone on the steps of the courthouse. He agreed to allow several members of the group to search the county buildings for Peck. Failing to find him, they retraced their steps to the City Building, still demanding the prisoner.

Many of the rioters had retreated only to return later with dynamite stolen from a construction site and guns and ammunition looted from a hardware store. Although the crowd had grown to 4,000–5,000, only 300–400 were actively involved in the demonstration while another 1,000–2,000 egged them on. Placing explosives around the foundation of the building, they hoped to breach the walls, but they proved to be too thick.

Another group of men set fire to the next-door Columbia Building. When firemen responded, the rioters shot at them, struck them with bricks, and chopped their hoses to pieces. Ultimately, the building collapsed. The violence did not end until four o'clock the next morning at about the same time that Chief Harrison fled from Akron, never to

Failing in their efforts to lynch Louis Peck, an Akron mob burned down the Summit County courthouse in 1900.

return to his job. The City Building, the Columbia building, the downtown fire station, and the courthouse were totally destroyed by fire. The mob finally broke up on Thursday morning, by which time the National Guard had begun arriving.

The chief of police had encouraged Washer with his wife and friends to go out on the town so he could tell the mob that the prison keeper had taken the prisoner away. As a result, Washer was at one of the summer resorts south of Akron when trouble broke out. Anxious about the situation at the jail, he tried calling the city building, but got no answer. Apparently, a very conscientious employee, he decided to return to Akron with his wife and drove directly into the mob on Main Street at about nine o'clock in the evening. Both of them were dragged from the buggy and two revolvers were shoved into his face. "It's blood we want, blood, blood, blood," one man said as he scratched Washer's face repeatedly.[57]

Mrs. Washer, meanwhile, her clothes half torn off, managed to fight her way to their apartment. Her husband tried to address the angry mob, but was struck on the side of a head with a brick. They carried him into a nearby drug store.

There was then a lull for a couple of hours, during which various city officials fled the premises, leaving the police chief and seven or eight of his men. But the crowd began to return around eleven o'clock. Although dynamite was set off at the City Building, it had little effect. At intervals, a police officer would step to a window and fire off five or six shots at the ground. Several more explosions occurred and some of the police slipped away into the darkness, each man looking out for himself.

The fire might not have been as devastating if it weren't for the fact that Columbia Hall, originally built as a roller skating rink, was of wood frame construction and acted as a tinderbox. Then there was the fact that the firefighters had been prevented from containing the blaze, forced to retreat under what was described as a "perfect fusillade" maintained by the rioters. The behavior of the mob led the *New York Times* of August 24, 1900, to speculate that there might possibly be a microbe that causes riots under the right conditions.[58]

Other fire companies responded and ignored the ruffians who tried to scare them away with their guns. The fire had now spread to the City Building, which was quickly enveloped in flames as well. It also fell. By four o'clock in the morning, nearly all of the thousands who had thronged the streets were gone and the policemen began to emerge from hiding.

Three hours later, Company C of the Eighth Regiment arrived from Canton. "The President's Own," as they were called, were welcomed by all of the law-abiding citizens of Akron. Although the city had two full companies of militia and some other semi-military organizations, efforts to call them out had failed. Only three or four reported to the armories. Most of them preferred to stand with the crowd and watch the fire.

After Probate Judge George M. Anderson found the mayor holed up in his house, he persuaded him to place a call to Governor George K. Nash for reinforcements. The Fourth Regiment of the Ohio National Guard was dispatched from Columbus on a special train and arrived at nine o'clock on the morning of August 23, 1900. All of the saloons were closed, law and order was restored, and Akron began to recover.

The next day, Peck was brought back to Akron, secretly tried, and in thirty minutes, and without benefit of legal counsel (no one would represent him), found guilty. He was immediately placed on a train for the Ohio Penitentiary in Columbus.

Forty-one men and boys were indicted as leaders of the rioters, which filled the county jail to overflowing. There were thirty convictions with penalties ranging from fines to imprisonment. The city councilman who had participated in the riots, however, was not one of them. He went free, as politicians are wont to do. Washer was subsequently awarded damages for the loss of his personal property.

Although many blamed the riot on outside agitators, ten days earlier members of a citizen's "Vigilance league" had posted notices on the home of African Americans living on the north side of town, warning them to leave within one week or they would be forcibly ejected. The ad-hoc group was upset that some blacks were buying houses in "the fashionable residence district of North Hill, which they occupy until their white neighbors pay an exorbitant price for their property to get rid of them."[59]

Thirteen years later on May 6, 1913, Louis Peck was pardoned by Governor James M. Cox because he had not received a fair trial.

Attempted Lynching, Delaware County, September 1900—Beeks, F. [B]

F. Beeks, a black barber, was forced to leave the city of Delaware on September 19,

1900, by "an enraged mob of 30 citizens."[60] They believed he had attempted to hypnotize G. Fauber, a white girl. Although he had been warned by the mayor and the marshal to get out of town, Beeks had not done so. As a result, armed citizens "with six ropes" seized Beeks, escorted him to the Hocking Valley Depot, and placed him on a train for Columbus.[61] There was little doubt a "hanging bee" would have taken place had he offered any resistance.[62]

On Thursday night, the African American citizens of Delaware threatened vengeance for the mistreatment of Beeks who continued to maintain his innocence. Having returned from Columbus that evening, Beeks was placed under the protection of 100 black men who assembled in the south end of town.

A mile or so north, 200 armed white men waited in the vicinity of Ohio Wesleyan University, ready to take some form of action if necessary. They had heard the threats by Beeks's defenders to shoot if any attempt was made to injure him.

One reporter warned that a race war was brewing in Delaware. The town was humming with excitement. It was rumored that Beeks had "assaulted several white girls" whose relatives had taken active roles in organizing the mob against him.[63] Later that same evening, a gang of white men stoned the house of a man named Alford. He was Beeks's employer and was giving him shelter. Several shots were fired, but no one was injured. After the police arrived, the crowd was persuaded to leave.

Despite the ruckus, Alford stated that Beeks would be back on the job Friday morning. While further trouble was anticipated, nothing else apparently transpired.

Mob Violence, Richland County, July 1900—Fockler, Cyrus B. [W]

John Alexander Dowie was an American religious figure who claimed to be "The Third Elijah." Born in Scotland, he moved to the United States in 1888 following an arson scandal. (A church he had built conveniently burned to the ground, enabling him to pay off his debts.) He soon developed a large following and a lucrative ministry as a faith healer in a pre–Pentecostal mode.

Setting up shop in Chicago, Dowie rented space adjacent to the World's Fair where he conducted "Divine Healings" of a fraudulent nature. He then founded what would become the Christian Catholic Apostolic Church in 1896, and four years later announced the creation of Zion, Illinois, a city which would operate on a theocratic political and economic model. Among its prohibitions were smoking, drinking alcohol, eating pork, and participation in modern medicine.

Zion would later be denounced as "a carefully-devised large-scale platform for securities fraud requiring significant organizational, legal, and propagandistic preparation to carry out."[64] At the time, he had some 6,000 followers.

During the summer of 1900, some followers of Dowie settled in Mansfield. The community may have already been suspicious of these strangers, but there were no reported incidents until the son of a sect member died because his mother declined medical help and another mother who had refused medical help went insane after her baby died at birth. As a result, some citizens of Mansfield made it known that the Dowieites were no longer welcome to settle among them. Sect members were subjected to harassment from residents of the city.

This was not unique. When Dowie went to Hammond, Indiana, he had been mobbed in the streets. While lecturing to medical students in Chicago, he required a police escort after he was met with stones, dead cats, and foul-smelling chemicals. He dubbed Mansfield

"Devilsfield" because of the frequency with which his elders came under attack. The propensity for his followers to die due to lack of medical care had generated so many lawsuits that he decided to abandon his Chicago base.

As early as July 21, 1900, Elder Cyrus B. Fockler, who was Dowie's representative in Mansfield, was attacked by an angry mob, but managed to escape. When he returned from Chicago ten days later, he was forcibly taken from his room in the Vonhof Hotel to the gas house, stripped of his clothing, and smeared with oil. He was finally rescued by the fire department who spirited him away on the hose truck. Although the mayor and several police officers drove him out of town, Fockler said he would return. A week or so later, a mob interrupted a Dowieite meeting, kidnapped two elders, stripped them naked, and painted them blue.

Mob Violence, Richland County, September 1900—Bassinger, Ephraim [W]; Leiby, E.H. [W]

Twenty-five members of the Christian Catholic Church were holding a meeting at the Mansfield home of Dowieite E.H. Leiby on the morning of September 16, 1900, when the house was surrounded by a stone-throwing crowd. Elder Ephraim Bassinger of Bluffton, who was conducting the service, was specifically threatened.

For three Sundays in a row, the police had sent him out of Mansfield in an attempt to head off trouble. After rescuing him from the mob, they shuttled him to the railroad station where some 500 people gathered.

Foiled in their attempt to lay hands on Bassinger, the mob returned to the Leiby home, broke open the doors, and seized him and two other members of the church. Returning with their captives to the station, they were greeted by a crowd that had expanded to 1,500 people.

The three men were taken by the police and placed on a train to Crestline. According to the *New York Times*, the only thing that kept them from being tarred and feathered was the fact it was broad daylight.

Mob Violence, Richland County, September 1900—Moot, Silas [W]; Bassinger, Ephraim [W]

On the morning of September 23, 1900, Silas Moot of Lima and Ephraim Bassinger, two elders in the Dowieite church, were kidnapped by a crowd of 6,500 people, painted with bucketsful of tar, and paraded through the streets of Mansfield. When Moot resisted, he was beaten and kicked into submission. As they stumbled along arm-in-arm, tar dripping from their hair and beards, the two men were pelted with missiles and taunted with cries of "Two little boys in black," "Hang them!" and "Will you know enough to stay away from Mansfield now?"[65]

The men had arrived in Mansfield early Sunday morning and were recognized as soon as they stepped off the train. Rebuffed in their attempt to hire a carriage, they started walking into town. Soon, 200 people had collected, impeding their way. Both men were roughed up, particularly Moot, whose right eye and nose were disfigured.

Taken a mile away to the Richland Buggy Company, they were ordered to strip. Bassinger complied, but Moot did not and had much of his clothing ripped away. They were then placed in a vat and had tar poured over them and painted on with brushes. Afterwards, they were allowed to don what few clothes they had left.

Following their rescue, Moot and Bassinger were driven to police headquarters where over a period of two hours the tar was removed through the application of lard,

Vaseline, and benzene. Following a bath, they were dressed in a change of clothing donated by a local store.

Because it was rumored that William H. Piper, overseer-at-large for the Dowieites, would be arriving from Chicago, a throng of people continued to meet every train. Consequently, when Moot and Bassinger were escorted by police to the Erie depot at noon, they had to once more pass through jeering crowds. As the two elders were placed on the train to Lima, they said they would not be returning to Mansfield if they could avoid it.

Such was the disdain for the Dowieites, a large group of people visited the homes of local church members in search of other Dowie elders. Some of the local Zionists made it known that they would be moving to more "congenial towns."[66]

On September 24, 1900, two church elders from Hammond, Indiana, arrived in Mansfield and registered in a hotel. As soon as the police learned about their presence, they picked them up and drove them out of town to avoid any trouble. Attacks upon the members of Dowie's church continued through the summer and fall. Leaders were beaten, painted blue, and driven out of town. The police had to start providing protection during their services.

In October 1900, the Dowieites were making a determined effort to colonize Mansfield. About three a day were being kicked out of town and others were in hiding, holding religious services in secret. City police officers were putting them on trains out of town even as county sheriffs were rescuing others. It was not unusual for people to chase and stone them when they were out on the streets. There were gangs of citizens supplied with tar and fears, searching the city for them.

Mob Violence, Richland County, November 1900—Loblaw, Mark [W]; Unknown woman [W]; Lieby, E.H. [W]

At noon on November 4, 1900, a vigilance committee composed of several hundred men and boys captured Mark Loblaw, a Dowieite elder from Chicago, and a woman companion, assumed to be his wife, when they were discovered within the city limits of Mansfield. Held for two hours, they were then forced to buy train tickets for Galion, Ohio, and sent on their way.

E.H. Lieby, a local church member who was accompanying them, was chased to a swamp and evaded capture. Another unidentified elder was also apprehended by a citizen, conveyed to the Erie Depot, and placed on the same train. Both men were roughed up by the crowd. When the unknown elder tried to address the people from the rear platform of the train, they threw stones at him.

Seventeen people were indicted for these attacks, but nothing came of it. Incredibly, charges were filed against a number of Zion church members as a consequence of the "Dowie Riots." Those indicted included John Alexander Dowie, Overseer Piper, and a half-dozen elders including Fockler. The charge was "utterance of libelous matter."[67]

The charges were dropped a year later along with charges of complicity against eight Mansfield followers. Mayor Huntington Brown used his powers of persuasion to convince the Dowieites to abandon their attempts to establish a church in Mansfield.[68]

7

The United States of Lyncherdom (1901–1909)

Mark Twain wrote a short essay in 1901 entitled "The United States of Lyncherdom" after three men were lynched in his home state of Missouri. He planned to use it as an introduction to a proposed book on the topic. But he soon abandoned the project because he believed he wouldn't "have even half a friend left down there [in the South], after it issued from the press."[1]

Attempted Lynching, Morgan County, January 1901—Weinstock, Walter A. [W]

A young woman, Nellie Morris, age nineteen, was returning home from the post office in Hackney on January 4, 1901. While crossing a field, she encountered Walter A. Weinstock, a year younger, who lived near her. Justifiably wary of him (it is believed he had propositioned her), Nellie began to run, but Weinstock immediately grabbed her and threw her to the ground. Somehow, she managed to push the powerfully built young man off and got back on her feet. At this point, he drew a razor from his pocket and cut her throat, severing neck muscles and opening the jugular vein.

As her life ebbed away, Nellie continued to fight back, seizing the razor. Her fingers, wrist, and both arms were badly cut and her dress was shredded, leaving her practically naked. The daughter of Benjamin Morris, a local businessman, Nellie was "prominent in society in this city and Parkersburg."[2] Weinstock, on the other hand, had just been released from the Ohio State Reformatory after attempting to kill his father, Jacob Weinstock, a wealthy Morgan County farmer.

A crowd of men apprehended Weinstock and trussed him up, binding his hands and feet with rope. They then placed him in a building while more than 1,500 people collected outside. A phone call was made to McConnelsville, notifying law officers to come for him. In the meantime, the people of Hackney were growing impatient and at ten o'clock in the evening were thinking of transporting him to the jail in Marietta. They apparently didn't, for an hour later some of them began to organize a lynch mob.

A tree had been selected and a rope procured. As the *Akron Daily Democrat* reported, "A crowd collected at Hackney when the crime became known, and only a leader was needed to carry out the threat of lynching. Miss Morris saved her honor, but it was probably at the expense of her life."[3]

In the end, Weinstock wound up being taken to the county jail in McConnelsville where the influence of his father kept the girl's neighbors from hanging him. And, as it turned out, Nellie didn't die. Although she was badly mutilated, her father spoke out on behalf of allowing the justice system to handle the matter.

Expected Lynching, Guernsey County, July 1901—Bisby, William [B]

The Taylors were well known in Steubenville where they were married on July 4, 1896, with 5,000 people looking on. Grant Taylor had wed Mary Witherall to celebrate the opening of Pleasant Heights Driving Park by the Knights of Pythias. Afterward, they were presented with a handsome bedroom suite.

Five years later, the Taylors were the most reviled couple in the hamlet of King's Mines.

Early on the morning of July 29, 1901, William (or Lawrence) Bisby (or Busby), a black man, was accused of "criminal intimacy" with Taylor's wife.[4] It was not the first such accusation made against her—and with a number of different men. In fact, the Taylors had previously been served with White Cap notices. However, Taylor paid no attention to the warnings, but "armed himself and threatened to shoot anyone interfering with him or wife."[5]

This time the accuser was Mack Sheldon (or Shelton). He had run into Bisby at the company store and told him his neighbors were not going to put up with his behavior much longer. Angered by his remarks, Bisby picked up a stone and attacked Sheldon, knocking out an eye and fracturing his skull.

Sheldon's brother, Melvin (or Melville), and Joseph Reedon rushed to Mack's aid. However, Bisby had fled to his house, armed himself with a shotgun, and barricaded himself in an upper room. Meanwhile, Taylor appeared on the scene and defended his wife's conduct. In response, Sheldon and Reedon drew their revolvers and fired at Taylor who fell to the ground.

Though mortally wounded in the heart, hip, and shoulder, Taylor managed to prop himself up on one elbow and shoot Sheldon in the abdomen and Reedon in the stomach. Both were likely to die. A total of twenty-three shots had been fired.

At about 8:00 a.m., Sheriff Joseph B. Dollison of Guernsey County received a telephone call notifying him of the trouble at King's Mines. When he arrived, he was accompanied by Deputy Gallop, Marshal Wilken, and Coroner Vorhees. The miners—several hundred in number—were still quite agitated by the shootings and were talking openly of lynching Bisby.

Although the Sheldon brothers and Reedon had been carried to their homes, Taylor's body had been left to rot in the sun because of the public antipathy toward him. The coroner had to coax the miners to move it to Taylor's house.

If it had not been for the timely arrival of Sheriff Dollison, it is likely that Bisby would have been killed. Consequently, he happily surrendered to the sheriff and begged to be taken to jail as quickly as possible.

Expected Lynching, Muskingum County, September 1901—Unknown man [W]

An unidentified temperance orator was nearly lynched in Zanesville in September 1901. Nothing else is known about the incident.

Attempted Lynching, Summit County, May 1902—Brant, Will [B]; Upshaw, Thomas [B] Coney, Charles [B]

Three African American men attacked a young woman named Bertha Moore near Cuyahoga Falls on May 17, 1902. Scared off by her screams, the men fled with her purse containing $3. A group of workmen at the Cuyahoga Falls Wire and Steel Company gave chase.

Newspapers reported, "The negroes were seen to swim the river and run up the railroad tracks toward Hudson."[6] Commandeering a hand car near Metz, the workers soon overtook the woman's assailants and brought them back to Cuyahoga Falls. They were met by a huge crowd.

If it hadn't been for the arrival of Sheriff F.G. Kelly and a couple of deputies, the culprits would have been lynched in the opinion of the reporter. Will Brant (or Brent) and Thomas Upshaw were sentenced to the Ohio State Reformatory, while Charles Coney was sentenced to the Ohio Penitentiary. The details of the criminal assault upon the young woman were withheld from the public for fear they would give rise to a lynching.

Attempted Lynching, Franklin County, June 1902—Williams, Charles [B]

Andrew Jackson was in a Bad Lands saloon in Columbus on June 22, 1902, enjoying a can of beer. When he refused to share it with him, Charles Williams pulled a knife and slashed Jackson across the abdomen, killing him. "A frenzied mob of colored people" (both Jackson and Williams were African Americans) chased after Williams, catching him at the corner of High and Long Streets.[7] They were preparing to hang him from a telephone pole when Detective Richard Owens spotted them from a passing street car.

Leaping off the moving vehicle, Owens rescued Williams from the mob, but not before Williams tried to cut him. At that point, a member of the mob clobbered Williams over the head with a billiard cue, knocking him to the ground and, in all probability, saving the detective from injury.

Although unarmed, Owens fought back the crowd until he was joined by Officer Mike O'Rourke. They then took their prisoner to the city jail.

Jackson had come to Columbus from Roanoke, Virginia, where he worked for a white planter. The planter's daughter had fallen in love with the black man and they ran away together. Authorities from Virginia tracked them to Columbus and endeavored to have Jackson extradited back to Virginia. However, Governor George Nash refused to honor the request because the couple had married since arriving in Ohio.

Unfortunately, the mixed race couple did not live happily ever after. Since arriving in Columbus, Jackson had been arrested several times for beating his wife. And now he was dead.

Expected Lynching, Lucas County, June 1902—Potter, Reuben C. [W]

In June 1902, Reuben C. Potter was placed on trial in Toledo for the attempted murder of his mother, Elizabeth Potter, age eighty-four. When it was time for her to testify, she had to be helped into the courtroom. She related how her son had struck her repeatedly with his fist, breaking her jaw in three places, and then locked her in a room to die. A reporter believed that "all the crowd lacked was a leader to drag the son out of the courtroom to administer lynch law to him."[8]

Mrs. Potter said she made her escape at two o'clock in the morning, crossing the fields to the home of a neighbor. Potter responded that his mother sustained the injuries by falling down the stairs. In fact, he swore that his love for her was so strong that he kissed her whenever they parted, which she also denied. However, the only threat of lynching came from the pen of the reporter.

Attempted Lynching, Lucas County, July 1902—Bower, Charley [W]

Five-year-old Charley Bower was strung up on July 27, 1902, in Toledo by a group of boys age ten to fourteen who were playing at lynching. If it hadn't been for the chance arrival of some workmen, he likely would have died. He was hanging from a tree limb, his face purple, and his tongue protruding. His lynchers fled as soon as they saw the men coming. Police said they expected to arrest them, but there is no indication they did.

Attempted Lynching, Ashtabula County, August 1902—Crooms, John [B]

The *Akron Daily Democrat* found it hard to believe that there had been an attempted lynching in Jefferson. The town was "a veritable hot-bed of Abolitionists in the old days and if a lynching were to take place there now it is very certain that many a lamented citizen would turn over in his grave, if the dead ever do such things."[9] And, yet, it did.

Late on the evening of August 18, 1902, John Crooms (or Croons), an African American, broke into the home of Harriet and Sabina Hopkins, apparently to commit a burglary. The victims were two poor and feeble women over the age of eighty. It was feared they both would die from shock. However, they were able to identify their attacker and Crooms was quickly apprehended.

Confined in the local jail, Crooms was closely guarded while a mob surrounded the building, intent upon lynching him. The women in the crowd were especially vocal. The reason for the mob's outrage was the manner in which Crooms assaulted the women. He chewed the ear off one of them and bit a hunk of flesh from the arm of the other. He left his hat and part of his clothing behind when he fled their home.

But when the sun came up, reason prevailed. The mob was promised the prisoner would be dealt with in a speedy fashion. Crooms was arraigned the following afternoon on a charge of felonious assault. He immediately pled guilty and was sentenced to life in prison at hard labor on September 30, 1902. His victims ("the Misses Hotchkiss") had not fully recovered from the attack.[10]

Attempted Lynching, Lawrence County, November 1902—Glasco, William [W]

On Thanksgiving evening, 1902, William Glasco (aka Glassby or Glasso) assaulted Mary Maloney. Following the preliminary hearing, he was housed in the Scioto County jail in Portsmouth as a precaution against possible lynching, but then returned to Ironton for trial.

Shortly before three o'clock on the morning on November 29, 1902, a mob attempted to abduct Glasco from the jail, but was prevented by an armed force of officers and police. Just as they were readying their attack, Glasco was placed in a carriage that struck off toward the northwest. It was presumed he was being transported to the Portsmouth jail by a roundabout way.

Glasco admitted to assaulting Maloney in revenge for her brother hitting him. She remained in serious condition from a blow to the head. Alerted by her screams, people came to her aid and Glasco was tracked down by bloodhounds brought in from Dayton. They arrested him in a saloon. Thousands of enraged citizens had helped in the chase and continued to fill the streets throughout the night. The authorities sensed they were planning to lynch the prisoner.

Finally, the mob assembled at Engine House No. 2. Fifty men were selected as leaders as they moved en masse to the armory where they demanded the keys so they could obtain rifles and ammunition. Captain Thompson, commander of the militia, refused and they opened fire with pistols. He was lucky to escape uninjured.

Foiled in their attempt to obtain additional arms, the mob marched upon the jail. This time it was Sheriff Taylor who refused to surrender the keys. When the mob left to secure battering rams, the sheriff spirited the prisoner out of the rear of the jail and drove him to Portsmouth.

Sheriff Taylor then transported Glasco to Gallipolis by buggy, by which time the leaders of the mob realized it was futile to continue their pursuit. Instead, they decided to await his return to Ironton. In December, he pled guilty to assault with intent to kill and was sentenced to fifteen years in the Ohio Penitentiary.

Mob Violence, Wood County, February 1903—Elstadder, Harvey [W]

Harvey Elstadder, "a worthless fellow, who had accumulated little beyond a lot of debts, a bad reputation and a large family," lived near Trowbridge.[11] After nearly beating his wife and young son to death, Elstadder was paid a visit in February 1903 by fifteen to eighteen white-robed men with a rope and several horsewhips. They removed him from the hovel in which he lived, tied him to a tree, and whipped him soundly. His screams could be heard for half a mile.

The White Caps then gagged Elstadder, placed him on his stomach, and beat him with wooden paddles. When they had finished, they warned him that if he ever mistreated any family member again, they would return to tar and feather or even hang him. He promised that he would behave and then, unable to walk, was allowed to crawl home.

Mob Violence, Wood County, February 1903—Irene, William [W]

Two nights after Elstadder's encounter with the White Caps, William Irene of Portage was captured by a score of well-disguised men who dragged him to a spot outside the village. He stood accused of neglecting his invalid wife and sick child.

Having prepared a large bucket of tar and two pillow cases full of feathers, the party of vigilantes was ready to apply them to the struggling man. However, Irene was able to break free and run for his life. The White Caps were unable to recapture him.

Mob Violence, Sandusky County, March 1903—[TL] Sissie, Chub [W]

Some forty masked men took "Chubb" Sissie from his home near Rollersville in March 1903, and nearly whipped him to death. Sissie was so badly injured that he had to be carried home by several of his assailants, who warned him they would return to hang him if he ever abused his wife again. It was thought he would not be able to walk for a week.

Sissie purportedly was in the habit of getting drunk and mistreating his wife. He had driven her out of the house in the middle of the night with a knife, forcing her to seek refuge with neighbors. Sissie, it was said, liked to drag her about the house by her hair or pull her head back and draw a knife across her throat. On three occasions, he had drawn blood.

Mob Violence, Lucas County, March 1903—Higgins, Harvey [W]

The *New York Times* reported in March 1903 that "a band of White Caps, composed of 200 of the better class of young farmers, has undertaken the moral regenerations of Northwestern Ohio."[12] It went on to explain that it was organized into three or four sections and had the "quiet sanctions" of the authorities. There were also unconfirmed rumors of floggings near Kalida and Bettsville and numerous warning notices had been mailed out.

Harvey Higgins lived near Bono or Big Ditch. Described as a "worthless ne'er do well," he was said to beat his eight-year-old twin girls while drunk.[13] Consequently, a group of vigilantes took him from his home in March 1903, stripped off his clothes, and struck him with tree branches until the blood ran down his legs. They then coated his back and legs with tar and goose feathers. He was told his next punishment would be even more severe.

Expected Lynching, Madison County, May 1903—Eckles, Howard [W?]

Howard Eckles, wanted for the rape of Lillie Henry, age ten or twelve, was brought back to London on May 12, 1903, by Detective Maley Thompson. Upon learning of the assault, an uncle of the little girl had chased Eckles, age twenty-one, with an axe and would have slain him had not the suspect left town.

There was a huge crowd awaiting him at the depot. Eckles assumed they were there to hang him and was justifiably terrified. However, Thompson took his prisoner off the opposite side of the train and hurried him to jail.

Attempted Lynching, Crawford County, June 1903—Dilling, Frank [W]

Late on the afternoon of June 14, 1903, Frank Dilling, a Portuguese section hand for the Pennsylvania Railroad, was biding his time at the Emerson House Café in Crestline when George Cook, a plasterer, said something that offended him. In a flash, Dilling shot the twenty-eight-year-old man "through the heart" before he had a chance to defend himself.[14] Dilling then dashed out of the saloon with an angry band in pursuit.

As word of the shooting spread, the mob grew. Dilling must have been out of ammunition because his pursuers freely pelted him with stones and other missiles. Finally, they dragged him to the ground and began pounding him with clubs. Twice he escaped and twice he was retaken.

Just as a rope was being procured to hang him, the police arrived. So the would-be lynchers took off, leaving Dilling for dead in the street. The police carted the unconscious man to jail where they revived him.

When they heard that Dilling was still alive, a crowd began to assemble at the Crestline jail, threatening to hang him. For his safety, the police smuggled him out of the jail and into a closed carriage that set off for Bucyrus at a full gallop.

Late that evening, the vehicle arrived in the county seat. "The horses were covered with foam and showed very hard driving."[15] Inside were two officers with drawn pistols and their badly injured prisoner. Once he was lodged inside the jail, County Sheriff John Gebhardt ensured he had enough reinforcements to keep Dilling safe.

A dispatch from Bucyrus noted that people were arriving from Crestline via "electric cars and rigs" and forming a mob around the Bucyrus jail.[16] Still, the police were optimistic that they could prevent further violence and, apparently, they did.

Attempted Lynching, Lorain County, July 1903—Pleasant, Robert [B]; Hall, Charles [B]

Two African Americans, Charles Hall and Robert Pleasant, got in a dispute with a white man, Daniel Cronan, on July 28, 1903, in Lorain. One of the black men slashed Cronan on the face and neck with a razor. Almost instantaneously a mob appeared, threatening to lynch the two men. They fled at once.

Chased through the south end of the city, Hall and Pleasant ducked into a local saloon, which was barraged with stones. In the confusion, the two men managed to escape. Calling out both the day and night shifts of his force, the chief of police also deputized some local men to assist with the hunt.

About nine o'clock the same evening, Pleasant was picked up and lodged in the town jail. Hall, on the other hand, was discovered by Robert Stack hiding in the pantry of his home. The two men struggled over Stack's gun until Hall darted outside. Although a mob saw him behind Stack's house, he evaded them and dashed toward the railroad station.

Hoping to deescalate the situation, Mayor F.J. King addressed the citizens who were milling around in the in street. He informed them that Cronan would be all right and asked them go home. They did, but only after taking out their pent up anger on a black-owned saloon and barbershop.

Then signs began to be posted about town blaming the blacks who lived there for the increase in crime and urging them to leave town. In response the Legion of Laborers, an African American organization, passed a resolution stating that the black community would "aid at any time in ridding the city of all niggers, regardless of race, color, nationality or previous condition" who were part of the criminal element.[17]

Pleasant was subsequently charged with intent to kill, but Hall was never found.

Expected Lynching, Hardin County, August 1903—Nickolson, William [B]

William Nickolson, a "mulatto," was suspected of having shot Harry Minard to death in his home, three miles outside Kenton, on or before August 1, 1903. He purportedly confessed to his sister and then fled with $200 he had stolen from his sixty-year-old victim. A posse set out after him and there were threats that he would be lynched if found.

Expected Lynching, Darke County, August 1903—Potter, George [W]

At Hagerman, there were threats of lynching George Potter, the accused murderer of Daniel Randolph (or Rudolph), his employer. Randolph had hired Potter, age thirty-five, a few weeks earlier to help with the harvest. Since then, he had been living with the family and the two men slept in the same room. Daughter Sadie, age fifteen who served as the housekeeper, slept in an adjoining one.

During the night of August 13, 1903, Sadie was awakened by someone pressing something cold against her face before knocking her unconscious. She also may have been grazed by a bullet. When she came to, she woke up her brother and they entered her father's room together. They found him dead in a pool of blood. He had been shot and his skull had been crushed. Potter was asleep beside the lifeless body.

Upon being awakened, Potter leaped from the bed and expressed surprise that Randolph had been murdered. He then hurried to a neighbor's house to raise the alarm. After a posse was assembled, he told them that robbers had entered the house and stolen $30 and a revolver from his trouser pocket. However, Randolph's clothes, which contained about $50, had not been disturbed.

Although Sadie discovered that the pantry window was open and Potter suggested the burglar had entered through it, she later identified Potter as the guilty party in a statement to the coroner. He was promptly jailed in Greenville, the county seat.

Newspapers reported threats of lynching, but they were not carried out. Instead, Potter was convicted of murder in the first degree and sentenced to life in prison.

Mob Violence, Sandusky County, September 1903—Hush, John [W]

John Hush of Clyde was accused by his neighbors of mistreating his wife and ten-day-old baby, including driving them out of the house while drunk. As a result, the baby died on September 27, 1903. In retaliation, his co-workers at the sauerkraut factory shoved a hose down his shirt and up his pant legs and turned on the water full force. There was also talk that the White Caps might pay him a visit.

Attempted Lynching, Butler County, October 1903—Spivey, Joseph [W]

On October 1, 1903, the Spivey brothers from Kentucky were visiting Edward Richardson in Billingsville, Indiana, when they decided to go to Oxford, a few miles across the state line, for the annual street fair and farmers' exhibition. They arrived to find the town teeming with strangers.

While patronizing one of the saloons, the trio pulled their revolvers on a bartender who somehow managed to evict them from his establishment. They continued their misbehavior in other saloons until Marshall John Woodruff attempted to place them under arrest. They shot him dead.

Moving out into the street, the Spiveys began firing wildly into the crowd. Deputy Marshal Jacob Manrod endeavored to take them into custody, but was felled by a bullet in the back and a shoulder. Ernest Jotten, a school teacher, was shot in the abdomen as he attempted to return to his boarding house.

The Spiveys then fled in separate directions with men chasing after them and throwing rocks. Joseph Spivey sustained a skull fracture. Louis Spivey was seriously shot in the back. All three men were rounded up and conveyed to the village jail, although Richardson was released when it was realized he had not participated in their misdeeds.

When the three groups of pursuers met at the jail, they clearly had not cooled off. Soon they battered down the doors, removed Joseph Spivey from his cell, and wrestled him outside. A noose was placed around his neck and he was hauled from place to place about town.

On three separate occasions, Spivey was suspended from three different trees, but escaped with his life. The mob, in its haste, had neglected to bind his arms and legs, so he was able to use them to prevent his strangulation. On another occasion, he was granted a reprieve so he could write a farewell letter to his wife and children. And on a third, Deputy Sheriff Luke Brannon bravely broke through the crowd and cut the rope before the deed could be completed.

Upon learning that a lynching was in progress, Brannon had driven to Oxford from Hamilton. Undeterred by the mob, he forced his way to Spivey's side, wrested him away from the ringleaders, and pushed his way to the jail where the prisoner was safely locked in a cell. His actions no doubt prevented many people from committing murder and likely helped to elect him to the office of sheriff the following month.

Order was sufficiently restored that the crowd listened to speeches by Mayor Flannigan, the Reverend Thomas J. Potter, and the brother of the marshal. Whether their words would have appeased them is unknown because, while they were speaking, the officers had smuggled the Spivey brothers out of the building through the cellar and up the coal chute. From there, they were secretly transported to the Butler County jail in Hamilton, fifteen miles away.

Perhaps remembering the fate of Henry Corbin, newspapers reported that the black citizens of Oxford who were part of the mob protested every time that Joseph Spivey was given a reprieve. Some even said that, had he been a black man, he would surely have been lynched without any regard for his appeals. However, at least one reporter felt that the only thing that saved him was the appeal by Woodruff's brother to let the law take its course.

Physicians attending the Spiveys in Hamilton said that both men were in serious condition. Louis, who had been shot, was in such bad shape that no further probing of his wound for the bullet could be undertaken. Although Joseph was likely to recover, he would long suffer the effects of his scalp wound. They confessed they had been in previous shooting scrapes and had spent time at the penitentiary in Frankfort, Kentucky, for shooting to kill.

Attempted Lynching, Franklin County, March 1904—Anderson, William [B]

William Anderson, an African American barber living in Lockbourne, was lucky he had friends. A quiet, law-abiding fellow, age twenty-two, he enjoyed a good reputation in the village. However, that did not prevent him from being charged with attempting to rape twelve-year-old Martha Gouldner, daughter of George Gouldner, while she was walking home from the grocery store on March 15, 1904. He may have been accused of assaulting another young girl as well; the reports were jumbled.

As the story made the rounds, a group of about fifty men formed. Encountering Anderson while he was walking along the street, they began shouting, "Lynch him!"[18] As he endeavored to get away, he was twice knocked to the ground. Still, he kept going until he reached his home. He explained to Marshal Bobst that Martha had been startled when he ran into her, but that he had neither planned nor attempted to assault her or any other girl.

Fearing to leave his own home, Anderson was assured by Bobst and the prosecuting attorney that they would keep him from harm. If necessary, the marshal said he would "deputize a sufficient number of persons to protect the colored man."[19]

As it turned out, the men who were most vocal in threatening Anderson were employees of the Scioto Valley Traction Line who just happened to be in Lockbourne on Saturday night and did not reside in the community. Ultimately, Anderson was not charged with any crime.

Lynching [TI], Clark County, March 1904—Dickerson, Richard [B]

Richard Dickerson (aka Dixon) was lynched in Springfield on March 7, 1904.

A mob composed of more than 1,000 men stormed what was thought to be an impregnable jail, dragged Dickerson out in the street, and hoisted him up on a telegraph pole. They then finished the job by passing around revolvers and firing at his suspended body for half an hour. An African American, Dickerson had sealed his fate when he shot Police Sergeant Charles Collis of Lagonda.

Dickerson had been living with a black woman named Anna (or Mamie) Corbin. After a quarrel, he had left in a huff. When he returned to collect some clothing, the landlord barred him from entry. So Dickerson went to the police station and persuaded Sergeant Collis to accompany him when he went back to the apartment.

As he was gathering up his property, Dickerson became embroiled in another argument with Corbin. The previous year, she had filed charges against him for fornication because she was fed up with his drunken behavior and wanted him out of her life. It resulted in a five-dollar fine and a six-month suspended jail sentence. Their relationship became even more contentious after that.

In anger, Dickerson drew a revolver and shot her in the breast (she would later die). When Collis tried to arrest him for the crime, Dickerson shot him four times and then fled from the house. Despite being mortally wounded, Collis tried to pursue him, firing at the fleeing suspect and calling on others to assist him. After he fell, a number of people joined the chase. Desperate to escape them, Dickerson went directly to the police station and surrendered.

The announcement that Collis had died prompted some talk of lynching, but Sheriff

L. Floyd Routzahn did not take it seriously because no leaders had stepped up. However, he had misjudged the intensity of feeling in Springfield over the fact that there had been a number of murders in recent years and no one had been convicted. Also, the increasingly large African American presence in the city had begun to spark racial unrest.

When a crowd started gathering early in the evening, Sheriff Routzahn wasn't particularly concerned. Most of them were boys. However, by nine o'clock, a number of men had joined them and demanded that the sheriff hand over Dickerson. He refused and informed them that there was no point in trying to break into the jail. It was much too strong for that.

Besides, Routzahn was prepared to do whatever was necessary to protect his prisoner and hoped that he would not have to injure any good citizen of Springfield as a result. He suggested they just move along and, apparently, they took his advice.

By 10:45, Routzahn felt confident that the situation was well in control. A few minutes later, he realized he was wrong. The mob was back and had increased in size. A contingent of men rushed the south door and were able to break through. Before they even knew what was happening, the sheriff and his deputies had been captured and disarmed. At least 600 men were crammed inside the jail, equipped with railroad iron, cold chisels, and sledgehammers. They threatened to destroy every cell unless the sheriff handed Dickerson over to them.

Murderer Richard Dickerson was repeatedly shot both before and after he was lynched in 1904 (archives of the Clark County Historical Society, Springfield, Ohio).

Concerned about the safety of the others prisoners, Routzahn told the mob where Dickerson could be found. He was quickly extracted from his cell and trundled out into the yard surrounding the building. Unlike most lynching victims, Dickerson was spared an agonizing death. Instead, the leader of the mob cleared an area and directed twenty or so men to shoot him. They readily did so.

When it was obvious that the prisoner was dead, his body was carried to the corner of Main Street and Fountain Avenue. There, at one of the most prominent intersections in the city, a rope was tied around Dickerson's neck and he was hung from a telephone pole like a piñata. As the body danged some eighteen feet above the ground, many in the crowd took the opportunity to shoot it, passing around a couple of dozen revolvers.

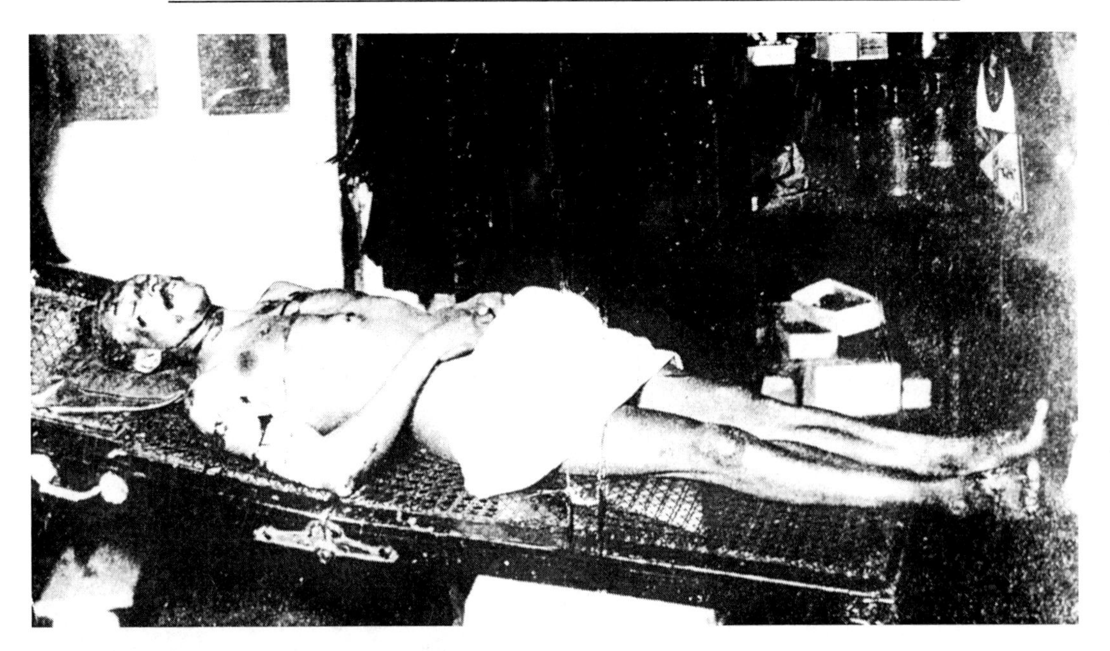

Top: Richard Dickerson's body was left hanging for four hours from a telephone pole at the corner of Main Street and Fountain Avenue (archives of the Clark County Historical Society, Springfield, Ohio). *Bottom:* The day after Richard Dickerson was lynched in 1904, a mob formed to drive all African Americans out of Springfield (archives of the Clark County Historical Society, Springfield, Ohio).

The mood was festive with much hooting and hollering as the body jerked and spun from the impact of the bullets. According to the *Dayton Evening Herald*, his tattered clothes fluttered in the wind "like shreds of a battle flag."[20] The mob "went fairly wild with delight" as Dickerson's "arms would fly up convulsively when a muscle was struck."[21] Having had their fun, the mob, which at one point was estimated at 4,000, dispersed early in the morning.

Dickerson's body was left hanging from the telephone pole for about four hours. After it was finally cut down, it was taken to an undertaker where it was prepared for shipment to Cynthiana, Kentucky, his former home.

Mob Violence, Clark County, March 1904—Race Riot

In the aftermath of the lynching, Mayor Charles J. Bowlus, Chief of Police O'Brien, and former Mayor W.R. Burnett held a private meeting in which they concluded that since the (white) citizens of Springfield were almost unanimous in their support of the lynching, they would not push for prosecuting anyone who participated. However, they allowed that County Prosecutor McGrew might choose to present the matter to a grand jury. And Judge J.K. Mower of the common pleas court was deeply upset by what had happened and was calling a special grand jury to review it.

The decision not to investigate the lynching and prosecute the ringleaders was not universally embraced. Still, as the *Lima Times Democrat* wrote: "While the lynching is deplored, the community is almost a unit in believing the lawless element of the city has learned a wholesome lesson."[22]

It was pointed out that Mayor Bowlus had tried to avert the tragedy. When he called Sheriff Routzahn to check on the situation, he was assured that he did not fear there would be mob violence. Then when he heard a mob had surrounded the jail, he contacted Chief O'Brien for reinforcements, as well as Major T.J. Kirkpatrick of the Third Ohio. The major had sought to mobilize Companies B and E of the Third Ohio, but it proved impossible to pull them together in time to prevent the lynching—that and the fact that they were reluctant to be placed in a situation in which they might have to shoot their friends.

The disgraceful behavior of the mob did not end with the lynching, however. On March 8, 1904, the day after, some who sympathized with the lynching victim were, purportedly, making threats to burn the jail and the courthouse in protest. These threats quickly became "common gossip," infuriating those who had supported the act of vigilante justice.[23]

Many white citizens of the city began to collect on the streets and talk of taking action against the blacks. By 10:30 that evening, the mob had swelled to 1,000 men, centered on the corner of High and Spring Streets. Father Crogan, assistant pastor of St. Raphael Church, spoke to those assembled, pleading with them to go home. But to no avail. Fifteen minutes later, the mob began to march on "the levee," the African American district of Springfield, "where many desperate criminals have been harbored by the illiterate and lawless inmates of the old dingy buildings."[24]

Reaching the tenements occupied by many blacks on the other side of the Big Four Railroad yards, the crowd started firing their revolvers. As they continued to move forward, they began hurling bricks and stones as well, breaking numerous windows and cheering as the glass showered the sidewalk. Although forty policeman were dispatch to the scene, they were powerless to control the rioting. The sound of revelry attracted more and more people who joined the mob.

A fire started in a saloon and quickly spread through the "negro quarters" of the city known as "the levee" (archives of the Clark County Historical Society, Springfield, Ohio).

Just before midnight, someone set fire to one of the saloons and the flames spread quickly through the building and those adjoining it, poorly maintained wooden structures ranging from one to three stories high. A mob had been firing at it for the previous half hour from a distance of 100 feet and it was not known whether any of the occupants of the building remained inside.

The efforts of the fire department to bring the flames under control were frustrated by threats by the rioters to cut the hoses if they did. As a result, a row of buildings, mostly apartments, from Spring to Gallagher Street were totally consumed at a loss of $20,000.

"It is understood that the negroes warned Sheriff Routzahn that the instant the torch was applied in Washington Street he had better remove his family from the jail, as that institution was to be immediately dynamited," the *New York Times* reported, but no attempt was made to do so.[25]

Mayor Bowlus had called out the local militia and Major Kirkpatrick arrived with thirty-five men within a few minutes of the fire being set. Under orders from Governor Myron T. Herrick, they were supplemented by companies from Xenia, Urbana, and Dayton. After midnight, the troops arrived by special train and rushed into the area, surrounding the levee. They drove the rioters back and disrupted their plan to invade another African American settlement.

Because the rioters interfered with the fire fighters, rows of buildings from Spring to Gallagher Street were destroyed (archives of the Clark County Historical Society, Springfield, Ohio).

The militia remained in Springfield for a week as 25,000 tourists flocked to the city to see the damages. Although several men were indicted, no one was ever convicted for his part in the lynching. There had been a dozen murders during the previous two years. The perception was that crime in Springfield was out of control.

In an interview with the *Dayton Daily News*, resident F.E. Snypp expressed the opinion that the lynching would "do Springfield good."[26] It was "but a culmination of the feeling of disgust and unrest that has been rankling in the hearts of many for months."[27]

For three days, race demonstrations had terrorized the black citizens of Springfield. Y.W. Smith, an African American, was arrested for urging black members of the community to set fire to white businesses and residential districts in retaliation for the lynching of Dickerson and the burning of the "negro quarters."[28] He was accompanied by "several strange negroes."[29] As more then twenty-five African Americans arrived in Richmond, Indiana, refugees from Springfield, hundreds of other were threatening to join them unless the demonstrations against their race ceased.

Attempted Lynching, Clark County, March 1904—Unknown boy [B]

A week after Dickerson was hanged, there was a terrifying incident that illustrated how the misbehavior of the so-called adult population of Springfield had influenced the city's youth.

At Shaffer Street School, two or more white boys grabbed an African American boy, tied a rope around his neck, and began dragging him along the ground. Fortunately, Principal B.G. Long stepped in to save him before he was seriously injured or killed.

Springfield was still occupied by two local companies of the Third Regiment and seven companies of the Second when the incident took place.

Attempted Lynching, Franklin County, March 1904—Jackson, Ben [B]

Ben Jackson entered Joe Stultz's saloon in Shadeville, on Sunday, March 13, 1904. An African American resident of the village, Jackson fell in with a group of white men who had been drinking heavily and invited him to join them. After he had consumed several alcoholic beverages and was in his cups, they persuaded him to entertain them by singing and dancing. Jackson readily complied, but one of the men decided his performance wasn't good enough. Since they had just been discussing the Springfield lynching, he suggested they lynch Jackson.

Bartender William Davis, believing it was all in fun, gave the men a twisted wet towel. Grabbing Jackson, they wrapped the towel around his neck and suspended him from a hook in the ceiling and then stood back to delight in their little joke. However, after a few minutes, they saw that Jackson's tongue was protruding from his mouth. Realizing they had gone too far, Stultz climbed on top of a slot machine and cut the towel. Jackson dropped to the floor.

When he finally regained consciousness, the men explained to Jackson that they had no intention of actually killing him. Even though Jackson declined to press charges, it is unlikely that he saw any humor in their actions. As Marilyn K. Howard observed, "Their request and the pretend lynching is an indication of the contempt which many whites still had for black people."[30]

Expected Lynching, Brown County, March 1904—Kelch, Joseph [W]

When the body of seventeen-year-old Inez Mathews was found in an old well on a farm near Ripley on March 14, 1904, some of those employed to search for her killer openly threatened to lynch the suspect.

The pretty teenager had been choked to death and there were two cuts above her eyes. She had last been seen with Joseph Kelch, age twenty-two, to whom she was purportedly engage. He had picked her up in a buggy at the Beasley home on Saturday night at about nine o'clock.

The story emerged that Mathews had refused to go with Kelch when he showed up that evening, but finally relented at the urging of Mrs. Beasley. She had employed the young woman as a live-in domestic and knew that Kelch, who worked for John Woods, had been dating her for about a year.

The following morning, the Beasley family began to search for her. Near the gate to their yard, they found signs of a struggle: pieces of clothing, ribbons, and hairpins. They raised the neighbors and search parties set off in several directions.

A few of them reached the home of John (or Charley) Woods, Kelch's employer. They found the horse Kelch had used was exhausted and the buggy contained bloodstains, pieces of clothing, and hair. The hubs of the wheels were bent, suggesting he had been driving with one hand and colliding with fences along the road. Furthermore, his overcoat was found in his room, covered in mud, indicating he had entered the house, then left again. He was wearing a blue suit and no coat, and, they suspected, headed for Cincinnati.

Upon hearing about the missing woman, Samuel Taylor, who lived four miles from the Beasley home, began to search his own property. Kelch had once worked for him. Along the highway, he found signs that a horse had been hitched there the previous night.

He also found the ground had been disturbed in the direction of an old well. When he investigated, he found the body of Inez Mathews had been dumped in it.

The search continued, but Kelch eluded them. Many believed he might have committed suicide. He had left a note in a trunk directing how he wanted $65 to be distributed. Then On the evening of March 24, 1904, Kelch's body was found in Straight Creek, five miles outside Georgetown. He had a bullet hole over his right ear.

False Report of Lynching, Montgomery County, March 1904—[FR] Unknown man [B]

A false report reached Springfield on the night of March 19, 1904, that a black man had been lynched in Dayton for assaulting a white woman. This caused a great deal of excitement for a time.

Expected Lynching, Clark County, May 1904—Fisher, Walter [B]

Despite the toll that the lynching of Dickerson had taken on the black citizens of Springfield, less three months later at midnight on May 30, 1904, a mob of African Americans surrounded the jail in Springfield, determined to lynch one of their own.

Walter Fisher had been arrested for the slaying of Edward Boone, also black, at George Hurley's honky tonk saloon. Boone supposedly refused to buy Fisher a glass of beer so he shot him.

After disguising Fisher's appearance, including shaving off his mustache, Sheriff Floyd Routzahn took him to Dayton for his own protection. When the sheriff told the mob he did not have Fisher, they said they would be back to get him when he was returned for trial.

In October, Fisher was convicted of second degree murder and sentenced to the Ohio Penitentiary for life.

Expected Lynching, Belmont County, October 1904—Terry, Jack [B]

A race war was feared when Jack Terry shot Carl Gitchell (or Getchel) dead at noon on October 2, 1904. Terry, who was black, and Gitchell, who was white, both worked as teamsters and lived in Cherry Alley in the town of Bellaire. When Terry returned home on Sunday, he encountered brothers Carl and Clarence Gitchell standing outside their residence.

For some reason, Terry began cursing all white men in the alley, claiming the alley was exclusively for the use of African Americans. He demanded that the Gitchells leave. Carl suggested they step to the "Commons" and settle the matter with their fists, but Terry began shooting. The first shot missed, the second struck Clarence in the hand, and the third pierced Carl's heart, killing him instantly. Terry took off at once.

Carl Gitchell was a popular individual and his friends wanted to avenge his death. Hundreds of men converged on the scene, crying for blood. The Gitchell brothers' father, armed with a rifle, was leading a large posse. "Kill! Kill!" they shouted.[31]

Thirty minutes later, Officer Goods and Marshal Mahone found Terry hiding in some willows along a creek. Drawing their revolvers, they formed a cordon, separating their prisoner from the angry mob as they hurried him to jail. The quick action by the police probably averted a race riot and a lynching. Terry was found guilty of first degree murder in December.

Expected Lynching, Muskingum County, November 1904—Hunton, John [W]; Jackson, Clyde [unk]; Wilson, Kid [B]; Carnes, Charles [W]

On November 21, 1904, John H. Hunton Jr. (or Huntington) was arrested in Roseville on suspicion of having set fire to four buildings in the past thirty-six hours. There had also been four similar fires at Zanesville and three at Nashport during the previous three weeks. Clyde Jackson, the initial suspect, was nearly lynched by an angry mob. He still was not thought to be totally innocent.

It was reported that Hunton was drinking heavily and might be on the verge of insanity. Saturday and Sunday night, threats to lynch the perpetrator had been made quite freely by the townspeople. For this reason, Sheriff Alonzo Swayne had kept Hunton under surveillance, but did not move to arrest him. When he finally did take him into custody, he rushed him to Zanesville for safekeeping.

Little was known about Hunton, despite his having lived in Roseville for two years. He was allegedly the son of the Reverend John Hunton of Lima and had once been a deputy sheriff of Allen County. He had been arrested previously for embezzlement while holding that office and served time at the Ohio Penitentiary, gaining his release in 1901.

Within a week or so of Hunton's arrest for arson, three more fires broke out in Roseville. This time, the suspects were a black man, Kid Wilson, and a white man, Charles Carne. They were promptly arrested, but feeling against them was running so high that the Reverend Luther J. Smith, the local Methodist minister, felt a need to stand on a box and urge the crowd to refrain from any unlawful activities.

Meanwhile, the authorities were suggesting they knew the name of the actual culprit, but were reluctant to arrest him because they weren't certain they could guarantee his safety.

Attempted Lynching, Knox County, April 1905—Copeland, George [B]

George Copeland, an eighteen- or twenty-year-old African American man, was arrested and jailed on April 25, 1905, for the criminal assault and murder Miranda Bricker, an unmarried white woman.

For years, Bricker, age fifty-five, had worked as the pastry cook at the Kenyon Military Academy in Gambier and was currently a housemaid for the Fairchild family. When Bricker's lifeless body was found, "There was evidence of a terrible struggle on the part of the woman and the marks on the lawn showed that she was dragged 500 feet from the point where she was first attacked."[32] Bloodhounds were used to track the path of her killer two miles to the home of Copeland.

A large crowd, estimated at 400, had followed along behind Deputy Sheriff James C. Shellenbarger and his officers.[33] The allegedly planned to lynch the suspect, but Shellenbarger wrapped him in a large overcoat, bundled him into an automobile, and raced twelve miles to Centerburg (or, possibly, Newark) where he was placed in jail under heavy guard. He would be placed on the next train to Columbus.

Although he was charged with first degree murder and rape, Copeland was released for lack of evidence just a couple of weeks later.

Expected Lynching, Coshocton County, June 1905—Dickerson, Benjamin [W]

Katherine "Kate" Hughes, age thirty-three, of Cooperdale was murdered on June 28, 1905, near Coshocton. Her mutilated body was found discovered either by her children or a neighbor woman who began looking for her when she did not return home.

Widely regarded as the prettiest woman in the vicinity, Kate was found in the thick underbrush near a spring with her neck pressed between two saplings. It was suspected her killer had also attempted to rape her.

A posse quickly formed, determined to "wreak summary vengeance" on the murderer.[34] Kate's husband, Simon, a miner, threatened to gather a mob to lynch her alleged murderer, Benjamin Dickerson. Bloodhounds brought in from Dayton went directly from the murder scene to Dickerson's bedroom some fifty yards away. A farmer, he was not home at the time, but was arrested later.

Kate had once been Dickerson's childhood sweetheart and he purportedly had been seeking to rekindle their relationship. He was subsequently found guilty of first degree murder and imprisoned.

Expected Lynching, Adams County, January 1906—Hayslip, Adelbert [W]; Hayslip, Owen [W]

Adelbert (or Delbert) and Owen (possibly Ona) Hayslip were indicted for the murder of Albert (or Alfred) Fisher in Adams County on January 1, 1906. Since there was a fear of mob violence, Deputy Sheriff Spencer McMillan transported them from West Union to Georgetown two days later, locking them up in the town's jail. They were convicted of murder and sentenced to the Ohio Penitentiary for life.

Because of the clamor in the community, a special grand jury was convened to hear the facts in the case. Fisher, age twenty-two, had been beaten to death near Cedar Mills on the way home from a New Year's celebration at church. Adelbert had used brass knuckles to smash the young farmer's skull while Owen kept people from intervening by training a revolver on them.

The Hayslip brothers would later claim that they pled guilty to the murder because they feared they were going to be lynched and seized upon the opportunity to go to prison in Columbus simply to escape from the situation.

Mob Violence, Clark County, February–March 1906—Ladd, Preston [B]; Dean, Edward [B]

Mark M. Davis, a railroad brakeman, was shot in Springfield on February 27, 1906. He was expected to die. The suspects were two black men, Edward Dean and Preston Ladd, and the city was up in arms. As a precaution, the prisoners had been quietly moved to Dayton.

In response, a mob of 2,000, purportedly led by railroad men, descended on the African American section of Springfield to exact vengeance. They burned eight buildings and terrorized all black men who dared to venture out on the streets, beating them and dragging them through the mud.

The ringleaders pushed ahead, firing their revolvers at random. When they arrived at Kempler's Saloon on East Columbia Street, the owner ran off, leaving his wife and three children asleep upstairs. The mob looted the place and were preparing to set fire to it when the fire brigade arrived and rescued the mother and children. Police Chief O'Brien immediately ordered all Springfield saloons closed.

Crossing the street, the lawless horde turned their attention to a five-story frame building. As the residents fled for their lives, the mob poured oil on the beds and burned it to the ground. The firefighters' efforts were ineffective because their hoses were repeatedly cut by the rioters. And the police felt powerless to do anything.

Major Horace Kiefer rallied two companies—B and E—of local militia, which were aided by contingents of National Guard. He cordoned off the endangered district, while the mob leaders led their men in shouting, "Burn the Jungles."[35]

By March 1, eight companies of militia were ordered in to assist with restoring order.

Although no one died as a result of the rioting, more than a dozen buildings were destroyed or damaged. City officials welcomed the rains which fell two days later, putting an end to the rioting.

Attempted Lynching, Warren County, October 1906—White, Henry [B]

George Basore, the town marshal of Franklin, was shot to death on the morning of October 30, 1906, while attempting to arrest Henry White. He suspected White, an African American, of being involved in some robberies that had taken place in the vicinity.

When Basore found him at the railroad depot preparing to go to Springfield, White drew a revolver and fired five shots into the marshal's breast. Chased through the streets, White evaded capture until he was shot in the right arm about a mile outside of town. His companion, a black woman, was also arrested. She had two suitcases full of stolen goods in her possession.

While White sat in a cell, a mob of 200–500 men and boys laid siege to the Franklin jail, hoping to get the prisoner and hang him. However, as they were breaking into the back of the building, Sheriff T.C. Patterson and two deputies rushed White out the front. Shoving him into an automobile, they sped off for Lebanon, the county seat, while shots were fired at the vehicle.

The townsfolk were so upset by the killing that they took their anger out on other black citizens, giving them no opportunity to defend themselves. Some of the rabble said they would go to Lebanon to get White. In the meantime, passengers on the traction line from Cincinnati refused to get off in Franklin.

White was found guilty of first degree murder in December and executed on July 19, 1907.

Mob Violence, Franklin County, January 1907—Bad Lands Riot

A mob of some fifty soldiers from Columbus Barracks swarmed the streets at about 6:30 on the evening of January 21, 1907, bent on avenging the shooting of one of their number by a black man. Armed with bricks, stones, and sticks, they poured into the adjoining Columbus neighborhood, known far and wide as the Bad Lands, and proceeded to wreck all of the stores, saloons, and brothels in their path, especially those operated by African Americans.

Led by James Sterns and a few others, the soldiers broke windows and assaulted many men and women while sending others fleeing for their lives. "Kill the Niggers," they shouted as they swept through the quarter.[36] Soon, the Columbus police and a squad of sixty soldiers converged on them. Twenty of the rioting soldiers were apprehended and marched back to the barracks. Ten others were rounded up later.

As it turned out, the shooting that precipitated the riot wasn't true. However, there had been a fight between a white soldier and a black man and the soldier had lost. The commander of the post, Major Edwin F. Glenn, downplayed the riot, chalking it up to a "boyish prank" and had the damage claims deducted from the soldiers' pay. The victims were also discouraged from filing claims.

Expected Lynching, Washington County, March 1907—Savage, Walter W. [W]

Walter W. Savage of Syracuse, New York, came to Marietta in late February to work as a sketch artist in the window of the Dime Saving Society Building. He specialized in persuading young girls to allow him to draw them. On March 3, 1907, he was found to have six girls between the ages of twelve and sixteen years in his room.

When the police arrived, the girls were lying together on the floor. Purportedly from good homes, they were all so drunk they could not stand up. Physicians administered an emetic to the girls to aid them in regaining consciousness. Savage and a second man, Andy Carothers, were arrested and taken to the city jail.

The girls all said that the men had forced them to drink whiskey, wine, and beer, which had allegedly been drugged. Three of them—Alma Rex, May Rex, and Ada Boots—became the focus of the investigation. At least two were thought to be the victims of attempted assault.

Some accounts compared Savage to Stanford White, who had been charged by the model Evelyn Nesbit Thaw of having done much the same thing to her. Along with Carothers, he was locked up in the county jail on the fifth floor of the courthouse. The entire police force stood guard against an anticipated Lynching.

When his case came to trial, Savage, who "begged for leniency and promised to leave the county if they let him off," received the most severe sentence the law would allow.[37] He was fined $100 and given thirty days in jail. The judge told a cheering crowd that he would have punished him more if it were within his power.

Savage's plans to relocate to Parkersburg, West Virginia, were at least temporarily placed on hold while he served his sentence.

Possible Lynching, Stark County, March 1907—Unknown Italian [W]

On March 4, 1907, an unknown Italian man was found hanging from a tree in Holbein's woods, several miles north of Canton. Originally, it was thought he had committed suicide. However, that was before Acting Coroner Barry discovered that his body was badly bruised and his skull had been fractured.

The *Stark County Democrat* reported, "The body when found was stripped of everything that might lead to identification and the condition of the body itself showed that it had been hanging from its suspended position for several days or possibly a week."[38] He had a heavy leather belt around his neck and his feet were touching the ground.

Authorities were investigating whether he had been murdered by the Black Hand, a purported band of Italian criminals.[39]

Expected Lynching, Clark County, April 1907—Jones, Will [B]; Cain, Peter [B]

On the morning of April 2, 1907, Will Jones, an African American, was fleeing through the streets of Springfield. He had wounded a black police officer, James Paine, and a throng of angry people were chasing him, urging others to join in a lynching. However, Jones ran into the arms of a police officer who got him safely to jail.

Alternatively, two African Americans, Peter Cain and Will Jones, got into a squabble. Cain fired three shots at Jones, who fell as he was running away. Thinking he had killed him, Cain tried to flee, but was pursued by a crowd estimated at 300. He likely would have been lynched if a former city fireman hadn't intervened.

Mob Violence, Madison County, April 1907—Ward, George H. [W]

As he was returning from his wife's funeral on April 19, 1907, George H. Ward, age fifty, was dragged from his rig by sixteen women from the village of Resaca. They beat him with buggy whips until they broke, leaving him in serious condition. One woman placed a noose around his neck and cried, "Will you pray now?"[40] Most of his clothing was torn from his body and his skin painted with black paint.

Ward, a prosperous farmer in Madison County, had been accused by his gravely ill wife in a divorce petition of forcing her to leave her sick bed, inadequately clothed, to feed the stock. After she was removed from his home by authorities, she died of consumption. He subsequently refused to allow any religious services to be held for her.

Mrs. A.W. Bradley freely admitted she was one of the women: "We punished the man because he treated his sick wife brutally, and, when she was dying, refused her nourishment. No, we needed no men to help us. This women of Resaca can well take care of themselves."[41] They were thought to be some of the most prominent women in the county.

Ward was a tenant on a farm owned by John Florence. Early in May, Florence discovered a crudely made sign posted on his property, warning him that his house might be burned down. Apparently, someone thought he was in sympathy with Ward, which he denied.

A month after he was assaulted Ward was notified that he was the missing heir to a half-million dollar estate in Portsmouth, England. Apparently, the newspaper coverage of his whipping had brought him to the attention of those who were attempting to locate him.

While Ward was still threatening to sue the women involved, it was thought that nothing would come of it because many people thought he deserved worse.

Expected Lynching, Miami County, April 1907—Earl, Frank [W]; Walker, Frank [W]

The citizens of Sidney were outraged by the murder of William B. Legg on April 20, 1907. At about 10:30 in the evening, two men entered his store, guns drawn, and ordered him to hand over the money. Legg resisted and was shot twice.

As the perpetrators were being sought, there was strong sentiment on the street for lynching. The next morning, Frank Earl (aka Dalton) and Frank Walker (aka Whiting) were appended in Lima after a brief skirmish.

While Walker was allowed to plead guilty to second degree murder, Earl was convicted of first degree murder. By then, talk of lynching had ceased. He was executed on December 20, 1907, at the Ohio Penitentiary.

Expected Lynching, Allen County, April 1907—Myers, George [W]

Forty-five-year-old George Myers was charged with sexually molesting Gladys Ryan, age four, near Elida. The daughter of Clifford Ryan, a farmer, she was reported to be near death.

Myers was arrested early on the morning of April 20, 1907, while being pursued by a mob of enraged neighbors. Sheriff Henry Van Gunton feared that an effort would be made to seize the prisoner and requested that Captain Gale of Company "C" Second Ohio Infantry provide a guard for the jail.

Mob Violence, Hancock County, July 1907—Smith, Clem [W]

For unknown reasons, Clem Smith (or McSmith), age forty-five, of Van Buren ran afoul of his neighborss wrath. On July 20, 1907, they expressed their disfavor when 100 to 150 of them tore off his clothes and covered him in tar and feathers. Afterward, they hung him in effigy and fired their guns at the dummy. The whole incident was witnessed by his wife who left town with him on an interurban car.

Twice before while a resident of nearby Findlay, Smith had been driven out of town and threatened with tar and feathering for unspecified offenses.

Expected Lynching, Delaware County, September 1907—Dalton, Henry [B]

Henry Dalton shot Chris Horn, an engineer for the Big Four Railroad, at Delaware, on September 23, 1907. The incident occurred when James Knowlton and Henry Dalton, both employees at a quarry in Sunbury, were traveling in a buggy that collided with a carriage driven by Horn. (Alternately, Horn was walking along the street when Dalton narrowly avoided running over him.)

When Horn chewed them out for their recklessness ("It's a wonder you wouldn't look where you are driving"), Knowlton got out of the buggy.[42] The two men exchanged words and then began exchanging punches. Seeing that Knowlton was losing, Dalton pulled out a revolver and shot Horn. He then attempted to escape by running up the street, but was quickly nabbed by Patrolman Williams and locked in the city jail.

Horn died of his wound on Sunday morning and the news quickly spread throughout the community. The situation became so volatile that "Sheriff" (likely Chief of Police William B.) Mathews thought it best to move the prisoner elsewhere. So he secretly conveyed Dalton to Columbus to "save the prisoner from violence at the hands of some of Delaware's enraged citizens."[43]

Driving a buggy around to the back of the jail, Matthews loaded the anxious prisoner into it and hurried along a little used road to Stratford. They then boarded the Columbus, Delaware & Marion interurban car. Handcuffed to the sheriff, Dalton sat silently in the smoker section for the entire trip. He seemed relieved when he was delivered to the jail in Columbus.

According to Dalton, a thirty-five-year-old black man, he was drunk when he committed the murder. The *Marion Star* observed that, "He had the heavy, sullen face which betokens the ignorant negro."[44] Horn was ten years older, white, and generally well liked.

Knowlton, Dalton's companion, was also arrested and jailed in Delaware, but Sheriff Matthews wasn't concerned about his safety. Dalton, he said, was the only prisoner he ever had that he was fearful he would not be able to protect. In November, Dalton was sentenced to eighteen years in the penitentiary for manslaughter.

Attempted Lynching, Washington County, November 1907—Sweeney, John [W]

On Sunday afternoon, November 3, 1907, John Sweeney was caught assaulting Anna Koon, age fourteen, in a building at the fairgrounds in Marietta. The thirty-five-year-old father of five barely escaped with his life.

"A crowd gathered, bound Sweeney with a rope and started for the Muskingum River."[45] Their plan was to throw him in. However, someone had notified the police who swooped in. They took him to the police station, battling the crowd all the way.

Fortunately, there were a few reasonable citizens who convinced the crowd to let the law handle the matter. Meanwhile, the little girl's condition was described as precarious. Described as a wealthy operator, Sweeney was sentenced to one year in the Ohio Penitentiary for assault.

Mob Violence, Adams, Brown, and Clermont Counties, 1908—Night Riders [W?]

By the 1890s, the American Tobacco Company controlled 90 percent of the country's tobacco sales. Owing to this virtual monopoly, tobacco farmers in Tennessee were being paid less for their crop than it cost to produce it.

In response, the farmers formed a collective—the Dark Tobacco District Planter's Protective Association of Kentucky and Tennessee—to try to control production and sales and, thereby, drive up prices. However, when it did not have the desired result, a splinter group within the association took action against those farmers who continued to sell their crops to the American Tobacco Company.

In the spring of 1908, these Night Riders started venturing across the Ohio River from Kentucky into southern Ohio and Indiana, burning and scrapping the tobacco beds and terrifying farmers. For example, in the village of Rural on April 25, 1908, about fifty men from Kentucky crossed the river and set fire to a couple of tobacco beds owned by Albert Newman. Newman shot at one of them with a revolver and was struck by a shotgun blast in the head.

A month later on May 23, 1908, Walter Hook, who lived about six miles from Ripley, fired upon the riders. They shot back, riddling his house with bullets and nearly wounding his child.

Due to these and other Night Rider raids, Governor Andrew Harris dispatched National Guard troops to southern Ohio in February, May, and June to protect Ohio's independent tobacco growers. Few of the riders appear to have been from Ohio.

Expected Lynching, Seneca County, March 1908—Hoffman, William H. [W]

Patrick Sweeney, a Tiffin police officer, age forty-five, was shot to death while attempting to arrest William H. "Butch" Hoffman on Friday, March 27, 1908. He had surprised Hoffman while he was burglarizing J.M. Beckley's grocery store.

Spurred by a $500 reward for his apprehension, a posse of local citizens was on the man's trail and there was talk of lynching him when they caught him.

A former convict, blind in one eye, Hoffman was purportedly captured at Cygnet, hiding in a boxcar, and returned to Tiffin. However, in November it was reported he had been captured in Williamsville, Missouri.

Attempted Lynching, Licking County, May 1908—Terwiliger, Ernst [W]

On the morning of May 24, 1908, Ernst Terwiliger was arrested for the murder of his wife. Her body had been found in her room, strangled to death. By afternoon, he had made a full confession.

The Terwiligers resided at the home of Mr. and Mrs. Charles Nutter. At breakfast, one of the Nutters went to wake the couple, only to find Mrs. Terwiliger dead in bed, her tongue protruding from her mouth and finger marks clearly visible on her throat. Ernst had been heard leaving the house shortly after midnight, but there had been no sounds of a struggle.

Only eighteen years old, Mrs. Terwiliger had been married to her husband for a year and was pregnant. She was purported to be a very attractive young woman and her husband was insanely jealous of her. They had separated as a consequence of domestic problems, but had recently reconciled.[46]

It was soon learned that Ernst had been drinking the previous evening and returned to the Nutters' house in a highly intoxicated state. Asked for money by his wife, he replied that he had none. She then harangued him for his failure to adequately provide for her due to his lack of employment. Angered by her remarks, he admitted seizing her by the throat in a drunken rage as she lay on the bed and killing her.[47]

Locked up in the Newark city jail, Ernst was aware of the burgeoning crowd of Newark citizens who were gathering outside. He became a "nervous wreck," fearful they might make good on their threats to lynch him.[48] A special guard of police reserves was provided to ensure his safety. Soon, the crowd dispersed, leaving the law to dispense justice.

Less than a year later, Ernst Terwiliger was one of "four insane criminals" who escaped from the Columbus State Hospital.[49] They were armed with knives they had fashioned from the steel in their shoes.

Attempted Lynching, Wyandot County, August 1908—Goodlove, James [W]

The lynch mob that swarmed the streets of Upper Sandusky on Friday evening, August 7, 1908, was led by "two pretty girls, belles of this city."[50] Their names were Ada F. Isaacs, age twenty, and Anna Edessa "Dessa" Isaacs, twenty-two. Their intended victim was James F. Goodlove who had shot Frank McCormick to death at the railroad depot where they both had gone to meet hotel guests.

Business rivals, Goodlove, former proprietor of the French House and currently of the Hotel Keber, called McCormack, a hotel bus driver, a vile name. McCormack struck him, and Goodlove fired his revolver. "Women on the depot platform fainted and a panic followed the shooting," the Washington, D.C., *Evening Star* reported.[51] Goodlove fled to the hotel where he readily surrendered to authorities.

There was bad blood between David Isaacs, the father of the young women, and Goodlove, who would tell potential customers, "You don't want to put up with a nigger" (Isaacs had a dark complexion).[52] However, several extra deputies were quickly sworn in to protect him from the lynch mob that Ada and Dessa were forming and their efforts came to naught.

Indicted for McCormack's death, Goodlove grew sick in the county jail and a week later was thought to be on the verge of death. He wasn't. Instead, he was convicted of first degree murder. However, as *Collier's Weekly* reported, Goodlove, in an Ohio Supreme Court ruling, benefited from a technicality. While evidence proved he had murdered Frank McCormick, the victim's true name was Percy Stuckey. His sentence was first reduced to fifteen years on the basis of "grammatical chaos," and later overturned.[53] Goodlove was turned loose. *Collier's* argued that Judge Sheets could have and should have remanded Goodlove for another trial, but had misapplied the statute.

Meanwhile, the "belles" of Upper Sandusky apparently did not marry, but lived together for much of their lives with Edessa, who had attended the conservatory of music at Denison University, working as a stenographer.

Mob Violence, Tuscarawas Ohio, September 1908—Welsley, Christian [W]; Martin, Harriet [W]

Christian Welsley, age seventy, and Harriet Martin, age fifty, were attacked by four masked men at their home in Wainwright on September 24, 1908, while they were sorting potatoes. Martin was stripped of her clothing, tied to the ground, and then tarred and feathered. Tar was poured down Welsley's shirt before he was able to escape.

The men did not say anything that would explain their actions. Martin had served as the housekeeper for the Welsleys for thirty years. At the time of the assault, Welsley's wife was away from home.

Mob Violence, Richland County, October 1908—Couts, Frank [W]

James Kennedy, an elderly man, tipped off local authorities that a band of White Caps would be going after Frank Couts on the night of October 18, 1908. The two men lived together in East Mansfield. The previous night, Kennedy had been visiting someone up the street. When he returned home, he was met by some eighteen or twenty men, all but one of whom wore a white mask and robe. Thinking that he was Couts, they had surrounded him. No doubt they wanted him because he had been arrested for cruelty and failure to provide for his three children.

However, when the White Caps discovered their error, they simply questioned Kennedy regarding Couts's whereabouts. They did not believe him when he said Couts was uptown, so they thoroughly searched the house. The next night, Sheriff Gustav Baer was lying in wait for them, but they did not show up.

Mob Violence, Wyandot County, March 1909—Kiefer, Peter D. [W]

Before daybreak on March 9, 1909, twenty-five White Caps rode into McCutchinville and riddled the home of Constable Peter D. Kieffer with bullets. They objected to the presence of a black servant in his home. Their horses were covered with mud, having been ridden for a considerable distance. The riders were well drilled and moved with military precision.

Attempted Lynching, Allen County, May 1909—Beam, John W [B]

A couple of the more prominent African American citizens of Lima were brothers Ulysses S. and John W. Beam, the former a physician and the latter an attorney. Born in Kentucky, they, along with another brother, also a doctor, came to Ohio in search of greater opportunity. While the third brother soon moved on, Ulysses and John became well established in the community.

On Sunday evening, May 23, 1909, John Beam paid a visit to the home of Mrs. Estella "Maude" Diltz, age thirty-five, who was either a widow or separated from her husband. She had moved to Lima from Waynesfield and operated a boarding house. Mrs. Diltz was described as a handsome woman. Although Beam was the rental agent for the property, the reason for his visit is unknown.

The previous Friday, Beam had stopped by and rung the bell. When no one answered, he tried to enter, but the door was bolted and he left. This time, the door was unlocked and he forced his way inside even as Mrs. Diltz was trying to lock it.

Pursuing the woman through the hallway and up the stairs, Beam fired his revolver at her five times and struck her three. She died while being transported to the hospital. After he left the house, he ran down the street pursued by several neighbors. Pausing to fire one shot at them, he then disappeared into the darkness.

Sheriff Henry Van Gunten organized a posse of deputies, aided by 150 citizens. At about 3 o'clock a.m., several bloodhounds arrived from a neighboring town and the chase was on. The dogs had no difficulty picking up the killer's scent and following his zigzagging trails through streets and alleyways.

At around 8 o'clock, the posse was approaching Beam's house when they heard three shots fired from the direction of the barn. Believing they were under attack, they fell back, then cautiously approached when there were no more gunshots. They found the lawyer beneath the barn floor with three bullets in his head.

The initial reports were that John Beam had committed suicide to escape capture. He was already under indictment on a conspiracy charge for robbing James Yoakum of $6,000, as well as obtaining a deed by fraudulent means. With respect to the robbery, Maude Diltz had testified against Beam before the grand jury and there was speculation that was why he killed her.

Some 500 people surrounded the county jail, calling for Beam's death. It is likely they would have lynched him, too, when the sheriff returned with him in custody. The mood in Lima was sufficiently ominous that Dr. Ulysses Beam was urged to leave out of fear he might be lynched. That evening, he closed his office and returned to his home in Kentucky.

Fears for his prisoner's safety caused the sheriff to transfer the wounded man from the hospital to the jail. However, no one dared approach the building. The area around the jail was festooned with electric lights. The sheriff had posted double guard and given them orders to shoot anyone who crossed the "deadline." Encouraged by Kevin Atkinson, Mrs. Diltz's grandfather, a gang of twenty-five men came from Waynesville, her former home, swearing to extract vengeance. But they did not challenge the sheriff and dispersed at dawn.

Rumors of Beam's impending death were greatly exaggerated. He didn't die from shooting himself in the head and seems to have recovered fairly quickly, leading some people to suggest it was all fake. A letter was produced in which Beam claimed he had slain Mrs. Diltz out of jealousy because he was in love with her. While Sheriff Van Guten branded it a forgery, Beam stuck to that story when he was arraigned the next day.

In November, Beam was convicted of first degree murder. However, the jury recommended mercy and he was sentenced to life in prison. A month later, he hanged himself in his cell sat the Ohio Penitentiary.

Attempted Lynching, Hamilton County, July 1909—O'Neal [B]

On July 29, 1909, an African American named O'Neal found himself on the run in Cincinnati after he stabbed Mrs. Benjamin Winer and knocked down several others. He had attacked her after she objected when he slapped his own daughter. O'Neal was set upon by a mob of white men numbering more than fifty.

"Brandishing an ugly looking knife, the negro held pursuers at bay and at a later hour the police had not apprehended him," the newspapers reported.[54] Other black men had rushed to his assistance, joined by the police, which may have saved him from being lynched.

Attempted Lynching, Licking County, October 1909—Underwood, Leroy [W]

A mob of sixty farmers, masked and heavily armed, were determined to lynch LeRoy Underwood on the night of October 11, 1909, for the brutal beating of Amel Dillman (or Amos Billman), a local farmer. However, several prominent citizens in the village of Purity talked them out of it. Dillman later sued his wife for divorce, charging her with conspiring with Underwood to kill him.

Attempted Lynching, Allen County, November 1909—Haring, Herbert [W]

On the evening of November 21, 1909, someone attacked seventeen-year-old Myra Smith on the streets of Lima as she was returning home from the telephone exchange where she worked. She did not see her assailant because he grabbed her from behind and nearly strangled her to death. Soon, the chase was on with several bloodhounds employed to follow the suspect's trail.

The police searched most of the night until they found Herbert Haring crouching in a box car. They were ready to string him up when someone in the group suggested they make certain they had the right guy. As it turned out, Haring had an ironclad alibi. His race was not mentioned, which suggests he was white.

In July 1910, police suggested that the culprit was Dan F. Dans (aka Davis) whom they had recently arrested for assault. He told police that he was "subject to strange and unaccountable spells at times, and that he had just been through one of them."[55]

Cincinnati police had already charged him with the murders of Anna Lloyd (choked, throat cut) and Dona Gilman (strangled), as well as the choking of Mary Wilson and Ethel Schear. He readily admitted to the assault on Wilson. Each of the crimes was committed along the C.H. & D. railroad on which he was a freight conductor. Dans told the police, "There seems to be two of me. At times spells come on and I am a demon. I don't know what to make of this. If often fight this other self, and sometimes I win and get over it."[56]

8

The Great Migration (1910–1938)

From 1910–1940, over 1.6 million African Americans fled the South in pursuit of better jobs and greater educational opportunities. They also sought to escape poverty, violence, and oppression.

Many of them migrated to cities in the North and Midwest. Many chose to settle in Ohio, particularly the cities of Cleveland, Cincinnati, Columbus, Dayton, and Akron. In Ohio, the African American population grew from 111,452 in 1910 to 339,461 in 1940, and from 2.34 percent of the overall population to 4.91 percent.

Attempted Lynching, Fairfield County, April 1910—Wallace, Harry [W]

Half the population of Bremen surrounded the town hall on April 12, 1910, threatening to lynch Harry Wallace. A shoemaker, Wallace was charged with the murder of Samuel Rosenberg, a driller of oil wells.

The slaying had occurred earlier in the evening at a keg party in a wooded area a half mile from town. As three other well drillers looked on, Wallace and Rosenberg got into an argument. Suddenly, Wallace turned on Rosenberg with his knife, stabbing and gashing him at least six times, and removing his heart and lungs.

Taken into custody by Marshal Lee Hankinson, Wallace was confined in the village jail. A mob of 500 people quickly gathered. Realizing he could not adequately protect his prisoner, Hankinson placed a call for help.

Led by Fairfield County Sheriff James W. Deffenbaugh, a posse forced its way through the crowd, revolvers drawn, in order to rescue Wallace. They had to outmaneuver the would-be lynchers by pretending to sneak the prisoner out the rear of the building before rushing him out the front to a waiting automobile.

As the party sped off to Lancaster, Wallace loudly cursed and bragged about what he had done.

Lynching [TI], Licking County, July 1910—Etherington, Carl [W]

The Ohio General Assembly passed the Rose County Local Option Act in 1908, permitting individual counties to decide for themselves whether they would permit the sale of alcoholic beverages. Two years later, the voters of Licking County came down soundly against alcohol sales, save for Newark, which was overwhelmingly in favor of it. Now, the "drys" (those who supported prohibition) were battling the "wets" (those who didn't).

As Anna Sudar observed in the *Newark Advocate*, the alcohol industry was at the foundation of the city's economy. Two thousand residents worked for the American Bottle

Company manufacturing beer bottles. There were also at least eighty saloons, fifty-four of them right downtown.

Once the law took effect, however, the Newark saloons were permitted to sell only near beer and soft drinks. Not everyone complied and everyone knew it. Mayor Herbert Atherton and Police Chief Robert Zergebiel charged the bar owners $10 a week to sell alcohol illegally. They termed it their "working agreement."[1]

Local prohibitionists were outraged and asked the Anti-Saloon League, based in Westerville, Ohio, for assistance in enforcing the law. Seventeen-year-old Carl Etherington, from Willisburg, Kentucky, was hired by the League as a private detective (or "secret service officer") to sniff out the "blind tigers" or "speakeasies" (illegal dispensaries of alcohol) operating in Newark.[2]

Despite his age, Etherington was a former Marine who claimed to be nineteen in order to get the job. He and several other detectives spent several days cruising the local bars, mingling with the customers and gathering evidence.

Then on the morning of July 8, 1910, twenty detectives brought in from Cleveland collected on the west side of the courthouse where they were deputized by Granville Mayor E.J. Barnes and Marshal Edwards Evans. Five warrants had been issued, authorizing them to raid five speakeasies.

As the detectives went about rounding up saloon owners and bartenders, many local residents responded by threatening to injure them. They were incensed that a handful of outsiders were interfering in local affairs. To make matters worse, the city police didn't recognize the deputies' authority and turned the prisoners loose. Instead, Chief Zergebiel had twelve of the twenty special deputies arrested and locked up in the city prison. They were later turned loose without their weapons at the peak of the disturbance and told to leave town.

In 1910, young Carl Etherington was hired by the Anti-Saloon League to uncover speakeasies operating in Newark.

Etherington was with a party of detectives who had staged a raid on Henry's Saloon on the west side of the courthouse square. They ran the customers out of the place so they could arrest the owner. However, the crowd collected outside the saloon, becoming angrier by the minute.

Sensing the tide was about to turn, the detectives fled out the back door and split up. At about one o'clock in the afternoon, Etherington tried to board a train near Idlewilde Park when he was grabbed by the crowd which began to beat him.

William Howard, owner of the nearby Last Chance Saloon, witnessed the assault on the detective and decided to get some licks in himself. A former Newark police chief himself, Howard took out his blackjack and began

A crowd gathered outside the Newark jail the morning after a teenage Carl Etherington was lynched.

striking the young man on the head. Somehow, Etherington was able to draw his revolver. He shot the forty-one-year-old Howard squarely in the chest.

Two bystanders said to Etherington, "We are officers, surrender yourself and you will be taken to the county jail and there protected."[3] Thoroughly exhausted, he gave his weapon to them and they used it to club him over the head. While Howard was rushed to the hospital, the mob continued to vent their anger on the hapless teenager. Finally, the police pulled up, loaded him into their wagon, and transported him to the county jail with the mob trailing behind.

Outside the county jail, several thousand people milled around, waiting for word of Howard's condition while officers patrolled the area. At 8:15 p.m., they learned he had died. In a matter of moments, the mood changed and the angry horde began acting out, cutting the telephone lines. A few began chanting death to Etherington.

By the time Mayor Atherton spoke to them at nine o'clock, asking them to go home, their numbers had increased to 5,000. A frequenter of the city's "houses of ill repute," the mayor bore the nickname "Hub," presumably because of his key role in protecting local vice, including prostitution, white slavery, gambling, pornography, and prize-fighting.[4]

When it was evident that no one was going to listen to him, Atherton went home to bed and Chief Zergebiel went to a saloon to play cards, in effect signaling that they had no intention of standing in the way of whatever the rabble wanted to do.

Employing railroad ties and rails as battering rams, the mob attacked the outside door of the jail. Sheriff William Linke tried to send word to Governor Judson Harmon of the situation, but he was on vacation in Michigan and unavailable. Adjutant General Charles Weybrecht would later say that Linke could have prevented the mob's actions had he called out the Newark Company of the Fourth Regiment. But in the governor's absence, no one else was authorized to mobilize the Ohio National Guard. Even if the guard had been dispatched, it was too late.

Wayne B. Wheeler, attorney for the Anti-Saloon League attorney, insisted that the jail could have been easily defended with just one firearm had anyone wanted to do so. However, after an hour, it was breached and the mob surged toward Etherington's second floor cell. In a panic, Etherington tried to kill himself, first beating his head against the wall and then wrapping himself in his bedclothes and setting them on fire. But by then the rioters had captured him.

Carrying their prisoner to courthouse square, the lynchers were unable to find a suitable tree. So they decided to take him Judge Charles Seward's house. A leader declared they would hang the detective and then the judge (one of the few officials who wasn't corrupt). By that time, they heard the militia was on its way—a false alarm—so nineteen-year-old William Wurster, who later admitted he had been drinking, placed the rope around Etherington's neck.

As Mabel McManiway stood on the seat of an automobile and shouted, "Pull him a little higher so I can see," Etherington was quickly hanged from a telephone pole at the corner of South Park Place and South Second Street as cheers erupted from the mob.[5]

"It is believed that Etherington asked for permission to make a statement to the mob, and as he attempted to speak somebody struck him a vicious blow on top of the head with a hammer, felling him to the ground, and this blow is believed to have killed him."[6] His last words were, "Send my love to mother and tell her that I died in the performance of my duty."[7] By 10:35 p.m., he had breathed his last.

The body was allowed to dangle from the pole for an hour. Slowly, the crowd lost interest in it and drifted away. Finally, the rope broke, dropping the lifeless body to the ground. A city ambulance then transported it to the city morgue. The *Delaware Gazette* declared, "The state of Ohio stands disgraced today in the eyes of the nation because of what a lawless crowd was permitted to do in Newark, Friday, as a result of the negligence and inefficiency of the authorities in that city."[8]

In response, Governor Harmon suspended the mayor and the sheriff for gross neglect of duty three days after Etherington's death. Both men would resign their offices. Etherington's mother, already sickly, died soon after she heard of his demise. His grief-stricken father would hang himself a year later.

"Now it is the eye of the world," one publication declared, "because of the lynching which occurred on its public square on Friday, July 8, which will henceforth be known as Newark's Black Friday."[9] Shamed by this episode, a grand jury moved quickly, returning fifty-eight indictments, nearly half of which were for first-degree murder. It was easy to assign collective guilt, but not individual responsibility.

Levi Valentine, a deaf mute, and Vance Miller, both African Americans, were arrested for being instrumental in the lynching. Miller allegedly struck Etherington in the head with a hammer.

The grand jury, sheriff, and attorneys examining the telephone pole on which Etherington was lynched.

In a sense, Montelle Watha was also a lynching victim, although he lost his freedom, not his life. Nobody knew quite what to make of Watha. He was a dark man, forty nine years old, but beyond that there wasn't much agreement. Some said he was an Indian from Bombay, although the 1910 census listed him as a native of West India. There was general agreement that his grasp of English, not to mention of American law, was limited.

As this editorial cartoon suggests, the mayor, sheriff, and chief of police of Newark did little to prevent the lynching.

Watha was the first tried and sentenced for the lynching of Etherington because, "Earlier in the evening he mingled with the crowd, and being called upon to speak by other colored men, he got up and gave utterance to language which had a criminal effect."[10] It was a rambling denunciation of the detectives. However, he was not present when Etherington was seized or killed. The judge sentenced him to twenty years for manslaughter, but later said he should have made it for no more than five.

Of the fourteen men indicted with Watha, only one other received a sentence equal to his, Walter Diehl. Both men were pardoned within four years of their convictions.

Still, there would be no other lynchings in Licking County. To protect it from souvenir hunters, the telephone pole was wrapped in metal before finally being taken down in 1953. The *Newark Advocate* reported having a piece of the noose and Etherington's bloodstained necktie in its own "museum of curiosities," but these have been lost over the years.[11]

Attempted Lynching, Athens County, July 1910—Kline, Thomas [W]

"Get a rope! Let us do what they did at Newark," was the cry of the Nelsonville mob which called for the lynching of Thomas Kline.[12]

A member of the local police force, Kline had killed John Lanning a few days earlier. Then, on July 12, 1910, while out on bail, he attempted to arrest Wendell Kelly for drunkenness. At the time, Kelly was in front of Amos Nelson's residence. During the ensuing struggle, Kelly and Kline tumbled into Nelson's house and Nelson joined in on the side of Kelly.

Kline summoned Police Chief Eddington to the scene. Nelson told Eddington that the arrest could not occur without a warrant. After one was obtained, Eddington and Kline started to escort Kelly to jail. En route, they were surrounded by a mob that called for Kline to be lynched. One of them threw a brick. However, the law officers continued on their way. It is unknown whether he was convicted of Lanning's murder.

Expected Lynching, Logan County, February 1911—Beers, John [W]; Beers, Gibson [W]

Someone was stealing corn from the cribs of farmers near Bellefontaine.

While standing guard one night, a wealthy farmer named Burr Kerns caught John Beers trespassing on his farm and knocked him down. Later, Kerns, along with his brother Daniel, a cousin Charles, and a neighbor Charles Bussart, paid a visit on Beers to warn him to stop the theft.

Beers denied the accusation and they began to fight. According to Beers, one of the men came at him with a shovel and another knocked down his wife. His son, Gibson Beers, fired a shotgun at Kerns and the blast nearly took off his head.

Following the shooting, the farmer's friends formed a lynch mob and descended on the Beers farm. John and Gibson barricaded themselves inside their home with rifles until the sheriff arrived with a posse. They surrendered to him and were rushed off in an automobile.

Expected Lynching, Erie County, June 1911—Winne, John [W]

If it hadn't been for the quick action of Mayor H.R. Williams and Marshal Melvin Gross, sixty-year-old John Winne, an admitted tramp, might have found himself hanging at the end of a line.

Accused of a felonious attack on Luella Storms, age ten, by her father, Frank Storms, Winne came close to being lynched in Vermillion on June 14, 1911. Instead, Mayor Williams and Marshal Gross whisked him away to jail in Sandusky. He pleaded guilty to the charge.

Mob Violence, Wayne County, June 1911—Heilman, Michael [W]

On Tuesday evening, June 20, 1911, Michael Heilman, age twenty-eight, of Fredericksburg was abducted from his home by a band of twenty men and women dressed as White Caps. Stripped of his clothing, they tied him to a post and flogged with a whip until his flesh was raw. His wounds were then doused in carbolic acid and red pepper. Pepper was also thrown into his eyes.

After being tarred, feathered, and ridden on a rail, Heilman was turned loose to run for ten miles, screaming in agony. He finally collapsed into unconsciousness.

Authorities were waiting to see if Heilman recovered before making arrests. At the very least, it was feared he might be permanently blinded, having lost the sight in one eye. And his body was described as "a mass of blisters."[13]

Heilman lived near a group of Amish in the village of Trail and it was initially thought that religious differences may have had something to do with the assault. However, it later turned out it was in retaliation for his relationship with Mrs. Rebecca Volk, a mother of seven children.

Mob Violence [TI], Cuyahoga County, June 1911—Jordon, John [B]

Some 200 white men and boys engaged in a gun battle with three African Americans on June 27, 1911, in the city of Cleveland. The black men had entered the orchard of John

Decker and begun picking cherries. When Decker ordered them to leave, an ex-con, John Jordon, drew a gun.

Decker and his hired hand, Arthur Beamish, then borrowed two revolvers from neighbors and pursued them. They were soon joined by others. Gunfire erupted at Lorraine Avenue and West 98th Street. When Jordon ran out of bullets, he was rushed by the crowd and knocked down several times. He later died at a hospital.

While Jordan was not hanged, his case is frequently cited as a lynching because he died at the hands of a mob. And just ten years later, newspapers were reporting (incorrectly) that he "was lynched for murder."[14]

Attempted Lynching, Stark County, July 1911—Mickens, Harvey [B]

Harvey Mickens, a black man, was charged with assaulting sixteen-year-old Myra Evans, daughter of Richard Evans, a miner. He was captured on July 10, 1911, by a posse of officers who chased him several miles on a railroad hand car. They then placed him on a locomotive and shipped him to jail in Massillon.

Word quickly got around of the suspect's capture and a crowd was already awaiting him. When Mickens was seen entering the town, the crowd swarmed in his direction, but was driven back by law enforcement. By evening, a mob of several hundred people had assembled in the northern part of the city, threatening to avenge the attack on the white girl. Cries of "Hang him!" and "Lynch the brute!" rent the night air.[15]

For several hours, 100 policemen and deputy sheriffs, armed with riot guns, held the mob at bay as it converged on city hall. However, the mob, it was said, lacked adequate leadership. Nevertheless, in anticipation of further trouble, the entire police force was called out and a number of special deputies sworn in. The following day, Mickens was taken to Canton for his protection.

Expected Lynching, Summit County, August 1912—Unknown man [W]

Near Stop 35 of the Akron interurban line, just over the Cuyahoga County line, a manhunt took place in August 1912. A volunteer posse of farmers armed with guns and carrying ropes, diligently searched for a man who "attempted an assault" on Gertrude, the ten-year-old daughter of Dr. R. Somers on August 16.[16] The girl's father and two uncles led some seventy-five men over the marshy ground.

However, Sheriff Dave Ferguson of Summit County, two deputies, and a detective were also on the scene to prevent any harm befalling the suspect. "There will be no lynching," the sheriff declared. "That's all there is to it."[17]

Meanwhile, the girl was recovering at home with black and blue marks on her throat. Presumably, the suspect, a light haired man in a blue suit and straw sailor hat, was never apprehended.

Mob Violence, Huron County, August 1912—LaValley, Minnie [W]

A young girl who purportedly had been flirting with several men in Clarksfield was persuaded to take a walk with three of them on the evening of August 30, 1912—only the men were actually women in disguise. They had gone but a short way when they were joined by five other women in male attire.

Taken to a remote spot, the girl was stripped of her clothing, tarred and feathered, and warned that if she didn't leave town "worse would follow."[18] The girl, age eighteen, subsequently did leave town, accompanied by her sister. The authorities refused to investigate the case because they said they had warned her to leave.

The girl was Minnie M. LaValley, daughter of Henry and Marietta LaValley, who planned to ensure her attackers were prosecuted. Following the incident, she purportedly had gone to Cleveland. The prosecuting attorney for Huron County said that unless her parents made a complaint, nothing could be done.

Eventually, six men (not women) were indicted for "riotous conspiracy," including Constable Reginald Thomas.[19] Their ages ranged from twenty to forty. The first, Ernest Welch, was convicted of assault and battery in November and sentenced to the Toledo workhouse.

Shortly before the verdict was reached, LaValley said she would commit suicide if the men were acquitted because her life would be ruined. She lived another sixty years.

Expected Lynching, Wood County, November 1915—Willey, John Henry [W]

Officially, John Henry Willey committed suicide, but his widow, Olive, never believed it. When his corpse was found suspended from a tree by an old clothesline near Bradner on the morning of November 28, 1915, the first thought was that he had been lynched. After all, there had been several threats, including a letter which read:

> Mr. Willey: I take pleasure in informing you that a "lynching bee" will be pulled off one of these evenings at Henry Saam's, and without a doubt the mob will make a clean sweep of it while they are at it. Yours from "Thirty Good Neighbors."[20]

Willey and his wife lived with Saam, who was her father.

Nine months earlier on February 12, 1915, and just a short distance away, Willey's grandmother, Eva Kimbel, age eighty-six, had been shot in the head and his grandfather, Joel Kimbel, age seventy-two, severely beaten. Suspicion fell on Willey.

In his defense, he said that he had left his home near Rollers shortly after seven o'clock that evening and arrived at Gibsonburg, five miles away, about two hours later. However, this would not have precluded him from committing the crime.

Initially charged with first degree murder and assault with intent to kill, Willey was eventually tried on second degree murder. A total of 171 witnesses were subpoenaed at a cost of $2,000 to $3,000. After twenty-two hours of deliberations, the jury found him guilty of assault and battery (or, perhaps, manslaughter) in the killing of Eva Kimble.

Attorney B.F. James immediately made a motion for a new trial which was granted by Judge Elmer McClelland. In setting aside the verdict, he said that Willey was either guilty of homicide or not guilty of anything. Willey was released on $5,000 bond.

In the week before his death, Willey had gone to Bowling Green and then Pemberville in a futile attempt to borrow money for his defense. He had started for home about 5:30 Saturday evening and wasn't seen again until the following morning when his dead body was discovered by a neighboring farmer. His horse and wagon were nearby.

This is where accounts diverge. According to one, a heavy leather strap hung from Willey's left wrist and his right hand was badly swollen. Speculation was that his hands had been bound behind him, but he had managed to wrest them free. His clothing was torn to shreds and the ground beneath him had been thoroughly trampled by a crowd of people.

However, a different story would emerge at the inquest conducted by Wood County Coroner Dan B. Spitler of Hoytville. After the body was taken to an undertaker for examination, no marks or bruises were found on it, although his neck was broken. His clothing was in good order down to his necktie which was not disarranged in any fashion and his shoes were polished. Supposedly the only footprints on the hard scrabble ground beneath him were his own. His feet were about eight inches off the ground.

After hearing dozens of witnesses who testified to Willey's state of mine and conduct in the hours before his death, Spitler concluded that he had taken his own life.

> "I am certain he did not commit suicide," B.F. James, Willey's attorney, countered. "He was in my office yesterday afternoon and we discussed the coming trial on the assault and battery charge. He was in high spirits, declaring he expected an acquittal. He was elated over being at liberty under bond."[21]

In reaching his decision, the coroner disregarded testimony from Dr. Black that he had observed definite depressions on Willey's wrists when he examined the body in the woods, although they were not evident at the undertaker's. He also ignored the claim of Samuel Hiser, a neighbor, who said he heard several automobiles pass his house early that morning, followed by gunshots. And he also dismissed the well-known threats to lynch the victim.

Without knowing anything about the character of Dr. Spitler, there is no reason to suggest that his ruling was motivated by anything other than the quest for the truth.

However, as a consequence of the Smith Act, Mrs. Willey, left alone to raise two infant daughters, would be entitled to compensation of up to $5,000 if her husband's death was categorized as the result of a lynching rather than suicide. In 1917, she sued the board of commissioners of Wood and Sandusky counties for $5,000 each, charging laxity of law enforcement. She lost her case on appeal.

Mob Violence, Mahoning County, January 1916—Davis, Robert [W]; Get, George [W]; Rosa, Frank [W]

It is remembered as the East Youngstown Riot.

On New Year's Day 1916, a Saturday, local tube mill workers walked off the job, although some may have done so a few days earlier.

Following the depression of 1913–1915, the workers, many of whom were immigrants, had demanded an increase in wages, reduced hours, and other concessions. When they didn't get them, they went on strike.

Three days later, the strikers were joined by workers at Republic Iron & Steel and Youngstown Sheet & Tube.

On Wednesday and Thursday, confrontations occurred between the strikers and the police or detectives hired to guard the plants. Although an increase in wages for steel workers was announced, not all the workers were willing to compromise on the other issues. By now, large quantities of whisky and weapons were adding to the volatility of the situation.

The next day, January 7, the strikers forced the authorities of East Youngstown to release an accused rioter who had been locked up in the village jail. With thousands of idle and disgruntled workers milling about, fights were inevitable. It soon became apparent that village police could not handle the situation.

At about 4 o'clock in the afternoon, as darkness was falling, a throng of men and women gathered at the east end of the bridge leading from East Youngstown to the Youngstown Sheet & Tube plant on the other side of the railroad tracks. They faced off the with an armed force guarding the entrance to the plant.

At shift change, a few workers tried to enter the plant in defiance of the strikers and their supporters. Allegedly, someone in the crowd fired a revolver at the guards stationed on the bridge. They returned fire with their rifles and the people broke ranks and ran. And, for all intents and purposes, that was the end of the hostilities between the strikers and the guards. However, that was the just beginning of the riot.

Militia dispersing rioters in East Youngstown after they caused more than $1 million worth of damage in 1916 (Library of Congress).

As Joseph Green Butler described it:

> The crowd that broke under rifle fire apparently forgot the cause of its grievance. It became a mob, and the mob members, already filled with drink, broke into saloons and plied themselves still more. Almost an hour after the clash at the bridge a flame burst out in a nearby building and in a moment the mad attempt to burn down a city was on.[22]

At least three people were killed: George Get, age twenty-three, who was shot through the head, Frank Rosa, who was shot through the lungs, and Robert Davis, age twenty-four, who was struck in the chest by a stray bullet. More than fifty others were wounded and in excess of a million dollars' worth of property was destroyed.

Many who fled from the gunfire took refuge in the East Youngstown saloons, breaking into them in some cases. Almost an hour later, one of the buildings in East Youngstown caught fire. After that, one building after another was set ablaze by the drunken mob, while others fetched their wagons and began looting the stores.

For six hours, anarchy held sway in East Youngstown until a volunteer group of citizens took action. While they could not check the spread of the flames, they did manage to curb further acts of destruction.

At dawn, some 2,700 National Guard troops with fixed bayonets were in place, supported by machine guns. They quickly dispersed the remaining rioters and instituted martial law for the next week. Over 400 people were taken into custody. Although the town of East Cleveland was reduced to ashes, little attempt had been made to damage the property of the steel plants.

A week after the rioting, two Austrians—Dan Fleck and John Brisky—confessed that they had been sent from New York to start a strike, thereby preventing the manufacture of war munitions for the allies. It was suggested that they might be German agents.

When it was all over, charges against the companies were dismissed. However, five rioters were sentenced to the Ohio State Reformatory and one to the Ohio Penitentiary on a murder charge.

Mob Violence, Knox County, April 1916—Clark, Samuel [W]

At about nine o'clock on Saturday evening, April 29, 1916, Samuel Clark of Knox County was about to fall asleep when he heard a "pounding on his door."[23] Rising from bed, he asked who it was. "I'd like to buy that cow of yours," a man said.[24]

As soon as he opened the door, Clark was seized by a group of seven masked men. "Come on boys, we've got him."[25] They stripped off his underclothing and carried him into the front yard, secured by a rope. A half-gallon of tar had been warmed at a fire on a neighboring hill and they proceeded to apply it to Clark's body, inflicting painful burns. Chicken feathers were then smeared all over the tar until he was completely covered.

Clark, age fifty-six, had a large quantity of whiskers and long hair. The men made sure to mix the tar thoroughly through the locks of hair, twisting it into tight knots. He was then told he had ten days to leave the country or he would be hanged.

After he was released, Clark tried to remove the tar with coal oil, but large patches of skin also came away. His whiskers showed where they had been ripped out in spots. He complained to anyone who would listen of severe stomach pains and said his back was covered with bruises from the kicking he had received. One of his assailants had even walked over his body. Still covered with tar from the shoulders down on his back, he said the men had done it for "Just damned orneriness."[26]

Within the week, Edward Boyd and Earl Rine (or Ryan), prominent citizens from the southeastern portion of the county, were arrested by Deputy Sheriff Walter B. Mossholder on assault and battery charges. It was reported they had been intoxicated when they assaulted Clark.

Rine had fought with Clark after the farmer accused Mrs. Rine of feeding his hogs "pounded glass."[27] However, the wife insisted she had never been on Clark's farm and that this was just one of a number of lies he had spread since moving from Coshocton to Knox County. (In response, Clark claimed that he was the victim of rumors and had not accused Mrs. Rine of poisoning his hog.) Boyd had also clashed with him over some matter.

A resident of New Castle claimed that Clark was in the habit of telling one man he had seen a neighbor coming from his cellar and then immediately telling the neighbor the opposite. This would result in a fight between the two men. Clark had a brother in the insane asylum and his neighbors felt the brother had more sense than he did.

In fact, the whole section of the county was in agreements that Clark had to leave. Sheriff John F. Woolison and Deputy Mossholder planned to investigate the matter thoroughly.

Not long afterward, Clark's wife, Isabelle, expelled him from their home and instituted divorce proceedings. His son, John Clark, who had not seen him for fourteen years ostensibly because he had been traveling, offered to allow him to live with him in Mt. Vernon rent free.

A little over two weeks after the incident, Woolison and Mossholder made the last arrests in the case: John Spang, Melvin and Roy Toothman, and Joseph (or Josias) and Melvin Jones.

In June, all of the details regarding Clark's marriage started to come out and it was apparently not a happy one. He was wed to Isabelle Toten, a widow with three daughters and a son, on April 21, 1910. They had no children together. According to Isabelle, she owned two cows, one calf, one sow, seventy-five chickens, together with most of the household goods. Her husband, on the other hand, had a farm in Coshocton County with five horses, one heifer, three hogs, and a buggy.

Isabelle charged Clark mistreated her, called her unprintable names, and prevented her daughters from visiting. When one did, he choked her and threatened to beat her brains out with a stick. She said he did not want her to have contact with her children, the neighbors, the church—anyone—and he always carried a shotgun.

In August, Boyd, Spang, the Toothmans, the Joneses, and Rine were indicted for the assault on Clark.

After New Year's, Samuel Clark came into town, complaining he had been suffering from the grip, all alone without the comfort of his wife or neighbors. He had a rope wrapped several times around his waist and tied in knots to keep his overcoat closed. He was a pitiful sight, but he still took pride in his five horses which he claimed were the fastest steeds in the county…

Clark's estranged wife, Isabelle, died of paralysis in March at the age of sixty. She had suffered her first stroke three years earlier and a second just a month before. Her maiden name, as it turned out, was Rine, suggesting she might have been related to Earl Rine. Since she had sued him for divorce, Clark had not been allowed to come near her, but did attend the funeral.

Following Isabelle's death, Clark applied to acquire to the cow and the sow on her farm. He claimed the animals were rightly his and she had been keeping them on her property in Coshocton County. "I've got $124 'lapped up' in that cow and sow and they're starvin' to death."[28] He said the sow had lost six of twelve piglets and the cow was hardly recognizable. This led to more conflicts with the law.

"I know every hill, holler, and dugout in Jackson Township," Clark told Deputy Sheriff Burr H. Lytle at the courthouse on Thursday morning, "and if you come to get me, I'll get you."[29]

"You say I won't come back?" the deputy responded.[30]

"You might come back a carcass," Clark threatened.[31]

A year after the incident, Clark asserted that he suffered injuries from which he would never recover. When his case went to trial in May, five of the accused entered vigorous denials. They also claimed that Clark was a resident of Coshocton County. However, by June, all but Melvin Toothman pleaded guilty to charges of assault and battery, and were fined $10 each and court costs for "riotous conspiracy."[32]

Attempted Lynching, Allen County, August 1916—Eley, Sherman [W]; Daniels, Charles [B]

Charles Daniels wasn't the sort of person you'd want to stick your neck out for, but Sheriff Sherman E. Eley of Allen County did just that—literally—thwarting one lynching, while nearly precipitating his own.

A "negro giant" (by some accounts), Daniels had allegedly attacked a twenty- (or twenty-two)-year-old pregnant white woman, Vivian A. Baber (or Barber), the wife of a local farmer.[33] She said that she was alone in her kitchen on August 30, 1916, when Daniels entered her house and demanded food. Incensed by her refusal to give him anything, Daniels beat her over the head, slashed her throat with a razor, gouged out one of her eyes, and left her to die. According to court records, she was also raped.

Later that morning, one of a dozen posses of angry farmers numbering some 200 men with bloodhounds captured the suspect in a woods not far from the Baber house in Shawnee Township, three miles from Lima. A "transient," he could not explain what he was doing there.

Sheriff Eley was apparently close to the scene for he quickly took Daniels into custody. Given the mood of the crowd, the sheriff feared the situation was likely to escalate. He elected to transport the prisoner to Putnam County Jail in Ottawa, eighteen miles away, rather than returning with him to Lima.

Public opinion of the sheriff hinged upon how a person felt about the temperance issue. Eley had been elected by the "dry" vote—those who felt Allen County should not allow the sale of alcohol. However, there were also a sizable number of citizens who represented the "wet" vote. Among their number were individuals of what the newspapers branded the "outlaw" and the "sporting" element. Sheriff Eley had already antagonized them earlier in the year when he had asked for the National Guard to stop the staging of a prize fight in Lima.

As the *New York Times* reported, Company C drove promoters, employees, special policemen, and spectators from Murphy Street ballpark and put a halt to preparations for the battle between Jack Dillon and Yankee Gilbert. Resentment toward Eley had been smoldering ever since. The assault on Vivian Baber (combined with copious consumption of alcohol in the Lima saloons) galvanized them into action.

While the sheriff was away, an angry crowd—estimated at 1,000 to 3,000 (or even 5,000) people—began to assemble outside the Allen County jail just before dusk, armed with shotguns, rifles, and revolvers. Historian James Bowsher asserts that some of them were members of the local Ku Klux Klan. When it was announced that the sheriff had taken the prisoner to the Ohio State Hospital for the Criminally Insane in Lima, they refused to believe it.

Breaking into the jail, which was guarded by a single deputy, the mob forced the sheriff's wife, Hazel Eley, to open all the cells. When they did not find Daniels, they proceeded to break into the courthouse and the sheriff's residence, forcing Mrs. Eley to flee into the night with her daughter and her younger sister.

When the sheriff returned from Ottawa at about 9:40 p.m., he found an angry mob waiting for him at the city limits. They demanded that he disclose the whereabouts of the prisoner, but he refused. He was chased through his own house and into the Elks Club. Seizing Eley, the horde stripped off his clothes and beat and kicked him in an effort to make him tell them where Daniels was. He still wouldn't.

The mob resisted all efforts to make it disperse. Chief of Police Kinney had called out his entire force, but his officers were overpowered by the heavily armed rioters.[34] They even fought off the fire hoses trained on them by the Lima Fire Department. Bravely, Eley continued to refuse to disclose what he had done with his prisoner.

Stripping a length of rope from an interurban car, the throng placed a noose around Eley's neck, strung it over the cross arm of a telephone pole or lamppost or transit pole, and pulled it tight. Cries of "Kill the nigger protector!" split the darkness as the crowd surged, knocking him over and preventing those who had the rope from stringing him up.[35] He was then trampled. Finally, he admitted he had taken Daniels to Ottawa.

While the mob held Eley prisoner under the pole, Chief Kinney called upon the citizens to join the force, but they wouldn't. The fire department was called out, arriving just as the mob was departing. The motorized fire trucks were run three abreast down

Allen County Sheriff Sherman Eley was nearly killed in preventing the lynching of Charles Daniels in 1916 (Jim Bowsher collection).

the streets at twenty miles per hour, spraying chemicals on those that had not joined the motor procession, and the men on foot were dispersed.

Having lifted the sheriff into a truck, the rioters drove off. More than fifty and possibly as many as 100 carloads of rioters set out for the Putnam County Jail. Those who made the trip were frustrated in their efforts to locate Daniels.

Even as they were arriving, Sheriff Miller had placed Daniels in a fast automobile headed for Toledo. They suspected he was one of the two huddled figures seen in the vehicle.

While their guard was lowered, Eley managed to escape. He made his way to a hotel, where his captors searched for him, but by then he had been spirited away by friends so he could receive medical attention for his cuts, bruises, a broken arm, and two broken ribs.

Evidently, Eley was treated for his injuries elsewhere for when he returned to Lima he learned that his three-year-old daughter, Doris, had passed away from a combination of pneumonia and shock. She had become seriously ill when the mob was searching his house. His sister-in-law, eighteen-year-old Cecil Kephart, was also a patient in the hospital, having become a nervous wreck during the violence.

That evening, Governor Frank B. Willis and Adjutant General Benson W. Hough of the Ohio National Guard were notified of the situation in Lima. Although no official request had been made, Willis authorized Hough to arrange for troops to be transported to Allen County if needed.

The day after the riot, County Prosecutor Ortha O. Barr called on Governor Willis to send in the National Guard to keep the peace. However, no action was taken because only the sheriff, mayor, or county judge could make such a request. Local government officials had already ordered all saloons to clock at six o'clock on August 31. African American residents of Lima were warned to stay off the streets and scores of them had taken the additional precaution of leaving town.

As a Grand Jury was expected to indict as many as 200 people for their involvement in the lynch mob, the entire police force of Lima was joined by fifty special deputy sheriffs in patrolling the streets. Although a large crowd did form in front of the county jail again, they did not misbehave. Meanwhile, Daniels was safely housed in the Henry County Jail at Napoleon, where he had been transferred when word reached Ottawa that the mob was on its way.

A week later, Eley ordered the prisoners from the county jail, chained together, and paraded past Vivian Baber to see if she could pick out her assailant. Mrs. Baber was still recovering from her injuries in the city hospital, but she did not hesitate to identify the culprit. However, the man she accused was not Charles Daniels, but an individual who had been locked up for the past three months.

Seven days after that, Daniels "stood a three hour grilling" by Prosecutor Barr. Not only did he continue to deny assaulting Mrs. Baber, but insisted he had never even seen her before.[36] Nevertheless, he was arraigned before Common Pleas Court Judge Klinger, held without bond, tried, convicted, and sentenced to the Ohio Penitentiary. After all that had happened, they weren't about to set him free.

Of the thirty-four rioters indicted, half pleaded guilty. The rest were tried over the following months in various venues on charges of assaulting Sheriff Eley. Some of them were found guilty and sentenced to the Ohio Penitentiary.

Only a couple of weeks after the attack on Mrs. Baber, Ida Knittle, age twenty-three, reported that another African American man, James Smith, age thirty-one, had entered her home and assaulted her. She said she grabbed up her five-year-old son, Henry, and fled. The suspect was quickly apprehended and "held in secret confinement by the police" as a precaution against more mob violence.[37]

Apparently, the Grand Jury did not believe Mrs. Knittle's allegation for it did not indict Smith and he was turned loose. Perhaps her husband, Grover, was not as prominent as John Baber.

The Cleveland *Advocate*, a black newspaper, was quick to heap praise on Sheriff Eley:

> [L]uckily, in the town of Lima there was a MAN WHO DARE TO DO HIS DUTY AS HE SAW IT … In the midst of the maelstrom of frenzy which had engulfed the citizens of Lima stood a pillar of manhood, Sheriff Sherman Ely, the hero of the hour.... Think of it! This was surely HEROISM if there ever was such.... IN ALL TIMES LIKE THESE, GOD GIVE U.S. MEN LIKE ELY.[*sic*][38]

The NAACP subsequently presented Sheriff Eley with a silver loving cup while Governor Willis added that the world appreciates a man "who stands squarely with a heart unafraid and his face to the front at times of stress."[39]

When Eley's term of office ended in 1918, he left law enforcement to become a teacher in a one-room school house for the next thirty-three years. The modest hero, who always said he was only doing his job, died at the age of seventy-eight. As for Vivian Baber, she went on to have thirteen children with her husband, John W., quietly passing away at the age of seventy-nine.

Mob Violence, Hamilton County, November 1917—Bigelow, Herbert S. [W]

Herbert S. Bigelow of Cincinnati was abducted on November 4, 1917, by white-clad vigilantes opposed to his pacifist politics. The following day, he was found near Florence, Kentucky.

Bigelow had been stripped of his clothes and lashed a dozen times with a blacksnake whip "in the name of the poor women and children of Belgium"—or so one of his abductors said.[40] Afterward, they gave him the names of two other prospective victims, pointed him toward Cincinnati, and told not to go anywhere for ten minutes.

Bigelow was hospitalized for at least a week while recovering from his injuries. While many people disagreed with his pacifist stance, most felt that the actions of the night riders should be condemned. They purportedly had 800 members, forty percent of whom lived in Cincinnati and the rest in Newport and Covington.

Expected Lynching, Auglaize County, June 1917—Anderson, William [B]

Fourteen-year-old Emma (or Ruth) Pester was out picking wild strawberries on June 16, 1917, when she was "criminally assaulted ... by a burly negro."[41] The daughter of a well-known farmer living near Wapakoneta, Emma was alone by the railroad track that passed through her father's property when she was touched on the arm by a man she didn't know. She began to run and yell for help.

The man pulled a pistol from his pocket and ordered Emma to stop or he would kill her. When she didn't, he chased her several hundred yards, seized her by the neck, and threw her to the ground where he raped her. As he made his escape, the girl ran home and told her family what had happened.

Immediately, Sheriff Ora Hinton organized a posse and set out after the suspect. Soon, they had overtaken and arrested two black men. Emma was then taken to the county jail in Wapakoneta to view the two men and identified one as her attacker. Fearing a possible attempt to lynch him, the accused was taken to another jail.

The suspect, William Anderson, was later released when workmen on the railroad corroborated his alibi on the day of the assault. Afterwards, Emma admitted she might have been mistaken in her identification "because of fright."[42]

In all, five African American men were arrested and released.

False Report of Attempted Lynching, Fulton County, September 1917—Lehman, Fred [W]

Up through World War I, the most notorious murder case to take place in Fulton County involved Frederick "Fred" Lehman. Lehman, a twenty-six-year-old German farmer, lived just outside Swanton with his wife, Grace Hall, twenty-two, on one of several farms owned by his father.

A member of the Gleaners Lodge, Lehman was an outspoken anti-interventionist when it came to the war then ongoing in Europe. So far, he had not been drafted into the military because he was married. However, by the middle of September 1917, he knew he could be called up at any time. Then on September 18, 1917, the unthinkable happened.

At three o'clock that morning, Chet Mills, whose house was directly across the road from Lehman's, heard several shots and cries coming from the direction of the Lehman farm. When he got up to investigate, he found Frederick Lehman, wounded by the mailbox, and his wife, Grace, dying in her bed.

Sheriff W.S. Boone arrived from Wauseon, the county seat, a half hour later. By then,

Grace was deceased, while Fred had slugs in his left arm and leg, as well as knife slashes to his chest and abrasions on his forehead.

Lehman said he did not know how long he lay unconscious, but when he came to he crawled toward the road and called for help. When Mills found him, he immediately summoned his wife and placed a call to Dr. Cosgrove from Swanton. Entering the house, Mrs. Mills found Grace Lehman, a bullet hole in her temple, her arms folded and the bedding in perfect order. There were no signs of a struggle.

Fred claimed that he had gotten up in the night because his stomach was upset and heard noises in the barn. Going outside to investigate, he noticed the barn door was opened wider than it should have been. No sooner had he stepped inside than he was knocked to the ground by a blow to the head. Looking up, he saw three men standing over him, one holding a pitchfork.

"You damned draft-dodger," one of them said. "We got called up and are bound for camp. And we'll be damned if we'll leave you behind with that big bank roll on you."[43] The men then robbed him of $55. After that, they produced a rope, tied a slipknot in it, and said they were going to hang him.

However, he managed to break free and run for his life, only to be cut down with gunfire after about 100 feet with a bullet in his arm and another in his leg.

When Sheriff Boone and Deputy McQuillen arrived, they found that many tracks and other possible clues at the crime scene had already been obliterated by those who came before them. Several drawers in the house had been rifled through and the contents dumped on the floor. However, $25 in cash and a couple of watches remained untouched in one of them.

Feeling the case was beyond his abilities, Boone called the chief of police in Toledo and asked for assistance. Two detectives soon arrived and began reviewing the evidence. Lehman's empty pocketbook was found in the hayrack. A fifteen-foot piece of rope was looped over a rafter. And the telephone wires had been cut. However, they found it curious that neither Lehman's nor Mills's dogs had barked.

The sheriff also found a .22 caliber revolver under the milk house with three cartridges missing. An old knife was also turned up with blood on one blade which could have caused the abrasions on Fred's forehead and breast. The bullet wounds in her arm and leg were probably sustained as Grace Lehman was running away from her attacker. An analysis of Fred's clothing showed he had been shot from the front—not the back—and at close range.

Dr. F.S. Bishop, coroner, had been called to the Lehman farm on the morning of Monday, September 17, 1917. When he arrived, he found Mrs. Lehman had been dead about two hours. He observed the autopsy performed by Drs. Cosgrove and Brailey which determined that she died from a .22 caliber bullet to the brain. It came from the pistol found under the milk house, as did Fred's wounds. A witness was prepared to testify that he saw Frederick Lehman purchase a similar revolver at a store in Delta.

Everything was pointing to Fred as the culprit, but the detectives lacked a motive. Then they received a tip: "Look into Fred Lehman's shananigans with Louise Bell."[44]

Louise was a neighbor's wife and would later admit she had become involved in a sexual relationship with Fred. In fact, he purportedly told her, "I like you better than my wife. And anyhow, she's sick all the time and wouldn't live long."[45] He was also rumored to have been paying attention to a woman in the eastern part of the county, Mrs. Elsie Fenton.

The prosecution would argue that Fred shot his wife while she slept then faked the attack on himself. After forty-one hours of deliberation, the jury found Fred Lehman guilty of murder, but with a recommendation of mercy. He served twenty-five years as a model prisoner at the Ohio Penitentiary.

Mob Violence, Allen County, March 1918—Linderman, Barney [W]; Jettinger, Carl [W]; Marks, J.C. [W]

German-Americans during World War I often had to defend themselves from allegations that they were pro–German. While some of them unquestionably were, others undeniably weren't.

In Delphos, an ad-hoc group of "patriots," the Delphos Vigilance Committee, took it upon themselves to make a house-to-house canvas of the town on March 25, 1918. Some 450 strong (including fifty women), the mob would drag out of bed anyone suspected of having pro–German sympathies and transport him/her downtown to city hall to salute and/or kiss the American flag.

The irony is that Delphos was founded by German immigrants and the accusations were being made against German Americans largely by German Americans. And these incidents weren't confined to Delphos or even Ohio. Newspapers of the era report similar demonstrations occurring throughout the country. Amazingly, the committee was formed in the Kaiser Café, owned by a Delphos resident named Kaiser Wilhelm, who was also a leader of the vigilantes. Given his name, he probably thought this was a good way to keep from having his own loyalty challenged. The committee was working from a list which contained a score of names.

Led by Richard L. Linderman, son of a former common pleas court judge, the Delphos group forced five men to kiss the flag and promise to display it in their homes (three others escaped). One wealthy merchant, Barney Linderman, Judge Linderman's cousin, had a flag nailed to his shoe store. For a time, he tried to hold the mob at bay with a revolver, but was finally persuaded to lay it down by Police Chief Clark Thompson. The accused was then compelled to kiss the flag twice and salute it. He was also warned that if the flag were taken down, he would be pitched into the canal and drowned. The attack had been prompted by the shoe salesman's refusal to buy war bonds.

Carl Jettinger, president of the Delphos newspaper (as well as the Buckeye Printers Association), disappeared the night after a flag was nailed to his door. His crime was not printing materials supporting the Liberty Loan program in his newspaper. In his absence, his assistant editor continued to publish the paper and devoted a fair amount of column space to denouncing him. The next night, four more alleged pro–Germans were forced to kiss the flag while 1,000 citizens looked on. Those who refused were threatened with hanging from nearby telephone poles.

Several days after the public demonstrations had subsided, J.C. Marks placed an ad in the *Delphos Herald* offering to pay $100 to anyone who would identify the person who accused him of having pro–German sympathies. After a few days passed, he was contacted by W.C. Baxter who admitted he had been the one who gave Marks's name to the vigilance committee and wanted to claim his $100. Marks refused. Baxter sued and was awarded $100 when the matter went to trial.

Mob Violence, Lucas County, April 1918—Beattie, John J. [W]; Hall, Perry J. Jr. [W]; Wagner, William [W]

Three residents of Holland were tarred and feathered on Saturday night, April 13,

1918. The victims were: John J. Beattie (or Beatty), age thirty-two; Perry J. Hall, Jr., age twenty-five; and William Wagner, age forty-four. The men were then marched to Liberty Court on Madison Avenue, made to kiss the American flag and swear fealty to the government of the United States. Afterward, they were turned over to the police.

Beattie, a socialist, openly opposed to the war. He not only refused to buy bonds, but had encouraged men to avoid the military draft. Those who favored the war felt that such actions should be punishable by law, but President Woodrow Wilson declared that their freedom of speech was protected. Nevertheless, Beattie had incurred the rancor of a group of Lucas County residents who were associated with the "White Hats" or Ku Klux Klan. Ironically, Beattie's brother-in-law was the chairman of the Liberty Bond Committee in Holland.

Hall was the marshal of Holland, which had purportedly been named after his grandfather ("Hall Land"). And Wagner, being the son of a German immigrant, was probably the most obvious target for a group that questioned the trio's patriotism.

Toledo's Ku Klux Klan had a committee, the "Supreme Thirteens," which maintained a "blacklist" of alleged German sympathizers. Eighty-six Klansmen in seventeen vehicles left Toledo at eight o'clock in the evening to drive to Holland.

When Hall learned that there were fifteen or twenty strangers in the village looking for Beattie, he armed himself and started for Toledo with Wagner to find him. They found him changing interurban cars and started back to Holland with him.[46]

About midnight, the Klansmen intercepted a car in which Beattie was being driven by Wagner in the company of Hall. Although they denied Beattie was with them, one of the Klansmen identified him. Placed in the truck, the three men were driven to a point near Ottawa Park where they were "tried" before a kangaroo court.

Although Beattie was the only one they were after, they were told they would all be treated the same. After the crowd pronounced them guilty, the "judge" said:

> You pretty little gang of pro-Germans, Socialists and what-not, you've heard the verdict. The sentence of this court is that you be smeared with tar from head to toe, with the exception only of that part around your eyes, and showered with feathers until you resemble the tribe to which you belong.[47]

Despite the presence of 500 onlookers, including some Toledo patrolmen, the vigilantes did not hide their identities. A federal attorney, Edwin J. Lynch, urged citizens to notify federal authorities in the future if they had a tar and feather party planned to ensure they were not disrupting an ongoing government investigation.

Less than a month later, Beattie was elected president of Holland's Loyal American Club. Among its members were Hall and Wagner. Two years later, Beattie lost his $20,000 damage suit against twelve "prominent citizens of Toledo."[48] A year later, he collected a $50 judgement and Hall a $500 one.

Mob Violence, Lorain County, May 1918—Rankey, Gus [W]

On May 6, 1918, Patrolman "Gus" Rankey attempted to arrest Louis Ritter, a soldier on furlough from Camp Sherman, in Elyria. When Ritter refused to comply, Rankey struck him on the head with his club, fracturing his skull. An angry mob quickly formed and tarred and feathered the patrolman, who was described as German.

Attempted Lynching, Marion County, February 1919—Warner, George Washington [B]

Early in the morning on January 30, 1919, the lifeless body of Rose Belle Scranton was found at the edge of an ash heap near the Erie Railroad roundhouse in Marion. She had died within seventy-five feet of her house. The previous day, Mrs. Scranton, age twenty-eight, had attended a funeral of a friend in Bucyrus and was walking home from the railroad depot when she was attacked. The killer apparently struck her on the head with a sandbag. The wife of Clyde Scranton, an inspector for the railroad, Rose Belle was also a member of the National Protective League, an anti-immigrant organization.

The railroad workers were incensed over Scranton's murder and threatened to roast her killer alive if they caught him. However, the *Marion Star*, a newspaper owned by U.S. Senator Warren G. Harding, urged the citizens to remain calm and refrain from taking matters into their own hands. At the same time, the newspaper denounced the slaying as one of the most appalling crimes ever to take place in Marion.

The police believed that the key to solving the murder was tracing Scranton's stolen jewelry. Owing to the amount of grease on the woman's clothing, they suspected her killer was a workman with greasy hands. They quickly narrowed their focus to African American men—railroad workers—who lived nearby. Apparently, they dismissed the possibility that she was killed by a white man, especially an immigrant who might have a grudge against her for her anti-immigrant activities.

Two black men, James Steele of Marion and Harry E. Dunlap of Bucyrus, were immediately detained. Law enforcement officials stated they would be taking every precaution to protect the prisoners. However, they were subsequently released following their preliminary hearing. The police investigated at least a dozen or so other black men and one Mexican, but had few leads and nothing to pin the crime on any of them. Fearing an outbreak of vigilantism, the police were simply anxious to show some progress on the case.

The *Marion Star* reminded its readers that Marion had changed. It was no longer the kind of town where everyone knew everyone. It had become a city with the problems that cities face, i.e., murders by persons unknown. The newspaper urged the citizens of Marion to remain calm and not make the mistake of lynching an innocent man.

Then late on the afternoon of February 2, 1919, Margaret Christian accused George (aka "Squires" or "Esque") Washington Warner, an African American, of having attacked her in the door-yard of her home. When arrested Sunday night following the attack, Warner had straw on his clothing, but denied being at the straw stack, a hangout for transient men, near the Christian home.

The police immediately tried to connect twenty-two-year-old Warner to the slaying of Rose Belle Scranton. He was a railroad laborer and black, which fit their rudimentary profile. A false rumor soon spread through town that he had confessed. That night, a mob gathered outside the Marion police station, demanding that action be taken. This forced the police to spirit Warner out of town to the Richland County jail for safe-keeping.

While Warner admitted having seen Mrs. Christian, wife of A.E. Christian, while she was walking along the street in Marion, he denied having attempted to attack her in her door-yard. As far as the Scranton murder was concerned, he claimed he was in Galion that night and provided the prosecutor with the names of two men who could vouch for him.

Anxious to restore order, Judge Mouser convened a special grand jury the following morning. During arraignment, Warner finally confessed that he had intended to assault Margaret Christian. Officers suspected he knew more than he was saying about the Scranton murder, as well. Finally, he told them he had heard about it while visiting "one of the

Negro shanties" at Crestline.[49] He said a man named Luci told him that after the murder, all people of color had been forced to leave the city.

Although exonerated of the Scranton murder, Warner was sent to the Ohio State Reformatory in Mansfield three hours after his indictment for the Christian affair.

Over the next half year, many others would be arrested on suspicion of the Scranton murder, including her husband (the charge had been worked up by a private investigator, Mrs. M.E. Fitzinger). But there was not a scrap of evidence linking any of them to the murder and it remains unsolved.

Mob Violence, Marion County, February 1919—Black Pogrom [B]

With warnings posted to be out of town by six o'clock, there was full "exodus of negroes" from Marion on February 3, 1919.[50] This followed threats of lynching George Washington Warner earlier in the day. While details are sketchy, the *Columbus Dispatch* reported that a mob of 200 assembled in the city, demanding Warner, but when they could not locate him, they went on a rampage, burning a saloon, breaking windows, and terrorizing the African American population. Most of them attacked a saloon on the west side owned by James Hagan and catering to blacks. As a result, the Marion sheriff placed the city under "semi-martial law."[51]

An angry horde of 300 then collected at the jail, but learned Warner had been transferred to Mount Gilead. A dozen members of the mob, most of them recently discharged military veterans still in uniform, hurried to Mount Gilead, but did not find him there, either. The *Dispatch* called it a "lynch mob" and noted that the "few colored families who remained in the city that night were barricaded in their homes."[52]

The *Marion Star* reported that some 200 black families fled for their lives, leaving behind all their property including paychecks.[53] Any of them who ventured out on the streets could not fail to notice the "TNT" signs posted prominently which stood for "Travel Nigger Travel."[54] Practically overnight, Marion had become an all-white community.

When William Estabrook Chancellor, a professor from the College of Wooster, made his muckraking expedition to Marion in an effort to prove President Warren G. Harding had black ancestry, he arrived in a town that had recently lost more than 200 African American families.[55] As historian Philip Payne has pointed out, "Chancellor conducted his investigation in a virtually all-white town whose citizens were fully captured by the tensions that gripped post-war America."[56]

Through their investigation of the Scranton murder, Payne suggests that the local police "perhaps inadvertently" set in motion the circumstances that would result in the outbreak of violence. Since they focused all of their attention on black men, systematically and, seemingly, indiscriminately arresting them, the citizens of Marion focused all of their pent-up anger on them. On one hand, the *Marion Star* reported that the railroad workers were maintaining a fire to burn the culprit alive and, on the other, it acknowledged "there is little evidence to fasten the crime to any of them."[57]

As their impatience grew, it wasn't much of a leap from suspecting one (so far unidentified) black man was to blame for the murder than to ridding the town of all black men. Frustrated by their failure to lynch Warner, the prime suspect in her death, many of them vented their anger on predominantly black bars and then black homes. After each incident, the mob was dispersed by the police, only to reassemble later.

Major A.J. Sautter didn't help matters by refusing to acknowledge what was taking place within his city. He minimized the seriousness of the situation and the *Star* supported him, referring to the pogrom as a "request" for black families to leave.[58] He suggested that property-owners and "residents of good standing and reputation" had nothing to fear because the mob wanted only to rid Marion of those of "a certain class," i.e., railroad workers from the South who were not legal residents of the town.[59]

Order was restored primarily because the mob had accomplished what it set out to do—force an exodus of black Marionites. Furthermore, the Erie Railroad cut about 100 employees of the roundhouse and the transfer station from the payroll, some of whom were so frightened by what had transpired that they feared to pick up their pay before departing. At least one saloon owner who depended upon African American customers complained that his business was ruined.

Mob Violence, Butler County, October 1919—Steiger, John E. [W]

White Capping continued well into the twentieth century, in spirit if not in name.

After being chloroformed early on the morning of October 20, 1919, John E. Steiger, a socialist leader in Hamilton, was taken to a woods north of town where he was tarred and feathered. He later received a letter warning him that if he didn't leave Hamilton within ten days, he would be subjected to even more severe treatment.

The Butler County grand jury could not identify anyone who was involved and Public Safety Director Henry B. Grevey believed Steiger was lying.

Expected Lynching, Belmont County, April 1920—Carie, Sarte [W]

Mrs. Augusta Burkhart, a seventy-four-year-old widow, and her daughter Lillian, age forty, were found murdered in their Martins Ferry home on April 17, 1920. Their faces had been hacked and crushed with a piece of iron and their throats cut. Robbery was suspected.

Sarte Carie, an Italian steel mill employee was arrested because he was "alleged to have kept a woman" and wanted to rent one of their houses, but he insisted he was innocent.[61] Fear of an attempt to lynch the suspect led Prosecutor W.T. Dixon to address the angry crowd that collected outside the Burkhart home on April 19. Carie was later released.

In December, the coroner received an anonymous letter claiming the murderer was in Bellaire. They were looking for a "foreigner." Eventually, Andrew Surgent was charged after being accused by his wife, but he was later acquitted.

Mob Violence [TI], Lucas County, July 1920—Harris, Milton [B]

The Lucas County coroner ruled the death an unavoidable accident. Milton Harris, age thirty-five, a chef aboard the City of Toledo, had not been "thrown overboard, as was first reported," but had fallen off the dock during a scuffle on July 13, 1920.[60] Harris had purportedly attacked a seventeen-year-old white boy and the accident occurred when members of the crew tried to intervene.

Although charges were dropped against all involved, the Tuskegee Institute logged this incident as a lynching based, presumably, on the initial report.

Expected Lynching, Defiance County, July 1920—Botkins, Joshua [W]

About July 10, 1920, mob violence was anticipated in Defiance after Joshua Botkins, age fifty, was arrested on a charge of beating to death the three-year-old son of his housekeeper, Mrs. Ida May Bullock. Botkins, a prosperous farmer, denied intentionally killing the child. He had held him by the ankles and struck him with a heavy harness tug.

Mrs. Bullock, who was pregnant, defended Botkins, pleading for his release. He purportedly had promised to marry her. Rumor had it that he had repeatedly beaten the dead youth and Bullock's two other children.

Preparations were made to call out special deputies if the crowd gathering around the jail became unruly. He was subsequently convicted of second degree murder.

Threatened Violence, Tuscarawas County, November 1920—Wife-beater warning

Calling themselves "The Avengers," an eighteen member group composed of seven Republicans, seven Democrats, and four Socialists announced their intention on November 17, 1920, to punish wife abusers.

In an anonymous letter to a Uhrichsville newspaper, the group, whose motto was "Equal justice to all," invited all abused wives to contact them to have their complaints addressed. They were characterized as a "Ku Klux Klan to avenge injuries done their wives by wife-beaters."[62]

Mob Violence, Cuyahoga County, December 1920—Fanner, George K. [W]; Sly, William C. [W]

At times, the Smith Act was applied quite broadly. For example, in May 1923, Mrs. George K. Fanner was awarded $2,500 by Cuyahoga County for the "lynching" of her husband two years earlier on December 31, 1920. Fanner and his business partner, William C. Sly, had been shot to death by five men during a payroll robbery.

Mob Violence, Clark County, March 1921—Springfield Riot

An eleven-year-old white girl, Marge Ferneau, allegedly suffered "mistreatment at the hands of an unknown negro" on the night of March 7, 1921, in Springfield. The investigation into the crime engendered such bad feeling between the races that a riot ensued—Springfield's third. In a city of 60,000, one eighth of the population was African American. By the time it was over, some twenty to thirty arrests were made.

James White, age fifteen or seventeen, was captured just north of Springfield on March 12, 1921, following a running gun battle. The black youth admitted to shooting Patrolman Joseph Ryan three times the night before. At the time, Ryan was attempting to disperse a crowd of black men. White was then taken back to town and locked in the city jail where he was surrounded by national guardsmen. Not long afterward, he was taken to the Boys Industrial School in Lancaster (or, alternately, the Ohio State Reformatory in Mansfield).

The same day, Clark County Sheriff David Jones was placed in charge of the situation in Springfield at a combined conference of military and civil officials. An order was immediately issued forbidding all public gatherings after six o'clock and the stoppage of all vehicles after seven o'clock. All movie houses and theaters were also to close. Only pedestrians with military passes were allowed to move about.

Three additional companies of National Guard arrived at noon, swelling their numbers to 550. Colonel Robert Haubrics of the Fourth Ohio regiment was in command. They patrolled the streets in automobiles and army trucks outfitted with machine guns. Chief of Police O'Brien felt the situation was under control and did not expect any additional trouble.

Many African American residents of Springfield insisted that the trouble was caused by "drifters" from the south and that no local African Americans had participated. However, according to the police, many of the blacks were armed with Springfield rifles they

Opposition to the KKK in Ohio was reflected in this 1922 Harry Westerman cartoon for the *Columbus Dispatch*.

had purchased following the previous riots. Asa Smith, a white man, was found to have dynamite on his person and was arrested as well.

Blame for the race riots was, in the opinion of the grand jury, due to a lack of determined action by the local police department. Marge Ferneau's assailant was, apparently, never apprehended.

Expected Lynching, Franklin County, July 1923—Two prohibition agents [W]

When two prohibition agents arrested W.A. Cary at the Deshler Hotel in Columbus on July 26, 1923, a crowd collected in the street. Their shouts of "Lynch them!" weren't directed at the suspect, but at the two "dry officers" who had taken him into custody.[63] The situation was described as a "near riot" by Columbus police.[64] Cary surrendered five quarts of whiskey and was fined $500.

Mob Violence, Jefferson County, August 1923—Steubenville Riot [W]

On the night of August 15, 1923, a riot occurred on the streets of Steubenville. A

The 1924 funeral of Creighton "Crate" Leathers in Van Wert included a procession by the Ku Klux Klan (Jim Bowsher collection).

caravan of roughly 100 Ku Klux Klansmen from East Liverpool, Ohio, and Chester, West Virginia, had paraded through town in twenty-five vehicles, led by a band. Their cars were decorated with electrically illuminated crosses, stars and stripes, and Klan insignia. Afterward, they met at a hotel and went inside for dinner.

Meanwhile, a large crowd assembled outside, including members of the Knights of the Flaming Circle, an anti–Klan group. It was composed largely of Italians, Catholics, and bootleggers who were opposed to the Klan's pro-temperance, anti-immigrant stance.

When the Klan meeting broke up and the Klan members went to their cars, one of them was challenged for draping the American flag over the front of it. A fistfight quickly ensued. The mob overturned a half-dozen or so of the Klansmen's automobiles while pelting them with bricks, bottles, and clubs. As many as 3,000 people may have participated in the melee.

Darwin L. Gibson, leader of the Klan and a conductor on the Pan Handle railroad, was shot in the neck when the two groups began firing at each other with revolvers. The bullet lodged at the base of his brain. At least two others were shot as well. John de Santis, twenty-seven, had a bullet in his left eye; Moscino Spinetti, twenty-six, was shot through the wrist.

The police arrested three suspects immediately and five others near East Liverpool just before daybreak. They were found to be heavily armed. A dozen Klansmen were injured and, perhaps, forty members of the anti–Klan group sustained black eyes, cuts, and bruises.

Mob Violence, Stark County, April 1924—Shaw, Lloyd [W]

Lloyd Shaw, age twenty-two, was horse-whipped on the night of April 9, 1924, by a gang of masked men. He was walking in Canton's public square when he was invited to take a ride with Robert Webb in his car. Webb drove him to a woods near Massillon, stopped the car, and stuck a gun in his side.

Surrounded by a group of men, Shaw was knocked unconscious and tied to a tree. After they administered a severe beating, the men fetched Webb's twenty-three-year-old wife and forced her to watch as Webb "brandished a knife and threatened to operate on [Shaw] right off."[65]

Shaw and Mrs. Webb were accused of being lovers, which they both denied. One of the men then lashed him with a black snake whip some fifteen or twenty times before he was returned to Canton.

Mob Violence, Trumbull County, August 1924—Meredith, Steve [W]; Niles Riot (Part I)

The troubles began at a Klan Konklave at Mineral Ridge early in August 1924, culminating in the beating of Steve Meredith, a resident of Niles. In retaliation, the Knights of the Flaming Circle, an anti–Klan group, purportedly burned a circle in front of a Klansman's home.

Then on the night of August 4, 1924, the two groups got into a squabble on the streets of Niles. Two were seriously injured and several others beaten. When the police moved in to disperse the crowd, estimated at 1,000 or some, they found that many of the participants were brandishing many firearms.

Mob Violence, Trumbull County, October–November 1924—Niles Riot (Part II)

Owing to violent outbreak when the Ku Klux Klan paraded through Niles in May, the organization was denied a permit for a second parade the following month. Consequently, the Klan scheduled its next parade for November 1, 1924. However, the Knights of the Flaming Circle responded by announcing its own march, with 10,000 participants. Then on October 29, someone bombed the home of Mayor Harvey C. Kistler because he would neither issue a parade permit to the Knights nor revoke the Klan's. Fortunately, both the mayor and his wife escaped injury.

Nevertheless, Dr. B.A. Hart, head of the Trumbull County Klan, stated the parade would go on as planned. Unable to deputize enough men to provide security, Sheriff John E. Thomas tried to talk the Klan into limiting their parade to the field where they were organizing. He was certain there would be trouble if they entered the city.

On November 1, at two o'clock in the afternoon, two unidentified Klansmen were purportedly shot to death on the outskirts of Niles. As the Klan moved into town, they were challenged along the way by the Knights of Flaming Circle.

When the two factions met, a full-blown riot ensued. Newspapers reported, "Two hundred anti–Klansmen armed with sawed off shotguns and swords were masses at these street intersections a strategic point which all traffic bound to the Klan rally must pass."[66] As they tried to stop the Klan's vehicles, shooting broke-out. Three men died. Colonel E.A. Watkins, a Klan leader from Youngstown, was surrounded by an angry mob and had to leave town under police escort. Mayor Kistler purportedly spent the night outside the city.

After eighteen hours of lawlessness, Governor Victor Donahey organized a regiment of National Guard to mobilize and placed the city under martial law.[67] Donahey immediately sent a telegram to United States District Attorney Benson W. Hough, commanding officer of the Ohio National Guard, to go to Niles to take control of the situation. Colonel

C.S. Connelly of Cleveland, overseeing the National Guard, began dragging Mosquito Creek on November 4 in response to rumors that several bodies may have been dumped there.

Thirteen people were known to have been shot and wounded. A special Trumbull County grand jury handed down ninety-five (or, perhaps, 104) indictments. Twenty arrests were made on charges of intoxication and carrying concealed weapons. The jury also recommended that Mayor Kistler and Police Chief L.J. Rounds be removed from office. Martial law was finally lifted after ten days.

Mob Violence, Lucas County, November 1924—McKay, R.A. [W?]

An itinerant Methodist preacher named R.A. McKay had been holding services in several African American churches in Toledo. Apparently, someone did not approve for he was summoned to the Third Baptist Church late on November 5, 1924, seized and blindfolded. He was then taken by automobile to a desolate part of the city, tied to a tree, and horse-whipped. Threatened with death if he told the police, McKay was believed to have fled the area.

Mob Violence [TI], Cuyahoga County, November 1925—Morrison, Albert [B]

Early on the morning of November 12, 1925, Albert Morrison, age forty, was slain in Cleveland's "Melting Pot"—Woodland Avenue and East 65th Street. It was an area "where newly arrived Immigrants from Europe brush elbows with kings of the gambling and vice worlds."[68]

An African American, Morrison and three companions were driving through Cleveland when they stopped at the Diana Restaurant to get something to eat. The men, presumably, didn't know they had "entered a restaurant where the patronage of negroes was unwanted."[69] When they failed to receive prompt service, they purportedly threw some dishes.

Very quickly "a gang appeared and a fight ensued just outside the restaurant."[70] During the melee, in which some twenty men participated, Morrison was stabbed three times, beaten over the head, and left in the gutter to die. "A call to police headquarters brought out the riot squad but by the time the officers arrived, Morrison's assailants had fled."[71]

Two days later, the *Hamilton Evening Journal* announced that the Cleveland police had declared war on "Cleveland crookdom."[72] They had rounded up 100 "characters of shady repute in that vicinity."[73] The police were holding three of Morrison's friends as material witnesses and expected to charge nine of the gang members with manslaughter. As one newspaper put it, "A race war started which ended with Morrison's death."[74]

However, according to the *Plain Dealer*, "Common Pleas Judge Walter McMahon yesterday instructed a jury to return a verdict of not guilty in the cases of four men—Aaron Goldstein, Larry Rubin, Sam Mobile, and Morris Fisher—charged with manslaughter in connection with the killing of Albert Morrison."[75]

Mob Violence, Summit County, August 1927—Harris, Alfred [W]

Eight masked men brandishing knotted ropes dragged Alfred Harris, age fifty-five, from his workshop on August 30, 1927. They ordered him to surrender a petition he had circulated which demanded that Governor Victor Donahey investigate a murder that had occurred two years earlier. Some 700 people had signed it. When Harris refused, the men drove him to a remote area of the county and severely beat him.

Attempted Lynching, Belmont County, September 1928—Wheeler, Mrs. Goldie [W]; Berry, Lester [W]

Lester Berry, his girlfriend, Hannah Gallagher, and a visitor, Mrs. Goldie Wheeler, were taken from a buggy in which they were riding on the evening of September 16, 1928, just outside Barton. While Gallagher managed to escape, Berry and Wheeler were kidnapped by a band of about twenty masked men wearing white robes trimmed in red. The group boasted that they were a "night riders club" and accused the trio, all between the ages of eighteen and twenty-one, of illicit relations.[76]

Berry and Wheeler were taken to a clump of trees about a half mile away, ropes were fastened around their necks, and the ends thrown over tree limbs. The victims were then hauled up until their toes barely touched the ground. While this was going on, the leader's mask slipped down and they recognized him. He then ordered that the couple be cut down. They were told to go home and not mention the incident to anyone.

A week later, John Eberhardt, forty, a mine foreman and the father of eight children, was arrested as the leader of the night riders. He denied knowing anything about them. County Prosecutor Paul Waddell then revealed that this was not the first report of the gang's terrorizing the village and that several women had been lured from home and beaten.

Having received several letters threatening her life if she testified against Eberhardt, Gallagher moved to Marion the following month where she married Edward Conrad, a carpenter from Wheeling, West Virginia. Eberhardt was subsequently acquitted when his wife and his mother provided him with an alibi.

A year later, a jury awarded Mrs. Wheeler $100 for indignities she sustained when she was mistreated by the night riders. It took longer to select the jury than to hear the case.

Mob Violence, Belmont County, April 1929—Van Horn, Pete [W]

About midnight on April 3, 1929, Pete Van Horn and a friend set out to get a drink. Just as they were passing the Belmont County courthouse, two cars pulled up beside them. Several men jumped out and dragged the painter into one of the cars. Taken to an abandoned school house, Van Horn, in his mid-thirties, claimed nine people, including two women, beat him unconscious with hickory clubs.

After he came to, Van Horn walked back to St. Clairsville where he received medical attention. In the end, he agreed to drop charges against the men in exchange for $500, the amount of money he stood to gain if he sued the county under the Smith Act.

During the same period, a Morristown man who paid too much attention to someone else's wife was escorted to Barnesville and placed upon a train headed south. In addition, a girl living in Morristown was tarred. And a Woodsfield resident was abducted and forced to leave the state.

Expected Lynching, Wayne County, February 1930—Horst, Melvin [W]

Four-year-old Melvin Horst of Orrville went missing on December 27, 1928. Although hundreds of volunteers looked for him, his case remained unsolved until 1930, when Charles Hannah, age fifty, "town musician, fish peddler, bootlegger and ne'er do well," confessed that he had clubbed the boy to death with a piece of wood.[77] He claimed that Akron bootleggers had disposed of the body.

Before Hannah's confession, seven other suspects were nearly sent to prison. Hannah had even coached his own son to lie about the Horst boy's death. But after the truth was known, three automobiles filled with townspeople gathered on February 26, 1930, planning to kidnap or lynch Hannah when he was moved to Akron. But the police foiled their plans by keeping Hannah in the county jail.

Attempted Lynching, Belmont County, August 1930—Janik, "Chicago Joe" [W]

Sheriff Ford Moore of Belmont County initiated an investigation in the attempted lynching of "Chicago Joe" Janik on or about August 1, 1930. Janik, age twenty-nine (or thirty-eight), was rescued by his friends from a "court of moonshiners" operating in the hills outside St. Clairsville who had accused him of stealing a still.[78] A man posing as a sheriff purportedly had placed a noose around his neck and strung the rope over the limb of a large tree.

Mob Violence [TI], Lawrence County, June 1932—Murray (aka Marion), Luke [B]

Luke Murray (aka Marion), an African American man in his early twenties, drew a pen knife on two white men in South Point on June 7, 1932. His body would later be found in the Ohio River. What happened in between is a matter of conjecture.

Murray was a chauffeur from Macon, Georgia. He frequently drove his employer, Howard G. Davidson, of Atlanta, and the employer's wife and daughter on trips in their automobile. He had driven the Davidsons to Ohio to check on some agricultural interests. He was staying with them in their farm house in the countryside.

South Point was a town of 500, mostly poor laborers, who worked for the wealthy farmers. It did not have any black residents. Murray stood out in the community for two reasons. First, he was unusually well dressed, especially for a black man. And second, he had been observed occasionally driving Mrs. Davidson or Nancy Davidson, the seventeen-year-old daughter, alone. In fact, he was purportedly warned to discontinue doing so by many of the white residents.

Then one day Murray got into a quarrel with a hired hand on the Davidson farm and both men were arrested. As soon as it was learned that he was being held in jail, a crowd began to collect. For reasons of his own, the town marshal removed Murray from his cell and placed him in a hallway. He then announced he was going home to dinner and would be back in two hours, leaving the prisoner unguarded. Shortly, thereafter, several members of the crowd grabbed a crosstie, broke down the door to the building, and abducted Murray.

The marshal did not seem to be concerned that Murray was gone. Neither did he bother to report his missing prisoner to any county officials. They found out about the jail-break three days later when Murray's badly decomposed body was fished of the Ohio River, although defense attorneys would dispute that the dead man was actually him.

According to the newspapers, sixteen white men were either arrested or under suspicion and six were later indicted. The suspects would grudgingly confess that they had removed Murray from the jail for the purpose of taking him across the river and out of state. However, they insisted he had jumped out of their boat on his own volition and drowned.

A post mortem examination revealed that Murray had received a blow to the base of the brain and that the second vertebrae of his neck was dislocated. However, the coroner ruled that the cause of death was drowning. It was also remarked that the prosecutor seemed poorly prepared and disinterested in pursuing the case.

Louie McKee, age sixteen, was subsequently found guilty of delinquency, but everyone else was acquitted. The jury may have been influenced by a newspaper report that the administrator of Murray's estate "proposed to sue Lawrence county for $5,000 under the 'death by mob' statute of Ohio" if any of the defendants were convicted.[79]

Although he was not hanged, Murray was, according to the Tuskegee Institute, the last person lynched in Ohio. An investigator from the NAACP concluded he was killed because he was "too popular with white employers."[80]

Attempted Lynching, Mahoning County, July 1934—Johnson, George [B]

On July 19, 1934, George Johnson, a black man in his mid-fifties, was rescued by police from an East Alliance lynch mob numbering some 700. A drifter from Steubenville, Johnson was accused of attacking a thirteen-year-old-girl near the "showgrounds," a local park. Overpowered by four men, he was swarmed by a mixed-race crowd of men and women who began striking him, inflicting cuts and bruises. Just minutes before, they had been spectators at a night game at the Blue Bell Baseball Park.

After an officer drew his revolver, Johnson was seized by deputy sheriffs who rushed him through the angry mob which was shouting, "Hang him!"[81] Once they reached the Alliance jail, the deputies kept the crowd occupied at the front door while they smuggled him out the back. Johnson was then whisked away to the Mahoning County jail in Youngstown for safekeeping.

Attempted Lynching, Hardin County, August 1934—Odell, Okey [W]

Okey Odell (or O'Dell) sued the Harding County commissioners for $5,000 under the Smith Act because of what he claimed was an attempt to lynch him.

A citizen of McGuffey, Odell, age thirty-eight, worked "the world's largest onion patch."[82] Men, women, and children would crawl down the onion rows planted in the Scioto marsh, weeding them in the summer and picking them at harvest time. There were very few onion farmers and a great many workers. He felt that the laborers weren't being adequately paid for their efforts and organized a union.

Installed as the group's president, Odell promptly asked for a thirty-five cent an hour wage and an eight-hour workday. When they didn't get it, he called a strike. Allen Edwards, owner of the largest operation, responded by brazenly threatening violence against the workers.

A mob numbering 200 abducted Odell on August 25, 1934, two months into the strike. Odell had been arrested earlier because it was believed his union was complicit in the recent bombing of Mayor Godfrey J. Ott's home. As he was being booked, a throng of anti-union men stormed the jail and wrested him away from the deputies, who offered little or no resistance.

As Odell later testified, his abductors kicked him, forced him into a truck, and drove him out of the county to somewhere near Waynesville. "He said the group placed a rope around his neck and threatened to lynch him."[83] They then warned him not to return. Too weak to walk, he was picked up by a passing motorist who, at his request, drove him back to McGuffey. Securing a revolver, Odell walked through town, accompanied by his brother, and challenged the vigilantes to come after him.

While recovering at home with broken ribs, Odell threatened to shoot anyone who tried to come into his house. Soon, the mob arrived. According to news accounts, they made "a long parade of shouting, club-waving strike breakers and land owners, shouting, 'Let's lynch O'Dell.'"[84] Twice they approached his house, but did not dare to enter.

On August 23, 1935, Odell agreed to accept $500 in compensation for his injuries the previous summer. Although a jury had awarded him $750, the amount was reduced by a judge to $250. Odell would later be sentenced to ninety days and fined $100 or $400 for pointing firearms at those who approached his house.

Mob Violence, Athens County, April 1935—Thompson, Harley [W]

Harley Thompson, age fifty-five, an Athens insurance agent, had purportedly written a series of articles in the *Ohio Examiner*, accusing the members of the Ohio University chapter of Pi Kappa Alpha Fraternity of having improper relations with their cook.

In retaliation, Robert C. Moore, the fraternity's president, allegedly led a band of five students who abducted Thompson on April 2, took him to a local cemetery, and tarred and feathered him. However, a grand jury refused to return an indictment against Moore.

Meanwhile, the publisher and editor of the muckraking newspaper were charged with "intent to corrupt the morals of the people of Athens County."[85]

Expected Lynching, Trumbull County, May 1935—Jutila, Ray [W]

On May 25, 1935, the Warren police department heard through the "grape-vine" that an attempt would be made to lynch Ray Jutila, the confessed slayer of Marie T. Tobin.[86]

Just a few hours earlier, Jutila, age twenty, had signed a statement admitting he had beaten the twenty-two-year-old woman with an ash can. He also set fire to the bed on which she lay and killed her dog. Jutila said he became angry when Tobin, the wife of his friend, rejected his advances. He would later claim they were having an affair.

Chief of Police B.J. Gillen put his officers on notice that they might be summoned at any moment and he had machine guns at ready to put down any disturbance. However, they were not needed. Jutila was sentenced to life in prison. When the jury recommended mercy, the former high school athlete said with a smile, "Gee! That's swell."[87] He had bet Deputy Sheriff Harry Dixon he would get the electric chair and gladly paid off his fifteen cent wager.

Expected Lynching, Montgomery, November 1935—Martin, Thomas [W]

After being ordered to work on Saturday, instead of Monday—which was Armistice Day—some 200 WPA workers walked off the job at Wright Field in Fairfield on November 8, 1935.

At about the same time, Thomas Martin, the foreman of a WPA project at the Northridge School stadium, asked the sheriff's office for protection after his workers threatened to lynch and tar and feather him. He said they, too, were angry about having to work on Saturday to make up for the holiday.

Consequently, Sheriff Phil Kloos and Montgomery County deputies, armed with shotguns and machine guns, rushed to the school on November 9 to quash a threatened riot by thirty-five workers.

Attempted Lynching, Tuscarawas County, October 1937—Matthews, Vandy Lee [B]

Vandy Lee Matthews was arrested in Dover on October 3, 1937, for assaulting a married couple. A nineteen-year-old African American, Matthews was accused of severely beating Forrest Lantzer with a shotgun and raping Elsa Lahm Lantzer, age twenty-nine, "in a lonely section of the city."[88]

Unaware that Matthews had been locked up in the Jefferson County jail in Steubenville, some 150–250 angry citizens began searching for him in the jails of Dover, New Philadelphia, and Cadiz. He was finally moved to the Cuyahoga County jail in Cleveland.

Fearing "a turbulent court scene," judicial authorities decided to try Matthews outdoors in a New Philadelphia picnic grove where everyone could witness justice in action.[89]

He was found guilty of rape and subsequently served fifteen years in the Ohio Penitentiary.

But his life came to an end in 1968, when he was shot to death by police in Century, Florida. Matthews had purportedly been loitering near the post office and was thought to have been reaching for a gun.

Mob Violence, Washington County, October 1938—Dixon, Joseph A. [W]

Joseph Dixon, a fifty-two-year-old evangelist, was found beside a highway in Washington County on October 11, 1938, suffering from shock. He said that he had been conducting a revival the night before at nearby Mill Creek when a dozen men seized, beat, and stripped him before covering him with tar.

Dixon, from Madison, South Dakota, was conducting the revival to celebrate his marriage to Opal V. Hasley, age twenty-two. He had married the young woman over the objections of her father, Wesley Hasley. The girl's father and eight of his relatives were acquitted of the crime.

Afterword

In 1938, the total number of lynchings nationwide, as tallied by the Tuskegee Institute, dropped to six. It had been a half dozen years since Ohio had a lynching. There would be no others. But the story of mob violence in Ohio doesn't end there because the underlying causes—anger, distrust of law enforcement, frustration—remain.

Case in point: sometime after midnight on February 18, 1968, a little more than a month before Martin Luther King, Jr., would be gunned down in Memphis, Tennessee, a cross was burned on the lawn of London city council president William C. Holton. The previous night, his daughter, Janet, had attended a high school dance with Dale McNeal. Janet was white and Dale was black.

While the Holton family might have easily concealed the damage, Bill chose not to. He wanted the scorch mark left there so the citizens of London could see it for what it was: a visible manifestation of the community's deep racial divide. Neither were the Holtons interested in identifying and prosecuting those who had committed the deed because they believed their actions were a reflection of attitudes held by many of the town's citizens. Bill may have even known that this was not London's first cross-burning.

Nearly forty-five years earlier on October 29, 1923, the Ku Klux Klan had erected a flaming cross on the grounds of the London High School. Not to be outdone, female members of the Klan burned a cross of their own the following week in front of the courthouse. Ironically, Bill Holton, a lifelong resident of London, was just five months old at the time. A historian of the town, he likely could have heard of these incidents.

The Tuskegee Institute stopped tracking lynchings altogether in 1968 because there had been none anywhere in the United States during the previous four years. But racial tensions remained. Before the year was over, race riots would break out in 125 cities throughout the country, including in Cleveland and Cincinnati.

Prior to the Holton incident, the young people of London, both black and white, had been brought together in interracial fellowship for many weeks through youth groups at London's two Methodist churches, the First United Methodist Church and the African Methodist Episcopal Church. Then on Sunday, February 10, the First Methodist Youth Fellowship invited their African American friends to help plan Brotherhood Sunday.

The youth also discussed doing more activities together and the subject of dating came up. Tom Holton was in his senior year of high school and one of the group's leaders. He had been interested in dating Mary Freeman, a black cheerleader who was also a participant in the group. Dale McNeal, Mary's cousin, was another one. So was Janet Holton, Tom's younger sister. Once the dating topic had been broached, Dale called Janet while she was on a babysitting job and asked her for a date.

A sophomore, Janet was shocked that Dale, the star of the school's basketball, baseball, and football teams, would invite her to a Saturday night dance at the fairgrounds. But both sets of parents gave their approval. Tom was already planning to go to the dance with Mary. Still, there was some apprehension about the reception they could expect. To ensure the couple was not harassed, the Madison County sheriff had two uniformed officers on duty, as well as three others in plain clothes. However, the evening proved to be uneventful. As Tom recalled, it was all about getting through the door.

The Holton family of London awoke to find a cross had been burned in their lawn during the night (Holton family collection).

Janet remembers her father waking her for church on Sunday morning and telling her that there was a gift for her on the front lawn. Someone had either used a blowtorch or gasoline to burn a cross in the grass. It did not take long for word of the incident to spread throughout the community. That afternoon, a parade of cars drove by their home and several pastors dropped by to offer their sympathy and support (although their own minister was not one of them). However, they could do nothing to help Janet who quickly found herself losing friends. One by one they said they had been forbidden by their parents to associate with her.

When Janet was invited to the prom a year later by another black classmate, a school administrator went so far as to tell her they would not be allowed to attend because the country club where it was being held did not admit African Americans. But Janet and her date went anyway. The county sheriff met them at the event, quietly ensuring their entry without incident. The sheriff was there also when they left. Janet never learned how he knew of their coming and going.

Mary Holton, Tom and Janet's mother, was quoted in *Jet* magazine as saying interracial dating had been taking place in London for the past year and some twenty teenagers of both races were involved. Following the cross-burning, she asked that everyone "help [the young people] grow in their freedom of friendship, quietly and in their own way."[1] While there were no more overt acts of hostility, the Holtons did not detect any change in people's attitudes.

Upon returning to London for her 45th high school reunion, Janet was taken aback when a half dozen former classmates approached her to apologize for shunning her all those years before. Perhaps, there were others who had a change of heart as well. She could only hope.

Appendix I: Lynchings (1772–1968)

By Tuskegee's count, Ohio had twenty-six lynchings between 1882 and 1968—ten white (38 percent) and sixteen black (62 percent).[1]

Using our narrower definition, we have identified twenty-eight lynchings during the period 1772–1968, but others may have gone unrecorded. The victims, all male, appear to have been evenly divided between black and white, but still disproportionately African American.

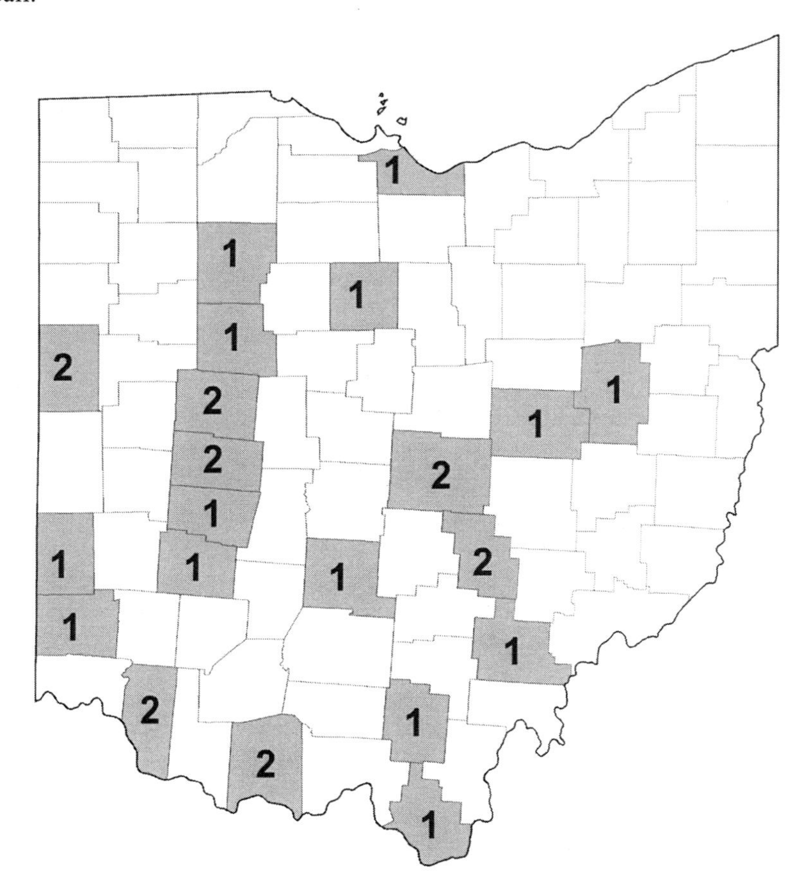

Known lynchings in Ohio (Elise Meyers Walker).

Race	*Name*	*Sex*	*County*	*Year*
B	Unknown man	M	Jackson	1803
W?	Unknown man	M	Licking	Early 1880s
B	Terry, William "Old Bill"	M	Adams	1856
W	Kimmel, Absalom	M	Mercer	1872
W	McLeod, Alexander	M	Mercer	1872
W	Davis, Jeff	M	Tuscarawas	1873
B	Ullery, George W.	M	Champaign	1875
W	Schell, James W.	M	Logan	1875
W	Mangrum, George	M	Clermont	1876
B	Taylor, William	M	Erie	1878
W	McDonald, Thomas	M	Pickaway	1880
B	Davis, Christopher C.	M	Athens	1881
W	Wagoner, John	M	Lawrence	1882
B	Fisher, Frank	M	Crawford	1882
W	Hickey, Richard	M	Perry	1884
W	Guest, Albert	M	Perry	1885
B	Howard, Henry	M	Coshocton	1885
W	Mussel, William	M	Preble	1886
B	Betters, Peter	M	Greene	1887
W	Boles, William	M	Hardin	1891
B	Corbin, Henry	M	Butler	1892
W	Lytle, Joseph	M	Hancock	1892
B	Parker, Roscoe	M	Adams	1894
B	Newlin, Seymour	M	Logan	1894
B	Anderson, Noah	M	Clermont	1895
B	Mitchell, Charles "Click"	M	Champaign	1897
B	Dickerson, Richard	M	Clark	1904
W	Etherington, Carl	M	Licking	1910

Appendix II: Attempted Lynchings (1772—1938)

Attempted lynchings represent a tinder box situation. Once a lynch mob formed, sometimes all that kept it from accomplishing its goal was either an absence of leadership or a strong response from law enforcement. Any of these incidents could well have culminated in a lynching. This list includes one woman, Mrs. Goldie Wheeler.

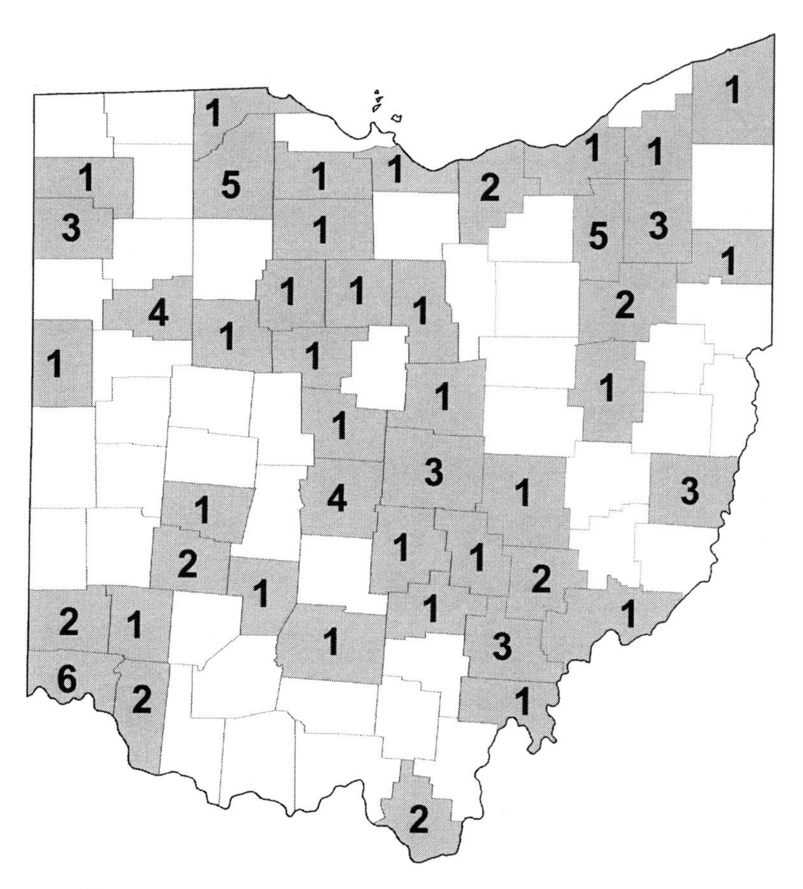

Known attempted lynchings in Ohio (Elise Meyers Walker).

Race	Name	Sex	County	Year
W	Unknown soldier 1	M	Hamilton	1846
W	Unknown soldier 2	M	Hamilton	1846
W	Lohrer, Constance	M	Hamilton	1861
W	Lohrer, Romain	M	Hamilton	1861
W	Kimmel, Jacob	M	Mercer	1872
B	Unknown male	M	Hamilton	1876
B	Garnett, Jim	M	Butler	1877
W	Scott, Luther	M	Geauga	1877
W	Storey, William	M	Clermont	1879
W	Zeek, Bill	M	Lawrence	1882
B	Holmes, William "Bill"	M	Meigs	1882
unk	Unknown man 1	M	Athens	1884
unk	Unknown man 2	M	Athens	1884
W	Reddy, Joseph	M	Perry	1884
W	Muntz, Charles	M	Sandusky	1885
W	Horn, John	M	Erie	1886
W	Haley, Bill	M	Paulding	1886
W	Dolph, Simon	M	Richland	1886
B	Umphreys	M	Franklin	1888
W	Martin	M	Wood	1888
W	Carn, Joseph	M	Summit	1888
B	Jackson, Sherman	M	Greene	1889
B	Gardner, Richard	M	Ross	1890
W	Burkett, William	M	Wood	1890
W	Stottsberry, George	M	Licking	1892
W	Cook, William	M	Wood	1893
W	Davidson, Curtis	M	Stark	1893
W	Cheadle, Madison	M	Morgan	1894
B	Dolby, William "Jasper"	M	Fayette	1894
B	O'Neill, Charles	M	Defiance	1894
W	Hart, Charles	M	Paulding	1894
B	Cain, Leo	M	Paulding	1894
W	Martin, Leander J.	M	Seneca	1895
unk	Murray, Rome	M	Greene	1896
B	Wald, Edward	M	Cuyahoga	1896
W?	Unknown tramp	M	Clermont	1897
W	Samson, Dr. S.H.	M	Hocking	1898
W	Wright, E.S.	M	Muskingum	1899
W	Zeltner, Paul	M	Wood	1899
W	Zeltner, John	M	Wood	1899
W	McGowan, Joseph	M	Portage	1900
W	Snyder, Dan	M	Portage	1900
W	Summers, Frank	M	Portage	1900
B	Peck, Louis	M	Summit	1900
B	Beeks, F.	M	Delaware	1900
W	Weinstock, Walter A.	M	Morgan	1901
B	Brant, Will	M	Summit	1902
B	Upshaw, Thomas	M	Summit	1902
B	Coney, Charles	M	Summit	1902
B	Williams, Charles	M	Franklin	1902
W	Bower, Charley	M	Lucas	1902
B	Crooms, John	M	Ashtabula	1902
W	Glasco, William	M	Lawrence	1902
W	Dilling, Frank	M	Crawford	1903
B	Pleasant, Robert	M	Lorain	1903
B	Hall, Charles	M	Lorain	1903

Race	*Name*	*Sex*	*County*	*Year*
W	Spivey, Joseph	M	Butler	1903
B	Anderson, William	M	Franklin	1904
B	Unknown boy	M	Clark	1904
B	Jackson, Ben	M	Franklin	1904
B	Copeland, George	M	Knox	1905
B	White, Henry	M	Warren	1906
W	Sweeney, John	M	Washington	1907
W	Terwiliger, Ernst	M	Licking	1908
W	Goodlove, James	M	Wyandot	1908
B	Beam, John W	M	Allen	1909
B	O'Neal	M	Hamilton	1909
W	Haring, Herbert	M	Allen	1909
W	Underwood, LeRoy	M	Licking	1909
W	Wallace, Harry	M	Fairfield	1910
W	Kline, Thomas	M	Athens	1910
B	Mickens, Harvey	M	Stark	1911
W	Eley, Sherman	M	Allen	1916
B	Daniels, Charles	M	Allen	1916
B	Warner, George Washington	M	Marion	1919
W	Wheeler, Goldie	F	Belmont	1928
W	Berry, Lester	M	Belmont	1928
W	Janik, "Chicago Joe"	M	Belmont	1930
B	Johnson, George	M	Mahoning	1934
W	Odell, Okey	M	Hardin	1934
B	Matthews, Vandy Lee	M	Tuscarawas	1937

Appendix III: Tar and Feathering (1772–1938)

Like lynching, tar and feathering was terrifying, painful, and occasionally deadly—mini-lynchings, as we have called them. And women weren't exempt. Of the seventy-three individuals known to have been tarred and feathered in Ohio (there were likely more), at least twenty-seven (37 percent) were women. They were nearly always tarred and feathered for prostitution or other sexual behavior—and sometimes women participated.

African Americans, on the other hand, account for only seven or so (10 percent) of the reported incidents.

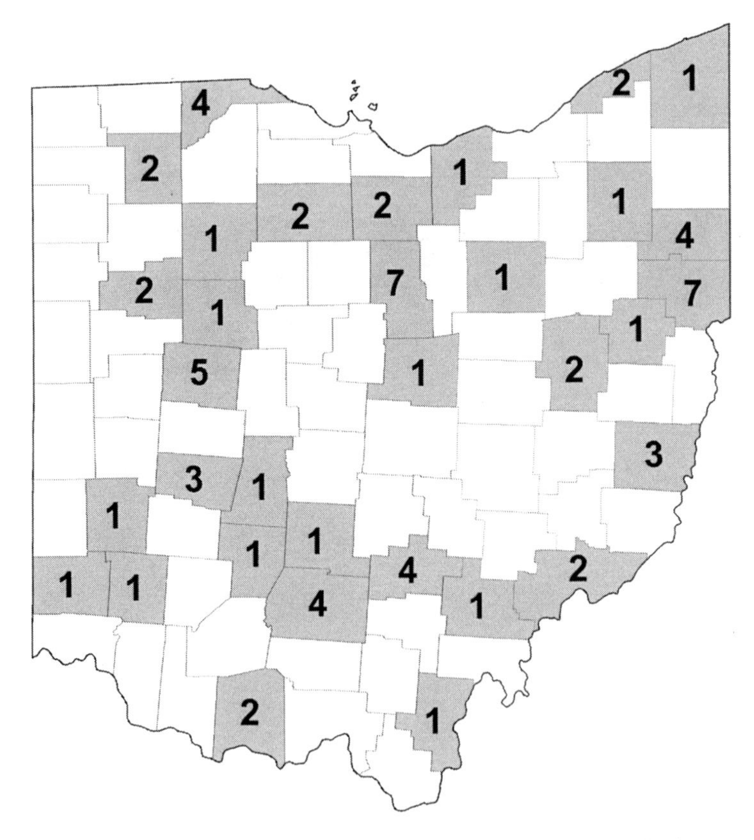

Known tar and featherings in Ohio (Elise Meyers Walker).

Race	*Name*	*Sex*	*County*	*Year*
W	Smith, Joseph	M	Lake	1832
W	Rigdon, Sidney	M	Lake	1832
W	Robinson, Marius	M	Mahoning	1837
W	Fall, Chancey	M	Clark	1844
W?	M.N.	F	Montgomery	1851
B	Unknown man	M	Madison	1857
W	Galton, Sarah	F	Belmont	1859
W	Galton (son)	M	Belmont	1859
W	Galton (daughter)	F	Belmont	1859
W	Richmond, Dr. B.W.	M	Ashtabula	1859
W	Tousley, Franklin	M	Portage	1860
B	Lett, Joshua	M	Hocking	1861
W	Pumphrey	F	Hocking	1861
B	Mabray, Thomas	M	Hocking	1861
B	Gross, Abraham	M	Hocking	1861
W	Morris, Mrs.	F	Columbiana	1863
W	Lee, Mrs.	F	Columbiana	1863
W	Unknown woman 1	F	Columbiana	1863
W	Unknown woman 2	F	Columbiana	1863
W	Unknown woman 3	F	Columbiana	1863
W	Unknown woman 4	F	Columbiana	1863
W	Unknown woman 5	F	Columbiana	1863
W	Ross, Emma	F	Mahoning	1864
W	Stearn, Louisa	F	Mahoning	1864
W	Herder, Ella	F	Gallia	1885
W	Hathaway, Ray S.	M	Huron	1885
Unk	Gray, Al	M	Allen	1886
Unk	Gray, Mrs.	F	Allen	1886
W	Dolph, Simon	M	Richland	1886
W	Follis, John W.	M	Ross	1886
W	Potts, Henry	M	Ross	1886
W?	Strunk	F	Hardin	1888
W	Wycoff, James	M	Carroll	1888
W	Mormon Elder 1	M	Adams	1888
W	Mormon Elder 2	M	Adams	1888
W	Milligan, William	M	Pickaway	1888
W	Miller, Sarah	F	Seneca	1890
W	Henson, Solomon	M	Warren	1891
B	Jackson, John	M	Logan	1892
W	Rutherford, Mrs.	F	Clark	1893
W	Rutherford, James S.	M	Clark	1893
W	Criestlay	F	Ross	1894
W	Rogers, C.H	M	Washington	1895
W?	Cummings, Bertha	F	Fayette/Pickaway*	1895
W	Martin, Leander J.	M	Seneca	1895
W	Benton, Mrs.	F	Logan	1896
W	Irey, William	M	Mahoning	1896
W	Roberts, May	F	Henry	1897
W	Roberts, Edith	F	Henry	1897
B	Rickman, Dave	M	Logan	1899
B	Jackson, Edward	M	Logan	1899
W	Jackson, Nell	F	Logan	1899
W	Kiniman, William	M	Ross	1899
W	Loblaw, Mark	M	Richland	1900
W	Bassinger, Ephraim	M	Richland	1900
W	Moot, Silas	M	Richland	1900

Race	*Name*	*Sex*	*County*	*Year*
W	Fockler, Cyrus B.	M	Richland	1900
W	Unknown woman	F	Richland	1900
W	Lieby, E.H.	M	Richland	1900
W	Higgins, Harvey	M	Lucas	1903
W	Smith, Clem	M	Hancock	1907
W	Welsley, Christian	M	Tuscarawas	1908
W	Martin, Harriet	F	Tuscarawas	1908
W	Heilman, Michael	M	Wayne	1911
W	LaValley, Minnie	F	Huron	1912
W	Clark, Samuel	M	Knox	1916
W	Wagner, William	M	Lucas	1918
W	Hall, Perry J. Jr.	M	Lucas	1918
W	Beattie (or Beatty), John J.	M	Lucas	1918
W	Rankey, Gus	M	Lorain	1918
W	Steiger, John E.	M	Butler	1919
W	Thompson, Harley	M	Athens	1935
W	Dixon, Joseph A.	M	Washington	1938

*Shown on map as Fayette

Chapter Notes

Preface

1. Scientists now regard race as a social construct and racial categories as a crude approximation for racial diversity.
2. By contrast, a Kansas jury had awarded a father $2 for the lynching of his son just two years earlier.
3. Thompson. *General Code of the State of Ohio*, 1858.
4. Gonzales-Day. *Lynching in the West*, 2006, 11.
5. In what is considered the worst mass lynching in U.S. history, eleven Italians died in New Orleans, but only two were hanged. The other nine were shot or beaten to death. See Meyers. *Ohio's Black Hand Syndicate.*

Introduction

1. Fite. *History of the United States*, 100.
2. Knepper. *Ohio and Its People*, xi.
3. Babbidon. *Race and Crime*, 48.
4. Charles Lynch was a Virginia planter and politician who presided over his own informal court during the American Revolution, although he is not known to have hanged anyone.
5. Rothestein. "Museum Review." *Times.*
6. Wells-Barnett. *Red Record*, 1.
7. *Ibid.*
8. During the first territorial assembly in 1802, a bill to give the black citizens of Ohio the right to vote failed by just one vote. However, some African Americans voted anyway during the first few decades.
9. Douglass. *Why Is the Negro Lynched?*, 7.
10. *Ibid.*
11. "Justification for Lynching." *Times*, 6.

Chapter 1

1. Taylor. *Frontiers of Freedom*, n.p.
2. Nelson. *History of Cincinnati and Hamilton County*, 364.
3. Williams. *A History of Jackson County*, 46.
4. *Ibid.*, 139.
5. Huff. *Memories of Old Newark*, n.p.
6. *Ibid.*, 377.
7. *Ibid.*, 379.
8. *Ibid.*
9. *Ibid.*, 385.
10. Taylor. *Frontiers of Freedom*, n.p.
11. $500 in 1829 would be about $13,000 today.
12. Feight. "'Black Friday'" *Scioto Historical.*
13. Evans. *A History of Scioto County*, 613.
14. Feight. "'Black Friday'" *Scioto Historical.*
15. Howe. *Historical Collections*, 427.
16. *Ibid.*, 428.
17. Brodie. *No Man Knows My History*, 119.
18. *Ibid.*, 428.
19. Howe. *Historical Collections*, 428.
20. *Ibid.*
21. Hill. *History of Licking County, Ohio*, 469.
22. Brister. *Centennial History of the City of Newark*, 288.
23. King. "The Abolitionists in Granville." *Times*, 1.
24. For some reason, James Emmitt used a pseudonym in his memoir.
25. Emmitt. *Life and Reminiscences of Hon. James Emmitt*, 281.
26. *Ibid.*, 281.
27. *Ibid.*
28. *Ibid.*, 285.
29. Weed. *Faith and Works*, 38–39.
30. Nelson. *History of Cincinnati and Hamilton County*, 365.
31. *Ibid.*
32. Stowe. *Harriet Beecher Stowe*, 107.
33. Bushnell. *History of Granville*, 302.
34. Galbreath. "Anti-Slavery Movement in Columbiana County," 365.
35. MacLean. *Shakers of Ohio*, 249.
36. Graham. *History of Richland County*, 427.
37. *Ibid.*, 437.
38. *Cincinnati Daily Gazette*, September 6, 1841, n.p.
39. Prince. *A Standard History of Springfield*, 316.
40. Humphrey. "Randolph Slaves," n.p.
41. *Ibid.*
42. Estimates of crowd size were often unreliable.
43. Greater Cincinnati Police Historical Society Museum, n.p.
44. *Brooklyn Daily Eagle*, June 28, 1854, 2.
45. Greve. *Centennial History of Cincinnati*, 732.
46. *Ibid.*
47. *Ibid.*, 733.
48. Lee. *History of the City of Columbus*, 62.
49. *Ibid.*
50. *Ibid.*
51. "Know-Nothing Outrages." *Sentinel*, 2.
52. *Ibid.*

53. Evans. *A History of Adams County*, 444.
54. "A Horrible Case of Rape and Lynching." *Times*, 2.
55. *Ibid.*
56. Evans. *A History of Adams County*, 444.
57. *Ibid.*, 454.
58. *Evansville* (Indiana) *Daily Journal*, November 2, 1857, 3.
59. *Ibid.*
60. "A Disgraceful and Shameful Affair." *Intelligencer*, 3.

Chapter 2

1. "Police Investigation." *Daily Press*, 2.
2. "Terrible Times in Ward Township!" *Statesman*, 2.
3. "Riot at Dayton, Ohio." *Intelligencer*, 3.
4. In 1871, while preparing to demonstrate how an allegedly murdered man accidentally shot himself to death, Vallandigham inadvertently died doing the same.
5. Kanuckel. "Draft Riot at Fort Fizzle," n.p.
6. "Riot at Dayton, Ohio." *Intelligencer*, 3.
7. "Bloody Affray at Lancaster." *Standard*, 2.
8. "Outrage Upon Mr. George Spence of Springfield." *Democrat*, 2.
9. *Ibid.*
10. "Exciting Trial in Mahoning County." *Statesman*, 1.
11. *Ibid.*
12. *Ibid.*
13. *Ibid.*
14. Graham. *History of Richland County*, 375.
15. *Ibid.*
16. *Ibid.*, 376.
17. *History of Van Wert and Mercer Counties*, 313.
18. *Ibid.*
19. Day. *Lynched!: A Fiendish Outrage*, n.p.
20. Kimmel. "Mary Secaur." Accessed 5/19/2016.
21. Day. *Lynched! A Fiendish Outrage*, n.p.
22. *Ibid.*
23. "The Evils of Lynch Law." *Republican*, 2.
24. "Lynch Law in Ragersville." *Democrat*, 3.
25. "From Cincinnati." *Gazette*, 3.
26. "Brutal Outrage on a Young Girl." *Chicago Tribune*, 5.
27. "That Lynching." *Enquirer*, 1.
28. Middleton. *History of Champaign County*, 1143.
29. *The Marion Star*, February 25, 1902, 5.
30. "The Bellefontaine Tragedy." *Jeffersonian*, 2.
31. *Ibid.*
32. "Lynch Law in Ohio." *Times*, n.p.
33. *Ibid.*
34. *Ibid.*
35. *Ibid.*
36. *Marion* (Ohio) *Star*. February 25, 1902, 5.
37. "A Horrible Murder." *Herald*, 2.
38. "A Young Girl Outrage." *Advance*, 7.
39. *Ibid.*
40. *Stark County* (Ohio) *Democrat*, January 27, 1876, 8.
41. "Along Ohio 39." *Record*, 1.
42. Knepp. "A Serial Killer." *Journal-Press*, n.p.
43. "Lynch Law in Ohio." *Times*, n.p.
44. Knepp. "A Serial Killer." *Journal-Press*, n.p.
45. *Ibid.*
46. *Ibid.*
47. *Ibid.*
48. *Ibid.*
49. *Ibid.*
50. *Ibid.*
51. *Ibid.*
52. *Ibid.*
53. (Clermont County, Ohio) *Courier*, November 17, 1877, n.p.
54. "Democratic Attack on Negroes." *Times*, n.p.
55. *Ibid.*
56. "Horrible Crime." *Jeffersonian*, 1.
57. "Jim Garnett." *Appeal*, 1.
58. *Ibid.*
59. "Mob Law at Oxford, O." *Star*, 1.
60. "Horrible Crime." *Jeffersonian*, 1.
61. "A Mob at Oxford Ohio." *Press*, 1.
62. *Ibid.*
63. "Horrible Crime." *Jeffersonian*, 1.
64. *Ibid.*
65. "A Mob at Oxford Ohio." *Press*, 1.
66. "Ohio Ku-Klux." *Enquirer*, 5.
67. *Ibid.*
68. *Ibid.*
69. "Lynch Law in Ohio." *Times*, 5.
70. *Ibid.*
71. "Hanged, but Not Killed." *Herald*, 1.
72. "Lynch Law in Ohio." *Times*, 5.
73. "The Scott Outrage in Ohio." *Times*, 1.
74. *Ibid.*
75. "Lynch Law in Ohio." *Times*, 5.

Chapter 3

1. "Terrible Murder Near Mansfield Ohio." *Tribune*, 2.
2. Howard. *Black Lynching in the Promised Land*, 73.
3. *Ibid.*, 74.
4. Graham. *History of Richland County*, 375.
5. "A City Under Mob Rule." *Times*, 1.
6. *Ibid.*
7. (Minneapolis) *Star Tribune*, September 9, 1878, 2.
8. "An Attempted Outrage." *Jeffersonian*, 2.
9. *Tiffin* (Ohio) *Tribune*, September 12, 1878, 3.
10. "Brutal Outrage by Tramps." *Times*, 1.
11. *Ibid.*
12. "Ohio Ku-Klux." *Enquirer*, 5.
13. *Ibid.*, 449.
14. "Ohio KuKlux." *Democrat*, 1.
15. (Memphis) *Public Ledger*, April 28, 1879, 1.
16. "Alleged Attempt at Rape." *Enquirer*, 1.
17. *Ibid.*
18. *Ibid.*
19. *Ibid.*
20. *Ibid.*
21. "Lynching in Clermont County, Ohio." *Democrat*, 4.
22. "Very Nearly Lynched." *Times*, n.p.
23. "Storey's Sad Story." *Star*, 1.
24. "Very Nearly Lynched." *Times*, n.p.
25. "Lynching in Clermont County, Ohio." *Democrat*, 4.
26. "Very Nearly Lynched." *Times*, n.p.
27. "Crime." *Kansas Valley Times*, 4.
28. "A Human Wolf." *Herald*, 1.
29. *Ibid.*

30. *Ibid.*
31. *Ibid.*
32. *Ibid.*
33. *Ibid.*
34. *Ibid.*
35. *Ibid.*
36. *Ibid.*
37. *Ibid.*
38. *Ibid.*
39. "A Human Wolf." *Herald*, 1.
40. *Ibid.*
41. "Horrible Lynching in Ohio." *News*, 1.
42. *Ibid.*
43. *Ibid.*
44. *Ibid.*
45. *Ibid.*
46. Meyers. *Carrying Coal to Columbus*, 84.
47. *Jackson* (Ohio) *Standard*, December 23, 1880, 2.
48. *History of Hocking Valley, Ohio*, 294.
49. "The Ohio Lynching." *Critic*, 3.
50. *Jackson* (Ohio) *Standard*, December 29, 1881, 1.
51. *Ibid.*
52. "Preliminary Examination." *Tribune*, 1.
53. This was the first year in which the Tuskegee Institute began tracking lynchings.
54. *Columbus Press*, June 10, 1897, n.p.
55. *Ibid.*
56. *Ibid.*
57. *Ibid.*
58. "Lynching at Ironton, O." *News*, 1.
59. "More Lynch Law." *Standard*, 1.
60. *Ibid.*
61. Dastardly Murder." *Enquirer*, 1.
62. "Mob Law." *Exponent*, 2.
63. "A Sunday Lynching in Ohio." *Times*, 1.
64. "The Minneapolis Plan." *Globe*, 1.
65. "Mob Law." *Exponent*, 2.
66. *Ibid.*
67. Harris. *Selected Works for Ida B. Wells-Barnett*, 211.
68. "Horrible Outrage in Meigs County." *Advocate*, 1.
69. *(Napoleon, Ohio) Democratic Northwest*, July 26, 1883, 1.
70. "Butterfield Gets Four Years." *Journal*, 3.
71. Risch. "Descendants of John Butterfield," n.p.
72. "Exit Johnson." (Napoleon, Ohio) *Democratic Northwest*, 1.
73. "Rife for a Lynching." *Bulletin*, 1.
74. *Ibid.*
75. *Ibid.*
76. *Ibid.*
77. *Cincinnati Enquirer*, March 25, 1884, 1.
78. Howe. *Historical Collections*, 86.
79. "Mob Rule." *Tribune*, 4.
80. *Haber. "Cincinnati: Not Porkopolis." Authority, n.p.*
81. Shepard. "Popular Explanation of the Causes of Lynch Law." *Reporter*, 112.
82. "A Father's Unnatural Crime." *Times*, n.p.
83. *Ibid.*
84. "The Ohio Riot." *Astorian*, 1.
85. *Eaton* (Ohio) *Democrat*, November 6, 1884, 3.
86. "Ohio Regulators." *Intelligencer*, 4.
87. "A Reporter Tarred and Feathered." *Appeal*, 3.
88. "The Ohio Tarring and Feathering Affair." *Union*, 2.
89. *Ibid.*
90. "The Career of Guess." *Dispatch*, 1.
91. *Ibid.*
92. "The Valley Tragey." *Dispatch*, 1.
93. "Killed by a Mob." *Capital*, n.p.
94. *Thomas County* (Kansas) *Cat*, June 25, 1885, n.p.
95. "Died of a Broken Heart." *News*, n.p.
96. "Killed by a Mob." *Capital*, n.p.
97. (Pittston, Pennsylvania) *Evening Gazette*, June 27, 1885, n.p.
98. "Died of a Broken Heart." *News*, n.p.
99. Hancock. "Biography of Nicholas Wynant Mills," n.p.
100. "Lynch Law in Ohio." *Journal*, 1.
101. "Died Like a Dog." *Democrat*, 3.
102. The men covered their faces with scarves, traded hats, and turned their coats inside out to disguise themselves.
103. "Lynch Law in Ohio." *Journal*, 1.
104. *Ibid.*
105. "Lynched for Rape." *Globe-Republic*, 1.
106. "Died Like a Dog." *Democrat*, 3.
107. *Hocking* (County, Ohio) *Sentinel*, September 3, 1885, 3.
108. "Threatened with Lynching." *Eagle*, 9.

Chapter 4

1. "Narrowly Escape Lynching." *Times*, n.p.
2. "A Girl's Experience with Gypsies." *Times*, n.p.
3. *Ibid.*
4. (Owosso, Michigan) *Times*, July 23, 1886, 8.
5. "Frozen Out of His Hiding Place." *News-Herald*, 2.
6. "A Murderer Lynched." *Bulletin*, 1.
7. *Hicksville* (Ohio) *News*, July 22, 1886, 4.
8. *Ibid.*
9. (Napoleon, Ohio) *Democratic Northwest*, November 18, 1886, 8.
10. *Journal of the Senate*, Volume XCII, 26.
11. "Henry Schwers Spits Out Bullet." *Towpath*, n.p.
12. *Ibid.*
13. "A Girl Murdererd." *Times*, n.p.
14. (Point Pleasant, West Virginia) *Weekly Register*, August 25, 1886, 2.
15. "A Farmer Tarred and Feathered." *Star*, 4.
16. Career. "Tales of the Mohican Country." *News-Journal*, 47.
17. Nelson. "The Story of Rendville," n.p.
18. "Killed by His Hired Man." *Times*, n.p.
19. "Captured!" *Democrat*, 2.
20. "Judge Lynch." *Transcript*, 9.
21. *Ibid.*
22. *Ibid.*
23. "Killed His Landlady." *Register*, 2.
24. "Met His Deserts." *Critic*, 3.
25. "Lynched by Negroes." *News*, 1.
26. "A Midnight Mob." *Republic*, 1.
27. "Met His Deserts." *Critic*, 3.
28. "Lynched by Negroes." *News*, 1.
29. *Ibid.*
30. *Xenia* (Ohio) *Democrat News*, June 18, 1887, n.p.
31. *Ibid.*
32. "Knights of the Switch." *Democrat*, 1.
33. *Ibid.*
34. (St. Paul, Minnesota) *Western Appeal*, September 3, 1887, 1.

35. Rusler. *A Standard History of Allen County*, 279.
36. *Allen County Democrat*, April 6, 1888, 1.
37. *Ibid.*
38. "Election Day 1888 Ends in Violence." *News*, n.p.
39. *Ibid.*
40. *Ohio Law Reporter*, Volume 10, 128.
41. "Almost a Lynching." *Gazette*, 2.
42. "Mobbed by Fellow Prisoners." *Bulletin*, 4.
43. Smith. *Women's Political & Social Thought*, 263.
44. *Ibid.*
45. *Ibid.*
46. Wells-Barnett. *The Red Record*, 6.
47. "A Diabolical Outrage." *Bulletin*, 4.
48. *Ibid.*
49. "Black Caps vs. White Caps." *Bulletin*, 4.
50. "'White Caps' Beaten." *Times*, 1.
51. *Ibid.*
52. *Ibid.*
53. *Ibid.*
54. *Ibid.*
55. "Crazed by a Whipping." *Gazette*, 2.
56. Live exhibits—from human curiosities to Indians—had been popularized by P.T. Barnum.
57. "The Ohio White Caps." *Northwest*, 9.
58. *Ibid.*
59. *Ibid.*
60. "More Warnings." *Northwest*, 9.
61. *Ibid.*
62. "White Caps." *Northwest*, 1.
63. "White Caps." *Journal*, 2.
64. *Ibid.*
65. "The Ohio White Caps." *Democrat*, 8.
66. *Ibid.*
67. *Ibid.*
68. *Ibid.*
69. "White Caps at Leipsic." *Northwest*, 5.
70. "Ohio White Caps." *News*, 3.
71. "Hopedale, Ohio Terrorized." *Bulletin*, 1.
72. "Outrages of Ohio White Caps." *Review*, 2.
73. "The White Caps." *Northwest*, 9.
74. "Ohio 'White Caps.'" *Times*, 2.
75. (Napoleon, Ohio) *Democratic Northwest*, January 10, 1889, 7.
76. Karcher. *A Refugee from His Race*, n.p.
77. "Rough Treatment." *Northwest*, 7.
78. "Ohio White Caps at Work." *Daily Post*, 5.
79. *Ibid.*
80. "Ohio White Caps." *Star*, 1.
81. "Wild Disorders." *Democrat*, 2.
82. *Salem* (Ohio) *Daily News*, March 13, 1889, 1.
83. "'White Caps' in Our Midst." *Daily Times*, 2.
84. "Murder and Riot at Xenia, O." *Journal*, 1.
85. "Whipped by White Caps." *Times*, n.p.
86. "Whipped by White Caps." *Dispatch*, 1.
87. (St. Clairsville, Ohio) *Belmont Chronicle*, October 10, 1889, 3.
88. (St. Clairsville, Ohio) *Belmont Chronicle*, November 21, 1889, 3.

Chapter 5

1. "Threatening a Teacher." *Gazette*, 2.
2. "Warned by White Caps." *Bulletin*, 1.
3. "Cold-Blooded Murder." *Enterprise*, 2.
4. "To a Shocking Crime Negro." *Bulletin*, 1.
5. "Sheriff's Ruse Foils a Mob." *Sentinel*, 2.
6. "Richard Gardner Spirited Away." *Bulletin*, 1.
7. *Ibid.*
8. "Real White Caps in Ohio." *Dispatch*, 5.
9. "A Weak Female." *Enquirer*, 1.
10. "Caps the Climax." *Argus*, 2.
11. "Engineer Vandevanter's Murder." *Critic*, 1.
12. "Wicked Defiance!" *Northwest*, 1.
13. "A Slanderer Lynched." *Times*, n.p.
14. "Wicked Defiance!" *Northwest*, 1.
15. "A Slanderer Lynched." *Times*, n.p.
16. "Wicked Defiance!" *Northwest*, 1.
17. "Trained Mob." *Globe*, 5.
18. *Ibid.*
19. "Lynch Law in Ohio." *News*, 11.
20. *Ibid.*
21. "Summary Justice." *Star*, 3.
22. "Murder, Cold Blood." *Sentinel*, 3.
23. *Ibid.*
24. *Ibid.*
25. "Put Tar and Feathers on Him." *Ocean*, 1.
26. "Female White Capism in Ohio." *Record*, 2.
27. "Hanging Not Enough." *Journal*, 1.
28. *Ibid.*
29. "An Ohio Lynching." *Journal*, 1.
30. *Ibid.*
31. *Ibid.*
32. *Ibid.*
33. *Ibid.*
34. "Swift Justice." *Register*, 2.
35. *Ibid.*
36. "A Soldier Lynched." *Dispatch*, 7.
37. "Another Lynching." *Journal*, 1.
38. *Ibid.*
39. *Ibid.*
40. *Ibid.*
41. "He Stared at People." *Newspaper*, 1.
42. *Davenport* (Iowa) *Democrat and Leader*, April 5, 1892, 5.
43. "Another Lynching." *Journal*, 1.
44. "Clamoring for His Blood." *Journal*, 2.
45. *Ibid.*
46. "Averted the Lynching Bee." *Independent*, 2.
47. "Clamoring for His Blood." *Journal*, 2.
48. Meyers. *Wicked Columbus, Ohio*, 21.
49. "Tarred and Feathered." *Sentinel*, 2.
50. "Narrowly Escaped Lynching." *Democrat*, 8.
51. *Ibid.*
52. "Bloody Wood." *Northwest*, n.p.
53. "Deed of a Drunken Brute." *Call*, 1.
54. "Beaten with Clubs." *Enquirer*, 1.
55. "Attrocious Crime Committed." *Democrat*, 5.
56. Evans. *A History of Adams County*, 393.
57. *Ibid.*
58. "Strung Him Up." *Dispatch*, 1.
59. *Ibid.*
60. "Colored Boy Lynched." *Banner*, 6.
61. *Ibid.*
62. "Up and Down Ohio." *Beacon*, 6.
63. "Vengeance." *News-Herald*, 3.
64. "They Strung Him Up." *Dispatch*, 1.
65. "At a Mob's Mercy." *Logansport*, 10.
66. "Ohio White Caps Still at Work." *Sun*, 9.
67. "Given Fifty Lashes." *Herald*, 1.
68. "Policeman Shot Dead." *Star*, 1.
69. Grant. *The Anti-Lynching Movement*, 51.
70. "Riot and Bloodshed." *Register*, 6.
71. *Ibid.*

72. "Ohio Troops Fire on a Mob." *Times*, 1.
73. *Ibid.*
74. "Riot and Bloodshed." *Register*, 6.
75. Burba. "A Wild Night at Washington C.H." *News*, n.p.
76. "The Ohio Lynching Riot." *Tribune*, 6.
77. (Columbus) *Ohio State Journal*, October 23, 1894, 1.
78. (Columbus) *Ohio State Journal*, October 30, 1894, n.p.
79. *Newark* (Ohio) *Daily Advocate*, October 20, 1894, n.p.
80. "Murder of Innocents." *Tribune*, 1.
81. "Girl Tarred and Feathered." *Bulletin*, 1.
82. "Girl in Tar and Feathers." *Journal*, 2.
83. *Ibid.*
84. "Lynching in Ohio." *News*, 1.
85. (Prescott) *Arizona Weekly Journal-Miners*, June 5, 1895, 5.
86. *Orleans County* (Vermont) *Register*, June 24, 1895, 2.
87. "Crimes and Casualties." *News*, 5.
88. *Marion* (Ohio) *Star*, July 11, 1895, 1.
89. The *New York Times* datelined its story "New-Richmond, Ky.—Aug. 21."
90. "A Lynching in Ohio." *Press*, 5.
91. *Ibid.*
92. "Swift and Sure Vengeance." *Dispatch*, 10.
93. *Ibid.*
94. *Ibid.*
95. "Guarded by Troops." *Call*, 2.
96. "Visited by Whitecaps." *Daily Times*, 1.

Chapter 6

1. Jim Crow was a derogatory term for African Americans and laws passed after Reconstruction to enforce racial segregation were called Jim Crow laws.
2. "An Age Couple Brutally Murdered." *Union*, 1.
3. *Ibid.*
4. *Ibid.*
5. "Romulus Cotell." *Leader*, 4.
6. "*Ibid.*
7. "Abbreviated Telegrams." *Argus*, 6.
8. *Marysville* (Ohio) *Journal-Tribune*, May 28, 1896, 1.
9. "Escaped a Lynching." *Eagle*, 1.
10. "White Caps." *Northwest*, 1.
11. *Ibid.*
12. *Ibid.*
13. Pearl Bryan was a twenty-two-year-old woman from Indiana whose headless body was found in Fort Thomas, Kentucky, in 1896. Her murder was the inspiration for the folk song, "Pearl Bryan."
14. (Shreveport, Louisiana) *Semi-Weekly News*, June 4, 1897, 1.
15. "Civilization in Ohio." *Times*, n.p.
16. Campbell. *The Year That Defined American Journalism*, 61.
17. "Bloody Lynching Bee." *Statesman*, 1.
18. "The Lynching at Urbana." *Times*, n.p.
19. "The Tragedy at Urbana." *News*, 1.
20. "Bloody Lynching Bee." *Statesman*, 1.
21. "Quickly Done." *Dispatch*, 1.
22. "The Tragedy at Urbana," *News*, 1.
23. *Ibid.*
24. "The Lynching at Urbana." *Times*, n.p.
25. "Lynching Party Foiled." *Call*, 3.
26. "Lynching Threatened in Ohio." *Times*, n.p.
27. "Chance for a Lynching." *Democrat*, 4.
28. "Lynching is Expected." *Star*, 2.
29. "Feeling is Intense." *Bulletin*, 1.
30. "Chance for a Lynching." *Democrat*, 1.
31. *Xenia* (Ohio) *Daily Gazette*, April 26, 1897, n.p.
32. "Wm. Carter." *News-Herald*, 7.
33. "A White Cap Outrage." *Mist*, 4.
34. (St. George, Utah) *Union*, November 13, 1897, 2.
35. "Ohio Lynching." *Journal*, 1.
36. "Death Due to a Doctor." *Miner*, n.p.
37. "The Mob Demands Him." *Times*, 1.
38. "May Be a Lynching in an Ohio Town." *Times*, n.p.
39. *Ibid.*
40. (Ardmore, Oklahoma) *Daily Ardmorite*, November 20, 1898, 4.
41. "A Case in Point." *Herald*, 2.
42. "After Rapist Smith." *Recorder*, 5.
43. "Fierce Farmers." *Republican*, 3.
44. "Tramp Kills an Ohio Woman." *Times*, n.p.
45. "Austin's First Cry." *Republican*, 3.
46. "A Very Cautious Opinion." *Republican*, 3.
47. *Ibid.*
48. "The Austin Aftermath." *Republican*, 3.
49. "Murdered His Parents." *Republic*, 1.
50. "Tarred and Feathered." *Gazette*, 2.
51. "It Looks Bad." *Beacon Journal*, 5.
52. "Coils Tightening." *Democrat*, 7.
53. "Lynching in Ohio is Probable." *Post*, 2.
54. *Ibid.*, 84.
55. *Ibid.*
56. Doyle. *Centennial History of Summit County*, 83.
57. *Ibid.*, 89.
58. *Ibid.*, 90.
59. Collins. *The Truth About Lynching*, 117.
60. "Race War at Delaware." *News-Herald*, 2.
61. *Ibid.*
62. *Ibid.*
63. *Ibid.*
64. Morton. "The Big Con." African Studies Center, n.p.
65. "Mob Tars Dowie Edlers." *Tribune*, 1.
66. *Ibid.*
67. "Dowie Cases Are Nollied." *Globe*, 5.
68. "In Mansfield History." *News-Journal*, 83.

Chapter 7

1. Clemens. "The United States of Lyncherdom," n.p.
2. "Wounded in Defense of Her Honor." *Acantha*, 1.
3. "Mob." *Democrat*, 1.
4. "Miners Talk Lynching." *Globe*, 3.
5. "Shooting Affair." *Jeffersonian*, 3.
6. "Attempted Lynching in Ohio." *Eagle*, 10.
7. "Lynching Threatened in Ohio's Capital." *Democrat*, 4.
8. "Anticipated Lynching." *Democrat*, 8.
9. *Akron* (Ohio) *Daily Democrat*, August 19, 1902, 4.
10. "Life Sentence." *Democrat*, 6.
11. "White Caps in Ohio." *Gazette*, 4.
12. "Punished by White Caps." *Times*, 3.
13. *Ibid.*

14. "Murder by a Section Hand." *Democrat*, 1.
15. "Safe from an Ohio Mob." *Sun*, 1.
16. "Riot at Crestline, O." *Journal*, 1903.
17. *Lorain* (Ohio) *Times Herald*, August 1, 1903, 1.
18. (Columbus) *Ohio State Journal*, March 15, 1904. n.p.
19. *Ibid.*
20. Robinson. "Lynchings Didn't Happen Only in the South." *News*, n.p.
21. "Mob Wild with Delight." *Press*, 5.
22. "Mob Leaders Not Under Arrest." *Democrat*, 1.
23. "The Torch Used." *Democrat*, 1.
24. *Ibid.*
25. "Ohio Mob Sets Fire to Negro District." *Times*, n.p.
26. "Mob Wild with Delight." *Press*, 5.
27. *Ibid.*
28. "Mobs Held at Bay." *Argus*, 1.
29. *Ibid.*
30. Howard. *Black Lynching in the Promised Land*, 202–203.
31. "Crowd Chases Negro." *Tribune*, 4.
32. "Ohio Lynching Averted." *Eagle*, 1.
33. A month later, Shellenbarger was shot to death in the line of duty.
34. "Jammed Between." *Democrat*, 6.
35. "Lynching Mob in Ohio." *Times*, n.p.
36. Meyers. *Wicked Columbus*, 42.
37. "Sketch Artist Is Sentenced." *Mirror*, 7.
38. "The Black Hand." *Democrat*, n.p.
39. See Meyers. *Ohio's Black Hand Society*.
40. "Brutal Widower Lashed by Women." *Enquirer*, 1.
41. *Ibid.*
42. "Delaware Citizens Aroused by a Murder." *Mirror*, 4.
43. "Saves Negro Murderer." *Times*, 4.
44. "Delaware Citizens Aroused by a Murder." *Mirror*, 4.
45. "A Narrow Escape from Lynching." *Mirror*, 2.
46. *Ibid.*
47. "Threaten to Lynch Confessed Murderer." *Tribune*, 2.
48. "Slayer of Wife Closely Watched." *Times*, 8.
49. "Insane Murderers and Burglars Make Escape." *Call*, 2.
50. "Two Girls Lead Mob." *Mirror*, 2.
51. "Lynching Averted." *Star*, 4.
52. "Murder is Sequel to Bitter Rivalry." *Star*, 10.
53. "Free of Murder Charge." *Dispatch*, 8.
54. "Race Riot May be the Result." *Tribune*, 1.
55. "Think Davis Also Assulted Girl at Lima." *Gazette*, 1.
56. "Fred Davis Thought to be Slayer." *Gazette*, 1.

Chapter 8

1. Wheeler. *Newark Lynching*, 1.
2. *Ibid.*, 20.
3. *Ibid.*, 16.
4. *Ibid.*, 2.
5. "Hold Woman for Part in Etherington Lynching." *Herald*, 16.
6. "The Lynching Tragedy in Ohio." *Sun*, 1.
7. Sudar. "100 Years Ago," 1.
8. *Ibid.*
9. Warner. "Lawlessness Breeds Anarchy," 1.
10. *Journal of the Senate of the Eighty-First General Assembly*, 71.
11. Baker. "The Thin Crust of Civilization." *Magazine*, 691.
12. "Urged Lynching of a Former Mt. Vernon Man." *Banner*, 3.
13. *Alexandria* (Virginia) *Gazette*, June 22, 1911, 2.
14. "Lynchings Become a National Menace." *Union*, 18.
15. "Jail Surrounded by Vengeance Seeking Mob." *Journal*, 1.
16. "Posse Seeking Assailant of Child in Ohio." *Times*, 1.
17. *Ibid.*
18. "Eight Married Women Tar and Feather Girl." *Eagle*, 1.
19. *Ibid.*
20. "Find Lynchers' Victim." *Times*, 4.
21. "Man Recently Tried For Murder." *Times-Dispatch*, 3.
22. Butler. *History of Youngstown*, 531.
23. "Ordered to Go Away." *Banner*, 5.
24. *Ibid.*
25. *Ibid.*
26. "Expelled Like Rip Van Winkle." *Banner*, 3.
27. "Two Arrests Are Made." *Banner*, 5.
28. *Ibid.*
29. "Deputy Lytle Is Threatened by Sml. Clark." *Banner*, 5.
30. *Ibid.*
31. *Ibid.*
32. "Indictments Nolied." *Banner*, 7.
33. "Picked Out Wrong Man." *Banner*, 1.
34. "Guard Negro from Ohio Mob Violence." *Star*, 6.
35. "Sheriff Badly Wounded by Mob." *Review*, 3.
36. "Negro Claims Innocence." *Banner*, 8.
37. "Guard Negro from Ohio Mob Violence." *Star*, 6.
38. Dray. *At the Hands of Persons Unknown*, 222.
39. "Sheriff Eley." *The Crisis*, 184.
40. "White Gowned Men Thrash Pacifist." *Herald*, 1.
41. "Auglaize County Girl Victim of Vicious Negro." *Democrat*, 8.
42. "Negro Held for an Assault on Wapak Girl." *News*, 9.
43. "The Strange Mystery of the Nocturnal Ambush." *Blade*, 6.
44. *Ibid.*
45. *Ibid.*
46. "Tar Party Quiz Begun by Jury." *Blade*, 1.
47. *Ibid.*
48. "Loses Suit for Tar Party." *Advocate*, 1.
49. Reid. *Mystifying Murder*, 57.
50. "Drive Negroes from Town." *Republican*, 9.
51. "Marion Negroes Flee," *Dispatch*, 3.
52. *Ibid.*
53. "Quiet Night Follows Troubled Monday." *Star*, 3.
54. *Ibid.*
55. For his part, Harding said it was possible.
56. Payne. *Dead Last*, 108.
57. *Ibid.*, 109.
58. *Ibid.*, 111.
59. *Ibid.*
60. "Unavoidable Accident." *Enquirer*, 9.
61. "Degenerate Murders Two." *Tribune*, 6.
62. "Ku Klux Klan Now After Wife Beaters." *Journal*, 1.
63. "Seven Arrests by Ohio Drys." *Eagle*, 4.

64. "'Lynch Them' Crowd Yells." *Citizen-Times*, 1.
65. "Canton Man Tells." *News-Journal*, 1.
66. "Three Men Are Killed in Niles." *Evening News*, 1.
67. Governor Donahey received strong support form the Klan, but rumors that he was a Klansman remain unsubstantiated.
68. "Police Find Body in Gutter." *Review*, 1.
69. *Ibid.*
70. (New Philadelphia) *Daily Times*, November 12, 1925, 1.
71. *Ibid.*
72. "To Declare War on Cleveland Crooks." *Journal*, 1.
73. *Ibid.*
74. "Police Find Body in Gutter." *Review*, 1.
75. "Sets Four Men Free." *Dealer*, 4.
76. "Real Attempt of Night Riders." *Democrat*, 2.
77. "Hint Lynching in Horst Case." *Journal*, 2.
78. "Sheriff to Probe Attempt to Lynch." *News-Star*, 10.
79. "Sordid Story of Ironton." *Courier*, 19.
80. "'Too Popular' with Employers." *American*, n.p.
81. "Threats Made Against Negro." *Evening Review*, 1.
82. "Onion Marsh Under Guard of Deputies." *Journal-Tribune*, 1.
83. "Jury Panel at Kenton." *Journal-Tribune*, 2.
84. Tucker. "As I View the Thing." *Herald*, 8.
85. "Fleming, Snyder Face Indictments." *Gazette*, 9.
86. "Guard Slayer from Lynching." *News-Journal*, 1.
87. "Athlete Who Killed Friend's Wife." *Tribune*, 1.
88. "Ohio Mob Gives Up Search." *Record-Herald*, 8.
89. "Trial Held in a Tourist Camp." *Independent*, 12.

Afterword

1. "Burn Cross at Home of White Girl." *Jet*, 15.

Appendix

1. The *Chicago Defender* reported identical numbers for the years 1882 through 1946.

Bibliography

Articles

"Abbreviated Telegrams." *Rock Island* (Illinois) *Argus*, May 26, 1896.
"After Rapist Smith." (Zanesville, Ohio) *Times Recorder*, November 25, 1898.
"An Aged Couple Brutally Murdered." *Sacramento Daily Union*, March 30, 1896.
Akron (Ohio) *Daily Democrat*, August 19, 1902.
Alexandria (Virginia) *Gazette*, June 22, 1911.
"Alleged Attempt at Rape." *Cincinnati Enquirer*, April 10, 1879.
"Alleged Murderers of Merchant Goss of Edinburg." *Akron* (Ohio) *Daily Democrat*, January 18, 1900.
Allen County Democrat, April 6, 1888.
"Almost a Lynching." *Fort Worth Daily Gazette*, May 18, 1888.
"Along Ohio 39: Ax-Handle Murder Put Berlin in Limelight." *The Daily Record*, September 9, 1966.
"Another Account of the Tragic Affair." (Columbus) *Ohio State Journal*, January 15, 1892.
"Another Lynching." (Columbus) *Ohio State Journal*, April 2, 1892.
"Anticipated Lynching." *Stark County* (Ohio) *Democrat*, June 3, 1902.
(Ardmore, Oklahoma) *Daily Ardmorite*, November 20, 1898.
"At a Mob's Mercy." *Logansport (Indiana) Pharos-Tribune*, April 17, 1894.
"Athens." (Logan) *Ohio Democrat*, January 26, 1889.
"Athlete Who Killed Friend's Wife Is Saved from Chair by Mercy Verdict." (Coschocton, Ohio) *Tribune*, December 21, 1935.
"Atrocious Crime Committed in Lexington Township." *Stark County* (Ohio) *Democrat*, November 16, 1893.
"Attempted Lynching in Ohio." *Brooklyn Daily Eagle*, May 18, 1902.
"An Attempted Outrage on a Young Lady—The Scoundrel Escapes." *Findlay* (Ohio) *Jeffersonian*, September 6, 1878.
"Auglaize County Girl Victim of Vicious Negro." *Celina* (Ohio) *Democrat*, June 22, 1917.
"The Austin Aftermath." *Bellefontaine* (Ohio) *Republican*, January 5, 1900.
"Austin's First Cry." *Bellefontaine* (Ohio) *Republican*, May 26, 1899.
"Averted the Lynching Bee." *Helena* (Montana) *Independent*, April 13, 1892.
Baker, Ray Stannard. "The Thin Crust of Civilization." *The American Magazine*, Volume LXXI, Number 6, April 1911.
"Beaten with Clubs." *Cincinnati Enquirer*, August 24, 1893.
"The Bellefontaine Tragedy." *Findlay* (Ohio) *Jeffersonian*, October 1, 1875.
"Bid Them Good-Bye." (Maysville, Kentucky) *Evening Bulletin*, December 13, 1888.
"Big Riot in Ohio." *Brooklyn Daily Eagle*, July 5, 1907.
"Black Caps vs. White Caps." (Maysville, Kentucky) *Evening Bulletin*, September 14, 1888.
"The Black Hand." *Stark County* (Ohio) *Democrat*, March 5, 1907.
"Bloody Affray at Lancaster." *Hillsdale* (Michigan) *Standard*, March 8, 1864.
"Bloody Lynching Bee." *Austin* (Texas) *Weekly Statesman*. June 10, 1897.
"Bloody Wood." (Napoleon, Ohio) *Democratic Northwest*, July 20, 1893.
"Booker T. Washington." *Indianapolis Freeman*, August 28, 1897.
Brooklyn Daily Eagle, June 28, 1854.
"Brutal Outrage by Tramps." *New York Times*, October 3, 1878.
"Brutal Outrage on a Young Girl." *Chicago Tribune*, July 29, 1874.
"Brutal Widower Lashed by Women." *Cincinnati Enquirer*, April 21, 1907.
Burba, Howard. "A Wild Night at Washington C.H." *Dayton Daily News*, June 26, 1932.
"Burn Cross at Home of White Girl Dating Negro." *Jet*, Volume XXXIII, Number 24, March 21, 1968.
"Butterfield Gets Four Years." *Perrysburg* (Ohio) *Journal*, February 8, 1884.
"Canton Man Tells of Being Horsewhipped." (Mansfield, Ohio) *News-Journal*, April 12, 1924.

"Caps the Climax." *Rock Island* (Illinois) *Argus*, July 31, 1890.
"Captured!" *Eaton* (Ohio) *Democrat*, December 23, 1886.
Career, D.W. "Tales of the Mohican Country: Tarred, Feathered." *Mansfield* (Ohio) *News-Journal*, August 13, 81.
"The Career of Guess." *Columbus Dispatch*, May 23, 1885.
"A Case in Point." (Los Angeles, California) *Herald*, November 18, 1898.
"Chance for a Lynching." *Valentine* (Nebraska) *Democrat*, October 28, 1897.
(Charles Town, West Virginia) *Spirit of Jefferson*, January 16, 1894.
(Cincinnati) *Daily Gazette*, September 6, 1841.
Cincinnati Enquirer, March 25, 1884.
Cincinnati Police History. http://www.gcphs.com/cincinnati_police_history_1850_to_1874.html. Accessed May 20, 2016.
"A City Under Mob Rule." *New York Times*, September 8, 1878.
"Civilization in Ohio." *New York Times*, June 9, 1897.
"Clamoring for His Blood." *Indianapolis Journal*, April 12, 1892.
Clemens, Samuel. "The United States of Lyncherdom." http://people.virginia.edu/~sfr/enam482e/lyncherdom.html. Accessed May 16, 2016.
(Clermont County, Ohio) *Courier*, November 17, 1877.
"Coils Tightening." *Akron* (Ohio) *Daily Democrat*, January 16, 1900.
"Cold-Blooded Murder." (Wellington, Ohio) *Enterprise*, April 9, 1890.
"Colored Boy Lynched." *Abbeville* (South Carolina) *Press and Banner*, January 31, 1894.
(Columbus) *Ohio State Journal*, October 23, 1894.
(Columbus) *Ohio State Journal*, October 30, 1894.
(Columbus) *Ohio State Journal*, March 15, 1904.
Columbus Press, June 10, 1897.
"Crazed by a Whipping." *Alexandria* (Virginia) *Gazette*, November 23, 1888.
"Crime." (Rossville) *Kansas Valley Times*, May 28, 1880.
"Crimes and Casualties." (Napoleon, Ohio) *Democratic Northwest and Henry County News*, July 18, 1895.
"Crowd Chases Negro." *New York Tribune*, October 3, 1904.
"Dastardly Murder." *Cincinnati Enquirer*, April 22, 1882.
Davenport (Iowa) *Democrat and Leader*, April 5, 1892.
"Death Due to a Doctor." *Butte* (Montana) *Weekly Miner*, February 10, 1898.
"Deed of a Drunken Brute." *San Francisco Call*, July 15, 1893.
"Degenerate Murders Two." (Coshocton, Ohio) *Tribune*, April 19, 1920.
"Delaware Citizens Aroused by a Murder." *Marion* (Ohio) *Daily Mirror*, September 23, 1907.
"Democratic Attack on Negroes." *New York Times*, November 5, 1876.
"Deputy Lytle Is Threatened by Sml. Clark." (Mount Vernon, Ohio) *Democratic Banner*, April 13, 1917.
"A Diabolical Outrage." (Maysville, Kentucky) *Evening Bulletin*, September 7, 1888.
"Died Like a Dog." *Stark County* (Ohio) *Democrat*, June 25, 1885.
"Died of a Broken Heart." *Hicksville* (Ohio) *News*, September 24, 1885.
"A Disgraceful and Shameful Affair." *Wheeling* (West Virginia) *Daily Intelligencer*, June 9, 1859.
"Dowie Cases Are Nollied." *St. Paul* (Minnesota) *Globe*, August 11, 1901.
"The Dowieites Are Here." *Akron* (Ohio) *Daily Democrat*, August 23, 1900.
"Eight Married Women Tar and Feather Girl." *Reading* (Pennsylvania) *Eagle*, September 14, 1912.
"Election Day 1888 Ends in Violence." *Lima* (Ohio) *News*, February 25, 1888.
"Engineer Vandevanter's Murder." *The Daily* (Washington, D.C.) *Critic*, July 22, 1890.
"Escaped a Lynching." *Brooklyn* (New York) *Daily Eagle*, June 6, 1896.
Evansville (Indiana) *Daily Journal*, November 2, 1857.
"The Evils of Lynch Law." *Marshall County* (Indiana) *Republican*, April 23, 1874.
"Exciting Trial in Mahoning County." *Daily* (Columbus) *Ohio Statesman*, June 3, 1864.
"Exit Johnson." (Napoleon, Ohio) *Democratic Northwest*, May 29, 1884.
"Expelled Like Rip Van Winkle." (Mount Vernon, Ohio) *Democratic Banner*, May 5, 1916.
"A Farmer Tarred and Feathered." *Auckland* (New Zealand) *Star*, January 5, 1887.
"Fatal Elopement." (Maysville, Kentucky) *Daily Public Ledger*, September 23, 1893.
"A Father's Unnatural Crime." *New York Times*, July 29, 1884.
"Feeling Is Intense." *Maysville* (Kentucky) *Evening Bulletin*, October 26, 1897.
Feight, Andrew. "'Black Friday': Enforcing Ohio's 'Black Laws' in Portsmouth, Ohio." *Scioto Historical*, http://www.sciotohistorical.org/items/show/108. Accessed September 20, 2017.
"Female White Capism in Ohio." *Alma* (Michigan) *Record*, December 4, 1891.
"Fierce Farmers." *Bellefontaine* (Ohio) *Republican*, March 28, 1899.
"Find Lynchers' Victim." *New York Times*, November 29, 1915.

"Fleming, Snyder Face Indictments." *Xenia* (Ohio) *Daily Gazette*, April 24, 1935.
"Fred Davis Thought to be Slayer of Anna Lloyd." *Chillicothe* (Ohio) *Gazette*, June 29, 1910.
"Free of Murder Charge." *Mahoning* (County, Ohio) *Dispatch*, July 1, 1910.
"From Cincinnati." *Alexandria* (Virginia) *Gazette*, July 29, 1874.
"Frozen Out of His Hiding Place." (Hillsboro, Ohio) *News-Herald*, April 14, 1886.
Galbreath, C.B. "Anti-Slavery Movement in Columbiana County." *Ohio Archaeological and Historical Society Publications*, Volume 30, Number 22. Columbus: Fred J. Heer, 1921.
"Girl in Tar and Feathers." *New Bern* (North Carolina) *Weekly Journal*, January 10, 1895
"A Girl Murdererd." *New York Times*, July 24, 1886.
"Girl Tarred and Feathered." (Maysville, Kentucky) *Evening Bulletin*, December 13, 1894.
"A Girl's Experience with Gypsies." *New York Times*, March 19, 1886.
"Give Us a Rest." (Hillsboro, Ohio) *News-Herald*, December 6, 1888.
"Given Fifty Lashes." *Delphos* (Ohio) *Daily Herald*, June 27, 1894.
Greater Cincinnati Police Historical Society Museum. http://www.gcphs.com/cincinnati_police_history_1850_to_1874.html. Accessed May 20, 2016.
"Guard Negro from Ohio Mob Violence." *Seattle Star*, September 14, 1916.
"Guard Slayer from Lynching." (Mansfield, Ohio) *News-Journal*, May 25, 1935.
"Guarded by Troops." *San Francisco Call*, October 28, 1895.
Haber, Samuel. "Cincinnati: Not Porkopolis but Queen City, 1830–1880." *The Quest for Authority and Honor in the American Professions, 1750–1900*. Chicago: University of Chicago Press, 1991.
Hancock, Audrey. "Biography of Nicholas Wynant Mills." April 2010. http://freepages.genealogy.rootsweb.ancestry.com/~grannyapple/MILLS/BIO-Nicholas%20Wynant%20Mills.html. Accessed May 20, 2016.
"Hanged, but Not Killed." *New York Herald*, November 23, 1877.
"Hanged by Lyncher." *New York Times*, February 5, 1884.
"Hanging Not Enough." (Columbus) *Ohio State Journal*, January 14, 1892.
"He Stared at People." *Aurora Daily Newspaper*, April 5, 1892.
"Henry Schwers Spits Out Bullet." *Towpath*, n.p. http://www.newbremenhistory.org/Schwers,Hy.-bullet.htm. Accessed September 25, 2017.
"Hey, Gov. Foraker." (Hillsboro, Ohio) *News-Herald*, July 25, 1889.
Hicksville (Ohio) *News*, July 22, 1886.
"Hint Lynching in Horst Case." *Milwaukee Journal*, February 21, 1930.
Hocking (County, Ohio) *Sentinel*, September 3, 1885.
"Hold Woman for Part in Etherington Lynching." *Los Angeles Herald*, August 25, 1910.
"Hopedale, Ohio Terrorized." (Maysville, Kentucky) *Evening Bulletin*, December 12, 1888.
"A Horrible Case of Rape and Lynching." *New York Times*, December 4, 1856.
"Horrible Crime." *Findlay* (Ohio) *Jeffersonian*, September 14, 1877.
"A Horrible Murder." *Somerset* (Pennsylvania) *Herald*. September 29, 1875.
"Horrible Outrage in Meigs County." *Newark* (Ohio) *Advocate*, August 6, 1882.
"A Human Wolf." *New York Herald*, September 4, 1880.
Humphrey, Jim, and Wallace, Rich. "Randolph Slaves." Traveling Through Time. https://www.shelbycountyhistory.org/schs/archives/blackhistoryarchives/randolphbhisA.htm. Accessed September 26, 2017.
"Hundreds Surround Jail." *Mahoning* (County, Ohio) *Dispatch*, April 15, 1910.
"In Mansfield History." (Mansfield, Ohio) *News-Journal*, July 31, 1977.
"Indictments Nolied." (Mount Vernon, Ohio) *Democratic Banner*, June 15, 1917.
"Insane Murderers and Burglars Make Escape." *San Francisco Call*, February 8, 1909.
"Investigating." *Maysville* (Kentucky) *Evening Bulletin*, December 5, 1888.
"It Looks Bad." *Akron* (Ohio) *Beacon Journal*, January 16, 1900.
Jackson (Ohio) *Standard*, December 23, 1880.
Jackson (Ohio) *Standard*, December 29, 1881.
"Jail Surrounded by Vengeance Seeking Mob." *Albuquerque Morning Journal*, July 11, 1911.
"Jammed Between." *Stark County Democrat*, July 4, 1905.
"Jim Garnett." *Memphis Daily Appeal*, September 5, 1877.
"Judge Lynch." *Little Falls* (Minnesota) *Transcript*, December 31, 1886.
"Jury Panel at Kenton." *Marysville* (Ohio) *Journal-Tribune*, April 1, 1935.
"Justification for Lynching." *New York Times*, August 9, 1899.
Kanuckel, Amber. "The History of the Holmes County Draft Riot at Fort Fizzle." http://www.holmesbargainhunter.com/article/20160713/FEATURES/707139989/-1/hbh28. Accessed September 26, 2017.
"Killed by a Mob." *Topeka Daily Capital*, June 14, 1885.
"Killed by His Hired Man." *New York Times*, December 9, 1886.

"Killed His Landlady." *Iola* (Kansas) *Register*, June 17, 1887.
Kimmel, David. "Mary Secaur." http://listsearches.rootsweb.com/th/read/OHMERCER/2005-04/1114114627. Accessed May 19, 2016.
King, Horace. "The Abolitionists in Granville." *The Historical Times*, Volume III, Number 1, Winter 1989.
Knepp, Gary. "A Serial Killer in Clermont County." (Cincinnati) *Community Journal-Press*, July 22, 2015.
"Knights of the Switch." *Stark County* (Ohio) *Democrat*, June 30, 1887.
"Know-Nothing Outrages." *Weekly Portage* (County, Ohio) *Sentinel*, June 9, 1855.
"Ku Klux Klan After 'Bad' Citizens Only." *Bridgeport* (Connecticut) *Times and Evening Farmer*, August 28, 1922.
"Ku Klux Klan Now After Wife Beaters." (Salem, Oregon) *Capitol Journal*, December 20, 1920.
"Lawlessness in Ohio." *New York Times*, November 9, 1878.
Lawrence County Ohio. http://lawrencecountyohio.com/ironton/stories/lawton.htm. Accessed May 21, 2016.
Lawton, F.B. "Former Ironton Newspaper Man Writes of Good Old Day." *Ironton* (Ohio) *Sunday Tribune*, February 18, 1934.
"Life Sentence." *Stark County* (Ohio) *Democrat*, October 3, 1902.
Lima, Ohio. http://limaohio.com/archive/20316/news-news_lifestyles-795986-election-day-1888-ends-in-violence. Accessed May 21, 2016.
Lorain (Ohio) *Times Herald*, August 1, 1903.
"Loses Suit for Tar Party." *Newark* (Ohio) *Daily Advocate*, October 31, 1919.
"Lynch Law." *Rutland* (Vermont) *Daily Globe*, October 2, 1875.
"Lynch Law in Ohio." *New York Times*, September 26, 1875.
"Lynch Law in Ohio." *New York Times*, July 9, 1876.
"Lynch Law in Ohio." *New York Times*, November 22, 1877.
"Lynch Law in Ohio." *Perrysburg* (Ohio) *Journal*, June 26, 1885.
"Lynch Law in Ohio." *Salem* (Ohio) *Daily News*, April 11, 1891.
"Lynch Law in Ragersville." (New Philadelphia) *Ohio Democrat*, August 1, 1873.
"'Lynch Them' Crowd Yells as Federal Agents Begin Raid." *Asheville (North Carolina) Citizen-Times*, July 26, 1923.
"Lynched by Negroes." *Palataka* (Florida) *Daily News*, June 16, 1887.
"Lynched for Rape." *Springfield* (Ohio) *Globe-Republic*, June 21, 1885.
"Lynched the Negro." *Indianapolis Journal*, April 16, 1894.
"Lynching at Ironton, O." *Galveston Daily News*, January 21, 1882.
"The Lynching at Urbana." *New York Times*, June 6, 1897.
"Lynching Averted." (Washington, D.C.) *Evening Star*, August 7, 1908.
"Lynching Case Is Called." *Gazette Times*, December 6, 1910.
"Lynching in Clermont County, Ohio." *Eaton* (Ohio) *Democrat*, May 29, 1879.
"A Lynching in Ohio." *Pittsburgh Press*, August 22, 1895.
"Lynching in Ohio." (Indianapolis) *Evening News*, May 31, 1895.
"Lynching in Ohio Is Probable." *Houston Daily Post*, April 24, 1900.
"Lynching Is Expected." (Washington, D.C.) *Evening Star*, October 23, 1897.
"Lynching Mob in Ohio." *New York Times*, February 28, 1906.
"Lynching Party Foiled." *San Francisco Call*, June 10, 1897.
"Lynching Threatened in Ohio." *New York Times*, August 30, 1897.
"Lynching Threatened in Ohio's Capital." *Akron* (Ohio) *Daily Democrat*, June 23, 1902.
"The Lynching Tragedy in Ohio." *Springfield* (Kentucky) *Sun*, July 13, 1910.
"Lynchings Become a National Menace." *Rock Island* (Illinois) *Argus and Daily Union*, November 18, 1921.
"Lynchings North and West." *Staunton* (Virginia) *Spectator*, January 24, 1894.
"Man Recently Tried for Murder, Found Dead." *Richmond Times-Dispatch*, November 29, 1915.
Marion (Ohio) *Star*. February 25, 1902.
Marysville (Ohio) *Journal-Tribune*, May 28, 1896.
"May Be a Lynching in an Ohio Town." *New York Times*, November 18, 1898.
(Memphis, Tennessee) *Public Ledger*, April 28, 1879.
"Met His Deserts." *Washington* (D.C.) *Critic*, June 14, 1887.
"A Midnight Mob." *Springfield* (Ohio) *Daily Republic*, June 13, 1887.
"Militamen Overawe Police of Lima, Ohio." *New York Times*, September 7, 1915.
"Miners Talk Lynching." (Saint Paul) *Globe*, July 30, 1901.
"The Minneapolis Plan." (St. Paul, Minnesota) *Daily Globe*, May 1, 1882.
"Mob." *Akron* (Ohio) *Daily Democrat*, January 5, 1901.
"A Mob at Oxford Ohio." *Somerset* (Ohio) *Press*, September 13, 1877.
"The Mob Demands Him." (Washington, D.C.) *Times*, February 7, 1898.
"Mob Law." *Hagerstown* (Indiana) *Exponent*, May 3, 1882.

"Mob Law at Oxford, O." *Cincinnati Daily Star*, September 3, 1877.
"Mob Leaders Not Under Arrest." *Lima* (Ohio) *Times Democrat*, March 8, 1904.
"Mob Rule." (Cheboygan, Michigan) *Northern Tribune*, April 3, 1884.
"Mob Tars Dowie Edlers." *Chicago Tribune*, September 24, 1900.
"Mob Wild with Delight." *Pittsburgh Press*, March 8, 1904.
"Mobbed by Fellow Prisoners." (Maysville, Kentucky) *Evening Bulletin*, May 18, 1888.
"Mobs Held at Bay." *Rock Island* (Illinois) *Argus*, March 11, 1904.
"More Lynch Law." *Jackson Standard*, January 26, 1882.
"More Warnings." (Napoleon, Ohio) *Democratic Northwest*, December 20, 1888.
Morton, Barry. "The Big Con: John Alexander Dowie and the Spread of Zionist Christianity in South Africa." Paper Presented at the University of Leiden, African Studies Center, June 20, 2013.
"Murder and Riot at Xenia, O." *Indianapolis Journal*, April 4, 1889.
"Murder by a Section Hand Nearly Causes a Lynching." (Logan) *Ohio Democrat*, June 18, 1903.
"Murder, Cold Blood." *Hocking* (Ohio) *Sentinel*, August 6, 1891.
"Murder Is Sequel to Bitter Rivalry." *Marion* (Ohio) *Daily Star*, August 7, 1908.
"Murder of Innocents." *Scranton* (Pennsylvania) *Tribune*, November 6, 1894.
"Murdered His Parents." (Phoenix) *Arizona Republic*, December 19, 1899.
"A Murderer Lynched." (Maysville, Kentucky) *Daily Evening Bulletin*, July 20, 1886.
"Murderer Lytle Lynched." *New York Times*, April 1, 1892.
(Napoleon, Ohio) *Democratic Northwest*, July 26, 1883.
(Napoleon, Ohio) *Democratic Northwest*, November 18, 1886.
(Napoleon, Ohio) *Democratic Northwest*, January 10, 1889.
"A Narrow Escape from Lynching." *Marion* (Ohio) *Daily Mirror*, November 4, 1907.
"Narrowly Escape Lynching." *New York Times*, January 28, 1886.
"Narrowly Escaped Lynching." *Stark County* (Ohio) *Democrat*, June 8, 1893.
"Negro Claims Innocence." (Mount Vernon, Ohio) *Democratic Banner*, September 15, 1916.
"Negro Held for an Assault on Wapak Girl Now Released." *Lima* (Ohio) *News*, June 26, 1917.
Nelson, Charles H. "The Story of Rendville." *Buckeye Hill Country*, Volume 1, Spring 1996.
"New by Telegraph. Particulars of a Horrible Lynching in Ohio." *Indianapolis News*, September 2, 1880.
New Orleans Republican, July 19, 1872.
(New Philadelphia) *Daily Times*, November 12, 1925.
"Ohio Ku-Klux." *Cincinnati Enquirer*, November 14, 1878.
"Ohio KuKlux." *New Orleans Daily Democrat*, October 14, 1878.
"An Ohio Lynching." (Columbus) *Ohio State Journal*, January 14, 1892.
"Ohio Lynching." *Akron* (Ohio) *Beacon Journal*, November 17, 1897.
"The Ohio Lynching." (Washington, D.C.) *Evening Critic*, November 23, 1881.
"Ohio Lynching Averted." *Brooklyn* (New York) *Daily Eagle*, April 24, 1905.
"The Ohio Lynching Riot." *Chicago Tribune*, October 19, 1894.
"Ohio Mob Gives Up Search of Jails for Young Negro." *Washington Court House* (Ohio) *Record-Herald*, October 5, 1937.
"Ohio Mob Sets Fire to Negro District." *New York Times*, March 9, 1904.
"Ohio Regulators." *Wheeling* (West Virginia) *Daily Intelligencer*, April 16, 1885.
"The Ohio Riot." (Astoria, Oregon) *Morning Astorian*, September 3, 1884.
"The Ohio Tarring and Feathering Affair." *Sacramento Daily Record Union*, May 27, 1885.
"Ohio Troops Fire on a Mob." *New York Times*, October 18, 1894.
"Ohio White Caps." *Emporia* (Kansas) *Weekly News*, December 20, 1888.
"Ohio White Caps." *Marion* (Ohio) *Star*, December 1, 1888.
"The Ohio White Caps." (Napoleon, Ohio) *Democratic Northwest*, December 6, 1888.
"Ohio 'White Caps.'" *New York Times*, December 16, 1888.
"The Ohio White Caps." *Stark County* (Ohio) *Democrat*, December 6, 1888
"Ohio White Caps at Work." *Pittsburgh Daily Post*, December 20, 1888.
"Ohio White Caps Still at Work." (New York) *Sun*, June 27, 1894.
"Onion Marsh Under Guard of Deputies." *Marysville* (Ohio) *Journal-Tribune*, June 26, 1934.
"Ordered to Go Away." (Mount Vernon, Ohio) *Democratic Banner*, May 2, 1916.
"Outrage Upon Mr. George Spence of Springfield." *Dayton* (Ohio) *Daily Empire*, March 14, 1864.
"Outrages of Ohio White Caps." *New Ulm* (Minnesota) *Weekly Review*, December 19, 1888.
(Owosso, Michigan) *Times*, July 23, 1886.
"Picked Out Wrong Man." (Mount Vernon, Ohio) *Democratic Banner*, September 8, 1916.
"Pistols and Slung Shots." *Bismarck Weekly Tribune*, December 5, 1890.

(Pittston, Pennsylvania) *Evening Gazette*, June 27, 1885.
(Point Pleasant, West Virginia) *Weekly Register*, August 25, 1886.
"Police Find Body in Gutter." (East Liverpool) *Evening Review*, November 12, 1925.
"Police Investigation." *Cincinnati Daily Press*, January 16, 1861.
"Policeman Shot Dead." *Marion* (Ohio) *Star*, July 6, 1894.
"Posse Seeking Assailant of Child in Ohio." *Washington* (D.C.) *Times*, August 18, 1912.
"Preliminary Examination." *Cincinnati Commercial Tribune*, December 30, 1881.
(Prescott) *Arizona Weekly Journal-Miners*, June 5, 1895.
"Punished by White Caps." *New York Times*, March 16, 1903.
"Put Tar and Feathers on Him." (Chicago) *Inter Ocean*, September 6, 1891.
"Quickly Done." *Columbus* (Ohio) *Evening Dispatch*, June 4, 1897.
"Race Riot May Be the Result." *Bismark Daily Tribune*, June 30, 1909.
"Race War at Delaware." *News-Herald*, September 20, 1900.
"Real Attempt of Night Riders to Lynch Couple." *Sedalia* (Missouri) *Weekly Democrat*, September 28, 1928.
"Real White Caps in Ohio." *Pittsburgh Dispatch*, July 1, 1890.
"A Reporter Tarred and Feathered." (Carson City, Nevada) *Morning Appeal*, May 29, 1885.
"Richard Gardner Spirited Away from Athens to Avoid a Mob." (Maysville, Kentucky) *Evening Bulletin*, May 26, 1900.
"Rife for a Lynching." *Daily Cairo* (Illinois) *Bulletin*, December 15, 1883.
"Riot and Bloodshed." *Iron County* (Montana) *Register*, October 25, 1894.
"Riot at Crestline, O." *Indianapolis Journal*, June 15, 1903.
"Riot at Dayton, Ohio." (Washington, D.C.) *Weekly National Intelligencer*, May 7, 1863.
"The Riot in Ohio." *Brooklyn Daily Eagle*, September 17, 1853.
Risch, Sherrie. "Descendants of John Butterfield and Abigail Morse." http://wc.rootsweb.ancestry.com/cgi-bin/igm.cgi?op=GET&db=bing&id=I121.
Robinson, Amelia. "Lynchings Didn't Happen Only in the South." *Dayton Daily News*. http://www.daytondailynews.com/localnews/content/localnews/daily/1127lynch.html.
"Romulus Cotell." *Marietta* (Ohio) *Daily Leader*, July 28, 1896.
Rothestein, Edward. "Museum Review; Slavery's Harsh History Is Portrayed in Promised Land." *New York Times*, August 18, 2004.
"Rough Treatment." (Napoleon, Ohio) *Democratic Northwest*, January 3, 1889.
"Safe from an Ohio Mob." (New York) *Sun*, June 15, 1903.
(St. George, Utah) *Union*, November 13, 1897.
(St. Paul, Minnesota) *Western Appeal*, September 3, 1887.
Salem (Ohio) *Daily News*, March 13, 1889.
"Saves Negro Murderer." *New York Times*, September 23, 1907.
"The Scott Outrage in Ohio." *New York Times*, November 23, 1877.
"Sets Four Men Free." *Cleveland Plain Dealer*, January 29, 1926.
"Seven Arrests by Ohio Drys Cause Threats of Lynching." *Reading* (Pennsylvania) *Eagle*, July 26, 1923.
Shepard, Vinton R., ed. "Popular Explanation of the Causes of Lynch Law." *Ohio Law Reporter*, Volume II, No. 14, July 18, 1904.
"Sheriff Badly Wounded by Mob." *Bisbee* (Arizona) *Daily Review*, August 31, 1916.
"Sheriff Eley." *The Crisis*, Volume 13, Number 4, February 1917.
"Sheriff to Probe Attempt to Lynch 'Chicago Joe' Janik." *The Monroe (Louisiana) News-Star*, August 2, 1930.
"Sheriff's Ruse Foils a Mob." *Hocking* (County, Ohio) *Sentinel*, May 31, 1900.
"Shocking and Mysterious Crimes." *Fulton County* (Ohio) *Tribune*, September 21, 1917.
"Shooting Affair." *Cambridge* (Ohio) *Jeffersonian*, August 1, 1901.
"Sketch Artist Is Sentenced." *Marion* (Ohio) *Daily Mirror*, March 6, 1907.
"A Slanderer Lynched." *New York Times*, February 26, 1891.
"Slayer of Wife Closely Watched." *Washington* (D.C.) *Times*, May 25, 1908.
"A Soldier Lynched." *Pittsburgh Dispatch*, April 01, 1892.
"Sordid Story of Ironton Lynch-Orgy Is Retold." *Pittsburgh Courier*, August 6, 1932.
Stark County (Ohio) *Democrat*, January 27, 1876.
"State News Items." *Eaton* (Ohio) *Democrat*, November 2, 1882.
"Storey's Sad Story." *Cincinnati Daily Star*, May 21, 1879.
"The Strange Mystery of the Nocturnal Ambush." *Toledo Blade*, July 16, 1950.
"Struck the Wrong Man." *Pittsburgh Dispatch*, April 14, 1889.
"Strung Him Up." *Columbus Dispatch*, Friday, January 12, 1894.
Sudar, Anna. "100 Years Ago, Newark Streets Were Lawless." *Newark Advocate*, July 12, 2010.
"Summary Justice." *Marion* (Ohio) *Star*, April 10, 1891.

"A Sunday Lynching in Ohio." *New York Times*, May 1, 1882.
"Swift and Sure Vengeance Visited on a Brutal Negro Murderer." *Columbus Evening Dispatch*, August 22, 1895.
"Swift Justice." (West Virginia) *Weekly Register*, April 5, 1892.
"Tar Party Quiz Begun by Jury: Judge Backs It." *Toledo Blade*, April 15, 1918.
"Tarred and Feathered." *Alexandria* (Virginia) *Gazette*, November 20, 1899.
"Tarred and Feathered." (Indianapolis) *Indiana State Sentinel*, January 4, 1893.
"Tarred and Feathered." *Salt Lake Herald*, May 26, 1885.
"The Temperance Cause." *New York Times*, April 8, 1874.
Terrell, March Church. "Lynching from a Negro's Point of View." *North American Review*, Volume 178, June 1, 1904.
"Terrible Murder Near Mansfield Ohio." *Tiffin* (Ohio) *Tribune*, December 13, 1877.
"Terrible Times in Ward Township!—Exodus of Negroes!" *Daily* (Columbus) *Ohio Statesman*, May 19, 1861.
"That Lynching." *Cincinnati Enquirer*, January 19, 1875.
"They Strung Him Up." *The Columbus (Ohio) Dispatch*, April 16, 1894.
"They Visit Manchester." (Napoleon, Ohio) *Democratic Northwest*, December 6, 1888.
"Think Davis Also Assulted Girl at Lima [sic]." *Chillicothe* (Ohio) *Gazette*, July 2, 1910.
Thomas County (Kansas) *Cat*, June 25, 1885.
"Threatened with Lynching." *Brooklyn* (New York) *Daily Eagle*, December 27, 1885.
"Threatened with Lynching." *Hocking* (County, Ohio) *Sentinel*, January 4, 1906.
"Threaten to Lynch Confessed Murderer." *The Salt Lake (Utah) Tribune*, May 25, 1908.
"Threatening a Teacher." *Xenia* (Ohio) *Daily Gazette*, January 11, 1890.
"Threats Made Against Negro." (East Liverpool, Ohio) *Evening Review*, July 20, 1934.
"Three Men Are Killed in Niles Klan and Anti Klan Riot." (Wilkes-Barre, Pennsylvania) *Evening News*, November 1, 1924.
Tiffin (Ohio) *Tribune*, September 12, 1878.
"To a Shocking Crime Negro Murderer Under Death Sentence Makes Complete Confession." (Maysville, Kentucky) *Evening Bulletin*, October 29, 1900.
"To Declare War on Cleveland Crooks." *Hamilton* (Ohio) *Evening Journal*, November 14, 1925.
"'Too Popular' with Employers." (Baltimore) *Afro American*, June 30, 1932.
"The Torch Used." *Lima* (Ohio) *Times Democrat*, March 9, 1904.
"The Tragedy at Urbana." *Indianapolis News*, June 5, 1897.
"Trained Mob." *St. Paul Daily Globe*. April 11, 1891.
"Tramp Kills an Ohio Woman." *New York Times*, April 12, 1899.
"Trial Held in a Tourist Camp." (Massillon, Ohio) *Evening Independent*, October 16, 1937.
"A Triple Murder." *Cincinnati Daily Gazette*, June 25, 1877.
Tucker, Sam. "As I View the Thing." *Decatur* (Illinois) *Herald*, August 28, 1934.
"Two Arrests Are Made." (Mount Vernon, Ohio) *Democratic Banner*, May 5, 1916.
"Two Girls Lead Mob." *Marion* (Ohio) *Daily Mirror*, August 8, 1908.
"Unavoidable Accident." *Cincinnati Enquirer*, July 15, 1920.
"Up and Down Ohio." *Summit County* (Akron, Ohio) *Beacon*, February 15, 1894.
"Visited by Whitecaps." (New Philadelphia) *Daily Times*, December 19, 1895.
"Visited by Whitecaps." (Wellington, Ohio) *Enterprise*, December 18, 1895.
"Warned by White Caps." (Maysville, Kentucky) *Evening Bulletin*, January 11, 1890.
Warner, Thomas H. "Lawlessness Breeds Anarchy." *The Expositor and Current Anecdotes*. Volume XI, Number 12, September 1910.
"A Weak Female." *Cincinnati Enquirer*, July 1, 1890.
"Weinstock Indicted." (Hillsboro, Ohio) *News-Herald*, January 17, 1901.
Wells-Barnet, Ida B. "Lynch Law in America." *Arena*, Volume 23, Number 1, 1900.
"White Caps in Ohio." *Gastonia* (North Carolina) *Gazette*, March 20, 1903.
"'White Caps' in Our Midst." (New Philadelphia, Ohio) *Daily Times*, February 14, 1889.
"White Gowned Men Thrash Pacifist." *El Paso Herald*, October 29, 1917.
"Wild Disorders." *Barton County* (Kansas) *Democrat*, February 7, 1889.
Wilson, Woodrow. News release on lynchings. http://www.amistadresource.org/documents/document_07_06_030_wilson.pdf. Accessed May 18, 2016.
"Whipped by White Caps." *New York Times*, April 28, 1889.
"Whipped by White Caps." *Pittsburgh Dispatch*, August 3, 1889.
"White Caps." (Hillsboro, Ohio) *News-Herald*, January 10, 1907.
"The White Caps." (Napoleon, Ohio) *Democratic Northwest*, December 20, 1888.
"White Caps." (Napoleon, Ohio) *Democratic Northwest and Henry County News*, December 3, 1896.
"White Caps." *Perrysburg* (Ohio) *Journal*, December 14, 1888.

"White Caps Around." (Hillsboro, Ohio) *News-Herald*, March 23, 1893.
"White Caps at Leipsic." (Napoleon, Ohio) *Democratic Northwest*, December 13, 1888.
"'White Caps' Beaten." *New York Times*, December 3, 1888
"White Caps Disbanded." *Hocking* (County, Ohio) *Sentinel*, December 20, 1888.
"The White Caps of Ohio." *Mexico* (Missouri) *Weekly Ledger*, December 13, 1888.
"A White Cap Outrage." (Columbia County) *Oregon Mist*, November 19, 1897.
"Whitecaps Again." *Abilene* (Kansas) *Weekly Reflector*, January 3, 1889.
"Wicked Defiance!" (Napoleon, Ohio) *Democratic Northwest*, March 5, 1891.
"Wm. Carter." (Hillsboro, Ohio) *News-Herald*, October 28, 1897.
"Wounded in Defense of Her Honor." *Dupuyer* (Montana) *Acantha*, January 10, 1901.
"Urged Lynching of a Former Mt. Vernon Man." (Mount Vernon, Ohio) *Democratic Banner*, July 15, 1910.
"The Valley Tragedy." *Columbus Dispatch*, May 22, 1885.
"Vengeance." *The* (Hillsboro, Ohio) *News-Herald*, April 19, 1894.
"A Very Cautious Opinion." *Bellefontaine* (Ohio) *Republican*, January 5, 1900.
"Very Nearly." *New York Times*, May 22, 1879.
Xenia (Ohio) *Daily Gazette*, April 26, 1897.
Xenia (Ohio) *Democrat News*, June 18, 1887.
"A Young Girl Outrage and Afterwards Beaten to Death." (Redwing, Minnesota) *Grange Advance*, February 2, 1876.

Books

Babbidon, Shaun L., and Helen Taylor Greene. *Race and Crime*, 3d ed. Los Angeles: Sage, 2013.
Baughman, Abraham J. *History of Richland County, Ohio, from 1808 to 1908*. Chicago: S.J. Clark, 1908.
Beardsley, D.B. *History of Hancock County from Its Earliest Settlement to the Present Time*. Springfield, OH: Republic, 1881.
Brister, Edwin M.P. *Centennial History of the City of Newark and Licking County, Ohio*. Chicago: S.J. Clarke, 1909.
Brodie, Fawn. *No Man Knows My History*. New York: Alfred A. Knopf, 1945, 1957.
Bushnell, Henry. *History of Granville, Licking County, Ohio*. Columbus: Hann & Adair, 1889.
Butler, Joseph Green. *History of Youngstown and the Mahoning Valley, Ohio, Volume 1*. Chicago: American Historical Society, 1921.
Campbell, W. Joseph. *The Year That Defined American Journalism: 1897 and the Clash of Paradigms*. New York: Routledge, 2006.
A Centennial Biographical History of Crawford County, Ohio. Chicago: Lewis, 1902.
Coffin, Levi. *Reminiscences of Levi Coffin*. Cincinnati: Western Tract Society, 1876.
Collins, Winfield H. *The Truth About Lynching and the Negro in the South*. New York: Publishing, 1918.
Cone, Stephen D. *A Concise History of Hamilton, Ohio*. Middletown, OH: G. Mitchell, 1901.
Day, J.H. *Lynched! A Fiendish Outrage—A Terrible Retribution!* Celina, OH: A.P.J. Snyder, 1872.
Douglass, Frederick. *Why Is the Negro Lynched?* Bridgewater, CT: John Whitby and Sons, 1895.
Doyle, William B. *Centennial History of Summit County, Ohio and Representative Citizens*. Chicago: Biographical, 1908.
Dray, Philip. *At the Hands of Persons Unknown: The Lynching of Black America*. New York: Modern Library, 2003.
Emmitt, James. *Life and Reminiscences of Hon. James Emmitt: As Revised by Himself*. Chillicothe, OH: Peerless, 1888.
Evans, Nelson Wiley. *A History of Scioto County, Ohio*. Portsmouth, OH: Nelson W. Evans, 1903.
Evans, Nelson Wiley, and Emmons B. Stivers *A History of Adams County, Ohio: From Its Earliest Settlement to the Present*. West Union, OH: E.B. Stivers, 1903.
Fite, Emerson David. *History of the United States*, 2d ed. New York: Henry Holt, 1919.
Ford, Henry A., and Kate B. Ford. *History of Hamilton County Ohio with Illustrations and Biographical Sketches*. Cleveland: L.A. Williams, 1881.
Galbreath, C.B. "Anti-Slavery Movement in Columbiana County." *Ohio Archaeological and Historical Society Publications*, Volume 30, Number 22. Columbus: Fred J. Heer, 1921.
Gonzales-Day, Ken. *Lynching in the West, 1850–1935*. Durham: Duke University Press, 2006.
Graham, A.A. *History of Richland County Ohio: Its Past and Present*. Manfield, OH: A.A. Graham, 1880.
Grant, Donald L. *The Anti-Lynching Movement, 1883–1932*. San Jose, CA: R and E Research Associates, 1975.
Greve, Charles Theodore. *Centennial History of Cincinnati and Representative Citizens*. Chicago: Biographical Publishing Company, 1904.
Haber, Samuel. "Cincinnati: Not Porkopolis but Queen City, 1830–1880." *The Quest for Authority and Honor in the American Professions, 1750–1900*. Chicago: University of Chicago Press, 1991.
Harris, Trudier. *Selected Works for Ida B. Wells-Barnett*. New York: Oxford University Press, 1991.
Hill, N.N. *History of Licking County, Ohio*. Newark, OH: A.A. Graham, 1881.
History of Hocking Valley, Ohio. Chicago: Inter-State, 1883

The History of Tuscarawas County, Ohio. Chicago: Warner, Beers, 1884.

History of Van Wert and Mercer Counties, Ohio. Wapakoneta, OH: R. Sutton, 1882.

Hover, John C., Joseph D. Barnes, Walter D. Jones, Charlotte Reeve Conover, Willard J. Wright, Clayton A. Leiter, John Ewing Bradford, and W.C. Culkins. *Memoirs of the Miami Valley*. Chicago: Robert O. Law, 1919.

Howard, Marilyn K. *Black Lynching in the Promised Land: Mob Violence in Ohio 1876–1916*. Ohio State University, Ph.D. Dissertation, 1999.

Howe, Henry. *Historical Collections of Ohio*. Norwalk, OH: Laning, 1896.

Huff, W. Thomas. *Memories of Old Newark*. Newark, OH: W.T. Huff, 2000.

James, Sally L. *American Violent Moral Regulation and the White Caps*. Honors Thesis, College of William and Mary, 1969.

Journal of the Senate of the State of Ohio: Seventy-Second General Assembly. Volume XCII, Norwalk, OH: Laning, 1896.

Journal of the Senate of the Eighty-First General Assembly of the State of Ohio. Columbus: The F.J. Heer, 1915.

Karcher, Carolyn L. *A Refugee From His Race: Albion W. Tourgee and His Fight Against White Supremacy*. Chapel Hill: University of North Carolina Press, 2016.

Knepper, George W. *Ohio and Its People*. Kent, OH: Kent State University Press, 2003.

Lane, Samuel Alanson. *Fifty Years and Over of Akron and Summit County*. Akron, OH: Beacon Job Department, 1892.

Lee, Alfred Emory. *History of the City of Columbus, Capital of Ohio*. Chicago: Munsell, 1892.

Loewen, James W. *Sundown Towns: A Hidden Dimension in American Racism*. New York: New Press, 2005.

MacLean, John Patterson. *Shakers of Ohio*. Columbus: F.J. Heer, 1907.

McIntosh, W.H. *The History of Darke County, Ohio*. Chicago: W.H. Beers, 1880.

Meyers, David, and Elise Meyers Walker. *Ohio's Black Hand Syndicate*. Charleston, SC: The History Press, 2018.

Meyers, David, and Elise Meyers Walker. *Wicked Columbus, Ohio*. Charleston, SC: The History Press, 2015.

Meyers, David, Elise Meyers Walker, and Nyla Vollmer. *Carrying Coal to Columbus*. Charleston, SC: The History Press, 2017.

Middleton, Evan P. *History of Champaign County, Ohio*. Indianapolis: B.F. Bowen, 1917.

Middleton, Stephen. *The Black Laws: Race and the Legal Process in Early Ohio*. Athens: Ohio University Press, 2005.

Nelson, S.B., and J.M. Runk. *History of Cincinnati and Hamilton County, Ohio*. Cincinnati: S.B. Nelson, 1894.

Ohio Law Reporter, Volume 10. Cincinnati: The Ohio Law Reporter Company, 1913.

Payne, Phillip G. *Dead Last: The Public Memory of Warren G. Harding's Scandalous Legacy*. Athens: Ohio University Press, 2009.

Perrin, William, J.H. Battle, and Weston Arthur Goodspeed. *History of Crawford County, Ohio*. Chicago: Baskin & Battey, 1881.

Prince, Benjamin F. *A Standard History of Springfield and Clark County, Ohio*. Chicago: The American Historical Society, Volume I, 1922.

Quillen, Frank U. *The Color Line in Ohio*. Ann Arbor: Wahr, 1913.

Raper, Arthur F. *The Tragedy of Lynching*. Mineola, NY: Dover, 2003.

Reid, Phil. *The Mystifying Murder in Marion, Ohio*. Bloomington: Xlibris, 2011.

Roberts, Brigham Henry. *The Life of John Taylor, Third President of the Church of Jesus Christ of Latter-Day Saints*. Salt Lake City: G.Q. Cannon, 1892.

Rusler, William. *A Standard History of Allen County, Ohio*. New York: American Historical Society, 1921.

Shuler, Jack. *The Thirteenth Turn: A History of the Noose*. New York: Public Affairs, 2014.

Smith, Hilda L., and Berenice A. Carroll. *Women's Political & Social Thought: An Anthology*. Bloomington: Indiana University Press, 2000.

Stowe, Charles Edward. *Harriet Beecher Stowe: The Story of Her Life*. Boston: Houghton Mifflin, 1911.

Taylor, Nikki Marie. *Frontiers of Freedom: Cincinnati's Black Community, 1802–1868*. Athens, OH: Ohio University Press, 2005.

Thompson, Carmi A., et al. *General Code of the State of Ohio*, Volume II. Cincinnati: W.H. Anderson, 1910.

Van Cleaf, Aaron R. *History of Pickaway County, Ohio, And Representative Citizens*. 1906.

Warren, Marvin. *Ohio Criminal Law and Forms*. Cincinnati: Moore, Wilstach, Keys, 1857.

Weed, Edward. *Faith and Works*. New York: C.W. Benedict, 1853.

Wells-Barnett, Ida B. *The Red Record*. Self-published, 1895.

Wheeler, Wayne B. *The Newark Lynching: Its Causes and Results*. Westerville, OH: The American Issue Publishing Company, 1910.

Williams, Daniel Webster. *A History of Jackson County, Ohio*. Jackson, OH: self-published, 1900.

Index